D0938680

# Political Theory in
# Modern Germany

*For Hermione, Grace and John*

# Political Theory in Modern Germany

*An Introduction*

## Chris Thornhill

Polity Press

First published in 2000 by Polity Press in association with Blackwell Publishers Ltd

*Editorial office*:
Polity Press
65 Bridge Street
Cambridge CB2 1UR, UK

*Marketing and production*:
Blackwell Publishers Ltd
108 Cowley Road
Oxford OX4 1JF, UK

*Published in the USA by*
Blackwell Publishers Inc.
Commerce Place
350 Main Street
Malden, MA 02148, USA

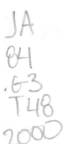

A catalogue record for this book is available from the British Library.

**Library of Congress Cataloging-in-Publication Data**

Thornhill, C.
   Political theory in modern Germany: an introduction / Chris Thornhill.
      p.   cm.
   Includes bibliographical references and index.
   ISBN 0–7456–1999–1.—ISBN 0–7456–2000–0 (pbk.)
      1. Political science—Germany—History.   I. Title.
JA84.G3T48   2000
320' .092' 243—dc21                                                                    99–32964
                                                                                                        CIP

Typeset in 10.5 on 12 pt Ehrhardt
by Kolam Information Services Pvt Ltd, Pondicherry, India
Printed in Great Britain by T. J. International, Padstow, Cornwall

This book is printed on acid-free paper.

# Contents

# *Acknowledgements*

During the writing of this work I have accumulated various senses of debt and obligation. I would like to thank the staff of the British Library and both state libraries in Berlin for their great assistance and good humour in finding the books and documents I have required. I would like to thank my friends, students and colleagues in the Department of German at King's College, London, for their support, and for providing a context in which I could pursue my research. Over recent years I have also profited greatly from discussions with Dan Burnstone, Simon Jarvis, Andreas Krampe and Drew Milne. The friendship of Ben Morris and Paul Key too has been very important to me during this time. My most abiding debt, however, is to my great friend Darrow Schecter, in whose company much of this book has been thought out.

# *Abbreviations*

| | |
|---|---|
| **CDU** | Christian Democratic Union |
| **CSU** | Christian Social Union |
| **DDP** | German Democratic party |
| **DNVP** | German National People's party |
| **DVP** | German People's party |
| **FDP** | Free Democratic party |
| **FVP** | Progressive People's party |
| **NSDAP** | German National Socialist party |
| **SPD** | Social Democratic party |
| **USPD** | Independent Social Democratic party |

# Introduction

This book addresses the major figures in the history of modern political thought in Germany, from Max Weber to Niklas Luhmann. The figures selected for special discussion are thinkers whose ideas are crystallized around specific structures and problems in German politics. They are, therefore, selected for their representative quality. Max Weber's thought, for example, centres on the dilemmas of German liberalism in its post-classical phase. Carl Schmitt is the representative figure on the extreme right of the inter-war era, linking the conservative movements of the late-Wilhelmine period with the populist dictatorship of the National Socialists. Franz Neumann and Otto Kirchheimer form a bridge which connects the debates in the unions and the socialist parties of the inter-war period with the critical theories, especially the sociological examinations of National Socialism, which developed around the Institute of Social Research in Frankfurt and New York. Jürgen Habermas's work provides the clearest overall reflection of critical, left-liberal debate throughout the history of the Federal Republic. Niklas Luhmann's ideas refract the administrative reforms and the neo-conservative theories of the state in the 1970s and 1980s.

Many important thinkers are left out of this work. Although attention is paid to certain aspects of the unorthodox forms of Marxism associated with the Frankfurt School, Theodor Adorno, Max Horkheimer, Walter Benjamin and Ernst Bloch are not treated separately in this book. Their works have been addressed very extensively in recent literature, and it is also debatable whether they write about politics. Similarly, for analogous reasons, neither Martin Heidegger nor Karl Jaspers are considered extensively here, despite their considerable influence on political debate. Such omissions do not imply that this work sets out to offer merely an intellectual history of the German political system. However, it seeks to illuminate the interrelations between political theory and political event in modern Germany, and the selection of the thinkers treated is always guided by this consideration. Although this book, also, is not intended primarily as a work of history, it is hoped that the fusion of social theory and political history which it employs will provide a clear set of analyses of the formations of political power in Germany in the course of the twentieth century.

Naturally, this work seeks to introduce readers to the defining characteristics of modern German political thought. This itself, however, is at times a complicated and paradoxical undertaking. In the post-1945 period, much political reflection in Germany has consciously turned away from what might be defined as the classical German forms of political philosophy. Neither Kantian liberalism, Hegelian statism, orthodox Marxist state-critique, nor simple nationalism are represented in their pure form amongst the thinkers treated here. The traditional 'primacy of politics' in German political thinking has been significantly diluted in modern theory (Beyme 1991b: 75). However, the theory of politics in modern Germany still has its origins in a determinately German history of thought, and the old antecedents are often visible just below the surface of even the most modern and innovative thinkers. Weber belongs to a tradition of liberalism which is marked by a reception of Kant, but which also has affinities with both Hegel and Marx. Schmitt's work is also coloured by a reception of both Kant and Hegel, although his ideas contain strong anti-Kantian and anti-Hegelian Roman Catholic elements. Neumann and Kirchheimer are influenced by a statist brand of Hegelian Marxism. Both Habermas and Luhmann, whose thought is characterized by its international eclecticism, still have their most important points of reference in the German tradition, and between them they owe heavy debts to Hegel, Marx, Husserl and various forms of neo-Kantianism.

Modern German political theory in general has its roots in the circumstances of modern German history. Not surprisingly, its characteristic features are various, complex and at times strikingly distinct from Western European political thought. The basic premise in modern German political thought is that the political sphere has a particular autonomy – that it is situated above the social arena, and that it cannot be reduced to the technical practices which determine the character of social or economic interaction. This idea, in different figurations, is at the very heart of the writings of Weber, Schmitt, Neumann, Kirchheimer and Habermas. Only in the postmodern – or post-political – writings of Luhmann does the political, in certain respects, forfeit its structural integrity.

The sources of the formal dignity accorded to the political sphere can be traced to the conditions of the genesis of the modern German/Prussian state. The German state in its twentieth-century form emerged from the post-medieval estate-based order of government (the dualist *Ständestaat*). This was a heavily protectionist system, in which both political authority and economic co-ordination were concentrated in the state, and in which independent economic activity was strictly regulated. In this system, which was reinforced after the religious wars of the seventeenth century, the monarchical executive arrogated central political and economic control to itself, and it protected this power by placing heavy fiscal burdens on the population, and by levying high customs duties on all imported commodities. This had a twofold function. Externally, the protection of the economy enabled the state to avoid competition with more advanced capitalist countries, especially Britain and France (Wallerstein 1980: 233). Internally, the absolutist mode of economic management created (at least in its ideal form) an embracing order, in which social and political positions were hierarchically graded in accordance with professional standing and privilege (Gall 1993: 5). The scope for the emergence of independent structures of authority outside the monarchical executive was therefore relatively limited. In the system of the *Ständestaat*, the estates – provincial deputations composed of property owners and notables – were empowered to influence taxation and to advise the monarchy in matters of common interest (Stolleis 1992: 110). The right to approve taxation was the cornerstone of this system (Rachfal 1902: 199). The estate-system was, therefore, in certain respects, a proto-parliamentary structure of governance, in which the financial sovereignty of the state was sustained by certain concessions to economic deputations (Spangenberg 1912: 130). The power of the estates increased in accordance with the reliance of the crown on taxation. During periods of warfare, for instance, the power of the estates increased as the crown relied upon them for revenue. However, it is notable, as F. L. Carsten (1959: 441) has argued, that in Germany the outcome of the balance of interests between crowns and parliaments (estates) was not – or only very belatedly – the transfer of power to parliament, and the distribution of power between state and society. The essential form of the *Ständestaat* survived well into the nineteenth century.

In these respects, the course of German history contrasts strikingly, but not uniformly, with that of other European nations. The key, and most common, point of comparison is Britain. In Britain, after the late-medieval period a political order developed which was characterized by a weak state, with limited fiscal revenue (Clay 1984: 140). The emergence of a relatively strong bourgeoisie, coupled with an increase in the power of the minor nobility (Stone 1972: 73), made it impossible for the British state to restrict the socio-economic influence of independent groups to the same extent as in Germany (Mooers 1991: 154–5). After 1688 a parliamentary order was cemented in Britain which guaranteed an 'exceptionally free society' for those with independent property (Atiyah 1979: 13), and which reinforced regional and traditional rights against the central monarchy (Dyson 1980: 39; Mooers 1991: 165–6). In the British system, the state was not strong enough to expand its authority over the civil arena. Rather, the state became an organ which oversaw, and which provided favourable conditions for, the expansion of the capitalist economy, and the capitalist classes. In France, by further contrast, although Louis XIV established a strong system of absolutism in order to combat the seigneurial power of the high aristocracy, by the 1780s the French monarchy was bankrupt, and extremely vulnerable (Doyle 1980: 114–15). The French Revolution itself, although it did not wholly remove the legacy of the ancien regime (Hinrichs 1972: 178), brought about the abolition of the feudal order, and the introduction of a political system which reinforced and reflected the liberation of the capital economy from absolutist control. Only modern Italy can be compared more directly with Germany. As late as the early nineteenth century, Italy, like Germany, had no central economy, and in some areas only a rudimentary exchange-system. Indeed, until 1861, when the Piedmontese system was imposed (Mack Smith 1997: 7), Italy did not have a customs union or a uniform currency (Greenfield 1934: 235–6). As in Germany, the processes of economic and political reform which marked the nineteenth century were, in Italy, carried out from above, often by enlightened landowners (Bellamy 1992: 105–6).

In Germany, even after the French Revolution, the provincial estate-system was re-established in modified form in most regions, with land-ownership the basis of rights of consultation and deputation (Koselleck 1989: 341). Importantly, also, through the early nineteenth century the economic influence of the estates in German politics was not coupled with equivalent political power (1989: 339–40). The role of the estates – at least in principle – was limited to the rights of economic deputation and consultative functions (Oestreich 1969: 280–1). German politics of the early nineteenth century was marked therefore by broad continuity with pre-1789 governmental forms, not by radical deviation from them (Scheuner 1977: 321). The earliest forms of constitutional organization in Germany, especially the Bavarian Constitution of 1818 and the Würtemberg Constitution of 1819 (Stolleis 1992: 100–11), were based expressly on the old estate-system, although they did make important additions to it. The concluding documents of the Congress of Vienna (1820) made provision for estate-based deputations – not for representative government (Boldt 1975: 21). Even the quasi-constitutional Prussian reforms of Stein and Hardenberg (1806–1821) only extended the legislative system to include the higher ranks of the bureaucracy. The Prussian council of state (*Staatsrat*), founded in 1817 by Hardenberg (Vogel 1983: 132), took the form of a parliament of civil servants, in which legislative decisions were made within the closed ranks of the bureaucracy.

Consequently, it has been widely argued that the broad division between state and society which inevitably marks monarchical systems was sustained in Germany considerably longer than in other European countries (Conze 1978: 214–15). In the nineteenth century, monarchical power in Prussia was naturally not unlimited, but the restrictions upon it were imposed by the bureaucracy, which fused legislative and executive powers, not by a free-standing legislature (Koselleck 1989: 264–6). Throughout the nineteenth century the Prussian state pursued processes of modernization from above

(Lütge 1966: 447). Through administrative innovation it adjusted gradually to shifts in economy and society (Breger 1994: 40–7). However, after the premature end of the reforms conducted by Stein and Hardenberg, the reformist administration of 1806–21 was soon restructured as a conservative wedge between state and society, which limited the openness of the state to alterations outside it (Vierhaus 1983: 40–1; Obenaus 1984: 519). Arguably, as Otto Hintze famously indicated (1962: 365–6), the strength of the Prussian bureaucracy obstructed the emergence of a genuine political society and prevented a coalescence of civil and political activity (Koselleck 1989: 331). Politics, in the early nineteenth century, became the province of the administration (Kehr 1965a: 38). The predominance of the bureaucracy was weakened gradually in 1847, when a united Prussian parliament was created (Koselleck 1989: 387), and by the 'revolutions' of 1848. However, the first Prussian Constitutions of 1848 and 1850 still contained a peculiar combination of provisions for social rights and for rule by an autocratic-bureaucratic elite (Bendix 1978: 427). These constitutions were organized around a three-level, estate-like division of the voting population (*Drei-klassenwahlrecht*), in which voting rights were allocated on the basis of contribution to public revenue (Boberach 1959: 150). Even those elected by the three-class system had only restricted influence on actual legislative processes. The highest level of legislative authority was still a ministerial bureaucracy. The estate-based concept that the socio-economic sphere is composed of a series of corporate formations which are properly distinct from the political arena thus remained a dominant aspect of the Prussian tradition of constitutionalism through the mid- to late nineteenth century (Boberach 1959: 150). The duality between the estates (the social sphere) and the imperial executive (the political sphere) was also a strong component of Bismarck's political outlook (Ellwein 1954: 314). The basic dualist scheme of the relation between politics and society remained (and was arguably reinforced) throughout the age of Bismarck (Scheuner 1977: 340).

Of particular significance for this work is the impact of the dualistic tradition in German history on the development of German law, especially the development of private law (see Brunner 1959: 124). The history of the private-legal system in Germany also underlines structural differences between German history and that of other European countries. In Britain, for example, the tradition of common law constituted an early, informal system of private law. This provided an important bastion against the centralization of power in the state (Pocock 1957: 49), and a crucial set of references for protecting property and private interests against the monarchy (Stone 1972: 103). Even the indictment of Charles I was in part articulated through reference to common law (Ives 1968: 121). Although a system of private-legal autonomy was not finally realized in Britain until the late eighteenth century, after 1688 rights of ownership, free disposition over property, and freedom of lateral contract were increasingly recognized as the foundation of the English legal order (Atiyah 1979: 87). Ultimately, the period 1770–1870, to follow P. S. Atiyah's argument, saw the development of a legal system which guaranteed maximum liberty of contract and which thus based law on the requirements of the free market (1979: 398). In this period of British history, significantly, the economic contract was detached from the political conception of a binding vertical contract between citizen and state, and transformed into a fluid consensual agreement, based on the mutual recognition of autonomy on the part of the contractual parties. By 1800, therefore, British legal thought had moved decisively towards a theory of legal obligation which was premised not on pre-established compacts, but on autonomy and personal consent (1979: 442). In France, although the system of private law lagged behind that in Britain, prior to the revolution of 1789 extensive plans had already been made to strengthen the bourgeoisie by means of economic reform (Grimm 1977: 1234). Ultimately, the *Code Napoléon* (completed in 1804) provided the foundations for a free private-legal order. The *Code Napoléon* was subsequently reinterpreted through the nineteenth century in a manner which drew out a theory of consensual, autonomous exchange as the basic element of economic legislation (Bürge 1991: 62). In Italy, again in part comparable to Germany, Napoleonic law was widely assimilated in the north, but a uniform *Codice Civile* was not introduced until 1865 (Coing 1989: 19). In Britain and France, however, the early power of the capitalist class was refracted by the legal system, which either gradually, in the case of Britain, or in revolutionary manner, in the case of France, adjusted its laws to the principles of free, rapid exchange.

In Germany, by contrast, the private-legal order was formalized more slowly, and much more erratically (Coing 1985: 40, 393). Although some of the South German states already included recognition of economic liberty in their judicial systems (1985: 116), the first Prussian legal code (*Allgemeines Landrecht*, introduced 1794) scarcely went beyond the formal codification of absolutist law. Before the French Revolution, also, there already existed a strong tradition of common law in Germany, which was anchored in Roman law. Common law gave limited recognition to personal freedom, and freedom of property. However, common-legal obligations under Roman law were of personal character, and they did not amount to the express liberation of economic activity (Coing 1989: 431). Germany had no uniform system of civil law until 1866 (1989: 20). The level of private-legal autonomy guaranteed in Britain by 1770, and in France by 1789, was not reached in Germany until 1848, and, arguably, not at all (Grimm 1977: 1239).

The reasons for this peculiarity of the German legal tradition can be seen in the political structures of early nineteenth-century Germany. The German estate-system revolved around the rigid demarcation between private and public spheres (Brunner 1959: 115). In the estate-system, naturally, definite concessions were made to private-legal interest. Indeed, an abstract doctrine of private law had already developed by 1800, resulting from the ius-naturalism of the Enlightenment (Stolleis 1992: 51). By 1810 the reforms of Hardenberg and Stein had set the terms for a capitalist private-legal order – for freedom of trade and freedom of contract (Vogel 1983: 165). The *Code Napoléon* was also widely, but unsystematically, received in the German states after 1807, especially in those under Napoleonic occupation (Wieacker 1967: 344; Fehrenbach 1974: 9). The *Code Napoléon* expressly guaranteed the inviolability of property-rights, and it remained the basis of private law in some areas of south-west Germany until 1900 (Wieacker 1967: 345). Despite this, however, the sphere of public law (the bureaucracy and the executive) retained a structural distinction from the private-legal operations of civil society (Dilcher 1977: 139). The civil sphere of economic activity had, for most of the nineteenth century, relatively limited impact on state-law. Indeed, although a private-legal sphere, with unrestricted commodity production, wage-labour and free circulation of commodities, was broadly (but not completely) developed in the early nineteenth century, this sphere existed separately from the strictly political order of the state (Habermann 1976: 4–5).

Generally, in the period of early European capitalism, the sphere of private law was a location in which anti-state energies were expressed, and through which property-relations were defined in opposition to the privilege- and obligation-based laws of the absolutist state. Through the separation of the economy from mercantilist state-regulation, private law, or common law, acted as formulae for differentiating the sphere of economic liberty (civil society) from the state (Stolleis 1992: 52; Grimm 1987: 198). In Germany, however, owing to the initial limitations placed upon the deputations of civil interest (the estates), the decorporation of the economy into a non-structured system of economic needs was a complex and tortuous process (Conze 1978: 248; see also Koselleck 1973: 80). Only relatively gradually did private law push back the limits of public law. Indeed, arguably, the sphere of public law retained its dominance through the nineteenth century. There remained in Germany during this century a body of non-liberal, social and autocratic legislation (especially in property law), which had its origins in the estate-system (Pohl 1977: 8), and which resisted the dominance of liberal private law (Wieacker 1967: 545). Although economic legislation was liberalized by the state in the period 1850–78 (1967: 468), as a result of the Great Depression (starting 1873) the impact of private law soon began to recede again. Bismarck's anti-liberal tariff- and welfare-laws after 1878 bear witness to the survival of a strong tradition of opposition to the recognition of the economy as the source of law. Bismarck continued the earlier tradition of administrative modernization from above, and he interpreted the economy, in neo-mercantilist manner (Pohl 1977: 24), as a subordinate component of political life (Krieger 1972: 24). This tendency is exemplified, theoretically, by the influential social-conservative writings of Lorenz von Stein (Lübbe 1963: 75–6), who postulated the need both for a strong state and for extensive social provision for the poor. Indeed, Stein imagined that the socio-economic sphere could be wholly integrated into the political order (Stein 1959: 138).

Above all, however, the primacy of the political sphere in nineteenth-century Germany is illustrated by the strong tradition of positivist legal theory which developed after 1815. In nineteenth-century Germany, the systematic elaboration of the principles of private law, contract law and property law, which had initially been theorized by Kant (Kiefner 1969: 25), was conducted by the Historical School, and later by the legal positivists. After 1815 a wave of attempts to systematize private law emerged from the pens of Germany's major legal theorists – firstly Savigny and Thibault, later Puchta, Jhering, Gerber and Laband. This culminated in the period immediately prior to 1848. It is notable, however, that these legal theorists, although committed to the clear separation of the private sphere of economic interaction from public or state-law, were not motivated by substantial liberal principles, or even by a strong sense that law contributes to the shaping of political conditions. Savigny believed that the formal liberty of the private-legal system could coexist with an authoritarian state (Dilcher 1977: 140). Puchta, Gerber, Jhering and Laband all saw law as a formally autonomous science. They argued that law should be separated from politics (Wilhelm 1958: 84), and they detached law from its foundation in the economy (1958: 101). Gerber, most significantly, belonged to the anti-liberal wing in 1848 (1958: 124). Laband supported the conservative-monarchical theory of state, and he was an admirer of Bismarck's anti-liberal policies (1958: 159). In nineteenth-century Germany, therefore, it can be argued that even the science of private law, which expressly intended to clarify the terms of socio-economic liberty, directly reflected and perpetuated the limitation of the social sphere which otherwise characterized German political life. Legal positivism implies, in essence, that no special status accrues to the private person or the private sphere and that these are defined only by the overarching public-legal order of the state (Wyduckel 1984: 280; Coing 1989: 270).

It is highly significant in this respect that whilst positivism emerged in the nineteenth century as the orthodox register for defining private activity, the nature of public life was widely represented in terms derived from historicism. By 1900 the Lutheran faith had broadly defined itself as the civil ethic of Prussian politics and Prussian culture (Hübinger 1994: 171–2). Cultural Protestantism, especially, saw national history and culture as an expression of the divine will (Harnack 1900: 128), and it saw the state as the highest achievement of national culture (Elert 1953: 168). Lutheranism, as a general ethic, represents national history as a series of collective historical reflexes, which are organically co-ordinated as political sovereignty. Out of Protestantism grew, by direct descent, historicism. Historicism, like Protestantism, also views national history as a fluid set of customs and beliefs which are united in the state. To a greater extent even than Protestantism, nineteenth-century historicism proposed itself as an ethic of integration which opposed the abstract values of the Enlightenment and sought to unite all the classes of the nation in the name of collective history and collective belonging (Iggers 1969: 35). The process of constitutional foundation in

Germany, after the failure of the liberal documents of 1848–9 (Hock 1957: 156), can itself be interpreted as a line of historicist projects which, until the revolutionary caesura of 1918–19, never made more than local adjustments to the fabric of state. In its ideology of statehood, continuity and collectivity, historicism directly obstructed the realization of democratic representation, which has its foundations in the tradition of natural law to which historicism is opposed. Even the founding fathers of the Weimar Constitution, in fact, especially Friedrich Naumann, saw their contributions as continuous components in the course of national history (*Verhandlungen der Nationalversammlung* 1920: 329/2189; Heilfron 1919: 964), in which the *Volk* wrote its own histories in law (Plessner 1969: 57). Naumann himself expressly linked the process of constitutional foundation back to the first political principles of Lutheranism (*Verhandlungen der Nationalversammlung* 1920: 328/1651). Broadly, in sum, it might be argued that positivism and historicism are in certain respects coexistent and co-emergent ideological structures. Positivism codifies private life, but it makes private life contingent upon public order. Historicism, analogously, sees public life as a series of reflexes, in which individual existence is passively assimilated into the national collective. It is no coincidence that historicism and positivism ultimately coalesce in the legal theories of the National Socialists (Rüthers 1994: 65).

Generally, the tentative systematization of private law in Germany can also be seen to reflect the defining traits of German liberalism and its limited theory of the legal state (*Rechtsstaat*). In the late *Kaiserreich*, German liberalism based its economic thinking on positivist assumptions and its political thinking on historicist ideas (Schieder 1980: 194). The German liberals ultimately accepted the legal preconditions for the capitalist private economy without a concomitant increase in political influence (John 1989: 89). The Civil Code (*Bürgerliches Gesetzbuch*) of 1896 marked the major systematic attempt of the Wilhelmine liberals to create an integrating ethic of politics based on the private-legal order. This Code was, however, notably marked by technical, positivist formalism rather than material values (1989: 254–5). The Code guaranteed freedom of property and freedom of inheritance. Nonetheless, it retained an attitude of compromise towards the old feudal structures and it framed the interests of the private economy in the vocabulary of positivist neutrality (Blasius 1978: 222). It barely recognized social issues (Wieacker 1967: 224; Kindermann 1981: 224).

The limitation of private law in the German tradition has important repercussions for twentieth-century political theory, on both left and right. Generally, the positivist conceptualization of private law in the nineteenth century forms the background to the chief preoccupation of all modern German political thought (excluding Luhmann) – namely, the attempt to propose alternatives to the pure formality of capitalist law. With the exception of Luhmann, all the major theorists of the twentieth century seek to develop a theory of politics which interprets law as a complex of positive relations to the state, not as the negative, static defence of non-political liberties. Such theories, for all their diversity, reject the political neutralization of law in positivism. Max Weber, for example, following in the footsteps of Ferdinand Tönnies (Tönnies 1887: 267), attempts to explain how the pure formality of law can be overcome, and how law can frame a common political ethic. Although Weber equivocates on the question of whether law can truly be constitutive of political order, he certainly implies that it can provide the general terms for the life of the national collective. Likewise, although Carl Schmitt retains the positivist conviction that the private order is a subsidiary moment in public power, Schmitt's radically anti-capitalist theory of substantial law also outlines how law can express a positive political will. Habermas also, analogously, grasps law as a series of value-rational norms which can (potentially) constitute the consensual basis of legitimacy for the political order. In legitimate law, Habermas argues, the private (or formal) autonomy and the public freedom of citizens are not inevitably segregated, but potentially co-original and co-constitutive.

In short, therefore, modern German political theory reacts against positivism by determining law as a substantial connection between particular and collective interests. Furthermore, modern German political thought reacts yet more emphatically against the implications of positivism by denying that the legitimacy of law can in any way be based in the relations of exchange in the capitalist economy. Weber, Schmitt, Neumann, Kirchheimer and Habermas all see law as a set of terms in which individual life is elevated above the particularity of private interests. All avoid upholding a sphere of private liberty which is given prior to political life. All try, in sum, to explain how law can connect private interests and public life, but all seek, equally, to show how it can escape its apriori reduction to the formal expression of property-interests. In this respect, thinkers on both left and right – from Schmitt to Kirchheimer – all share the same conviction that public/political life has primacy over the formal ordering of private needs.

It is in this respect that the most fundamental distinction between the German tradition of political reflection and that of other European countries can be identified. As a result of these broad historical, intellectual and sociological preconditions, German political thought is generally marked by a hostility towards the theory of the social contract. Contract-theory, at least in its classical form, derives the conditions of political legitimacy from the social sphere, and argues that the sphere of human liberty, which it is the duty of politics to defend, exists prior to political life.

The rejection of contractarian theory in Germany can be identified at the beginning of the nineteenth century. The theory of the social contract had, in fact, been strongly represented in the theories of the early German Enlightenment, especially those of Althaus, who based the legitimacy of the public order on private interests (Gough 1936: 72). Later, Kant's political philosophy, although it contains, in part, a substantial theory of public political life (J. Ritter 1970: 81–2; Riley 1982: 132; Gough 1936:

173), also saw legitimate public order as an order in which the private interests of citizens are stabilized and defended by public law (Kant 1966a: 238). Although Kant argued that a legitimate legal state depends on (or is born out of) the transition from the sphere of private antagonism to the sphere of public law, he also asserted that the contracts which are formed privately set the basic terms of agreement for the establishment of the system of public (or civil) law, and therefore for the constitution of a republican legal order (Kant 1966b: 424). The stabilization of property-rights, Kant explained, is only possible under the constitution of civil law.[1] Therefore, Kant can still be viewed as a thinker in the tradition of contract-theory, for whom private interest is prior to political life (Koslowski 1982: 200). The economy, most importantly, is recognized by Kant as an area of operation which is not subordinate to political regulation, and which in certain respects provides the preconditions for political life (Saage 1989: 210).

Despite this, it is notable that the development of individualist or voluntarist contract-theory in Germany ended with Kant. Indeed, even Kant's own theory of the social contract does not imagine that the contract is constituted by free agreement between citizens and the state, but rather by the compliance of citizens with universal moral principles (Kant 1966b: 431). After Kant, the tendency to interpret political legitimacy in terms of personal or collective consent diminished in importance. In fact, this was not exclusive to Germany at this time. By the end of the eighteenth century, traditional contractarianism was widely criticized in most European countries. In Britain, the legal practice of recognizing the authority of free, lateral contracts had moved British political thinking away from the statically normative assumptions of the vertical contract (Atiyah 1979: 60). In France, Rousseau's brand of contract-theory turned radically against the individualist assumptions of classical contractarianism (Sened 1997: 25). Rousseau asserted popular unity, not private rights of ownership, as the basis of political legitimacy (Riley 1982: 102), and he argued that genuine political life could only be grounded on the total transformation of private rights into public obligations. For Rousseau, therefore, the contract does not protect private property and private liberty: it renders such rights and liberties public. Importantly, Rousseau's contributions to the economic legislation of the revolutionary era were subsequently criticized and eliminated by the bourgeois legal interpreters of nineteenth-century France (Bürge 1991: 42).

In Germany at this time, however, the tradition of contract-theory underwent a far more thorough modification than in Britain or France. After Napoleon, German political philosophy returned in part to the classical conceptions of political life which had initially been undermined by contractarianism (F. D. Miller 1995: 29). With the emergence of Hegel as the most influential political theorist of the immediate post-Napoleonic

1 Kant 1966b: 366. See also Diesselhorst 1988: 67; Küsters 1988: 76; Saage 1989: 194.

period, German political philosophy moved against the individualist favouring of private rights against public ethics, and set out a strongly neo-Aristotelian theory of political life (Riedel 1982: 93). In Hegel's theory, collectively constituted ethical life (*Sittlichkeit*) is placed above private rights (J. Ritter 1969a: 297). Indeed, rights are not considered private, or in any way anterior to common political existence (J. Ritter 1969b: 114). For Hegel, rights, whether of property or nature, do not exist outside the political sphere (J. Ritter 1969c: 168), but are worked out only through common ethics and interaction. The political sphere, for Hegel, has complete primacy over the private sphere. For this reason, therefore, post-Napoleonic political philosophy in Germany can be seen to put forward a positive theory of human political life and liberty, in which freedom is not prior to political interaction, but rather realized through it. Above all, in post-Napoleonic German political theory, the state, and the common political life which is engendered by the state, pre-exist all other aspects of political existence. Hegel shares with Rousseau the anti-Kantian belief that political life can only be based on the substantial unity of the collective (Fulda 1991: 62). Indeed, in certain respects Rousseau's theory of the contract is also an assault on the individualist principles of contract-theory. However, Rousseau's idea that political order might be based upon voluntary agreement rests, Hegel argues, upon the erroneous presupposition that individual choices antecede political life. In fact, Hegel argues, the converse is the case. Lateral agreements between citizens cannot be translated into vertical agreements with the state. The state is prior to all agreements.

Hegel's critique of contract, therefore, demonstrates a paradigmatic unwillingness to accept the rationality of the economy as the foundation of the political order. His essential argument is that the state cannot be based upon contract, because a contract merely codifies the rationality of private law. Contract is based upon the particular interests and antagonisms which the private economy produces. Although Hegel acknowledges that certain forms of liberty are generated by the economy, the logic of the economy, he argues, is self-interest. The state, in contrast, embodies a higher general rationality, which can intervene in the economy and reconcile the antagonisms which the economy engenders. Genuine politics, thus, can only – Hegel argues – be established by the state and the state-administration, to which he imputes the ability to enact the general will of the people, beyond the divisions caused by the economy (Hegel 1986: 407). Hegel's political philosophy might, therefore, be seen to contain a political *anthropology*, in which the composition of collective political life is the defining fact of human existence. Hegel maintains a strong attachment to the estate-system of government. He sees the estates as hinges which operate at the interface between civil society and the state. Estates, however, he asserts, do not have true political dignity, and they cannot constitute the political will.

This tradition of anti-contractual theory in Germany has produced a history of very distinct political formations. The traditional critique of the individualistic political order grasps the social sphere (in the tradition of the *Ständestaat*) as a complexly composed set of organisms and spheres of activity, which are situated beneath the level of the state (H. Brandt 1968: 76), but which are also integrated into the state. Such theories were especially widespread in conservative German responses to the French Revolution (Bowen 1947: 18), and in reactionary thought prior to 1848. However, they also survived into the twentieth century, and they experienced a revival in the 1920s and the early 1930s, especially in Roman Catholic political theory (Spann 1921: 199). Nonetheless, there are also more radical versions of the organic – non-contractual – theory of law and state. The dream of a political order based on law-creating fellowship (national solidarity) rather than law-imposing sovereignty, grudging compromise between the classes, or mere formal contract, remained influential well into the twentieth century, especially in the Weimar Constitution (see Portner 1973: 236). Hugo Preuß's drafts for the Weimar Constitution, strongly marked by Otto von Gierke (H. Preuß 1926: 489; see also Gierke 1868: 1/135; Berman 1983: 219–20), sought to guarantee popular sovereignty by integrating all organizations into the state. The social legislation of the Weimar period also testifies to the survival of a corporate, or economic-democratic element in modern law. The social components in the Weimar Constitution attempted to bridge state and society by placing industrial relations on the juncture between private and public law, under the co-ordinating authority of the state, and by linking the political will-formation to active collaboration between social groups (classes) in the economy. The post-1945 political concept of the social-legal state, at the core of the founding documents of the Federal Republic, is itself in part indebted to this tradition of organic-corporate reflection. The relativization of private or contractual law remains therefore an active component even in the most recent German political tradition (Wieacker 1967: 545).

Many of the more recent theories of legitimacy addressed in this work also strongly recall Hegel's thought, and they mirror the Aristotelian recourse at the inception of modern German political theory. The plebiscitary dimensions to the thinking of Schmitt and Weber are also symbolic attempts to overcome the contractarian political order. Both Weber and Schmitt see the political dimension to human life as the manifestation and production of a collective political ethic. Neumann and Kirchheimer argue most radically in favour of a political order in which human life is not bound to any private obligations. Habermas's early assertion that the good polity cannot be anchored in the unmediated pluralism of interest contains a clear echo of Hegel's refusal to grant to technical reason the status of universality (Theunissen 1981: 27). German political thought after Hegel tends, therefore, to argue that the rationality of politics is distinct from other spheres of operation, and that the political sphere retains an autonomous status, as (ideally) a location of universal will-formation which is not categorically bound to prior concerns. Legitimate government is thus generally grasped as government which is not a mere clearing-house for different, vacillating interests, but a condensation of non-specific collective needs. In this respect, the nineteenth-century duality of state and society has been refracted into twentieth-century theory as an insistence that state and society, if they are to be connected, cannot be simply linked in easy fluidity. They must, rather, be reconciled in a sphere of action which either antedates, or is constituted beyond, the forms of association and antagonism which characterize the technical aspect of human life.

Even the German liberal movements, which elsewhere pioneered contract-theory, did not, at least outside the marginal post-Kantian line, develop a theory of contractual freedom. The liberals of the nineteenth century – strongly influenced by the spirit of historicism – argued, generally, that national political organization would provide the key to the resolution of economic antagonisms (see Gagel 1958: 67–8), and that liberty could not be envisaged outside the state. The German vision of emancipation – especially liberal emancipation – was thus imagined, broadly, in terms which were derived from the state itself. There are clear historical and conceptual reasons for this. The liberal 'revolutionaries' of the *Vormärz* and 1848 certainly endeavoured to secure their own economic emancipation. But German unity and the borders of the German nation-state were, necessarily, their equally pressing concerns (Nipperdey 1983: 669). After the failures of 1848, the middle class did not constitute itself in civil opposition to the state, but acquiesced in Bismarck's system. Even liberal programmes of the first decades of the twentieth century were still complicatedly rooted in the governmental structures of the Hohenzollern era. For these reasons, German liberals tended to view the state as the precondition of liberal success, not as a contractual or representative body. This is illustrated most perfectly by Max Weber, who grasps politics both as the administration of economic advantage and as a collective quality which condenses and serves the national will. Even the early radical groups of the mid-nineteenth century and the social-democratic movement of the late nineteenth century retained an attachment to the strong state (Nipperdey 1961: 394). Although Marx's theory of politics interpreted the political sphere as a mere superstructural reflex of the economy, the formative years of the German labour movement were strongly marked by Lassalle's particular brand of strong-state socialism (see Morgan 1965: 33; S. Miller 1964: 35–7).

The nature of these relations between public and private life in the German legal and political traditions in fact closely reflects certain aspects of economic organization in Germany. Significantly, the tradition of laissez-faire liberalism never attained the same level of popularity in Germany as in Western European countries. Even in the age of high liberalism – the mid-nineteenth century – the insistence that control of the economy should be devolved exclusively to private bodies found little support in Germany. Notably, the ordering of the German economy in the nineteenth century was marked by far higher levels of organization and regulation than elsewhere. Political reflection in Germany, thus, displayed a practical opposition to freedom of lateral contract, as well as a theoretical hostility to vertical contract-theory. In addition to the regulatory measures introduced by Bismarck after 1878, the period of accelerated industrial expansion in Germany (1870–1900) coincided with a rapid concentration of economic power in the hands of organized associations – cartels. These cartels were freely constituted bodies which were designed to limit competition and to fix prices in certain sectors of industrial production. The development of the cartels was the topic of fierce debate in the latter part of the nineteenth century. It is striking, however, that even most liberal thinkers approved of cartels, and saw them as mechanisms for protecting collective interests from the ravages of the unchecked private economy (Pohl 1979: 209). The cartels were originally viewed as semi-public associations which contributed to the will-formation of the state from the economy, but which remained just below the level of the political system (1979: 230). It can thus be inferred that the liberal class in Germany was not in principle opposed to the restriction of free trade and the imposition of limits on the competitive self-regulation of the economy. The cartelization of the economy increased rapidly through the early twentieth century, and it became a formal mode of economic steering during the 1914–18 war (Grossfeld 1979: 257). Significantly, the development of the cartel-system also had an effect on the structure of public law. In 1877 the cartels were declared legal by the Prussian judiciary, and were not deemed to be obstructions to the freedom of trade otherwise guaranteed in the system of private law (1979: 257). This judgement was reinforced by the Imperial Court in 1890 (Coing 1989: 181). The liberalization of the economy in the period 1850–75 was thus (in part) redressed by a system of cartel-based economic organization, which accorded semi-public status to bodies properly situated in the sphere of private law. In Germany, therefore, in parallel to the relativization of private law by the state (from above), private-legal associations quickly organized themselves (from below) in such a manner that they assumed a position on the intersection between public and private law. They were thus able to exercise quasi-legal authority over whole sectors of socio-economic activity. This meant, in short, that in Germany the sphere of private law was subject to a process of rigorous regimentation, and that an organized system of power emerged beside the state, which was able to regulate the economy, and which could also influence the decisions of the political executive. Not until the 1920s was it consistently argued that the cartels actually formed a mode of organization which did not reinforce the power of the state, but detracted from it. Gustav Streseman passed anti-cartel legislation in 1923. Similar legislation was again passed by Ludwig Erhard in 1957. In modern German political thought, notably, the cartel-system of organized capitalism is interpreted as a symptom of the absence of real political life in Germany. From Weber to Habermas, the technical and collective organization of the economy by bodies interposed between state and society is viewed as a poor surrogate for real political life, which prevents the mediation between the economy and the state that genuine political society presupposes.

The defining aspects of German political thinking, in sum – its historicism, its positivism, its statism, its integrative ethic, its positive theory of
liberty and its anti-contractual theory of politics – can in general be
interpreted as variations on the conviction that social rights do not exist
in a neutral space outside, or before, the political order, and that the
recognition of personal liberty always presupposes a political collective,
centred around the state. In such theories, the liberal–democratic relation
between interests and representation is inverted. Legitimate government,
following such ideas, is not the particular representation of social interests,
but rather a political life-form, in which particular interests have a subsidiary position.

The development of such ideas can, not lastly, be ascribed to the
relatively late period of industrialization in Germany. By the time a non-
aristocratic political class had developed, the Prussian state was secure
enough – having already absorbed certain sectors of the middle class
through administrative reforms (Nipperdey 1983: 31–82; Grimm 1988:
87) – to obstruct, at least until 1914, the assumption of power by anti-
conservative forces and interests. The Prussian middle class, in particular,
was assimilated rapidly into a politically restrictive, but economically bene-
ficial compromise with the Hohenzollern state. The middle-class parties
did not get hold of real power until after 1919, by which time the period of
unrestricted bourgeois rule was already over (G. Schmidt 1974: 277).

It might also be observed in this relation that in Germany the classical
arena for the expression of bourgeois interests – parliament itself – has
never occupied a position of absolute centrality in the political order. The
parliaments of the period 1849–1918 were really only budgetary chambers
with fluctuating influence on the executive, whose power did not finally
exceed rights of fiscal veto (Huber 1963: 776). Members of parliament were
not permitted ministerial status. These parliaments were also characterized
by low levels of party-political organization. Up until 1918 (and arguably
afterwards), the political parties did not develop either as effective links
between civil society and the state or as organs for intellectual/ideological
formation. The constitutional organization of the Weimar Republic, in
certain regards a model of popular democracy, did not recognize political
parties as public bodies. The Weimar Constitution contained heavy presidial checks on the strength of the legislative body, and it was based from
the outset upon extra-parliamentary compromises between the government
and the military, and between big business and the unions. These placed
prior limits upon the executive authorizations of the parliamentary government. Parliament, already effectively powerless by 1930, was dissolved
finally by the Enabling Laws of the National Socialists in 1933. Even in
the Federal Republic it has often been asserted that parliament has never
completely asserted itself as the true location of power, and that its influence has always been counterbalanced or determined by the corporate
functions of social and economic organizations. The separation of powers,
in Western European democracies the chief political accomplishment of the

bourgeoisie, was also not finally achieved in pre-1945 Germany. Even in more recent traditions of German conservative thought, the separation of the powers is by no means an unquestionable component of the good political order. In post-1945 political thought, the conviction that the unrestricted ceding of power to the parliamentary legislature is a mere technical device for appeasing the economic ambitions of the middle class, rather than a means for engendering true democracy, remains influential (W. Weber 1951: 43). This argument is right at the heart of much inter-war political theory. Analogously, much of the left-leaning theory of the Federal Republic is, despite its critique of parliamentary democracy, still concerned with the attempt to show how parliament might be transformed into the organ of real will-formation. The theory of politics in German thought is therefore always related to the position of the middle class. Schmitt, Neumann and Kirchheimer attempt to eliminate the systems of political life (private law) which the middle class has produced. Weber and Habermas attempt to revivify that space – public/political culture – which is customarily (or ideally) filled by the middle class, but whose weakness in Germany reflects the complex history of the German bourgeoisie.

The main question in German political thinking remains, therefore, the distance between state and society, and the difficult attempt to link the two. In the following studies, varying outlines are seen for models of democracy which unite both components. These include the charismatic integration of people into government by means of the personal qualities of leaders (Weber), the symbolization of politics as an aesthetically integrative appeal (Schmitt), the active mediation of civil society through political participation (Neumann and Kirchheimer), the production of radical-democratic discourse (Habermas), and the post-subjective functionalization of citizens for the technical needs of administration (Luhmann). In each case (except that of Luhmann), politics, conceived as radical-democratic politics, aesthetic politics, charismatic politics or discursive politics, is not reducible, merely, to the expression of already existing needs. It is the central dimension in varying forms of philosophical anthropology, in which human life is human only when it is political.

In each case, therefore, against the background of the wholesale dissolution of political action in modern society (see Narr and Schubert 1994: 215), the observer is invited to reflect upon the contemporary conditions of political liberty.

# 1

# *Max Weber*

Max Weber has entered intellectual history as the major sociologist of early twentieth-century Europe, and naturally his political thinking cannot be extricated simply from his general sociology. His sociological writings on economic history, law, religion and the city constitute the body of research upon which his political ideas are based. However, Weber's political works stand also as responses to political dilemmas of his own time, and in this work they will broadly be treated as such. This chapter will therefore focus especially on his theory of politics, and it will draw on his wider thinking mainly in order to situate and explicate his understanding of politics and the political sphere.

It is of the greatest significance for Weber's thought that his education coincided with the rapid expansion of industrial production in Germany and the corresponding rise in power of the industrial middle class. Weber's father was a municipal councillor and prominent member of the National Liberal party in Berlin, and in his youth Weber was introduced to many of the leading liberal politicians and intellectuals of late nineteenth-century Prussia (Bendix 1977: 1). Weber's thought exemplifies the complexity of liberal thinking during this period, and it provides an illuminating case-study of the peculiarities and problems of German liberalism in general.[1]

Nineteenth-century German liberalism never constituted a uniform political bloc, and its history was marked by division. Even during its period of fleeting triumph in the revolutionary parliament of 1848–9, it was characterized by a latent schism between a statist tendency, which

---

1 See Zwehl 1983: 91–2. See also Groh 1973: 31; Stegmann 1970: 127; Jones 1985: 1; Blackbourn and Eley 1984: 159; Dahrendorf 1967: 31.

simply sought to secure the influence of the middle class within a constitutional monarchy, and a radical-liberal contingent, which was more inclined to seek support amongst the growing proletariat (Schieder 1980: 556). After 1848, the differentiation of political positions within the German liberal movements became increasingly complex as the liberal class itself increased in numerical size and its interests became less homogeneous. Partly owing to the fragmentation of the middle class, the position of the liberal parties in the political system of imperial Germany was also complex and deeply compromised.

After the unification period, the National Liberal party (founded 1866) acted as senior coalition-partner of the Free Conservatives in the imperial parliament and it collaborated with Bismarck in introducing important liberal economic reform measures throughout the early 1870s (Wehler 1995: 866; Sheehan 1978: 135). Although the separation of government and parliament in the imperial electoral system meant that the National Liberals never gained direct access to the governmental executive, the 1870s were marked by the unique (albeit temporary) prestige of liberal politics and ideas, by the willingness of Bismarck to negotiate with the liberal parties, and by the short-lived centrality of the parliamentary system in political decision-making. However, this period was terminated by the famous anti-liberal turn in Bismarck's post-unification politics. In 1878 Bismarck discredited the market-oriented policies of the liberal parties and he dissolved the conservative–liberal coalition which had been sustained through the first decade of the united Germany. Following this, Bismarck introduced a series of anti-liberal laws, partly with the intention of weakening the influence of the liberal factions in parliament, and thereby of limiting the influence of parliament itself (Pack 1961: 27). These laws included the anti-socialist law (1878) which prohibited socialist political agitation. They also included the introduction of protective tariffs (1879) – intended to protect the internal market, increase governmental revenue, and weaken the autonomy of the liberal factions – and the welfare laws of 1883, 1884 and 1889, which established the foundations for an authoritarian welfare-system, designed both to palliate and undermine workers' movements (Ullmann 1995: 179). The second decade of the united Germany was thus characterized by anti-socialist and anti-liberal policies. The quasi-parliamentary order of the 1870s was replaced by a more conservative coalition, which checked the reformist ambitions of the liberals, and supplanted the nascent parliamentary system with a more Caesarist style of government (Winkler 1979a: 36–7; Stürmer 1974: 327). Bismarck's attempt to weaken the incipient parliamentary system also cemented the development of a corporate model of political and economic government (Wehler 1995: 936–7). In this system, the importance of personal connections between interest-groups and politicians in many instances outweighed parliamentary representation itself (Puhle 1970: 342–3). Notably, Bismarck's anti-parliamentary policies came soon after the foundation of the first organized bodies for the representation of industrialists' interests. The

Association of German Iron and Steel Producers was formed in 1874 and
the Central Association of German Industrialists was formed in 1876 (H.
Rosenberg 1967: 161; see also Sieling-Wendeling 1976: 77). Bismarck
himself toyed with the idea of reintroducing estate-based systems of corporate representation (Ullmann 1982: 146; Winkler 1972: 24; Pack 1961: 20).

The impact of the crisis-year 1878–9 on the liberal groupings was
devastating (Gagel 1958: 104; Nipperdey 1961: 131). The right wing of
the National Liberal party broke away in 1879. The members of the party's
left departed in 1880 and eventually fused with the left-liberal Progressive
party to form the Deutsche Freisinnige Partei in 1884, which itself dissolved into rival factions in 1893 (Pack 1961: 131). The remaining members
of the National Liberals regrouped and reformed the party in 1884, with an
avowedly pro-conservative, pro-Bismarck manifesto, which declared support for the anti-socialist law, for protective laws for agriculture and for
reinforcement and expansion of the military (Langewiesche 1988: 180). The
refounded National Liberal party collaborated extensively with the Conservatives, even forming a majority-coalition in the period 1887–90. Even
the left-liberal parties which emerged after 1893, primarily the Freisinnige
Volkspartei and the Freisinnige Vereinigung, were only hesitantly opposed
to the major political programmes of the conservative governments. After
1900 the left-liberal groupings became more acquiescent in their dealings
with the government, and even collaborated in part with the 1907–9
coalition-bloc with the Conservatives and the National Liberals (Elm
1968: 174). The history of liberalism in the *Kaiserreich* can therefore be
summarized as a history of decline. During this time, the right-leaning
liberals were at times willingly absorbed into the coalition-structure which
supported Bismarck's executive, and the left-liberals were left to dream
of expanding their influence by attracting support from the working class
in order to block the executive. Between 1893 and 1907 the percentage
of votes won by the left-liberals declined from 18 per cent to under 7 per
cent. Only after the recreation of a unified left-liberal party in 1910, the
Fortschrittliche Volkspartei (Progressive People's party: FVP), did the left-
liberal share of the vote again reach above 10 per cent.

Importantly for an assessment of Weber's thought, the liberal tradition in
Germany contains conceptual and historical traits which distinguish it from
the individualistic premises of liberal politics. Owing, in part, to the
enforced collaboration between the liberal parties and the Prussian executive, German liberalism did not seamlessly absorb the classical-liberal
(private-legal) proclamation of freedom of contract – or, freedom *from*
the state – as the foundation of political liberty. Nineteenth- and early
twentieth-century German liberalism retained a belief in the state-executive
as the co-ordinator of the public good. Similarly, traditional German
liberalism, both left and right, was strongly marked by its sympathetic
approach to welfare-policies. The Verein für Sozialpolitik (Association for
Social Policies), founded by Gustav Schmoller in 1872, was an important
forum for liberal debate in the *Kaiserreich*. This association attracted figures

from both left- and right-liberal orientations who proposed alternatives to the laissez-faire policies of the National Liberal era (Boese 1939: 20), and who approved the corporate welfare-system which Bismarck began to introduce in the 1880s (Lambi 1963: 88–9). Representatives of this association even harboured hopes of effecting greater co-operation between the liberal movements, the unions and the SPD (Feldman 1966: 22; Sheehan 1978: 153). Weber was close in outlook to certain doctrines of the Verein für Sozialpolitik, which published his first major work.

It is arguable, therefore, that liberal thinking in nineteenth-century Germany remained distinct from the general premises of European liberalism for the simple reason that it opposed the primacy of private law and the private economy. By the late 1870s, few influential liberal theorists showed unqualified support for free-market liberalism. For this, Weber's thought is exemplary. Weber argues that the crucial feature of modern political systems is that the state is increasingly rationalized in accordance with the private-legal order (1972: 506). The modern state, Weber explains, operates by purely formal norms and it creates its legitimacy by such norms. This formality of the modern state is due to its legal basis. Positive law, upon which the modern state is founded, has developed through a process of rationalization in which the state has assumed legal and functional responsibility for the economy (1972: 487). The state must therefore guarantee the conditions which allow the economy to function. Rather than viewing this, however, as a successful accomplishment of the bourgeoisie, Weber sees it as a process which undermines law's power to define political life in substantive terms (1972: 499). In keeping with the general climate of liberal debate in Germany after 1878, Weber insists that the state possesses a structural dignity above the economy, and that the integrity of political life is undermined wherever the basis of the state is placed exclusively in the private-legal order. Significantly, Weber's systematic reflections on law began to appear after the establishment of the *Bürgerliche Gesetzbuch*, which became statute in 1900.

The key aspect of late nineteenth-century liberalism in Germany can, however, be most accurately assessed as a problem of integration. Weber's thought again has exemplary status in this respect. After the failure of the proto-parliamentary reforms of the 1870s, parliament itself – and the political parties – declined rapidly in influence and prestige. The liberal parties, therefore, were (at least in part) deprived of the classical arena of liberal organization and integration. The middle-class share of political power was reliant either on the pursuit of blocking-tactics ('negative politics') or on the forming of unholy alliances with the Conservatives. After the secession of the left-liberals in 1880, the liberal movement was never again in a position to present itself as a united front against conservatism (W. J. Mommsen 1990a: 22–3; Schieder 1980: 199–200). Generally, in fact, the German political parties never performed the organizational and integrative function which they possessed in Anglo-Saxon political systems. Indeed, the organizational weakness of German parties can be viewed as a factor which directly played into the hands of the executive of the *Kaiser-reich* and which prevented the broadening of the political power-base (Grosser 1970: 15). Liberal intellectuals of the late *Kaiserreich* were there-fore forced to reflect on special means for the (re)establishment of an integral bloc representing middle-class interests. In many respects, Weber's entire opus can be interpreted as an endeavour to recreate liberal politics as a substantive ethic of integration, which encompasses private, public and social law and which thus appeals to, and involves, all sectors of society. However, here too the years of co-operation with the anti-liberal executive in the *Kaiserreich* left their mark on liberal thinking. Weber himself (as will be seen) affirmed many attributes of Bismarck's executive. Bismarck's employment of ideological processes of integration, such as autocratic welfare-measures, heroic nationalism, colonial policies and charismatic Caesarism, is strongly echoed in the technical nature of Weber's own theory of democratic legitimacy (Winkler 1979b: 34). Therefore, Weber's work can, on one hand, be viewed as an attempt to recast liberalism as a popular appeal. However, on the other hand, it also marks the end of liberalism as a set of more or less determinate convictions. It is, at the very least, a plan to deploy traditionally anti-liberal means of integration for the salvation of liberalism itself.

Weber's party-political connections were closely bound up with the career of Friedrich Naumann, for whom Weber acted both as political disciple and intellectual adviser. Naumann is remembered chiefly as an influential left-liberal political thinker and popular theorist of the early twentieth century, and as one of the founding fathers of the constitution of the Weimar Republic. In each of these respects, Naumann's closeness to Weber is important, and Naumann's activities often illuminate Weber's basic ideas. In 1896 Naumann founded the short-lived left-liberal Nation-alsozialer Verein (National Social party), a party which endorsed a policy of simultaneous external economic expansion and internal democratization in Wilhelmine Germany (W. J. Mommsen 1959: 145). Naumann's writings of this time, especially *Democracy and Empire*, are the most revealing reflec-tions on the problems confronted by the left-leaning German liberals around 1900 (Naumann 1900: 127). In *Democracy and Empire*, Naumann laments the archaic nature of the three-class electoral system in Prussia. He examines the emergence of the Social Democratic party (SPD) and the unions in the late *Kaiserreich*, and he advocates broader co-operation between the SPD (especially the revisionist wing, under the influence of Eduard Bernstein) and the various liberal parties.[2] He supports the creation of a system of political alliances, as an alternative bloc to the conservative executive (see G. A. Ritter 1985: 27; Kühne 1994: 282), able to connect all sections of society from the non-revolutionary industrial proletariat to the leadership of the National Liberals (Naumann 1900: 116). His plan for a coalition stretching from Bebel (leader of the SPD) to Bassermann (leader

---

2 See Theiner 1983: 131. Also: Gagel 1958: 99; Nipperdey 1961: 188; Düding, 1972: 194.

of the National Liberals) perfectly captures the spirit of the rather desperate left-liberal attempts to expand the legislative influence of the middle class in the early twentieth century (Heckart 1974: 16; see also D. S. White 1976: 162–3; Theiner 1983: 112). Naumann argues that a coalition between the SPD and the Liberals would provide a legislative counter-weight to the ministerial cabinet (G. Schmidt 1964: 251), and would thus facilitate electoral reform (see G. A. Ritter 1978: 367). A liberal-revisionist coalition, Naumann therefore claims (1911: 320), would be the most effective device for maximizing the power of the middle class. Ultimately, he asserts, a broader-based political system in Germany would also help secure the objectives of the German imperialist programme, as it would strengthen the spirit of national community (W. J. Mommsen 1959: 100). Naumann's interest in social-liberal co-operation, therefore, has an essentially functional character. A politically integrated proletariat, he projects, would enable the middle class to gain a hold on power, and would ultimately serve the economic interests of the middle class. In *Democracy and Empire*, Naumann also picks up the threads of social imperialism which derive from Lorenz von Stein and the members of the Verein für Sozialpolitik (Fehrenbach 1969: 186–7), and he grandly represents Kaiser Wilhelm II as the charismatic co-ordinator of social integration and external expansion.

Naumann's ideas gained especial significance at the end of the first decade of the twentieth century, after the dissolution of the liberal–conservative 'Bülow bloc' (due to differences in fiscal policy) and the renewed fusion of the left-liberal factions to form the FVP in 1910 (see Kühne 1994: 470, 540, 565). In this period the abruptly interrupted process of parliamentarization of the 1870s regained momentum. In 1907 the left-liberals and the Zentrum (the Catholic party) had both independently appealed for electoral reform to strengthen parliament against the executive (Pateman 1964: 15). Parliament itself had been in part responsible for the end of Bülow's tenure on power in 1909, and by 1912 there existed a large anti-government, reformist majority in parliament (Feldman 1966: 11). The prospect of a united liberal-socialist body was therefore an important component in the renewed move towards the consolidation of parliamentary power (Bertram 1964: 54). Naumann especially greeted the dissolution of the Bülow bloc as an opportunity for recementing the lost alliance between left- and right-liberals (Eschenburg 1929: 269–70). It is unlikely, however, that either Bassermann or Bebel seriously supported Naumann's plans (Langewiesche 1988: 225–7). Bassermann, for example, despite his apparent move to the left after 1909, evidently retained hopes of renewed co-operation with the Conservatives (Bertram 1964: 62).

Naumann was certainly not a great political theorist. His ideas comprise a rough fusion of revisionist Marxism, nationalism, cultural Protestantism, mythologizing monarchism and imperialist euphoria. However, his proposal for a political order combining internal integration and external expansion crystallizes the broad climate of liberal political debate in post-Bismarck Prussia (see Schustereit 1975: 221). For all the crudeness of his thinking,

Naumann, like Weber, recognizes the weakness of liberal politics in Wilhelmine society. He seeks accordingly to reinvent liberalism as an integrative ideology and thus to rescue the liberal movement from its assimilation into the Wilhelmine executive (Gagel 1958: 102; Kühne 1994: 276; Conze 1950: 355). In order to achieve this, Naumann combines aspects of diverse and even conflicting political positions. His thought assimilates both the social policies of the left and the constitutional and imperial legacy of the right (W. J. Mommsen 1975: 137). His endeavour to link social integration, aesthetic monarchism and imperialism perfectly underlines the ideological coalescence of Wilhelmine liberalism with the politics of its adversaries. Both Naumann and Weber recognized that purely liberal programmes had little appeal for the German middle class at the turn of the century, and that liberal groups would have to abandon liberal ideals in order to achieve their objectives (Rürup 1972: 222).

Weber was the intellectual mentor behind Naumann's political activities. Weber, like Naumann, belonged to the generation of middle-class intellectuals who drifted to the left after 1900, owing to their disillusionment with the failed reforms and the pragmatic accommodations of the National Liberals. Owing to his contempt for Kaiser Wilhelm II, Weber became an advocate of full parliamentary democracy in the first decade of the century (W. J. Mommsen 1963: 295–322). Although Weber was not a full member of the National Social Party (Düding 1972: 197), Naumann's vision of a cross-party anti-conservative alliance has clear similarities with Weber's ideas (Spael 1985: 43–4). Weber also shared Naumann's sense that a successful imperial programme could only be pursued if the proletariat was integrated into the political system. However, it was not until the revolutionary winter of 1918–19 that the relation between Naumann and Weber gained its greatest importance. After the collapse of the Hohenzollern monarchy in late 1918, and in the months prior to this collapse, Weber set out a number of proposals for the political reorganization of Germany. His favoured model was a system which combined parliamentary administration with plebiscitary rule. At the end of the monarchy, Naumann acted as head of the Commission for Basic Rights in the constitutional assembly in Weimar. Naumann's contributions to the new constitution strongly reflected the influence of Weber's more theoretical writings on constitutional law (Schiffers 1971: 12; Treippe 1995: 130–1; Theiner 1986: 75). Also at this time (1919), Naumann founded the DDP (German Democratic party). The DDP, true to Naumann's earlier dream of a unified non-Catholic, bourgeois bloc, was conceived as a party of national unity. In the early Weimar system, the DDP sought to play the role of a hinge-party between the interests of the SPD, the unions and the parties of big business (Jones 1988: 25), especially the DVP (German People's party), which emerged after the dissolution of the National Liberals (see Frye 1985: 45). Although Weber was not an active member of the DDP, he was close to the leading figures in the party, and he influenced its underlying conception (W. J. Mommsen 1959: 303–4). Neither Naumann nor Weber lived to see the outcome of their political projects, as both died before the Weimar Republic was much more than a year old. However, their political interventions between 1895 and 1919 mark the clearest threads which connect the debates surrounding the liberal movements in mid- to late-Wilhelmine society and the German (and liberal) experiment with democracy in the 1920s.

In short, therefore, Weber's political thought constitutes a set of responses to the antiquated nature of the German political system of the Wilhelmine period. Despite the rise in strength of German industry, and the industrial class, during the last decades of the *Kaiserreich* – by 1913 Germany had the second highest level of industrial production in the world (Wehler 1995: 610–11) – actual executive power was only rarely placed in the hands of figures who had not emerged through the dynastic families and the high ranks of the bureaucracy (W. J. Mommsen 1990b: 64). Although Weber never wholly abandoned the old-style Prussian liberalism of the National Liberals (Gagel 1958: 72), his political contributions focus on the need for the adjustment of the governmental apparatus to the conditions of modern Germany, with its altered class-configurations. Central to his thought in this respect is the conviction that Germany could only con-solidate its position on the international stage through vigorous constitu-tional modernization. Modernization, in Weber's national-political sense, means the consolidation of the role of the middle class in political admin-istration. Above all, Weber sought to create a political system which would facilitate the emergence of a middle class equipped with the skills and abilities required for the international reinforcement of Germany's power. Weber's thinking revolves around the classical liberal assumption that the political strength of the nation depends utterly upon the economic strength of the bourgeoisie (Gagel 1958: 15). He argues therefore that a system of representation should be created in which those responsible for the eco-nomic success of the nation are also entrusted with political authority.

Weber's commitment to the consolidation of middle-class power runs through all his work. All Weber's writings focus on the middle class. His sociological works provide an ideal history of the modern middle class. His economic works examine the preconditions for the emergence of the middle class. His political works address the conditions of the middle class in modern society. Weber expressly terms himself a 'bourgeois scholar' (1988a: 19), who is marked by the 'views and ideals' of the bourgeoisie (1988a: 20) and whose mission is to define and protect bourgeois interests. Weber's opus constitutes thus a set of systematic reflections upon the very nature and motivations of the bourgeoisie. However, it is also in his theory of the middle class that Weber's thought is at its most ambiguous. Indeed, it is in his theory of the middle class that his ideas move most emphatically away from the common positions of liberalism. Weber emphatically places his thought in the service of bourgeois interests, and he seeks to produce a system of government by means of which the bourgeoisie might legitim-ately assume power. Despite this, his work can also be read as a critical theory of the bourgeoisie, and of the German bourgeoisie in particular.

Weber's interpretation of the position of the German middle class is seen most clearly in his very earliest political writings, most significantly his inaugural address at the University of Freiburg in 1895. In this essay, he (like many far more conservative figures: see Röhl 1967: 256) examines how the German peasants in the eastern areas of Prussia are disadvantaged by the financial policies of the eastern aristocracy – the Junker class – and consequently lose influence to the less culturally and economically developed Polish peasants (see A. Rosenberg 1928: 46). This examination provides a context in which Weber develops his more general theories on the relation between political and economic concerns (see Puhle 1972: 59). The conditions of the eastern peasants, he claims, must be viewed as an issue in which the interests of the nation-state should prevail over local financial considerations. The post-Bismarck Junker class is, he explains, a class which is struggling for economic survival, and whose disproportionate influence on executive decisions is inimical to the national interest (1988a: 19). In questions of economic policy, he argues, 'the last and decisive vote' should be given to 'the economic and political power-interests of our nation and its bearers, the German nation state' (1988a: 15).

Weber thus uses his investigation on the eastern peasants as a vehicle both for attacking the archaic qualities of the Prussian executive and for interpreting the role of the bourgeoisie in modern Germany. Power, he implies, should be transferred to a class which is strong enough to represent the interests of the nation. However, his outline of the status of the bourgeoisie is not one of unrestricted enthusiasm. He recurrently condemns the rural bourgeoisie for being inattentive to interests of national well-being. He especially criticizes rural capitalists for employing foreign labourers because they are cheaper, thereby weakening the standing of the German-speaking peasants (1988b: 186). Despite his support for the political emancipation of the bourgeoisie, therefore, Weber rejects the pure economization of politics, and he insists that the economic power of the bourgeoisie must play a positive and unifying role in the political sphere. Although Weber expresses contempt for the old Junker class, he is not much more sympathetically disposed towards the new bourgeoisie. He explains:

> Throughout the whole of history the attainment of economic power has always made a class consider itself prepared to assume political government. It is dangerous and, in the long term, incompatible with the interests of the nation when a class which is declining economically has political power in its hands. Yet it is still more dangerous when classes, who are gaining economic power and are therefore likely to accede to political government, are politically not mature enough to lead the state. Both these things threaten Germany at the moment and provide the key to the present dangers of our situation. (1988a: 24)

Weber anticipates therefore that 'an enormous task of education' will be necessary in order to prepare the bourgeoisie for the assumption of power (1988a: 24).

This passage illuminates the very heart of Weber's political commitment. True to the post-1878 tradition of German liberalism, Weber claims that the political sphere has its own specific quality and autonomy, and he insists that matters of national importance should be regulated by more than mere private interest (see Aron 1965: 113–14). The state, he suggests, might in certain circumstances protect the population from the excesses of the capitalist economy and thus retain a co-ordinating, even neutral function in economic affairs (see Giddens 1971: 234). The national security and survival of the German-speaking eastern peasants are, he argues, a cause significant enough to override both the privileges of the Junkers and the investment policies of the modern capitalists (see Giddens 1972: 26). Weber's pledge to the bourgeoisie is therefore qualified. It depends upon the ability of this class to contribute successfully to the organization of both economic and national-political needs. In post-Bismarck Prussia, Weber argues, the aristocracy is no longer able to govern the nation, the bourgeoisie is prevented by the aristocracy from developing in such a manner that it could govern the country, and both the peasantry and the urban proletariat (and therefore the whole nation) suffer from these deficiencies of the political apparatus. The modernization of Germany is therefore, for Weber, the condition of its survival. It is not merely a process by means of which the bourgeoisie obtains influence.

The chief traits of Weber's brand of liberalism – and of German liberalism in general – are also illustrated in this early essay (Sheehan 1978: 34). Even at this early stage it is clear that Weber's liberalism combines both elements of classical liberal thought and elements of strongly anti-liberal positions. His theory of the bourgeoisie partially absorbs the protection- and welfare-related components of Bismarck's anti-liberal legislation, as well as principles of state-driven imperialism (W. J. Mommsen 1975: 128). The assumption of power by the bourgeoisie will, Weber intimates, not only herald the emancipation of the economy, and its most powerful class. It will also guarantee that the economy serves national purposes. In this respect, Weber ascribes two radically divergent functions to the middle class. He argues that the economic rationality of the middle class – the 'struggle for economic confidence' – should naturally form the basis of the relations between German and Polish peasants (1988a: 13). Indeed, he bemoans the fact that the German bourgeoisie has not proved itself sufficiently strong to combat effectively the groups which oppose it. At the same time, however, Weber argues that the middle class should serve interests higher than economic gain – that it should integrate and enact the demands of the national collective itself. In this respect, Weber's liberalism calls upon traditions of political reflection which have little or no connection with market-based liberalism. Like Hegel before him, Weber suggests that the political sphere possesses a dignity which differentiates it from the rational administration of the economy. The ethic of politics should, therefore, be elevated above the rationality of mere interest. The strongest class produced by the capitalist economy, he argues, is entitled to assume political power. To justify its assumption of political power, however, it must incorporate an ethic which extends beyond purely economic rationality. The formal ethic of economic rationality must, Weber indicates, be transposed into an ethic of substantive or collective obligation.

Historically, Weber's attack on the influence of agrarian interest-groups on Prussian politics is a rejection of the corporate style of government which characterized Imperial Germany. The circumvention of parliament in the post-1878 Bismarckian system gave organized interest-groups (of which agrarian bodies were amongst the strongest) direct personal access to the political executive.[3] This period saw a large-scale transfer of power from parliamentary organizations (parties) to corporate associations and interest-groups (Puhle 1970: 343). Weber's polemic against agrarian interests is therefore also an assault on Bismarck's personal-corporate system. This system, Weber implies, allows the favouring and balancing of particular interests to prevail over more general national commitments. Consequently, it prevents the production of a political will which is able to recognize and act upon genuine national interests. Weber's observations on the eastern peasants therefore touch the heart of the preoccupations of the Wilhelmine liberals. Weber indicates that a political system is required which will guarantee the effective transfer of power to the middle class, and which will adequately prepare the middle class for government. Only such a system is able to overcome the internal fragmentation of the political order caused by Bismarck's personal system of rule, a system which jeopardizes the future of the German nation itself (see Lindt 1973: 32). Weber argues therefore that only a system based on the classical administrative organs of the middle class – parliament and political parties – is capable of producing an integrating political will and identifying universal political needs. Weber especially condemns the relegation of parliamentary, and party-political, activity to purely 'negative politics' under the imperial system (1988d: 421).

Such reflections refer most directly to the special position of political parties and parliament in the corporate system of the post-Bismarck era. The anti-parliamentary measures introduced by Bismarck ensured that the political parties in late nineteenth-century Germany only gained limited experience of real government, and were not in a position to take hold of political power (G. A. Ritter 1976a: 105; Ullrich 1996: 30). However, the structural weakness of the political parties in imperial Germany was also due to factors which existed well before Bismarck's Chancellorship. The German parties only began to form systematically in the period immediately prior to 1848. During their period of formation, therefore, they had to position themselves within a pre-established bureaucratic state, for the construction and organization of which they had had no responsibility (G. A. Ritter 1976a: 104). Sociological historians have repeatedly stressed the peculiar character of pre-1945 German parties as milieu-specific interest-groups, rather than universalizing organs of representation (see esp.

3 See Stürmer 1974: 281; Winkler 1972: 31; Wehler 1995: 666; Fischer 1973: 139–61; Nocken 1978: 42.

Lepsius 1993: 47; Pickart 1972). At the same time as Weber, Otto Hintze, the constitutional theorist and historian, famously argued against the parliamentarization of Germany on the grounds that political parties in imperial Germany were themselves embedded in the corporate and personal system of rule – that they were 'not really political, rather economic-social or religious-confessional formations' (Hintze 1962: 368). Weber himself puts forward a liberal-reformist variant on the same problem. He sees parliamentarization as a crucial opportunity not only for creating a new political system of representation, but for establishing cross-class, truly national means of political integration. Behind all Weber's writings on the function of the party, therefore, is the demand that political will-formation should be liberated from the bureaucratic executive and placed in the heart of the social sphere. Only thus, he intimates, can a genuine political culture be engendered. Post-Bismarck Germany, he explains, is 'a nation which is absolutely devoid of political education, far below the level which it had already attained twenty years earlier. And above all a nation which is devoid of all political will, accustomed to thinking that the great statesman at its head would sort out its politics for it' (1988d: 319). Weber's personal objective is therefore to explain how 'parliament, damned by its present internal structure to purely negative politics', can be 'transformed into a bearer of political responsibility' (1988f: 221). The political party, above all, Weber argues, has the capacity to recreate the integrative function of responsibility which was taken from Bismarck's parliament after 1878. Weber's theory of the party is intended thus as a model for the transformation of the entire political tradition of Germany. The liberation of the party, he suggests, can overcome the fragmented, regional and particular character of political will-formation in Germany. It can, consequently, also contribute to the production of a genuinely national ethos. In short, Weber sees the party – albeit with reservations – as a crucial organ in the removal of political authority from the executive and in the re-establishment of the German state on integrative foundations.

Weber's reflections on such questions culminated in the period 1914–18. The quasi-autocratic character of the Wilhelmine executive was reinforced during the First World War. By 1918 executive power was concentrated in the hands of Kaiser Wilhelm II and, especially, the leaders of the military, Hindenburg and Ludendorff. Despite repeated promises of political change through the latter years of the war (see Patemann 1964: 63, 68, 89), the military junta around Wilhelm II disposed of the wartime Chancellors who attempted to restrict the authority of the monarchical executive (Patemann 1964: 93), and it is debatable whether they ever seriously countenanced the prospect of electoral reform (1964: 123, 143). However, beneath the level of the governmental executive the question of electoral reform became increasingly pressing during the war, especially as the possibility of a working consensus in electoral issues (a reform-majority) between the SPD, the left-liberals and even the Zentrum became ever greater as the war drew on (Bermbach 1967: 41; Grosser 1970: 208). In July 1917 a diffuse cross-party committee was created, including members of FVP, SPD, National Liberals and the Zentrum, to discuss issues of electoral change (Bermbach 1967: 67–9). By October 1918, the last imperial Chancellor, Prince Max von Baden, finally decided that ministerial responsibility should be given to members of parliament, including left-liberal and even SPD politicians (Elben 1965: 36). This involved a crucial alteration to Article 21 of the Imperial Constitution, which had previously ruled that members of parliament could not act as secretaries of state (Mußgnug 1984: 127; Elben 1965: 36). During the war period, therefore, the antiquated executive structures which Weber saw as inimical to national interest were in part reinforced. At the same time, however, the war also saw the beginning of a reformist coalition between the SPD, the left-liberals and the Zentrum (Bermbach 1967: 231). The war thus held out the prospect that the left-liberal movements might gain direct access to government, and even that a two-party English-style system might be created (Grosser 1970: 62). Indeed, the quasi-parliamentary situation created by Max von Baden was in certain respects very close to Weber's own intentions. It is against this background that Weber's most important political interventions were formulated. In the last months of the 1914–18 war, and in its immediate aftermath, Weber wrote a series of highly influential articles, in which he gave details of his model for the democratic reorganization of Germany. These had, especially via Naumann, significant impact on subsequent political events.

To understand Weber's proposals for the establishment of democracy in Germany in 1918 it is necessary, however, to look briefly at his broader sociological thinking. Weber, famously, argues that the intellectual foundations of Western capitalist society are to be found in the work-ethic of Protestantism, most especially the Calvinist variant of Protestantism. He argues that the key principles of individual life in the capitalist economy – the suspension of immediate pleasure, the purposive rationalization of individual behaviour in the interests of future reward, and the deification of labour as a calling – are motivated by the innerworldly asceticism of Protestantism (1986: 198). In his sociological writings, Weber describes the development of capitalist organization as the result of a social climate of rational demystification of the world (see Schluchter 1979: 251; Liebersohn 1988: 104), in which purposive thinking creates forms of order and management appropriate to the needs of the economy and its administration (see Hennis 1987: 98–9). Above all, Weber argues that the rationality of Protestantism is characterized by a specific relation between means and ends. Protestantism (and later capitalism) organizes individual action in order to fulfil purposes – spiritual in Protestantism, economic in capitalism. Common to both Protestantism and capitalism is therefore a proportioning (or even subordination) of means to ends – which Weber terms purposive rationality (*Zweckrationalität*). Like Simmel and Nietzsche before him, he argues, however, that the purposes of modern (capitalist/bureaucratic) rationality are ultimately without substance. Such purposes (*Zwecke*) are in fact merely the means (*Mittel*) to create functional codes which allow the systems of the economy and the administration to operate. The purposes, therefore, which economic agents give to themselves in order to justify their actions are not genuine purposes, but illusory motives, produced in fact by the capitalist economic system itself. Despite his clear similarities with Marx, Weber rejects the scientific explanation of capitalism as a self-propelling, instrumental dynamic, and he explains social and economic change as the result of an interplay between both normative (ideal) and instrumental (material) factors. Weber's sociological approach revolves around the attempt to understand social formations as 'action-orientations', in which subjective motivation is derived from general value-systems (1972: 16). The rationality of modern capitalist society is an 'action-orientation', in which agents order their behaviour according to specific means–ends prescriptions, in which all means and ends are subordinated to the production of profit.

The issue of rationalization also has a central position in Weber's political thought. The political manifestation of the rationalization of modern society, he argues, is the production of bureaucracy, in which each political task is accomplished by a system of appointed executives. The emergence of modern centralized, bureaucratic states, Weber explains, goes hand in hand with the expansion of the centralized economy (1988g: 558). Modern bureaucratic states develop in accordance with the need for smooth-running financial administration (1972: 571). In such states, both economy and state are organized by the principle of divided labour, according to which tasks are fulfilled in a purely functional, depersonalized manner (Rossi 1987: 171). Weber says thus of the development of the modern state: 'The whole process is a perfect parallel to the development of the capitalist firm by means of the gradual expropriation of independent producers' (1972: 510). He repeatedly compares the modern state to the factory, to the large firm and to the economic association. The modern economy and the modern state have, Weber asserts, emerged together (1972: 825), and economic rationality and calculability are the crucial action-orientations in the political life of modern states (1972: 118, 45). The positive legal orders of the modern state are therefore the most obvious products of the purposive systems of rationalization in the economy. Weber thus sets out a damning, quasi-Marxist and quasi-Nietzschean, critique of the legal state (the chief objective of liberal reform-policies), which, he argues, far from creating just government, has merely distributed power, in functional latency, through all spheres of social action.

In this relation, Weber also develops his sociological distinctions between different forms of political legitimacy. He asserts that in modern societies the legitimacy of the political order is guaranteed by technical/rational means – by its appropriateness to the fulfilment of prescribed political functions, rather than by the content of the norms upon which order is founded (Kronman 1983: 45). The bureaucracy is a decisive factor in the engendering of legitimacy in modern society (M. Weber 1972: 128). The bureaucracy, Weber asserts, complies with a technical logic of purposes, in which actions are justified insofar as they are regulated by purposive prescriptions. The actions of a civil servant, for instance, are justified by their usefulness in the accomplishment of a particular administrative objective, not by any inherent quality. Like Luhmann after him, therefore, Weber sees the bureaucratic positivization of law as the basis of modern politics (1972: 817). The positivization of law, he asserts, frees social systems from substantive and inherited structures of legitimacy. He contrasts this with the traditional legitimacy of archaic societies, in which political order is seen to be legitimate because of its time-honoured nature (1972: 122–76). Most famously, in addition to rational (modern/capitalist) and traditional (pre-modern/pre-capitalist) legitimacy, Weber also puts forward a third model of legitimacy – charismatic legitimacy. A political order can also be seen to be legitimate, Weber argues, because of the charisma of its figurehead. The ability to engender legitimacy through charisma is the attribute of the 'chosen warlord, the plebiscitary ruler and the political party-leader' (1988g: 507). Charismatic legitimacy is, expressly, 'anti-economic' (Kronman 1983: 49). It is, Weber explains, a form of legitimacy which predates the rational coalescence of capitalist economy and bureaucratic state. The influence of Nietzsche's critique of technical and instrumental rationality, and his attempt to salvage a last trace of real experience in modern life, are a constant influence on Weber's pronouncements on legitimacy (Nietzsche 1968: 314). In his examination of different modes of legitimacy, Weber (not unlike Nietzsche) shows a qualified enthusiasm for non-rational, charismatic forms of government. He sees in these a mode of authority which gives vitality to the sterile world of purely rational-bureaucratic administration. Above all, he sees in the charismatic mode of legitimacy the symbolization of an integral political life, which is not concerned exclusively with technical provision and administration. The appeal of the charismatic leader *integrates* citizens into the political system more effectively than mere technical modes of governance. It appeals, Weber implies, to the vital dimension of social and political life.

These distinctions have special relevance for Weber's observations on the contemporary circumstances of German politics. The German parliament in the late *Kaiserreich*, he explains, is condemned by its negative role in politics to exclusively artificial and bureaucratic activity. Above all, the domination of politics by the bureaucratic executive in Germany conforms to the model of purely rational legitimacy. In this regard, Weber distinguishes between questions of political importance and questions of mere administrative proficiency. The German civil service, he explains, has been remarkably successful in showing a 'sense of duty' and skill in the 'mastering of organizational problems' (1988d: 351). These attributes do not, however, translate into the ability to deal with matters of broader implication: 'The civil service has failed completely whenever it is confronted with *political* issues' (1988d: 351). In other words, Weber argues that the ability to develop a genuinely *political* culture depends on the addition of non-bureaucratic activity to the political arena. Political matters cannot be resolved exclusively by technical rationality (1988d: 340), and a strong parliament is required to ensure that the political power is not monopolized by the sub-political logic of the bureaucracy. Weber thus sets up an opposition between the political party and the executive bureaucracy. The active liberation of the party, he argues, is the means by which bureaucracy can be held in check.

The critique of bureaucratic rule – perhaps the most central position in Weber's sociology – is by no means peculiar to Weber's thought. It is also a common component in most liberal theory of the late nineteenth century. The critique of the bureaucracy has, in fact, complex historical origins, and it reflects the special (if not unique) position of the bureaucracy in Prussian history. The great proto-parliamentary reforms conducted by Stein and Hardenberg in the second decade of the nineteenth century were actually carried out by the state-bureaucracy. During this period the state-administration was broadly identified as the motor behind the rational-liberal reform-processes of the late Enlightenment (Stolleis 1992: 211). The reforms of Stein and Hardenberg attempted, in essence, to limit the power of the monarchy by transferring legislative competence to the administration. However, after the ultimate failure of the reform-projects in the early 1820s, Prussia was left with a significantly reinforced bureaucracy, which became increasingly compliant with the restorative politics of the post-Napoleonic age (1992: 220). Arguably, in fact, the modernizing reforms which had been implemented by the bureaucracy of Stein and Hardenberg ultimately created a system of conservative bureaucratic domination in Prussia. Through the reform-period the administration gained such legislative competence that it became the major obstacle in the path of subsequent modernization – especially of attempts to transfer power from the bureaucracy to a constitutional legislative body (Vogel 1983: 49). By the 1830s the belief – exemplified by Hegel – that the bureaucracy could act as a progressive organ of reform had been replaced by an attitude of liberal scepticism towards the governmental administration (see Vierhaus 1983: 40–1; Stolleis 1982: 386; Obenaus 1984: 519), which was viewed as the main opponent of popular political representation (Conze 1978: 220). In Prussia, therefore, after the reforms administration and political decision-making fell notoriously close together (G. A. Ritter 1976b: 175). The core of Weber's entire political argument is that political activity should be separated out from administrative operation. This argument links directly with the sociological foundations of Weber's thought. However, it is also a common aspect of the liberal critique of the bureaucratically dominated legislative, executive and judicial faculties of the Prussian state-administration, which were cemented during the reforms of Stein and Hardenberg (Koselleck 1989: 332).

Despite his rejection of the absorption of politics by administration, however, Weber's suggestion that parliamentary party-politics can act as an antidote to bureaucratic rationalization is not without ambiguity. In fact,

Weber actually implies that parliaments and parties are themselves necessarily bureaucratic, and that their functions can never finally exceed the
needs of mere administration. Weber describes parliament as a 'factory'
(1988d: 340). Modern parliaments, he explains, act as 'representatives of
people who are dominated by the means of bureaucracy' (1988d: 339).
Members of parliament, he argues, are primarily taken up with administrative tasks, and the deputations of interest-groups in parliament represent
technical issues, which are pre-formed and processed by the regulations of
the bureaucracy. Most importantly, Weber argues that parliamentary government itself is only the manifestation of a contract between social parties.
For this reason, in Weber's typology of institutions, parliamentary legitimacy remains ultimately bound to technical-rational or bureaucratic action-
orientations. Parliament, Weber indicates, is itself lastly only a subordinate
component of *genuine* government.

Weber, naturally, does not depreciate absolutely the role of parliament.
He suggests that parliament should be given greater influence over the
bureaucracy. Leading administrators, he argues, should be subject to parliamentary control, and should be politically answerable to, or even drawn
from, parliament itself. Through the institution of such measures 'the
leaders of the most influential parties of parliament necessarily become
positive contributors to the power of state' (1988d: 340). However, the
most vital function of parliament consists, Weber argues, in its ability to
prepare its finest members for the fulfilment of objectives of a higher order.
The political party, he indicates, has its true worth only insofar as it exceeds
the functions of a mere party – as it produces figures for leadership. The
true worth of parliament resides in its quality as a sphere of 'competitive
conflict' (1988d: 341) in which parties struggle for executive power, including power over the bureaucracy. In the 'negative' parliamentary system of
the post-Bismarck era, this is not possible, for parliament is 'powerless'
(1988d: 348). Nonetheless, despite his insistence that party-politics should
be radicalized, and that real power should be conceded to parliament,
Weber implies that parliament itself ultimately adheres to technical prerogatives, and that its genuine 'political' character is only realized when
parties produce leaders for 'highest power' (1988d: 349).

This is of great importance for Weber's outlines for representative
democracy in Germany. The institution of parliamentary-democratic elections leads, among other things, Weber argues, to ever more densely
ramified systems of bureaucratic administration. Influenced by the famous
sociological theories of Robert Michels (Michels 1911: 22), Weber laments
the fact that in the German party-system the organization of parties has
always been regulated by the principle of patronage, which has often
assumed a scheming or nepotistic character, and is symptomatic therefore
of the bureaucratic culture of 'negative politics'. However, he also states
that the introduction of mass-democracy actually heightens the bureaucratic nature of politics. Democracy and bureaucracy, he implies, always go
hand in hand. In the conditions of mass-democracy, he explains, 'it became

necessary to create an enormous apparatus of apparently democratic associations, to form an electoral association in every part of town, to keep business ticking over at all times, to bureaucratize everything efficiently (1988g: 535). Weber thus describes the bureaucratic future of politics as a 'cage of obedience' in which citizens are governed by a 'rational administration of civil servants', which forms 'the sole and final value which decides the manner in which their affairs are managed' (1988d: 332). In view of this 'unstoppable march of bureaucratization', Weber asks whether it is possible in modern society to salvage any freedom at all, whether it is possible to guarantee any kind of genuine democracy, and whether politics can be anything other than bureaucratic domination (1988d: 333–4). The parliamentary democratization of politics is, therefore, not a solution to the triumph of bureaucratic-technical rationality. It is itself a part of Weber's catastrophic vision of excessive technical control of human action-orientations. Weber sees parliamentarization, in part, as a means of overcoming bureaucracy – as a means of conducting real politics. However, parliamentarization itself ultimately produces bureaucracy and eliminates the vital 'political' dimension to human action.

To interpret such dilemmas in Weber's theory of democracy, it is necessary to look at a further key moment in his general sociology, the importance of which stands alongside his theory of bureaucratic domination – namely, his sociology of conflict, which is a constant undercurrent in his thought (see Ferber 1970: 56). In his earliest writings on the eastern peasants, Weber stresses the importance of conflict in national history (1988a: 14). In his wartime writings, he defines the struggle for power as the crucial trait of international politics: 'We too are a powerful state. And this fact is the final and decisive reason for the war' (1988c: 175). In his economic writings, he affirms conflict as the basis of economic activity (1972: 49). In the political arena, most especially, Weber views the fact of conflict not as a matter for lamentation, but as the external process through which national cultures are refined and strengthened. The state itself, he argues, is the 'monopoly of legitimate physical violence' (1972: 822). He defines 'politics', simply, as: 'The quest for a share of power or for influence on the balance of power, either between states, or in one state, between the groups of people which it incorporates' (1988g: 506). The worst bureaucratic excesses of Wilhelmine parliamentary politics can, according to Weber, be attributed to the fact that the parliamentary apparatus has little active involvement in actual political decisions and cannot assume 'leadership of the affairs of state' (1988d: 346). Bureaucracy, therefore, is characterized by a lack of conflict. Because of this lack of conflict, it is not *political* and cannot be given responsibility for *political* decisions.

Weber's sociology of conflict also feeds closely into his political works of 1918. A parliament with direct political influence on the executive is, Weber argues, more likely to provide an arena of genuine conflict and contention between political parties (see W. J. Mommsen 1959: 395). This arena would then serve to create a vibrant, conflictual political culture.

Most significantly, this would constitute a school of leadership for future politicians. The German parliament is, traditionally, he argues, a 'place full of bustling parvenus and job-seekers', without real political influence (1988i: 242). It cannot accommodate 'those with qualities of leadership – who do not seek sinecures, status and salary, but something completely different: power and political responsibility' (1988i: 242). Elsewhere, he states: 'It is of decisive importance that only those personalities are schooled for leadership who are elected through political conflict, because all politics is in essence conflict' (1988d: 392). For these reasons, Weber endorses a party-system based loosely upon the English model (Struve 1973: 134). This system, he claims, gives scope 'to political ambition and to the will for power and responsibility' (1988d: 403). It therefore, Weber argues, produces strong political leaders – it gives expression to 'the "Caesarist" traits in mass democracy' (1988d: 403). He explains: 'Strictly organized parties in particular, which genuinely wish to assert themselves in the power of state, have to subordinate themselves to people who are trusted by the mass, if they possess qualities of leadership' (1988d: 403).

Weber therefore approves extensive parliamentarization in Germany because he believes that a vital parliament, in which parties can claim real power through conflict, will operate as the breeding ground for future leaders (1972: 843). He states simply: 'The political purpose of parliamentarization is, of course, to create a place in which leaders are selected' (1988d: 424). Like most of his contemporaries, Weber addresses the relation between parliamentarism and democracy, and he makes a clear distinction between the two concepts. He interprets democracy (like Luhmann after him) as the inevitable sociological state of modernity (or capitalism), which has emerged through the disintegration of the feudal estates, the emergence of the mass-economy and the development of new powerful classes. Democratization, he argues, cannot be prevented, for it is a product of the development of universal capitalism. Parliament is, therefore, merely a technical structure appropriate to the administration of mass-democracy (see Nipperdey 1961: 90). The Germany of 1918, he explains, is confronted with the choice between a 'pseudo-parliamentary bureaucratic authoritarian state' and a democratic state which integrates its citizens into government (1988j: 291). However, Weber's assessment of the relation between democracy and parliament at no point indicates a whole-hearted endorsement of either of them. He sees democracy, neutrally, as the sociological condition of the modern age, but he does not propose a thorough parliamentarization of all the institutions of government in Germany. Parliamentary democracy, he argues, has its justification in the technical production of leadership-elites, not in its internal functions.

This throws complex light on the ideal constitution of politics in Weber's thought. As seen above, Weber indicates that genuinely political legitimacy is constituted by the presence of a dimension of charismatic leadership, and, consequently, by the overcoming of bureaucratic rationality. However, he also argues that strong leadership produces bureaucracy. Qualities of leadership, he asserts, create 'rigidly organized' parties (1988d: 403), whose internal cohesion depends on the identification of all party-members with the leader. Indeed, Weber argues that the chief virtue of the parliamentary system is that the parliamentary bureaucracy is rationalized in order to produce and preserve strong leaders. He supports ideally a parliamentary system in which all parties, and the parliamentary administration itself, strive to gain maximum efficiency in order to produce leaders. Far from advocating an abandonment of technical motivation, therefore, Weber argues that the technical systems of government in fact require further technical rationalization in order to generate nontechnical, or charismatic figures. The bureaucratization of parties is not, he explains, 'a stiff obstacle for the emergence of leaders' (1988d: 403). Weber, in short, advocates a model of political representation which does not derive its legitimacy from the rational processes of the economy and the bureaucracy. However, this legitimacy can only be constituted, Weber intimates, by means of the consolidation of precisely that rationality to which it is opposed.

Weber's theories of technical and charismatic legitimacy were ultimately reflected in his writings on the constitution of the Weimar Republic. Friedrich Ebert (SPD), first President of the Weimar Republic (1919–25) and head of the interim government before its establishment, convoked a conference of experts in December 1918, which was designed to open discussion on the new democratic constitution. Weber participated in this conference, together with, among others, the liberal constitutional theorist Hugo Preuß (FVP), to whose organic model of regional self-administration Weber was strongly opposed. For the governmental form of the new republic, Weber himself recommended the reinforcement of the central power of the state and the maintenance of a strong governmental executive (Elben 1965: 68–9; Grassmann 1965: 92). Despite his high regard for Weber (Schiffers 1971: 108), Ebert eventually chose Preuß instead of Weber to draft the founding documents for the new republic (G. Schulz 1963: 123–4). Nonetheless, partly through the prompting of Naumann and other figures in the DDP (1963: 173), and partly even through the intervention of senior military figures (Elben 1965: 134), Weber's elite-democratic model eventually had direct influence on the constitutional form of the Weimar Republic (Elben 1965: 48; see also Nippel 1994: 294), which, famously, gave far-reaching powers to the President, who was elected by a plebiscitary system. Preuß himself (1919: 13) paid lip-service to Weber's theory of elites. However, Preuß's ideas were much closer to the pure parliamentary model of democracy than to Weber's plans for a strong presidial executive (G. Schulz 1963: 124–5; Grassmann 1965: 110). Preuß had little time for geo-political theories of sovereignty and he was keen to limit the abstract authority of state. Preuß's constitutional theory in fact derives closely from Gierke's concepts of organic self-administration.

In contrast to Preuß's organic model, Weber's proposal for the retention of a Caesaristic executive dimension in the Weimar Constitution is clear enough. He explains: 'The fact that even, and indeed particularly, in democracies, precisely the important political decisions are made by individuals – this inevitable circumstance means that mass-democracy since the time of Pericles has always purchased its positive successes by making large concessions to the Caesaristic principle of leadership selection' (1988d: 395). Most emphatically, in 'Politics as a Vocation', his famous address to the student body at the University of Munich in 1919, Weber argues fervently that the Weimar Republic should be governed by a President, elected by plebiscitary means, who stands above the institutions of parliament. He states: 'The Imperial President could be the sole vent for the need for leadership, if he is elected by plebiscitary, not parliamentary election' (1988g: 544).

During the revolutionary period at the beginning of the Weimar Republic, Weber thus proposed that a democratic order should be instituted which combined both direct-democratic and parliamentary-democratic structures. Owing to his consultative role in the constitutional debates of this time, Weber's sociological insights had a precise impact on the political fabric of the Weimar Republic. Weber claims that the modern party-system inevitably contains forms of government which do not accord simply with the common notion of parliamentary order as discursive, rational government. There is, he asserts, always an element of demagogic politics in the party system (see W. J. Mommsen 1974: 87–8). Accordingly, Weber argues, there is, always and inevitably, a moment of plebiscitary rule in the parliamentary system. The party-leader makes a direct appeal to the electorate on the basis of his own leadership talents or personal charisma, and he organizes his own party in accordance with the same principles. The chief objective of the party-leader is to become President, and it is to this end that each political party is organized – the 'plebiscitary dictator stands . . . above the parliament and rallies the masses around himself by means of the party machine. The members of parliament are for him merely sinecured workers who belong to his following' (1988g: 525). In this respect, Weber clearly predicts the forms of mass political organization, structured around both charismatic party leadership and rationalized party bureaucracy, which emerged throughout the 1920s.

In keeping with this theory, Weber suggests that in the modern political arena there are two types of politician. There are party bureaucrats who make their living *from* politics – politicians who are thrown up by the mass-administration of the modern apparatus. There are also politicians who are not economically dependent upon the financial resources of the party – who live *for* politics. Both types of professional politician characterize the essence of the modern political system. Weber warns, predictably, against the propagation of a 'civil service spirit' by the representatives of the former category (1988d: 389). He asserts also in the clearest terms that genuine politicians – those who live for politics and are motivated by truly political, not pecuniary ambitions – live in constant tension with the principles of parliamentarism (1988d: 393).

However, although Weber acknowledges the superiority of those politicians who live *for* politics, who are blessed with a demagogic, or strictly *political* talent, he does not expressly endorse authoritarian government. Indeed, he is far from advocating a system of unchecked mass demagoguery. At various points in his work he warns against purely emotional appeals in the political sphere, both on the left and on the right.[4] The 'demagoguery of the streets, practised with specific means of the proletariat' (1988k: 305) is a constant source of apprehension in his writings of 1918. In reference to the English system he points out the advantage of a reciprocal balance between the highest executive and the parliament. He lists the functions of parliament as those of a body which regulates the power of the President, which preserves civil law as a check on presidential power, which provides a forum for leading politicians to demonstrate their ability, and, crucially, which contains peaceful means of deposing the dictator should he lose the trust of the masses (1988d: 395). Nonetheless, Weber sees the moment of political demagoguery as a means of integrating both the party-following and the general populace into the active praxis of politics. He states: 'Democracy and demagoguery belong together. This is, however, completely independent – we repeat – of the constitution of state. It will be the case as long as the masses cannot be treated as a purely passive object of administration, but have opinions which are of influence' (1988d: 395). Owing to the very nature of democracy, Weber argues, the forces of leadership are expected to legitimize their actions through an appeal to popular opinion. This is a natural consequence of the general move away from government by pure decree. Total consensus in the public sphere, however, is not possible, especially in a large state such as Germany. It is therefore necessary to *produce* forms of integrative consensus, or legitimacy, by other, non–consensual means. Weber argues that consensus, in the form of rational legitimacy, can be partially produced, or at least simulated, by the operations of the bureaucracy. The bureaucracy can at least create an atmosphere of rational-technical reliability. However, the appeal of the real politician, who lives *for* politics, represents an additional structure through which popular consensus and broad agreement with political measures can be engendered (1972: 122).

The underlying idea which informs Weber's model of plebiscitary government is a theory of political secularization. Weber argues that two processes of secularization underpin the development of European society. Protestantism, he explains, has been secularized as the rationality of capitalism and bureaucracy. Weber grasps Protestantism as a theology which has limited intrinsic content, but from which an ethic of means–ends rationalization arises, which justifies actions in the present according to the future purposes (however fictitious) which attach to them. Parallel to this,

---

4 Ernst Nolte argues that Weber's imagination does not stretch to Caesaristic leaders of the type of Hitler or Mussolini. However, as seen here, Weber certainly both understands and seeks to counter the threats posed by plebiscitary government. See Nolte 1963: 11.

however, Weber suggests that pre-rational theological contents also retain
an influence, as action-orientations, in the political sphere (1988g: 556).
The ethic of political charisma appeals to such orientations. The democratization of Western political systems has had, therefore, two conflicting but
related consequences. It has produced, Weber suggests, both rational/
bureaucratic and non-rational/charismatic forms of government. Indeed,
these two forms of authority exist side by side, one producing the other.
The course of democratization has produced a huge network of rational,
bureaucratic apparatuses, designed to facilitate the winning of mass-
support (Loewenstein 1965: 38). But, as a corollary of this, it has also
produced an increased need for demagogic forms of leadership (1972:
829; 1988g: 533). In each of these historical currents, distinct but related
processes of secularization are sedimented.

Weber thus ultimately comes close to affirming precisely those plutocratic forms of government which he criticizes in the Wilhelmine state
(1972: 830). He argues: 'The government of a state or a party by people,
who (in the economic sense of the word) live exclusively for politics and not
from politics, means necessarily a "plutocratic" recruitment of the leading
political strata' (1988g: 514). The traditional Prussian institution of a strong
state with a strong personal executive, and a limited parliamentary legislature, remains the model for Weber's theory of democracy. His fidelity to
inherited structures of governmental form is clear to see, even in 1919,
where he explains: 'The position of the Kaiser could be filled best by a
single person' (1988e: 468). The President, he outlines, should retain all the
special powers previously enjoyed by the Kaiser, including rights of sus-
pensive veto, the power to dissolve parliament, and the supreme command
of the military (W. J. Mommsen 1963: 302). He advocates, however, that
this model should be modified so as to render best service to the bourgeoisie: 'We also value the resolute rejection of monarchical legitimacy as a
means of finally letting the bourgeoisie stand on its own feet' (1988e: 454).

It is in such respects that the legacy of liberal politics in the Wilhelmine
era is most manifest in Weber's thinking. It is naturally reductive to trace
Weber's thinking exclusively back to the predicaments of nineteenth-
century liberalism.[5] Nonetheless, the proposed deployment of Caesaristic
measures in Weber's model of democracy can be linked closely to the
technical 'synthesis of democracy and autocracy' used by Bismarck himself
after the dissolution of the liberal–conservative coalition in 1878 (Stürmer
1974: 298). Similarly, the relegation of parliament to the level of a subsidiary chamber, beneath the level of the highest executive, has its origins in
the Prussian traditions of the constitutional rule. Certain key aspects of
Weber's constitutional theory are in fact strongly anticipated by the
National Liberal theorist Rudolf Gneist. Gneist, like Weber after him,
interpreted political freedom as the technical precondition of internal
and external economic success (Gneist 1894: 230–1). Gneist also viewed

---

5 See Wolfgang Schluchter's actualization of Weber's ethics: Schluchter 1991: 534.

political parties as interest-based instruments which dilute the pure political will of the national whole (Gneist 1872: 140; 1894: 230), and engender
excessive bureaucracy (1872: 182). He also saw the attempt to secure the
ministerial responsibility of politicians (not the representation of social
needs) as the cornerstone of the legal-democratic state (1872: 175). Most
significantly, Gneist, like Weber, sought to construct a nationally embracing category of political value, in which particular interests are subordinated to the authority of the executive, and in which elected interest-
deputations cannot claim the authority of state-power (1872: 182).

Weber was naturally not alone in his unwillingness to relinquish the
institutions of the Wilhelmine system. In the inter-party constitutional
committee of the period 1917–18, even SPD delegates (including Ebert)
were initially reluctant to sanction major changes to the political fabric of
Germany. They (like Weber) also viewed parliamentary reform primarily as
a means of limiting the power of the ministerial bureaucracy (Bermbach
1967: 73–4). In 1918, Weber was also not alone in proposing that the
gradation of power between parliament and government should be carried
over from the Wilhelmine system into the new republic (Grosser 1970:
218). It is therefore arguable that Weber's ambiguous attitude to the party-
system reflects widely held preconceptions regarding the limited possibilities for democratic reform in the late *Kaiserreich*. Although Weber clearly
seeks to liberate political organizations from their absorption into the
bureaucracy (Puhle 1970: 361), the 'anti-party attitude' characteristic of
the post-Bismarck system still reverberates through his thinking (Grosser
1970: 15). More pointedly, Weber implies that political parties are themselves not finally distinguishable from corporate interest-groups, and that
their position should not be cemented at the highest level of political
decision-making. The pinnacle of the political order, he stresses, should
be produced by plebiscitary election. Parties, Weber argues, should be
rationalized, and they should be given a more active role in government –
but, he suggests, they are not strictly *political* bodies. The Weimar Constitution itself, partly owing to Weber's input, did not distinguish political
parties from economic associations, and it did not recognize them as organs
of popular will-formation (Lohmar 1963: 5).

In fact, the plebiscitary component to Weber's theory of democracy can
be interpreted as a strategic response to the predicaments of German
liberalism in the nineteenth century. As outlined above, the corporate
system of the post-Bismarck period was characterized by the fragmentation
and particularization of parties, splinter-parties and interest-groups. The
crisis of liberalism in late nineteenth-century Germany was both a cause
and a product of such fragmentation. Weber's thoughts on the Weimar
Constitution simultaneously react against and reflect these aspects of the
post-Bismarck system. In the Weimar Republic, Weber wishes to see
greater power given to political parties (and parliament), but he also implies
that the parties are ultimately only deputations of technical interests. The
plebiscitary system, he argues, can embrace the more fundamental interests

and loyalties of the nation – energies which cannot be caught by mere parties. Weber's model of plebiscitary government thus marks, in one respect, an attempt to ground the political order on the free expression of the people, on the heart of the liberal-constitutional idea – not on the technical mediatization of the people by means of party-organizations (Schieder 1980: 204). However, significantly, in Weber's thought the classical-liberal idea of the free expression of the popular will undergoes a strategic transfiguration. In the classical idea of liberal constitutionalism, the plebiscitary leader *represents* the popular will. In Weber's thought, however, the plebiscitary leader *binds* the popular will to fixed political form, and *creates* the popular will through the symbolic production of consensus. Weber thus sets out a theory of charismatic integration, not representation (Rürup 1972: 235). It is the function of charisma to symbolize a unifying political ethic which embraces all areas (private and public) of national life, and secures more stable forms of national cohesion. Weber, clearly, sees the new republic as a situation in which democratic forces (especially the middle class) have finally obtained real power. Above all, he fears (as did indeed occur) that the democratic political organizations (parties) will immediately disintegrate and see their position of power once again dissipated (Jones 1985: 29). Weber's theories of plebiscitary government and the technical production of consensus can, therefore, certainly be viewed as residues of anti-democratic thinking. However, it might equally be argued that Weber endorses both parliamentary and plebiscitary institutions because he fears that the democratic forces in Germany are not strong enough to maintain a democratic political order if they are not systematically – or symbolically – integrated from above. Weber, therefore, can certainly be viewed as an anti-democratic democrat, or an anti-liberal liberal (Söllner 1979: 182–5). However, he might equally be viewed as a sceptical democrat, whose long experience of party-political fragmentation led to a theory of democracy in which the moment of integration is given greater importance than particular issue- or interest-based representation.

Contrary to many interpretations, in sum, Weber does not blankly endorse charismatic government as a means of engendering political legitimacy. In his own descriptions of the ideal-type of the politician there are few direct references to the quality of pure charisma. Weber actually represents the character of political actions in terms of their 'ethical' qualities. Political actions can, Weber argues (1988g: 551), fall into one of two categories. They can represent an 'ethic of conviction' (*Gesinnungsethik*) or an 'ethic of responsibility' (*Verantwortungsethik*). This means that actions can be motivated either by abstract ethical convictions which must be upheld regardless of their context or by the purposive sense of political responsibility, which seeks, pragmatically, to attain particular goals in a particular set of circumstances. In this counter-position, Weber gives clear privilege to the ethic of responsibility. 'The person motivated by an ethic of conviction', he explains, 'does not understand the ethical irrationality of the world' (1988d: 551; see Schluchter 1980: 101). Weber thus claims that a high degree of political pragmatism is the attitude most appropriate to the political sphere. Like Nietzsche before him, Weber argues that all values are finally grounded in individual volition and particular decisions. Political values are no exception to this (W. J. Mommsen 1974: 7). However, whilst Nietzsche adulates the charisma of the great artist, Weber outlines a transformation of pure charisma into the 'charisma of reason' (Breuer 1994: 57). It is, he intimates, the function of the politican to stabilize the charismatic dimension to politics within durable institutional forms. This, Weber implies, cannot be accomplished by charisma alone. 'Mere passion, however genuine,' he explains, 'is not enough. This does not make a politician, if it does not, in the service of a cause, make responsibility towards this cause the decisive guiding star of its action' (1988g: 546). Weber's figure of the politician, therefore, is by no means synonymous with the qualities of charismatic leadership. On the contrary, Weber argues that the political sphere has its own specific quality of rationality – that is, the rationality of power, responsibility and interest. Weber depicts the politician who is motivated by the 'ethic of responsibility' as a broad synthesis of pragmatic, rational and charismatic authority.

Weber thus asserts that a certain conceptual and practical autonomy accrues to the sphere of political activity. This is the thrust of all the sociological distinctions outlined above. Politics, he argues repeatedly, is different from administration. The political sphere cannot be assimilated to the rational logic of the bureaucracy. It is also different from the ethic of conviction, for it cannot be understood in terms of virtue and abstract belief. Similarly, politics is different from the economy. Political considerations must, in the extreme case, prevail over economic rationality. They are not deducible from the logic of private interest. In Weber's depreciation of politicians who live *from* politics and his advocacy of a small oligarchical or plutocratic elite who live *for* politics, he also implies that genuine political thinking should not finally accept the sociological interrelation between economic and political power. A sphere of political activity should be guaranteed which is not defined by, and exhausted in, bureaucratic or technical practices. The rationality of the economy should be counter-balanced by the charismatic-rational quality of a political sphere which is elevated above economic considerations. Although the modern state is largely a product of the economy, it, Weber argues, should also stand above the economy, as an autonomous power representing all interests (see Zängle 1988: 132).

Above all, for Weber, the defining feature of political action is that it sets its own purposes. By doing so, it exists in a mode of rationality which is distinct from economic and technical areas of human life. Following Nietzsche and Simmel (Simmel 1989: 304), Weber argues that actions in the bureaucracy and the economy follow fictitious purposes. In fact, purposes in the bureaucracy and the economy are not genuine purposes at all – they are the rational means by which these systems perpetuate themselves. In political action, in contrast, Weber identifies a mode of rationality which does not comply absolutely with the principles of predictability and prescribed purpose which characterize actions in the programmes of the economy or the bureaucracy. Political rationality (*Verantwortungsethik*) is capable of organizing behaviour around the accomplishment of substantive purposes, and it thus escapes the functional fictions of purely technical areas of operation. In this respect, Weber moves very close to certain aspects of Kant's political anthropology. Kant also sees purposive autonomy as the attribute which separates political life from mechanical life (Kant 1966a: 232). The true politician, Weber argues, is a figure who is able to stand outside or above technical systems and, if necessary, to guide these systems in accordance with his own purposes – whatever their content. Central to Weber's understanding of politics, therefore, is that the politician conforms – uniquely – to a means–end rationality in which purposes are not merely illusory.

Such reflections are also at the heart of Weber's conception of political citizenship. In his assessment of the merits of different electoral systems in 1918, he argues against proposals from certain sections of the SPD and the USPD (Independent Social Democratic party) that representation should be organized through shop councils, soviets or guilds, and he especially attacks the ideal of common-economic organization championed by certain liberal thinkers (especially Walther Rathenau). The terms of this argument throw important light on Weber's wider definition of the political sphere. He argues here that elections should reflect a political will, not a merely economic consensus. Equal 'electoral law means, in the first place,' he explains, 'simply that in this aspect of social life the individual, uniquely, is not, like everywhere else in life, considered on the basis of his particular professional or familial position . . . but simply as a citizen. The unity of the population of a state, instead of the dividedness of private life-spheres, is given expression in this' (1988j: 266). Weber's insistence on the autonomy of the highest level of political activity therefore links with a more general interpretation of political life. He sees a broad symmetry between the independence of the political elites and the independent quality of the political dimension to human life itself. Political elites, he suggests, have the ability to recognize purely political needs, because they do not have to think about immediate personal gain. Similarly, he argues that individual citizens, if temporarily extrapolated – in the process of election – from their private and economic life-contexts, also have the ability to recognize political interests (or purposes) as something other than economic or technical necessity. Weber's theory of elite government is intended therefore as a non-contractarian variant on Kant's political anthropology. The political quality of national life, Weber argues, is anthropologically distinct from technical, economic or pragmatic considerations. Unlike Kant, however, Weber does not believe that this common political quality can be realized through public (or moral) agreement. Rather, it is best represented by a figure not absorbed exclusively by technical concerns. The highest level of the political apparatus is, nonetheless, a distillation of the political quality of the entire nation and its members.

Weber's criticism of common-economic, soviet- or estate-based representation is also closely historically linked with his ambivalent attitude towards political parties. During the 1914–18 war the corporate nature of Wilhelmine government was intensified by the interventionist role which the state played in the war-effort. Throughout the war the state was forced to mediate between the demands of conflicting economic interest-groups, in order to maintain the food-supply and the production of armaments. One consequence of this balancing function, which the state assumed, was that the state devolved certain powers to corporate bodies (Feldman 1970: 320) – including cartels, syndicates, and industrialists' associations – as these, under state-supervision, were entrusted with responsibility for the distribution of raw-materials, with commissions and with the fixing of commodity-prices (Feldman and Steinisch 1985: 19–20). This strengthened the bargaining-power of the SPD and the unions. Rights of union representation were, for instance, cemented in the famous Auxiliary Service Law of 1916 (see Varain 1956: 151; Kocka 1973: 115). At the same time, however, the co-ordinating autonomy of the state in this period also reinforced the influence of major industrial associations on the executive (Zunkel 1974: 30). These developments consolidated still further the personal, collectivist character of governmental decision-making processes in Germany, as economic and political directives became increasingly interlinked during the war. A variety of economic theorists, from Kautsky and Hilferding on the left to the liberal Rathenau (1918: 28), and the proto-syndicalist Werner Sombart (and other figures attached to the Verein für Sozialpolitik, such as Schmoller, Adolf Wagner and Lujo Brentano; see Pohl 1979: 224–5, 230), saw in such corporate tendencies the emergence of a new brand of capitalism. They interpreted this as state-capitalism or even state-socialism, which they viewed as a system in which political and economic power could be perfectly co-ordinated by means of common-economic or syndicalist modes of government (Zunkel 1974: 51–2). The wartime co-operation between unions and business had far-reaching consequences. The later corporate agreements upon which the Weimar models of social capitalism (Kocka 1973: 115), and social partnership, were based – especially the famous Stinnes–Legien Pact of November 1918, and the resultant Central Community of Labour (Zentralarbeitsgemeinschaft; see Feldman and Steinisch 1985: 53) – emerged directly from the mode of economic organization which developed during the war, and even from personal relationships forged during the period of wartime co-operation.

Weber, however, despite his enthusiasm for partial state-administration of the economy, rejects all ideas of government by professional councils or syndicates. He insists instead that the political sphere should not become a mere bartering house for particular economic interests. The administration of political power by economic bodies leads, according to Weber, directly to the usurpation of the state by the most economically powerful, capitalist bodies (cartels) (1988j: 267; 1988l). Weber's symbolic limitation of political power to the highest level of the executive is thus, in part, an attempt to prevent the illegitimate arrogation of power by economic groups. Equally, it is an attempt to constitute political legitimacy as a distillation of the collective will, not as a set of fluctuating bargains between adversaries. In this respect, Weber's concept of genuine politics as a mode of non-technical praxis has more than a passing overlap with Marxist anti-corporatism, and his ideas are taken up later by the Austro-Marxists, by Franz Neumann, Otto Kirchheimer and by Jürgen Habermas.

Weber imagines, therefore, that the plebiscitary leader can symbolically incorporate the genuine political interests of the nation, which are only particularly represented by technical parties, by common-economic councils or by corporate organs. However, in this theory the actual nature of politics – or political interests – remains unspecified. The political sphere is outlined by Weber merely as a set of practices, attitudes and strategies which do not rely on expressly rational or technical action-orientations. The specific quality of politics is that it is able to use the means of violence to attain certain goals. Despite this, however, Weber scarcely describes politics in substantive terms. Apart from broad references to national interest, there is no basis of content or value in Weber's reflections on political life. Indeed, a clear idea of the actual implications of Weber's theory of politics only emerges, ultimately, through his observations on issues of foreign policy and overseas expansion (W. J. Mommsen 1975: 128).

It is, therefore, of the greatest significance that Weber's concept of politics, and his promptings for political reform, depend largely upon the interests represented in external politics. The dignity which Weber accords to the political sphere is itself directly linked with foreign expansion. He states: 'A nation which imagines that the leadership of state is exhausted in adminis-tration, and that politics is an occasional occupation for amateurs or a peripheral activity of civil servants, should renounce world politics and adapt for the future to the role of a principality' (1988j: 289). Indeed, Weber's entire commitment to democratic reform is presented as a component in his more general enthusiasm for overseas economic expansion:

> A people of masters, however – and only such a people can and is permitted to pursue 'world-politics' – has no choice in this regard. For the time being, it is certainly possible to thwart the democratization-process. For strong interests, prejudices and cowardices are allied against it. But . . . the price for this would be Germany's future. All the forces of the masses are engaged against a state, in which they are merely objects, not active contributors. (1988j: 291)

Ultimately, therefore, Weber justifies democratization because democracy, he argues, would engage the masses in the state – and this engagement would strengthen the international standing of Germany (Breuer 1994: 30).

It is almost impossible, in this respect, not to associate Weber's thinking with the broad tendencies of both German imperialism and liberalism in the period 1870–1914. The ideological contribution of colonial policies to the stabilization of the political system in Wilhelmine Germany has been very thoroughly addressed and documented, and it cannot be treated at length here. Weber's ideas, however, can be interpreted as a political model which is closely linked with the overseas economic and military expansion, which was pursued during Bülow's tenure as state-secretary for foreign affairs (1897–1900), and Tirpitz's authority over the navy, after 1897 (Canis 1997: 223; Hillgruber 1977: 62–3). It has been widely argued that the German programme of external expansion was consciously designed as a means of producing an illusory – or at best social-imperialist (see Wehler 1969: 488) – basis of legitimacy for a political order which was devastated internally by class conflict and by the broad divide between society and the political order (Wehler 1973: 176). The concerted development of colonial policies in the period 1897–1900 coincided with a broad move to the right in the imperial executive (Röhl 1967: 251). The colonial policies were thus employed in order to draw disparate areas of German society together and to reinforce the prestige of the increasingly reactionary and autocratic executive, around Kaiser Wilhelm II (1967: 255–9). Bülow himself described the development of German imperial programmes in the following terms: 'I give the greatest weight to foreign policies. . . . Only successful foreign policies can help, reconcile, pacify, integrate, unite' (cit. W. J. Mommsen 1993: 140). The integrative aspect of national prestige which Bülow attached to overseas expansion is thus clear to see. Colonial policies brought only limited gain and were scarcely systematically practised. However, they enjoyed great popularity in the 1890s, and they served, at least to some extent, as a means of uniting conservative and bourgeois elements of German society in the name of a powerful 'Weltpolitik' (1993: 141–3).

Weber's theory of politics can be assessed against this background (see also Berghahn 1973: esp. 5–24). Especially in his earliest writings, Weber expressed strong support for German expansion overseas and the enlargement of the navy after 1896 (Röhl 1967: 253). Unlike his more conservative contemporaries, Weber does not suggest that colonial policies should be pursued simply because they have an integrating effect on the broader social life. On the contrary, he argues that society – especially its disadvantaged members – should be politically integrated because this is likely to further the pursuit of colonial policies. However, both Weber and more conservative advocates of colonial policies suggest that the political unity of the civil sphere in domestic politics is not a value in itself. Unity, or social integration, is merely a useful quality – to be engineered by various means and for various ends. It is ultimately subordinate to economic prerogatives. At the heart of Weber's theory of politics, therefore, is the implication that trained elites and plebiscitary leaders should be allowed to practise politics and to make political decisions in financial independence, because these decisions are required to further the interests of the nation on the international stage.

Weber's argument that the political sphere possesses its own quality of autonomy depends upon a technical reflex. The political sphere in domestic politics is only autonomous because it is subordinate to the economic sphere in external politics – expressly to international programmes. Real politics, Weber implies, is whatever enhances and furthers the national (economic) interest. Those responsible for the national political interest should, therefore, be trained in an environment conducive to the development of appropriate skills.

Weber's theory of politics therefore raises a question which has far-reaching implications for his overall sociology. Weber asserts, on one level, that the political sphere is attached to charismatic and charismatic-rational forms of operation which distinguish it from the economic-administrative rationality of general society. By virtue of this quality, he suggests, the political sphere represents and integrates the general interest of the nation. Implicit in this is not only a critique of bureaucracy as an emasculating dimension to modern politics, but also of the economy as a system of purposive calculation. Weber expressly differentiates between the qualities of economic management, the type of the 'boss', and the qualities of political government (1988g: 539–40). He warns repeatedly (in quasi-Marxist terms) against the placing of political power in the hands of corporate-economic organizations – either in the form of cartels, syndicates, or common-economic executives (1988j: 267). The attributes of the bureaucrat are, Weber also outlines, historically and sociologically symmetrical with the qualities stimulated by capitalism (see Beetham 1985: 56). The logic of real politics, he implies, is therefore situated above both the bureaucracy and the economy. On a different level, however, Weber also explains that the modern form of politics is inseparably linked with the centralization of the economy (1972: 97). He repeatedly stresses the relation between the emergence of the rational-bureaucratic state, based on positive law, and the development of capitalist modes of calculation (Kronman 1983: 120). Ultimately, as seen in his contribution to colonial debates, Weber also argues that the rarefied sphere of political activity actually derives its determinate contents from its contribution to the organization of the national interest – to international politics, or, implicitly, imperialism (W. J. Mommsen 1959: 91–2). Politics, in Weber's thought, possesses two distinct implications. It is the collective interest of the nation, the sphere of human life elevated above simple needs. However, it is also – indeed primarily – the external administration of these needs.

In this respect, Weber's thought actually describes (almost unwittingly) the division of the state in modern capitalism into two distinct modes of operation – into the sphere of direction and the sphere of distribution (Kirchheimer 1964: 42–3). Weber argues that the fundamental orientation of the state is necessarily determined by foreign economic interests – by the sphere of direction. In this regard, the state follows technical, economic directives. It legitimizes itself ultimately by its ability to manage economic expansion. At the same time, however, Weber argues that in domestic politics the state conforms to a wholly different logic. In domestic politics, the state can intervene in the economy. It can regulate antagonisms in society and it can ensure that the collective will prevails over particular economic interests. In domestic politics, the state thus represents the collective – political – interest. It is formed, Weber implies, out of the heart of the collective political will. In this contradiction between the technical (external) operations of the state and the representative and distributive (internal) functions of the state, Weber, in essence, describes the collapse of the political legitimacy of the modern state. Legitimacy in domestic politics, he acknowledges, is sustained by means which are very different from those which ensure legitimacy in external politics. Moreover, what happens in the domestic political sphere is ultimately of limited significance. The legitimacy of the state, finally, stands or falls by the ability of its leaders to manage its economy in international politics. Weber tries to paper over this separation between directive (external/economic) and distributive (domestic/political) legitimacy. He argues that the political sphere in domestic politics (the sphere of distribution) is both intrinsically autonomous *and* absolutely determined by foreign matters (by the sphere of direction). However, the unspoken implication of Weber's thought is simply that the modern state is not, strictly, a political state, that its legitimacy cannot be constituted by political means, and that the collective interest and the national interest do not inevitably coincide. The special significance of charisma in Weber's typology of legitimacy can be seen, therefore, as a means of obscuring the fact that integral political legitimacy is no longer possible.

In Weber's very last writings, after the collapse of the Hohenzollern monarchy, this issue of the relation between the economy and the polity undergoes certain modifications, although its basic logic is sustained. Owing to the defeat of Germany in the war, Weber's support for German expansion became increasingly muted, and by 1918–19 he clearly aligned himself, in certain respects, to the SPD, which he saw as the likely party of government after the formation of the Weimar Republic (see Heinrich Potthoff 1972: 454). Despite this apparent shift to the left, however, Weber's theory of the relation between polity and economy remains constant, even after the war. After 1918, he demands the erection of a strong democratic state as a means of regulating the economy (1988e: 474). However, he underlines the fact, especially pressing in the economic conditions of late 1918, that the erection of a new German state will only be possible if this state is acceptable to foreign credit, particularly American credit (1988e: 458), and if the powers of big business can be successfully integrated into economic management (1988e: 460). Despite his assertion of the theoretical primacy of the polity over the economy, therefore, Weber indicates clearly that the polity itself has to be organized within the confines of economic pragmatism. This realism was in fact not at odds with the policies of the SPD executive. The leaders of the SPD also placed the immediate development of social policies above long-term socialization strategies (Schieck 1972: 155), and they gave only limited weight to the radical doctrines on the fringes of the party (Witt 1978: 96). Weber's qualified sympathy for the SPD after 1918 is still, therefore, restricted by the demand that the economy must serve the interest of the middle class (see W. J. Mommsen 1965). He states: 'When an order collapses due to the pressure of external enemies, it is certainly not difficult to overthrow it from within. It is much more difficult, and today, without the free co-operation of the bourgeoisie, impossible, to replace it with a new durable order' (1988e: 483). Although Weber's theory of the relation between politics and economics never expressly reduces national interest to the interest of the middle class, he assumes that political viability is always limited by economic viability. The political dignity which Weber gives to the state subsides therefore lastly into the tacit admission that the state cannot act as an economically neutral organ and that it cannot act against economic directives.

The sources of such complications in Weber's theory of political economy can be found in his sociological category of conflict. As shown above, Weber understands conflict as a sociological counter-weight to bureaucracy. Conflict is the foundation of both internal politics and international relations. However, the broad term 'conflict' has a rather undifferentiated anthropological quality in Weber's thought. Both his political plans for Germany, and his analyses of the relation between the polity and the economy, revolve around the belief in the primacy of foreign politics, and the inevitability of conflict within this sphere. He justifies his demands for a strong executive and for the relegation of parliament to a training ground for elites by claiming that the political system must be made serviceable to the conflictual sphere of foreign policies and to the overarching interests of the nation-state. In his political works Weber therefore represents conflict between nations as a universal fact, rather than as a product of material forces. This, however, contradicts the theory of conflict contained in his more detailed sociological works. In his sociological works, Weber explains how conflict between individuals and between nations is produced by the latency of violence in capitalist economic relations. 'The capital calculation in its formally most rational shape', he argues, 'presupposes thus the conflict between man and man' (1972: 49). He also explains how the monopolization of legitimate political violence by centralized states is due to their monopolization of the means of economic appropriation (1972: 72). In this regard, Weber approaches both a Marxist explanation of conflict as class-violence and capitalist expansion, and a Nietzschean theory of contract as rationally sanctioned antagonism. Conflict, according to this theory, is the original basis of economic and bureaucratic rationality. Economic and bureaucratic rationality can obscure and perhaps disseminate violence, he indicates – but they are also produced by it and they remain signifiers of latent violence. At the same time, however, Weber argues that conflict is also the original source of the dignity and autonomy of the political sphere. The political sphere, he suggests, has its dignity because it tests in conflict those leaders who later preside over the external conflicts of the nation-state. In sum, therefore, Weber criticizes the conflictual/contractual rationality of capitalism as sub-political, but he also asserts that the conflictual/contractual rationality of capitalism is, indirectly, the foundation of politics (1972: 832–3). In this regard, once more, Weber's thinking crystallizes most perfectly the predicaments of German liberalism. On one level, Weber condemns the entire system of rationality produced by the middle class. He also proclaims this same rationality, however, as the basis of the common good. His work is thus both a despairing history of the German middle class and a despairing attempt to argue that this class is the natural class of government.

Despite Weber's attempt to constitute a category of political life which is not reducible to particular and technical concerns, therefore, his theory of democracy is essentially a technical theory, which has little time for theories of consensual representation and for unstable forms of mass-political participation (see Dronberger 1965: 259). Weber's ideas look forward to those of Niklas Luhmann and, in particular, to Luhmann's technical theory of legitimacy (Luhmann 1964: 156). Weber sees parliamentarism as a means of training political elites, and his critique of the constitutional apparatus of Wilhelmine Germany is due to the fact that, technically, this apparatus has failed to do this (see Gilg 1965: 259). Similarly, Weber grasps the institution of the plebiscitary President as a device through which the populace can be emotionally engaged in the political sphere in an orderly, non-revolutionary manner (Beetham 1985: 96). The most essential function of democracy is also pragmatic and technical in character. It is to further the pursuit of successful economic policies (W. J. Mommsen 1959: 206), and to secure the emancipation of the most powerful economic class.

Weber's theory of politics is therefore itself a product and reflection of the purposive or systemic rationality which he detects and diagnoses in all areas of society (Bogner 1989: 118). Even after the collapse of the Hohenzollern monarchy, Weber's proposals for the new republic are marked by a startlingly technical conception of democracy. 'Plebiscitary presidential elections would', he states, 'naturally produce a strict bureaucratic party-organization, and the actual electoral conflict would, here too, be located increasingly in the parties themselves (in the nomination of presidential candidates)' (1988e: 469–70). Weber's model for a plebiscitary system thus actually intensifies the level of bureaucratic domination. It forces parties to rationalize their administration in order to compete with each other. The actual process of plebiscitary election is also little more than a technical procedure. The real conflict for power takes place within the technical apparatuses of the parties themselves. Elections merely confer formal legitimacy on figures who have already been competitively groomed for power through the parties.

This technical aspect to Weber's political theory is grounded in his theory of legitimacy. As outlined above, Weber argues that different governments legitimize themselves in one of three ways. There are traditional forms of legitimacy, in which governments are accepted because they have been there for a long time. These are specific to pre-modern society, although they clearly survive into the modern age. There are rational forms of legitimacy, in which governments are accepted because they fulfil certain functions, and conform to certain rules, which are themselves subordinate to overarching purposes. These are specific to internally differentiated, capitalist societies, which are organized around the division of labour. There are also charismatic forms of legitimacy, in which government is accepted because of the charismatic qualities of the leader. These are usually specific to revolutionary movements or forms of order which have not emerged directly out of traditional or rational systems (see Freund 1968: 243). In Weber's projects for the reorganization of government in Germany he calls upon two forms of legitimacy. The parliamentary bureaucracy, he explains, is the bearer of rational order, which mediates between people and power. The plebiscitary President is the charismatic leader (albeit with certain rational qualities) who is able to integrate the masses through direct appeal. In neither of these cases does Weber suggest that the legitimacy of power is based on reasoned or considered conviction on the part of those who are subject to this power. Each form of legitimacy is legitimate because it provides an action-orientation which, owing to personal qualities or habitude, is accepted as legitimate (1972: 122–3).

It can therefore be argued that Weber's theory of politics fails by its own internal criteria. His political ideas stand in marked contrast to the broader scope of his general writings, for they draw upon the technical rationality whose impact he elsewhere laments (J. C. Alexander 1983: 76). Although Weber argues that the political sphere can be interpreted as a set of practices and representations situated outside the limits of particular or technical-bureaucratic rationality, his conception of pure politics has its foundations in the economy and the bureaucracy. Weber (like Nietzsche before him) implicitly refers to two counterposed traditions of secularization, the demonic-charismatic and the technical-rational, which run through the entire emergence of European civilization. In his writings on politics these traditions are bound together in a single instrumental fusion, with *charisma* and *ratio* side by side. Indeed, the technical-functionalist dimension to Weber's political writings can be interpreted as an instrumental application of the spontaneous, creative relativism which he inherited from Nietzsche (M. Weber 1922: 490; Kocka 1986: 16).

More broadly, Weber's reflections on politics illuminate the problems of political thinking in the context of German liberalism, and liberalism in general. Like most German liberals of the late nineteenth century, Weber retains a strong attachment to the tradition of the Prussian power-state (*Machtstaat*), to the maintenance and reinforcement of which the National Liberals had contributed so much (Albertin 1972: 230). This itself – at least in part – explains his unwillingness to give autonomy to the legislature, especially the party-legislature. His affection for government by elites has its origins in older forms of Prussian liberalism (Gagel 1958: 141), and his fidelity to the formal structure of Hohenzollern government reflects historically the partial assimilation of the right-liberals into the old monarchical executive (1958: 104). However, in his commitment to the furtherance of the interests of both liberalism and the German bourgeoisie, Weber also introduces important innovations in liberal theory. He rejects classical-liberal, 'negative' or property-based models of economic emancipation, and he attempts instead, like Naumann, to cement the power of the bourgeoisie in a positive, interactive, and cross-class relation to the state. In particular, he refuses to see the grounds of citizenship in the economy, or in its distillation as contract, and he argues instead that the heart of political unity is constituted by a positive relation between people and power. However, as described above, Weber is not able to determine the quality of this pure political relation of positive liberty between people and state without recourse to the technical ideology of integration. Although he proclaims positive freedom as the basis of national politics, this freedom is always limited by the system of private law (externally) and by the technical processes of integration (internally). The people are integrated into the state through technical devices, and the quality of genuinely political activity is only substantiated through the economy. Weber does not overcome the formalization of politics, which he views as the chief problem of the modern order.

Weber, for these reasons, has been interpreted widely as the greatest representative of German liberalism, whose ideas, however, were most influential at a time when German liberalism had already demonstrated the inflexibility of its political forms (Gagel 1958: 175). Weber's attempt to compose a cult of leadership above the bureaucratic operations of the parliament reflects national-liberal theories of politics, in which a direct equation is made between the common good, the national interest and the personal executive. The differentiated social basis of the common good is not examined in this model (Millbank 1990: 92). Weber's commitment to the personal representation of collective interest relies upon the belief that collective interests and national interests are identical (Albertin 1972: 233), and that the state represents and enacts both sets of interest simultaneously.

Weber, like Naumann in *Democracy and Empire*, looks back through the nineteenth century at all the issues which have contributed to the exclusion of the liberals from power in Germany – to the undermining of the party-political apparatus, to the fragmentation of the middle class, to the symbolic popularity of representative figures, to the rapid emergence of a strong labour-movement, and to the integrative weakness of liberal ideology. Against this background, he attempts to develop a technical-ideological plan, which will rectify the deficiencies of liberalism, and thus help the liberals to gain power at last (Gall 1975: 352). In each respect, Weber's thought shows a strong attachment to liberalism, but also a recognition that liberalism can only be salvaged by means other than its own. In each respect also, Weber argues that the liberal class is the natural class of government. It can only legitimize itself as such, however, by deploying devices of integration. Real power, implicitly, has already left the political sphere. Politics arranges people in the service of the national economy.

## Selected further reading

Beetham, David (1985) *Max Weber and the Theory of Modern Politics* (Cambridge: Polity Press).

Bellamy, Richard (1992) *Liberalism and Modern Society: An Historical Argument* (University Park, Pennsylvania: Pennsylvania State University Press).

Bendix, Reinhard (1977) *Max Weber: An Intellectual Portrait*, introduced by Günther Roth (Berkeley/Los Angeles: University of California Press).

Dronberger, Ilse (1971) *The Political Thought of Max Weber: In Quest of Statesmanship* (New York: Appleton-Century-Crofts).

Freund, Julien (1968) *The Sociology of Max Weber*, translated by Mary Ilford (Harmondsworth: Penguin).

Giddens, Anthony (1971) *Capitalism and Modern Social Theory: An Analysis of the Writings of Marx, Durkheim and Max Weber* (Cambridge: CUP).

Giddens, Anthony (1972) *Politics and Sociology in the Thought of Max Weber* (London: Macmillan).

Kronman, Anthony T. (1983) *Max Weber* (London: Edward Arnold).

Liebersohn, Harry (1988) *Fate and Utopia in German Sociology, 1870–1923* (Cambridge, Mass.: MIT Press).

Mommsen, Wolfgang J. (1974) *The Age of Bureaucracy: Perspectives on the Political Sociology of Max Weber* (Oxford: Basil Blackwell).

Mommsen, Wolfgang J. (1984) *Max Weber and German Politics, 1890–1920*, translated by Michael S. Steinberg (Chicago: University of Chicago Press).

Mommsen, Wolfgang. J. and Osterhammel, Jürgen (eds) (1987) *Max Weber and his Contemporaries* (London: Allen & Unwin).

Sica, Alan (1988), *Weber, Irrationality and Social Order* (Berkeley/Los Angeles/London: University of California Press).

Struve, Walter (1973) *Elites against Democracy: Leadership Ideals in Bourgeois Political Thought in Germany, 1890–1933* (Princeton: Princeton UP).

# 2

# Carl Schmitt

Carl Schmitt remains today not only the most important political theorist of the Weimar period, but the most influential of all political theorists in Germany between Weber and Habermas. Outside Germany, Schmitt is known chiefly as the most prominent intellectual spokesman for the National Socialist state. His theory of the friend–foe relation is seen by many as the defining moment in the state-theory of the early period of the NSDAP (National Socialist party) and in the authoritarian and anti-Semitic ideologies of the late-Weimar 'conservative revolutionaries', who were centred around the conservative Catholics and the DNVP (German National People's party). Schmitt's ideas were diversely appropriated by the major theorists and protagonists of late-Weimar conservatism, with which he clearly identified. Moreover, Schmitt organized his career in an extremely opportunistic manner after the assumption of power of the NSDAP, and he became, for three years, the leading spokesperson, in Germany and abroad, for the judicial system of Hitler's state (Noack 1993: 197). Despite his earlier friendships with certain eminent Jewish intellectuals, Schmitt cleansed his writings of positive references to Jewish thinkers after Hitler came to power. He also worked for Göring during the early years of the National Socialist regime. Schmitt's subsequent influence on reactionary theory in Germany has also been profound. From Forsthoff to Luhmann, the scope of post-1945 right-wing reflection on politics in Germany falls largely into the category of Schmitt-reception, or can be viewed at least as a continued preoccupation with Schmittian themes (see Saage 1983).

Although this chapter does not offer an apology for Schmitt, or for his opportunistic actions during the early 1930s, it seeks to give a comprehensive picture of his work, and of its historical context. It also underlines the fact that interest in Schmitt's ideas is not exclusive to the right. On the contrary, aspects of his thought have been assimilated both to left-oriented voluntarism and to recent versions of radical pluralism. His more recent advocates, especially outside Germany, have been on the left. This chapter also asserts that Schmitt's sociological and intellectual-historical roots are not to be found in the late-Weimar DNVP or the NSDAP, but rather in the Roman Catholic party of the *Kaiserreich* and the Weimar period – the Zentrum. Most especially, however, this chapter offers a critique of Schmitt, which argues that the problems of Schmitt's thought cannot be grasped exclusively through reference to his political collusions. The strongest critique of Schmitt's ideas can be articulated through a more immanent representation of his failure to resolve the problem which concerns him (like Weber) above all others – the problem of technology, and the technical neutralization of human life.

Schmitt's ideas draw together a variety of influences. They connect a Rousseauian theory of the general will, a Hegelian critique of the social contract, and ideas derived from the tradition of conservative Catholic thought. Although Schmitt roundly criticizes neo-Kantianism, his ideas also carry a very heavy debt to some aspects of Kantian legal theory. Similarly, although Schmitt belongs to a broad tradition of Roman Catholic conservative thinking, Kierkegaard's radical Protestantism also forms an important undercurrent in his writings. His debate with Thomas Hobbes also constitutes a strong theoretical influence on his development – although it is by no means clear that he really understood Hobbes.

The basic position in Schmitt's thought is a critique of parliamentary democracy. Parliamentary democracy, Schmitt asserts, is a contradiction in terms. He argues that genuine democracy, which he grasps in Rousseauian manner as the general will of the people, cannot be expressed through the technical order of parliamentary discourse and compromise (1923: 20). Modern or parliamentary democracy, he explains, is not democracy, not rule by the people, but rather a 'heterogeneously composed construct' of democracy and liberalism, in which government is conducted not by the people, but *by discussion* (1923: 13). Even the classical-liberal conception of homogeneous democracy, in which public discussion provides the foundation for representative government, has, Schmitt argues, been replaced in modern society (the Weimar Republic) by a 'polycratic' system, in which discussion takes place outside parliament (1931a: 71). This system allows minority bodies, especially strong economic organizations (1923: 62), to gain disproportionate access to power. Modern parliament, Schmitt claims therefore, has abandoned its fundamental legitimation as a place where binding, determinate decisions are represented (1928: 319), and it has taken on the quality of an insurance house for the organs of capitalist economic power (1928: 312). For this reason, Schmitt argues, the composition of the collective will in modern democratic systems cannot be truly democratic – for the collective will is subject to processes of interest-based fragmentation before it has even been formed. The liberal-democratic vision of power legitimized by discussion, therefore, has been supplanted by a technical and temporary set of compromises and contracts which can be rescinded when they are no longer of use (1923: 10). Consequently, the operations of parliament, Schmitt argues (like Habermas in the 1950s), can no longer be viewed as democratic discussion in the true sense. The discussions which take place in parliament do not genuinely constitute power. Power is formed through extra-parliamentary deals and alliances.

Like Weber before him, Schmitt is especially vitriolic in his criticism of the technical character of the modern parliamentary system. The party system, he argues, has had no success in the task for which it was conceived – in resolving differences of interest in the civil sphere by means of party-mediation. He describes the Weimar state as a 'fragile coalition-party state', in which governments are based on technical compromise, not fundamental agreement. The parties in this state are merely 'social or economic power-groups' (1923: 11), and are therefore ultimately without responsibility and incapable of genuine representation (1931a: 88). The compromised, technical nature of parliamentary representation, Schmitt argues, therefore devalues its claim to legitimacy. This aspect of his political thought has been influential in subsequent left-leaning political theories (especially amongst thinkers connected with the Frankfurt School). Schmitt argues, in essence, that liberal democracy can never be genuine democracy, because it is merely an instrument which transposes the private-legal interests of powerful capitalist groups into the public-legal system of the executive. Because of this, liberal democracy cannot produce truly legitimate governments. It can at best engender systems of authority which justify themselves by the inferior, technical criteria of legality.

Equally fundamentally, however, Schmitt's critique of majority democracy revolves around the ancient argument that the majority is not always right, that a minority elite can protect the well-being of the majority – or the general will – better than it can itself, and therefore that even the ardent democrat is obliged to argue that democracy must in certain cases be suspended for its own protection (C. Schmitt 1923: 36). Parliamentary democracy, or party-democracy, therefore, cannot be legitimate, for it is limited by a sense of its own final insufficiency. These arguments, formulated most clearly in *The Crisis of Parliamentary Democracy* (1923), gained great importance in Schmitt's later reflections on the NSDAP. At the core of this critique is the suggestion that the executive should be strengthened in order to protect democracy itself (1923: 56). Schmitt argues that dictatorship, with the fullness of power in the hands of one person (1923: 56), is a more democratic means of protecting and representing the general will than the interest-based discussions of the party-political or paliamentary system (C. Schmitt 1921: viii).

Schmitt's proposals for the supplanting of the democratic balance between legislature and executive with an unchecked executive assumed various forms. Depending on the historical context, Schmitt saw the ideal

executive as the total state, as absolute sovereignty, as commissarial dictatorship, as sovereign dictatorship, or, most fatefully, as Hitler's *Führertum*.
After 1933, he defined Hitler's position in the National Socialist state in the
following terms: 'In a state based on leadership (*Führerstaat*)... in which
legislation, government and judiciary do not check each other distrustfully
as in the liberal state of law (*Rechtsstaat*), whatever is legal for an "act of
government" must be incomparably more valid for an action through
which the *Führer* has proved his status as both leader and judge'
(C. Schmitt 1940: 202). The homogenization of judge and leader is crucial
in this quotation. In his post-1933 writings, Schmitt affirms the National
Socialist conception of law precisely because it abolishes the difference
between executive and legislature, in favour of the unrestricted law-creating
authority of the executive. However, Schmitt's predilection for the strong
executive is not expressed uniformly. It is adjusted rather to analyses of
everyday politics. The broad trajectory in Schmitt's thought is marked by
his vacillations between various correctives to the technical order of liberal-
capitalist democracy. In the course of this trajectory, Schmitt assumes the
mantle of post-historicist legal theorist, decisionist, political theologian,
neo-positivist, concrete-order theorist, apologist for the Nazi state, anti-
Semite, critic of the Nazi state and, finally, the condemned man of German
politics. Owing to the Protean nature of Schmitt's work, efforts to represent
his ideas are usually highly reductive. Indeed, it is only in relatively recent
years that Schmitt has been treated with anything but the contempt deemed
due to the most high-profile theorist of Hitler's state.

Schmitt's dislike for the discursive structures of modern 'government by
discussion' (1923: 13) is connected with the philosophical and sociological
premises of his world-view. As background to his more specific political
interventions, Schmitt puts forward a theory of modern society which is
strongly indebted to Max Weber's theories of legitimacy and secularization
(see Ulmen 1991: 147). He explains how modern society is the product of a
process of transformation which has moved the centre-point of human
understanding from the metaphysical assumptions of Christian theology,
through the subject-centricity of the Enlightenment, to the political technicity of the modern age. The modern age is characterized both by the
technologization of industrial production and the technical rationality of
democratic government (1932b: 89). Like Weber, Schmitt sees the political
process of secularization as a process of neutralization, in which the substantial basis of genuine political order is undermined by shallow technicity.
In this respect Schmitt marks a bridge between Weber's (allegedly) value-
free description of the rationalization of theological contents through the
emergence of capitalism and Martin Heidegger's inquiry into the nature of
post-Cartesian ontology and the inauthenticity of modern subjective life.
For Schmitt, in broad analogy to Heidegger, genuine intellectual endeavour
in the state of capitalist modernity can only consist in the restitution of
substance to the formal procedures of democracy and political life. His
reflections on parliamentary democracy are therefore not only a political

critique, but a historiographical lament, in which technical democracy reflects the political conditions of the post-substantial age. The undercurrent of profound pessimism in Schmitt's theory of politics can therefore be grasped, theologically, as a counter-eschatology (*Verfallsgeschichte*; Meuter 1994: 392), in which forms of order which predate the neutralization-process of the modern age relentlessly recede into ever greater distance, leaving modern political life ever more neutral, and ever more secular (E. Kaufmann 1960: 377). Schmitt's theory of substantial and cosmological decline projects the original structure of political order as a theocratic order, in which God is *present* in the world (Meuter 1994: 87; see also E. R. Huber 1927: 19). In the modern age, Schmitt sees the Catholic church as the only durable form of order: 'With every change of political situation all principles are apparently changed, except one – the power of Catholicism' (1925a: 7).

The history of German Catholicism provides, in this light, a complex context for Schmitt's ideas. Anti-liberalism was a more or less inevitable component of Roman Catholic political perceptions in late nineteenth- and early twentieth-century Germany. Generally, the integrating power of the Catholic church had been severely undermined during the establishment of liberal ideas in the pre-1848 period (Sperber 1982: 318). Throughout the nineteenth century liberalism was widely represented as the main adversary of the church. However, the Roman Catholic background to Schmitt's thought can also be linked to the determinate cultural-political conditions of Roman Catholicism after unification (see Hartung 1920: 51–2; Buchheim 1963: 252). The first decade after Bismarck's unification of Germany was marked not only by the short-lived influence of the liberal parties, but also by a series of aggressive anti-Catholic laws and strategies, known as the *Kulturkampf*. These were designed to increase the state's control of the Catholic church (Sheehan 1978: 136), and to weaken the Zentrum, in order to cement the liberal–conservative hold on power (Stürmer 1974: 85; Winkler 1979a: 40–1). The temporary liberalization of the economic order in Germany in the 1870s, and the liberal–conservative coalition which effected it, were, therefore, firmly associated with anti-Catholic policies. Schmitt himself grew up in the Sauerland, an area strongly connected with the Zentrum, noted for its anti-Bismarckian tradition, and directly affected by the *Kulturkampf*.

After the fragmentation of the liberal parties following 1878, the bitter opposition between Catholics and liberals continued. After 1880, the Zentrum became a crucial force in imperial politics. Its political orientation – and especially its openness in issues of economic policy – allowed it to form anti-liberal coalition-governments with most other parties. Bismarck himself deliberately reintroduced the Zentrum into the fold of acceptable politics after the dissolution of the liberal–conservative government in the late 1870s, thus transforming the Zentrum into a banker against liberalism, and against liberal reform. The Zentrum was in many respects a natural ally of the conservative factions, as the electoral strength of the Zentrum relied in large part on the preservation of the three-class electoral system (Schauff 1928: 21). Although there were short-lived periods of co-operation between the National Liberals and the Zentrum, the bitterness between these parties remained an important political factor throughout the Wilhelmine era. The contribution of the Zentrum to the collapse of the Bülow bloc (Lerman 1990: 242) and the renewed formation of a Conservative–Catholic alliance in 1909 further reinforced the inherited antagonism between liberals and Catholics (Witt 1970: 160; H. Rosenberg 1967: 254). It was not until the Weimar period that the possibility of representative collaboration between liberals and Catholics was taken for granted. However, the period of collaboration between the Zentrum and the various liberal parties coincided directly with a loss of electoral power by the Zentrum (Plum 1972: 29). Schmitt's critique of the inorganic coalition-system of the Weimar state, his anti-liberalism, and his condemnation of economic theories of politics can therefore be viewed against the politics of Catholicism in the early twentieth century.

Schmitt's analysis of the neutralization of modern politics is most evidently, in short, a critique of liberalism. Yet – still more fundamentally – it is also a critique of Protestantism, and of the political forms which have emerged from Protestantism (of which liberalism is one). Like Weber's sociological diagnoses, Schmitt's condemnation of the neutralization of the modern state is an attack on the spirit of Protestantism, and on the technical-rational-capitalist culture which it (according to Weber) has produced. However, although Schmitt's position is heavily influenced by Weber, it is also a counter-Weberian sociology. Indeed, as Weber proposes himself as the bourgeois counterpart to Marx, Schmitt proposes himself as the Catholic counterpart to Weber. Despite his critique of modern political life, Weber nonetheless sees the rationality of Protestantism as the rationality of progress. Schmitt, in contrast, sees Protestantism as an inexorable logic of decline. For this reason, Schmitt's theory of political neutralization can also be interpreted as a critique of the modern German state itself, which emerged by direct descent from Luther's Reformation. Indeed, Schmitt is (by implication) especially hostile to Luther's political theology. Luther expressly detached the state from the transcendent order of natural law, and therefore initiated the shift to the insubstantial, which Schmitt deplores (Kober 1961: 168). In some quarters Bismarck's unification of Germany was equated with the final triumph of Protestantism (Windell 1954: 97). In view of the anti-Protestant dimension to Schmitt's thought, Schmitt's pact with the National Socialists should be seen in a discriminating light. Schmitt's thought, for all its temporary collusion with Hitler's judicial programmes, is at base a deep-rooted condemnation of the entire historical and sociological process which produced modern Germany, from the Reformation, through Protestant absolutism, to Bismarck, and thus to Hitler himself. Unlike Weber, Schmitt in fact rejects the suggestion that modern rational order can be legitimate at all. Whilst Weber suggests that the modern age has produced new forms of technical legitimacy which cannot be dismissed, Schmitt insists that the logic of the modern age can only neutralize political substance and depoliticize genuine politics.

Following these arguments, Schmitt implies that politics can only be genuine politics if it comprises a set of autonomous acts which are not determined by any non-political form of rationality (1925a: 24). Schmitt insists thus on the autonomy and the primacy of *the political*. Legitimate government must, he asserts, be more than a series of technical administrative devices. For the state to be legitimate, he argues, it must be *political*: it must be underscored by a guiding political ethos. Schmitt criticizes liberal conceptions of the political which reduce politics to the negative defence of liberties against the state (1932a: 70). He deplores polycratic definitions of politics, which grasp political order as fleeting compacts between technical or economic organizations. He criticizes conceptions of the political which reduce politics to the free contract of individuals (1923: 20), and he condemns all suggestions that the economy should be given primacy over political life (1932c: 11). The process of depoliticization, Schmitt outlines, resides in the prioritization of any technical, economic, juridical or 'factual' positions over the pure moment of the political itself (1958a: 359). The political moment is a mode of action which is ideally anterior to all other forms of association, even to the constitution of the nation itself. The moment of the political is prior to both law and the state (1932a: 20). The political, therefore, is a structure of action (or *existence*) which marks the last moment of substance in the secular crisis of the modern age (Beneyto 1988: 106). Genuine politics is resistance to the neutralization of modern life (M. Schmitz 1965: 242). Most especially, the liberal conviction that the 'legal order' (*Rechtsordnung*) is the foundation of politics omits, Schmitt argues, to notice that, in the juxtaposition of law and order, order comes before law (1922: 16). There can, in other words, be no law without order, and no order without politics.

Schmitt's position in Weber's wake is, in sum, the most radical argument against the formalization of law in liberal legal theory. Schmitt ridicules the liberal dream of the triumph of law over power. Moreover, Schmitt argues against the entire history of private-legal (capitalist) encroachment upon the power of the state. In this regard, again, Schmitt can be compared to Weber. Although Weber criticizes the pure formality of capitalist law, he reflects nonetheless upon the mechanisms through which the sphere of individual interest might be reconnected to the state. Indeed, arguably, Weber ultimately suggests that the state is subordinate to private interests. Schmitt, in contrast, summarily denies the law-giving authority of extra-political interests. Whatever happens outside the political sphere is, for Schmitt, not relevant to power. In his reflections on politics and order, therefore, Schmitt's arguments always turn against the liberal doctrines of legal positivism, especially against the suggestion that law itself might limit, or even replace, the power of the state. Indeed, it is in opposition to Hans Kelsen, the major exponent of twentieth-century positivism, that Schmitt develops the central traits of his own legal theory.

Kelsen's legal theory revolves around the argument that politics and law are identical. His theory of law rejects all suggestion that law is the product of ideological, or political, influence. In *The Pure Theory of Law* (1934), he argues that law can be viewed as a pure normative system, which does not refer outside the immanent structure of legal terms for its validity. The sphere of the norm – of the *ought* (*Sollen*) – is the sphere of law, Kelsen argues. Social reality exists in the sphere of *being* (*Sein*). The science of law is thus, for Kelsen, the pure interpretation of norms, situated exclusively in the mode of the *ought*, and the methods of legal technique need give no consideration to their social purpose. All non-positivist theories of law, such as natural-law theory, social contract theory, theory of law as will or as legal recognition, are rejected by Kelsen as ideological (Voegelin 1927: 275).

According to Kelsen's mode of critical positivism, all substantive theories of the law import non-legal contents into the legal sphere. Justice itself, Kelsen asserts, is a perhaps convenient, but ultimately ideological construct which has no real relation to the law (Kelsen 1934: 15–16; see also Moore 1978: 3–6). He sees natural law as a covert means of introducing conservative value-orientations into the essentially value-free sphere of legal operation (1943: 266). Similarly, Kelsen rejects sociological explanations of law, which explain law on the basis of the concrete obligations which it forms in the social sphere. He argues instead that the legal system conforms to a logic which is distinct from that of social or natural action. For these reasons, Kelsen is deeply opposed to any suggestion that the state and law can be segregated. The state itself, he argues, although an active constituent of the coercive order of law, cannot be conceived outside the legal sphere. State and law both constitute a common normative or ideal order (1922: 87–9), from which the state cannot be separated out as a personal agent of force. The ascription of meta-legal attributes to the state represents, Kelsen argues, a mere secularization of the illusions of metaphysics (1922: 227).

Kelsen's ideas mark an advanced position in the left-liberal defence of the legal state. He argues that the law itself is the guarantee of good order. The specific normative properties of the law, he explains, are derived from from an original norm (*Ursprungsnorm*). The operations of the law are determined by their coherence with this original norm of law, which confers authority on subsequent norms. The 'original norm', for Kelsen, means the stipulations of the constitution – the founding documents of the political order. The constitution, he asserts, is the fundamental assumption from which all interpretations of the legal order must proceed (1934: 65). The legal order is thus a static set of norms, in which the validity of the particular norm can only be ascertained if it can be traced to its original antecedent. Through the hypothetical assumption that this norm is valid, the entire legal order which is based upon it gains validity (1934: 66). In this respect, the influence of the neo-Kantian thinker Hans Vaihinger is manifest in Kelsen's thinking. Vaihinger's philosophy is a theory of the 'as-if', which asserts that the preconditions of human cognition and social being are shared ideal fictions, which have no ontological correlation with the sphere of being. Kelsen's theory of the original norm links closely with the cognitive preconditions of Vaihinger's 'as-if' form of Kantianism. It is, Kelsen asserts, not possible to make substantive pronouncements about the nature of the original norm. It is important merely that it should be interpreted *as if* it were the precondition of positive law.

Despite his commitment to formal positivism, however, Kelsen's theory of the hypothetical norm has paradoxical overlaps with Weber's theory of revolutionary legitimacy, and, more importantly, with Schmitt's decision-istic-sociological concept of order.[1] The original norm, Kelsen argues, has only ideal significance, as the norm to which the validity of subsequent norms can be traced. However, norms – despite the ideal formulation of Kelsen's theory – do not come from nowhere. They rely, originally, on authorship. Kelsen, in fact, was personally responsible for drafting the documents which transferred the power of government to the interim state-council at the inception of the first Austrian Republic (Ableitinger 1983: 150), after the collapse of the Habsburg monarchy in 1918 (see Goldinger 1986: 58; G. Schmitz 1981: 59; Ermacora 1982: 20). Kelsen himself therefore acknowledged (at least practically) that breaches in the ideal legal order inevitably occur – most obviously in the interim between the demise of one legal order and the foundation of a later one. The first Austrian Republic was, therefore, one crucial example of the refoundation of the original norm upon which the polity is based (Overdieck 1987: 37). By drafting a revolutionary constitution himself, Kelsen created an original norm, and he must have recognized that every original norm is limited both by the possibility of its overthrow, and by the possible production of new norms (Kelsen 1922: 98–9). In the historical moment of foundation, Kelsen's theory of the original norm is, therefore, directly parallel to the personal authority of sovereignty, which is theorized by Schmitt and Weber (see Raz 1980: 95).

Two particular factors in Kelsen's theory of the constitution are of especial historical importance for Schmitt's ideas. Firstly, the constitution of the First Republic in Austria was (like the Weimar Constitution) marked by an opposition to the classical-liberal separation of legislature, executive and judiciary. In his drafts for the Austrian constitution, Kelsen proposed that the executive committee of parliament, guided and restricted only by the basic norms of the constitution, should combine all powers, and that this unity of powers should not be undermined by the conferring of special authority on either plebiscitary figures or the bureaucracy (Overdieck 1987: 152–60). Kelsen thus rejected in principle the separation of executive and legislature in favour of a system in which both executive and legislature are regulated exclusively by the original norm of the constitution (Brauneder 1976: 197). To secure the adherence of executive and legislature to the

1 Weber also uses the 'as-if' category to examine the foundation of legal order. See M. Weber 1972: 192.

constitution, Kelsen proposed the creation of a constitutional court, to assess the compatibility of new laws with the original norm (Marcic 1966: 501). The constitutional court was the culminating moment in Kelsen's proposals for the First Republic (Kelsen 1923: 208), and it was the most durable legacy of his thinking. Secondly, in contrast to Schmitt's anti-party attitude, Kelsen's constitution gave express legal recognition to the political party as a legal subject of public law (Ableitinger 1983: 159). The party, in fact, has a central position in Kelsen's theory of democracy. The fundamental precondition of democracy, Kelsen argues, is the existence of a party-system. The party-system, he asserts, serves to integrate all of society into politics via broad-based democratic associations. It sublimates the social element of political conflict almost completely into the sphere of politics and law. The fact that the activities of political parties are regulated by the constitution transposes all social movements into the arena of legal order (Kelsen 1929: 23), and it thereby divests them of their radical or revolutionary content.

More broadly, however, Kelsen's pure theory of law has crucial importance for Schmitt because it illustrates the weakness of liberal attempts to limit power through law. Historically, legal positivism sought – at least in principle – to undermine the state's monopoly of power. It developed initially as a codification of private law. However, Kelsen's positivism (like that of Gerber and Laband before him) transposes responsibility for the restriction of state-power into the order of public law itself. In Kelsen's legal theory, all law is public law, because all law is derived from the objective legal order of the constitution. To Schmitt's perspective, Kelsen's thought therefore demonstrates the worst self-deception of German liberalism. Kelsen's positivism relies on the belief that the legal agency of the state can be translated into, and subsequently regulated by, pure legal codes. But it also claims that these codes, although formally neutral, possess the quality of public authority. In its attempt to circumscribe the power of the state, positivism thus succeeds only in giving power back to the state, in supposedly neutralized form. It makes the state responsible for maintaining the norms which are intended to limit its own authority. This, for Schmitt, perfectly underlines the inability of liberal thought to constitute a genuine ethic of politics. Legal positivism is, Schmitt implies, a classically disastrous attempt to transpose the formal rationality of the private-legal or anti-state interests sphere into the rationality of politics. The hostility to the theory of legal norms, as exemplified by Kelsen's legal theory, remains a key thread which connects the various periods of Schmitt's career. Through all his works, despite apparent overlaps between his own ideas and Kelsen's thought, Schmitt sets himself squarely against the positivist orthodoxies perpetuated by Kelsen, and he opts instead for a sociological orientation in the scrutiny of the connection between state and law. Schmitt rejects Kelsen's thought for its formulaic quality, for its repudiation of substantive theories of state-law, and most especially for its quality as purely normative legalism.

Schmitt's opposition to Kelsen assumes a different character at different points in his development. In his early writings, Schmitt's opposition to the pure ideality of positivism is markedly distinct from his later works. In these early works, Schmitt is still attached to juridical hermeneutics and late-historicist theories of law (see A. Adam 1992: 29–30). He argues here – against Kelsen – that positive law must be grounded in the 'moral world-view of the people' (C. Schmitt 1969: 88), and that the historical-cultural horizon of the nation must form the substantive base by which legal and political decisions (norms) are given authority (see Schmidt-Aßmann 1967: 23). Here, Schmitt simply reiterates the traditional historicist critique of Kantian ethics and natural law. At this stage, therefore, Schmitt's writings anticipate his later works only insofar as they put forward a late-historicist, or even hermeneutical value-relativism as the basis of law (see H. Hoffmann 1964: 43–4; Gadamer 1960: 379; Stolleis 1992: 148).

However, the positive essence of Schmitt's theory of politics (and thus his critique of positivism) is clarified by his observations on the politics of Catholicism, in *Roman Catholicism and Political Form* (1925). In this work, Schmitt states that the only genuine politics is based on the ethos of the Catholic church. Such politics, he argues, has been most severely attenuated by the culture of Protestantism (and capitalism). The foundation of legitimate politics, he explains, is only possible where politics is related to spiritual ideas and to systems of authority which represent and enact these ideas (see Mehring 1989: 51). Schmitt argues thus in anti-Weberian tone: 'No political system can last even one generation by the mere technical assertion of power. Ideas are fundamental to the political, for there is no politics without authority and no authority without an ethos of conviction' (1925a: 23). The Catholic church, therefore, perfectly encapsulates the moment of genuine politics – of *the political* (Bröckling 1993: 72). This pure political dimension to the Catholic church resides, Schmitt explains, in its representation of a transcendent idea, and in the positive enactment of this idea in the temporal world (see M. Kaufmann 1988: 108–9).

*Roman Catholicism and Political Form* also contains the philosophical basis to Schmitt's theory of political order. In this work, Schmitt sets out a theory of human life, in which he asserts that the rationality of the Catholic church encompasses the dimension of humanity which is not exclusively devoted to the technical processes of the economy, and to the reproduction of material needs (1925a: 19). The rationality of Catholicism, Schmitt argues, is situated above the progressive structures of Weberian rationality, as a static representation of a durable ethic, which is 'political in an eminent sense' (p. 22). The historical struggle of Catholicism against its adversaries is thus the 'reaction against the mechanism of time' (p. 23), against 'an age of economic thinking' (p. 26). Above all, Schmitt argues, Catholicism recognizes the need for government. Government under the rational-technical conditions of Protestantism, he claims, is not strictly necessary. In Protestantism, the power of political organization is not differentiated from the autonomous logic of material reproduction (p. 49). Protestant, or capitalist, government is, Schmitt implies, simply a system which balances or manages technical interests, and in which the state's ethical integrity is diluted by its constant involvement in the civil sphere. Protestant – or capitalist – government is therefore not strictly *political*: it is not informed by an ethic which differentiates it from the simply technical and material processes of economic utilization and natural need-satisfaction (p. 16).

In this respect, Schmitt's Catholic ethic of politics moves, almost paradoxically, close to Kant. Schmitt argues that human nature should be interpreted as a dual structure. Humanity is, on one level, a component of the natural-technical processes of the sphere of material reproduction. However, humanity is also a component of a natural-legal-political sphere, in which human nature is connected with divine grace, and so elevated above mere need. This second quality of human nature is signified by the representative ethic of the Catholic church. For Schmitt, as for Kant, nature thus exists in two forms (Kant 1966b: 350; Brakemeyer 1985: 28). Nature, firstly, is pure material need, from which human political life must detach itself. Secondly, however, nature is also the guiding reason of human politics, in which humanity sets itself above needs. Both Kant and Schmitt argue therefore that the political quality of human life overcomes and supersedes mere nature. In doing so, it realizes the natural potential of humanity itself.[2] Kant explains this political dialectic between first nature and second nature as a relation between different modes of natural law. Through the natural, ethical law of human reason, Kant argues, humanity can overcome the natural law of material antagonism (Kant 1966b: 515, 526; Riedel 1973: 338). Schmitt explains this same dialectic as a relation between material nature (need) and divine nature (grace).

This relation, for Schmitt, is also a dialectic between Protestantism and Catholicism. Catholic forms of order are required, Schmitt suggests, if humanity is to be represented politically as anything other than pure technical need (1925a: 49). Schmitt argues thus – like both Weber and Kant – that there exists an ideal political sphere, in which humanity bestows a political ethic upon itself which segregates humanity (initially) from the sphere of material reproduction, and (latterly) from the technical logic of the economy. However, unlike Weber and Kant, Schmitt argues that the genuinely political sphere can only be interpreted theologically. Weber's attempt to understand pure politics as a system of integration falls, for Schmitt, into the trap of technical reason. Likewise, Kant's interpretation of the political sphere as an arena for the rational justification of property-interests is also, for Schmitt, insufficiently political. For Weber and Kant, diversely, private needs are enacted through political systems. For Schmitt, the private sphere of needs must be kept rigidly apart from the political order. This separation symbolizes the separation of material and divine nature.

2 Kant, 1966c: 364. See esp. J. Ritter 1970: 81–2. See also Prauss 1983: 44; Sassenbach 1992: 58; Kaulbach 1970: 53.

These ideas are also at the heart of Schmitt's critique of liberalism. The systems of representation engendered by liberalism, Schmitt asserts, are in essence merely distillations of the process of material reproduction, in which government is employed to balance and satisfy fluctuating technical needs (1925a: 28–9). Moreover, Schmitt argues, government which is installed solely in order to balance interests will never be truly legitimate, for it is based on revocable economic contracts. Like Hegel and Weber before him, Schmitt indicates that the contract, as the abstraction of economic exchange, can never be genuinely legitimate, and can never be the foundation for trustworthy – *political* – order. The interests which are refracted into the contract are merely non-reconciled residues of the relations in the civil-economic sphere. For this reason, Schmitt (at least in gesture) declares sympathy for the late-medieval estate-based systems of representation – the *Ständestaat* – in which the representation of the political will is (as in the church) representation 'from above' (1925a: 35). The hierarchical principle of representation in the pre-constitutional *Ständestaat* serves, Schmitt implies (without great historical insight), to limit the impact of technical rationality on the political order, and to relegate the deputation of social needs to activities outside the state-administration (Schwer 1970: 8). The modern system of representative constitutionalism is, for Schmitt, merely a technical compromise between mutually exclusive forms of order – or between mutually exclusive social classes (C. Schmitt 1928: 211). For this reason, the constitutional system can never be truly legitimate, for it never evades the technical obligation to harmonize conflicting interests. In this regard, Schmitt's ideas can be closely compared to Hegel's philosophy of law (Hegel 1986: 172). The positive outline of good politics in Schmitt's work is – as in Hegel's thought – a model of hierarchical representation, in which the political ethic of representation does not attach itself to the representation of particular interests, but to the general or higher ethic of political life. At the base of this is a theological/anthropological concept of humanity, in which humanity has not yet been finally relinquished to the sphere of material technicity.

However, if the representative dignity of the church crystallizes the heart of Schmitt's political theology (and his anti-positivism), the most renowned position in his political trajectory is his 'decisionist' phase, especially of the late 1920s. Decisionism is a loose theoretical construct which informed varying traditions of political, legal and theological reflection in post-1918 Gemany. Its chief manifestations are found (apart from in Schmitt) in the Kierkegaard-inspired theologies of Karl Barth and Rudolf Bultmann, in the ethics of Karl Jaspers and in Heidegger's existential ontology. Although it assumes diverse character in each of these examples, decisionism generally is a term which indicates that, after the collapse of ontological, theological, ius-natural and constitutional certainties, the contextual *decision* of the individual subject has central status as the source of political/existential authentication and authorization. Decisionism – at least in its political form – can be perhaps best understood as a subjective refiguring of the national relativism which is at the heart of German historicism (Krockow 1990: 85). Historicism, generally, is a collective form of decisionism, in which the national whole, freed from the supra-positive constraints of enlightened ius-naturalism, shapes itself decisively into its appropriate national-political form. In both decisionism and historicism, the truth-claims of the political sphere are set against the abstract truth of natural law in the Enlightenment, or the juridical truth of divine law in Catholicism. The historicist theories of the state developed in the wake of Hegel by, for instance, Droysen, Dilthey and Meinecke sought to explain the state as an accretion of cultural-national experience (Meinecke 1963: 510; Dilthey 1883: 114–15), in which political actions – or decisions – are perpetrated outside theological or ethical certainty, and therefore possess only occasional or contextual validity. Subjective, or theological, decisionism is in many respects therefore little more than the internalization of the political principles of historicism.

However, the complexity of Schmitt's thought is underlined by the fact that even one of its apparently more consistent gestures – his decisionism – contains three distinct sub-categories. Rather than constituting a uniform dimension to his thinking, Schmitt's 'decisionism' in fact contains diverse features which can be separately categorized as sovereign decisionism, antagonistic decisionism and constitutional decisionism.

The first form of decisionism developed by Schmitt is set out in *Political Theology* (1924), in which he first outlines his famous theory of the state of exception. Here, Schmitt asserts that state-power can only be genuinely legitimized in the limit-case of normative order: that is in situations of internal or external emergency, where the order of the polis is directly threatened by siege or civil war. He outlines thus the most lapidary of all his theories: 'The sovereign is whoever decides over the state of exception' (1922: 11).

This theory is clearly marked by Schmitt's own political experience. Owing to the constant threat of political sabotage during the early 1920s, the politics of emergency was a crucial area of debate in the Weimar period. The Weimar Constitution itself contained extraordinarily far-reaching provisions for emergency legislation and the dissolution of parliament in cases of political threat to the government (Watkins 1939: 18). The notorious Article 48 of the constitution stipulated exceptional situations (the *Ausnahmezustand*) in which normal parliamentary executive and legislative processes could be suspended and the power of execution could be given directly to the President of the republic.[3] As a continuation of the nineteenth-century provisions for the state of siege, which had naturally been extended during the war (Boldt 1972: 325), Article 48 also gave the President supreme command over the military (H. Mommsen 1990: 70). Article 48 of the constitution was conceived initially as a means of protecting the republic against insurrection from extremist groups on both left and

---

3 See G. Schulz 1963: 190–1. See also: E. R. Huber 1981: 38; 1975a: 207; Oberreuter 1978: 43.

right. However, it soon became useful merely as a device for introducing legislation without the consent of parliament. Such deployment began under the presidency of Ebert, who used the article 135 times (Maser 1987: 266), in some instances to introduce anti-inflationary budgetary measures (H. Mommsen 1990: 150; Boldt 1980: 292–3). Ebert himself was well aware of the more authoritarian possibilities for governance which Article 48 presented, and he was not ill-disposed towards the use of the article to circumvent democratic procedure (Stürmer 1980: 313). Ebert's extensive employment of Article 48 led to early controversy about the legitimacy of such parliamentary suspension (Boldt 1980: 297), in which Schmitt was closely involved. However, the usage of Article 48 as a means of overruling the legislative body was taken much further under Hindenburg's presidency (1925–33), especially after the collapse of Müller's SPD-led coalition in March 1930. Article 48 ultimately became the basis for rule by emergency decree in the late-Weimar interim of 1930–33 (Conze 1967: 193), during which time Article 48 was routinely utilized to pass laws without parliamentary agreement.

Against this background, Schmitt argues that only the politics of the extreme can reliably constitute genuine order. It is, he argues, only in the limiting moments of normative order that the fundamental principles of this order rise above the technical dissolutions to which they are ordinarily subject. Only in the state of exception (*Ausnahmezustand*), in which Article 48 applies, can the authority of law be concentrated in the hands of one person. Only thus can this authority, legitimized by plebiscitary election, be asserted decisively against the common pluralism of government, in order to 'protect the unity of the people as a political whole' (1931a: 159). It is only in the state of exception, Schmitt implies, that the technical compromises upon which the political system is based are replaced – as revelation – by an unequivocal political imperative (1922: 43).

The technical apparatus of modern government is, Schmitt thus suggests, a merely normative order, which cannot by its own will force adherence to its own norms. Law, however, is not truly valid unless it can do this (1922: 38). For Schmitt, wherever the normative order of modern government is disrupted, only pre-technical – personal – sources of order have the strength to maintain the integrity of the state. Schmitt's theory of secularization therefore leads him to the conclusion that the state, as a substantive body, is already vanishing, or cannot at least be taken for granted. Order can therefore only be created through direct recourse to *the political* in the purest sense – which is conceived by Schmitt as a personal will, as revelation, not as technical organs of administration (see H. Hoffmann 1986: 231).

The second, and equally renowned, form of decisionism which appears in Schmitt's work is presented in *The Concept of the Political*. This component of Schmitt's ideas is almost universally (if incorrectly) identified as the defining trait of his thought. In this work, Schmitt sets out his theory of the friend–foe relation. He argues that a political decision between friend and foe constitutes the all-legitimizing basis of politics. The legitimacy of a political order, he explains, depends utterly on its ability to define itself against other forms of political order – to be decisively different (if necessary) from other modes of political life. The decision between friend and foe, Schmitt explains, is the final source of legitimacy in an age where even the state itself has been in part consumed by technical needs (1932a: 24). In the extreme case, Schmitt asserts, the stability of a particular political organization hinges on the ability of its representatives to decide resolutely that they represent *this particular* organization and no other. They must therefore be able to decide between friend and foe.

This theory of the friend–foe relation has been interpreted (even, at times, by Schmitt himself; 1928: 377) as a racial model of national-political belonging, or as a reduction of politics to warfare (1928: 371). However, it can (in connection with Schmitt's theological reflections) also be interpreted as an ethical model of political adherence. Schmitt's decisionism is not essentially militaristic (1932a: 34), and it does not revolve essentially around racial or international conflict (1932a: 35). On the contrary, Schmitt's theory of the friend–foe relation is little more than the argument that the positive cohesion of a political system depends upon its ethical unity. Constituents of a genuine political order must, Schmitt implies, *decide* to exist in a way which cannot simply be fused with any other. The details of this decision thus become concrete, integrative components of political order (1928: 378). Only by means of such a decision – if necessary against alternative structures of political life – can the constituents of the polity be *political*. It is only through the decision, Schmitt explains, that the polity confers upon itself an ethos which is distinct from the diversity of compromises in the sub-political, or technical sphere. In this regard, Schmitt's theory of the decision directly parallels the status of the social contract in classical liberal theory. For Kant, for example, by entering the contract the members of a polity elevate themselves above the sphere of private antagonism. Analogously, it is only through the decision *for* a unified ethic of political order, Schmitt asserts, that the polity distinguishes itself from the civil-economic sphere. The political body, for Schmitt, is founded at the moment where its principles are decided in such a manner that they cannot be harmonized by means of compromise or bargain with an alternative political body, where the interests of its constituents are ceded decisively to the collective (1932a: 38–9). At the point where such a decision is made, the economic, theological, cultural or national group becomes *political* (1932a: 39). It detaches itself from the exclusively material sphere of need and strategy. The decision for or against a friend or a foe is therefore, for Schmitt, the decision for a positive ethic of political life. In an age in which substantive principles of political order are in decline, the decision between friend and foe is the *last* principle of possible order.

Clearly, on one level, Schmitt's friend–foe relation provides the most striking of all proto-National Socialist theories of law and politics (see Sontheimer 1962: 94–8). Schmitt asserts that the basis of genuine politics (and therefore genuine order) resides in the ability of the law-giver to distinguish between friend and foe, be that the friend and foe of the collective or the friend and foe of himself or herself. This distinction is elevated to the basis of what Schmitt calls the 'ontological (*seinsmäßige*) facticity and autonomy of the political' (1932a: 28). The presence of an adversary produces unity and homogeneity, and homogeneity is itself a precondition of social and political order. War (or its threat) is the base of politics, Schmitt thus intimates, and the moment of difference or enmity is always a key integrative moment in the constitution and maintenance of a political order. The theory of the friend–foe relation implies that the state and law cannot be neutral, and that politics cannot be grounded in the assumptions of compromise, contract or mere trust. Liberal assumptions of social agreement, and positivist (Kelsenian) conventions of legal neutrality, are in the extreme case absolutely devoid of legitimacy.

However, despite its overlaps with anti-constitutional tendencies on both left and right, the friend–foe relation was only obliquely (or opportunistically) linked to any organized political grouping. In his theory of the friend–foe relation, Schmitt warns against the dangerous ideologies of liberalism – especially the conviction that compromise and interest can always be harnessed to the good of the polity. He explains how politics which does not mediate social antagonisms into a genuinely unified consensus will never attain internal stability (1923: 10). This theory is intended to warn against the inorganic forms of coalition which constituted the bedrock of the late-Weimar period. Liberalism, Schmitt argues, has fragmented the ethos of real political life by transforming economic interests into the base of political order. Liberalism, therefore, has replaced this ethos with a purely negative theory of politics – and therefore with a weak state and a weak political culture (1932a: 69). For this reason, Schmitt continues, liberalism always tends to produce anti-liberal governments – for it does not possess a decisive ethic which would enable it to obstruct organizations which are hostile to it (pp. 70–1). The distinction between friend and foe is, Schmitt argues, a means of recreating the state as a genuine political ethic (p. 44). It is a means of constituting the state positively, as something other than a balancing-apparatus for economic needs. Schmitt thus reflects on the friend–foe distinction as a final bastion against the subsidence of politics into the purely technical or neutral. The triumph of the technical over the ethical, Schmitt warns darkly, will be far more *total* than any simple political decision between friend and foe (pp. 24, 68). In part, therefore, Schmitt's critique of liberalism and his emphasis on the friend–foe relation can be viewed more as an admonitory description of the strength of National Socialism than as its unequivocal endorsement (see Taubes 1995: 139). Schmitt's theory of the friend–foe relation, for all its dramatic lip-service to theories of violence, turns back to the nineteenth century and argues, in essence, that the incursions of the private sphere upon the state have failed to produce a substantive theory of politics. What is more, they have destroyed the old one. Because of the damage done by liberalism, and its creed of private law, the state now *must* decide between friend and foe in order to survive, in order to free itself from complete annexation by the economy. Previously, Schmitt indicates, it was not forced to make this decision.

The third striking form of decisionism which emerges in Schmitt's thought is seen most clearly in *Theory of the Constitution* (1928). Like many of his works from the later years of the Weimar Republic, this work offers an altogether more favourable representation of constitutional democracy than his earlier works. This can be attributed to the partial stabilization of the republic during the years 1924–9. Even here, Schmitt does not wholly affirm the Weimar parliamentary system. He argues, however, that rule within the constraints of the constitution has, after all, a certain claim to legitimacy. The constitution, he argues, even the pleonastic Weimar Constitution, represents a collective *political* decision about the form and order of national politics. 'A constitution', he states, 'does not rest on a norm, the correctness of which is the ground of its validity. It rests on an ontological political decision about the manner and norms of our own being. The word "will" describes – in contrast to all dependence on normative or abstract correctness – the essentially *existential* moment of the ground of this validity' (1928: 76). A legitimate constitution is thus the reflection of the political will of the collective. The Weimar Constitution, Schmitt argues, derives its (partial) legitimacy from the fact that it (partially) represents the political form of the German people (1928: 121).

Schmitt's essential argument in *Theory of the Constitution* is that modern constitutions can be broken down into their technical components and their political components (1928: 220). If a constitution, he argues, is merely a set of provisions relating to the administration of the legal state, it possesses merely formal validity, and merely formal concepts of liberty (p. 200), which do not contain in themselves the grounds for their own enforcement. This is the heart of Schmitt's famous distinction between the constitution itself (*Verfassungsrecht*), which is the 'unique decision' over 'the political whole in respect of its particular form of existence' (p. 21), and constitutional laws (*Verfassungsgesetze*), which are merely the formal adjuncts to this decision, and which can be easily suspended (p. 26). A constitution is politically valid, Schmitt argues thus, if it contains principles of positive order and the means for the enforcement of these principles – if it marks a decision for a particular form of order, and no other. The constitutions of bourgeois legal states, he explains, contain a rough fusion of technical and political components (p. 216). Indeed, Schmitt continues, bourgeois legal states can barely constitute themselves as genuine decisions, because they are based on purely neutral concepts of freedom. Nonetheless, the Weimar Constitution, Schmitt asserts, 'is a constitution, not a series of constitutional laws. It contains the fundamental political decisions for a constitutional democracy' (p. 29). Schmitt thus imputes to the Weimar Constitution genuine, although technically diluted, legitimacy. It possesses, he suggests, a latent principle of positive order, which is not identical with the compromise-form of the social contract, and not identical with the simple securing of negative liberty against the state, which Schmitt otherwise defines as the chief traits of the bourgeois legal state (p. 67).

At this juncture, therefore, Schmitt argues that even constitutional systems can claim political legitimacy. Moreover, he indicates that the Weimar Constitution itself would be assured genuine legitimacy if the political decisions (*Verfassungsrecht*) at its heart were clarified in relation to the technical-administrative laws (*Verfassungsgesetze*) relating to their enforcement. He argues that the Weimar legal-political system should be replaced with a system in which the principles of legal governance (of the *Rechtsstaat* itself) are made subordinate to the vision of concrete, positive, political order which the constitution, Schmitt alleges, also contains. What preoccupies Schmitt in his most positive reflections on the nature of constitutional rule is that the constitution, as the political form of the people, might be invoked as a uniting set of principles of positive order, from which no law, and therefore no action, can ever be excluded. Constitutional rule might, therefore, represent a unified ethic of political life, which is not fatally constrained by technical compromise. To ensure that this is the case, Schmitt argues that all the compromise-elements of the constitution, or all aspects of the constitution which run counter to its quality as a pure political ethic, should be amended, or made subordinate to its principles of order. In the bourgeois legal state, this would mean that the basic components of the state – the separation of the powers and the catalogue of bourgeois liberties – would themselves have to be amended. The strict separation of the powers, Schmitt argues, reflects the internal fragmentation of the modern, bourgeois state (1928: 186; 1932a: 61). Moreover, bourgeois liberties, Schmitt asserts, are themselves ultimately liberties *against* the state, not *for* it (1928: 216). Schmitt's proposals for the transformation of the Weimar state into a genuinely legitimate political order therefore envisage a radical recasting of modern democracy itself. This transformation would include an annulment of the technical encroachments of private interest upon the state. The separation of powers, the catalogue of basic rights and the sanctity of private contract would all therefore be made subordinate to the overarching will of the state-executive. The state would, thus transfigured, constitute a decisive (quasi-theological) whole, substantively distinct from the sphere of needs and interest to which it is enchained by liberalism.

This constitutional dimension to Schmitt's decisionism also connects closely with the historical conditions of the Weimar Republic. Amongst the peculiarities of the Weimar Constitution was the fact that it was divided into two sections. The first section provided for the technicalities of administrative law and, significantly, for the regulation of parliament. The second contained a series of basic pronouncements about the rights and obligations of citizens in the new German state. Friedrich Naumann, Weber's acquaintance, was primarily responsible for drafting the second part. At one stage Naumann even sought to phrase the rights and obligations of citizens in vernacular speech, to make them accessible to all citizens as the unifying ethos of national-political life (Naumann 1919a: 156–7). Above all, Naumann accentuated the basic rights of citizens as structures of positive liberty, realized not against the state, but in interaction with the state – as principles of social integration. Even the bourgeois-liberal principle of the sanctity of private property was presented by Naumann not as a negative liberty, but as a pedagogic means of national improvement and production (Naumann 1919c: 142) – thus as a dynamic component in national will-formation. Naumann, too, like Weber, was determined to reorganize liberal law as an integrative system of positive order.

Schmitt's fluctuating attitude to the second part of the Weimar Constitution is an important and revealing aspect in his thinking. At times Schmitt accuses Naumann of great juridical naivety. But in his writings of the later period of the Republic he is clearly impressed by the vision which moved Naumann's actions – namely, the creation of a framing suprapositive order for the political life of Germany. By the end of the Weimar Republic, Schmitt's attention focuses on the discrepancies between the order implied in the second part of the constitution and the technical stipulations of the first part. Tellingly, he describes the second part as a 'counter-constitution' (1932c: 57), and he discusses various devices by means of which the basic decisions of the second part are undermined by the administrative provisions of the first part. Schmitt's constitutional works of the late-Weimar period thus set out a defence of the second part of the Weimar Constitution against the first. Schmitt indicates in these works that the political principles of equality, labour, justice and participation set out by Naumann might indeed be grasped as integrative principles of order. Schmitt, however, in contrast to Naumann's cautious sympathy for plebiscitary government (Naumann 1919d: 9), argues that the order-principles of the constitution are best realized by representative figures, bound to the constitution, who are not legitimized by technical, electoral consensus, but by the direct *acclamation* of the people (C. Schmitt 1928: 279).

Schmitt's ascription, thus, of legitimizing power to the collective decision, inscribed in the constitution, raises fundamental questions about the overall nature of his decisionism. In *Political Theology* the decision creates political order as a quasi-theological decision from above, made by the sovereign in the state of exception. In *The Concept of the Political* the decision also produces order as a decision from above, in which the decisive identification of the foe creates a structure of positive order. This theory, however, already suggests that the decision has a legitimizing force which is not restricted to the executive level of government. The fact of the friend–foe relation, conceived as the immutable base of the political, can transform any association into a political order. In *Theory of the Constitution*, the creation of order assumes the aspect of univocal political foundation from below, or at least of the direct correlation between foundation from below and organization from above (Hennis 1977a: 166). The general tendency of

Schmitt's decisionism suggests, of course, that it is the decision from above which is the real guarantor of political order. But his thought is both pragmatic enough and sensitive enough to changes within the political landscape of Germany that, in the period 1924–9, he endorses the collective decision as the ground of legitimate order. Above all, in each of these cases the crucial issue is that a decision is made at all – that an integral political will transfuses the ordering of political life.

It is very important to note, however, that Schmitt's descriptions and projections of a political system based on positive principles of order, and elevated above the system of technical and economic needs, have minimal symmetry with the actual modes of governance which he supported and approved in the late 1920s. Indeed the discrepancy between his prescriptions and the forms of domination which he endorsed throw telling light on his whole theory of politics.

Schmitt's treatment of exception-politics refers most directly to the employment of Article 48 of the Weimar Constitution during Heinrich Brüning's administration of the period 1930–2. Backed by Hindenburg, Brüning invoked Article 48 to introduce deflationary economic measures in the aftermath of the Wall Street Crash (C. Schmitt 1932a: 71). Brüning's presidial cabinet replaced the Grand Coalition, led by Hermann Müller (SPD). The collapse of the Grand Coalition in March 1930 had been due largely to differences between the DVP-representatives, the unions and the SPD-deputies regarding plans for a reduction of social spending (Conze 1968: 39). Before Brüning's assumption of the chancellorship, Hindenburg had assured him that he was prepared to suspend customary legislative processes in order to push through the economic measures which the SPD had previously resisted (Conze 1967: 203). Brüning's specific mandate as Chancellor was therefore to cut public expenditure, to increase German exports by reducing labour costs (Golla 1994: 28), and to stabilize the budget at the level of national growth (Rapport 1992: 414). It has been outlined above that, until his death in 1925, Ebert had also permitted frequent and varied use of Article 48. However, special legislation had been introduced in 1922 to prohibit anti-republican activities, and in most minor threats to the republic this legislation had been employed instead of Article 48 (Jasper 1963: 56–92). During Brüning's chancellorship, however, the use of Article 48 was very extensively expanded. It was implemented not to quell threats to political stability, or to protect the constitution, but as a systematic device for introducing economic decrees, or passing yearly budgets (G. Schulz 1980: lxvi). During Brüning's period of office, therefore, Article 48 was used mainly as a protective institute to prevent interferences in the operations of state (Jasper 1963: 286). In the period 1930–3, consequently, the legislative power of parliament was most severely undermined, as legislation was effected almost exclusively by direct presidential decree or prerogative, rather than by debated jurisdiction. Parliament assembled ninety-four times in 1930, but it assembled on only thirteen occasions in 1932 (Scheuner 1967: 248). Article 48 became the 'instrument of an economic-social practice of rule by emergency decree' (1967: 253). Importantly in this respect, the presidial system established by Brüning and Hindenburg was also pronouncedly bureaucratic in character. Presidial edicts, negotiated by Brüning and Hindenburg, were simply fed into the free-floating administration of state, which had been detached from the complicated machinery of parliament. This process gave great executive power to the civil service (1967: 279).

Thus, despite the grand gestures in his theory of pure politics, the actual functions which Schmitt ascribes to the presidial executive are substantially less dignified than he suggests (C. Schmitt 1932a: 85). Schmitt's theory of presidial democracy is itself closely modelled to the supplantation of parliament by the bureaucracy which was accomplished under Brüning and Hindenburg. During Brüning's period of economic dictatorship, therefore, the concrete implications of Schmitt's theory of the exception become clear. The use of Article 48 to introduce economic legislation gives to the President, Schmitt implies, greater legitimacy than can ever be claimed by the legal state (1932e: 71). Such employment of emergency powers, he indicates, transforms aspects of law which are based in the private economy into positive principles of public order. Schmitt criticizes parliamentary democracy because it is fragmented, precarious and technical – because it cannot unite the will of the people, except through technical balancing-acts, and because it marks the triumph of the economy over the polity. However, manifestly, Schmitt himself does not suggest with any seriousness that the acts of the sovereign in the state of exception (under Article 48) can truly reconcile the conflicts which are – in Schmitt's own terms – unsuccessfully mediated in party-politics. On the contrary, the President, like the parties, is an organ for passing economic laws (see Perels 1973: 72; V. Neumann 1984: 71). The sovereign who can distinguish between friend and foe in the state of exception is, Schmitt suggests, more purely political than any compromise which can be secured through parliamentary activity. Yet, as a point of historical fact, the acts of legislation which the sovereign (Hindenburg) introduced were not distinct in type or character from those passed by the parliamentary system. Indeed, in their quality as formal economic edicts, the laws passed by the sovereign were more strongly determined by the material system than parliamentary laws.

By endorsing the position of the President as the 'guardian of the constitution', therefore, Schmitt simply indicates that the President can institute a system of superlegality, in which presidial edicts override and circumvent the legal provisions of the constitution (1932c: 76; see also Kirchheimer 1932: 12). Despite Schmitt's (self-proclaimed) hostility to merely technical or administrative politics, however, his critique of technical government has little more than a metaphorical or gestural quality. Schmitt's vision of integral politics only suggests, ultimately, that the President should take control of the state-bureaucracy, and transform it into the instrument of his own will (or of the economic interests which he sanctions). 'The Imperial President', Schmitt explains, 'can pass general

norms and can take special steps and create extraordinary executive departments in order personally to ensure that they are applied and carried out. In
other words, he unites in himself legislation and legal execution and can
immediately execute the norms which he has set' (1932c: 68–9). Schmitt's
assertion that the sovereign can integrate and unite all components of
political will-formation thus, in reality, cedes far greater power to the
bureaucracy than would be possible under the government of a strong
parliament. In this respect, Schmitt simply endorses the gradual move
away from parliamentary rule towards bureaucratic domination which
characterized the politics of the Weimar state, and which was in part
responsible for its decline. Far from seriously indicating a path towards
government by a pure political will, in practice Schmitt's theory validates
domination by a bureaucratic executive, which is closely tuned to economic
directive. Rather than offering the possibility of real legitimacy in politics,
Schmitt (like Luhmann after him) accepts that conflicts within the social
sphere will be addressed (if at all) merely by administrative departments,
and he represents political unity, beyond these systems, through the strong
planning-executive (Beyme 1996: 101), concentrated around the President.

Schmitt's decisionistic theory of the strong executive, grounded in the
friend–foe relation, can therefore be interpreted as a mode of consciously
secular politics (see Nicoletti 1988: 120–1). Rhetorically, Schmitt argues
that the sovereign who can decide between friend and foe creates a unifying
ethic which pervades, as a principle of order, the entirety of political life. In
practice, however, the sovereign is merely a senior bureaucrat. The parliamentary system, Schmitt argues, cannot base itself on anything other than
fleeting agreements and coalitions, which are incapable of infusing the state
with a strong integrative ethic. Therefore, the bureaucracy and the judiciary are forced to detach themselves, in partial autonomy, from the
legislative body. If the judiciary and state-administration were to remain
closely joined to the legislature, Schmitt explains, they would be unable to
operate, owing to the constant alterations in the system of party-agree-
ments. Parliamentary democracy, Schmitt laments therefore, inevitably
produces highly technical-bureaucratic systems of government – far
removed from the original conceptions of popular sovereignty. By consequence, in modern democracy, Schmitt explains, the political apparatus
inevitably dissolves into distinct administrative departments, because these
are not organically fused by a binding political (or theological) ethic.
However, Schmitt's lamentation on the technical and bureaucratic nature
of modern government ultimately does not go beyond the assertion that a
dictator is required to maintain control over the prerogative system of
administration. 'The dictator', he argues, 'is more adequate and appropriate
to the administrative state, which manifests itself in prerogative practice,
than a parliament separated from the executive' (1932c: 81).

Thus, for all his political-theological rhetoric, Schmitt, like Hans Freyer,
proposes the sovereign decision, lastly, as a plan for the bureaucracy
(Freyer 1933: 22). Although in his reflections on the technical nature of

the modern age Schmitt sees technology as the final stage in the process of political neutralization, his own decisionistic theory of the sovereign does not oppose this process.[4] Schmitt's sovereign relies fully upon, and augments the power of, the technical departments of modern government. The instrumentalization of technology by the powerful is, Schmitt argues elsewhere, the 'definitive sense' of the modern age (1932a: 94). In sum, the theological surface to Schmitt's decisionism merely masks, aesthetically, the collaboration of Schmitt's thought with the technical systems which (he otherwise argues) define the political conditions of modernity. Schmitt's symbolic vision of charismatic leadership is scarcely more than a means for devolving power and influence to the administration, which is thus freed of its obligation towards the legislative body (C. Schmitt 1993: 114).

Schmitt's decisionism therefore constitutes a complex of highly contradictory political positions, which ultimately endorse a form of politics which is very different from the ideal preconditions of his theory of order. Confessing sympathy for the supra-positive ethic of the church, Schmitt approves politics based on contextual assertions of power. Professing hostility towards technical modes of government, Schmitt provides a model for rule by the bureaucracy. Declaring a commitment to transcendent representation as the guiding ethic of political legitimacy, Schmitt also recognizes (albeit half-heartedly) the legitimacy of the claim to popular sovereignty. In each of these respects, Schmitt's thinking undergoes a decisive move to the secular. Whilst the ideal foundation of Schmitt's theory of government is in the realm of theological representation, he is also prepared to find distorted reflections of these ideas even in the least sacral modes of political organization. Schmitt is, in principle, able to see *all* order as a dim reflection of real order.

This contradictory fusion of theological and secular ideas in Schmitt's thought can again be directly linked both with his Roman Catholicism and his neo-Kantian influences. In one of his earliest works, *The Value of the State and the Importance of the Individual* (1914), Schmitt puts forward a theory of the state which combines neo-Kantian legal theory and Roman Catholic ius-naturalism. In marked contrast to his later works, he asserts here that the state is obliged to effect the supra-positive norms of absolute right (1914: 38), and that the state is the executive which transfers right into positive political order (see also Rommen 1935: 159). The state, Schmitt indicates, must at all times act within the constraints of absolute law (see also Schilling 1933: 119), and it owes its dignity to its representation of legality, which is not derived exclusively from its own functional necessity (Pilch 1994: 69–70). The state, Schmitt continues, can only be defined through law (1914: 46), and it is only the mediator of law, never its author (p. 68). True authorship in law, he argues, is possessed only by the Catholic church (p. 44). The legal status of the Pope legitimizes, across national

---

4 Much recent literature has taken Schmitt's critique of technology at face-value. See esp. McCormick 1997: 4.

borders, resistance to acts of state which contravene *divine-natural law* (p. 82). At this point, evidently, Schmitt believes in supra-positive forms of right, which exist prior to individual political edicts. Relatedly, in another early work, *Political Romanticism*, Schmitt condemns the 'occasionalism' of the political ideas of Romanticism (1925: 23). Romanticism, Schmitt argues, transfers the substantive order of God to the fanciful character of the Romantic subject – a subject which erodes substantive certainties, and relegates the order of the world to the level of a mere 'occasion' for its interest and delight. Ironically, Schmitt even accuses Romantic thinking of too easily entertaining mutually exclusive political positions (p. 227). Schmitt sees in Romanticism a lamentable example of the secular process away from durable principles of order towards secularity and subject-centricity.

Schmitt's own thinking, however, follows exactly the same process of secularization as the world which he describes and laments (see Meier 1994: 192). Schmitt's own ideas chart the move from the substantial to the formal, from the ideal to the technical, from the representative to the conflictual, from the sovereign to the metaphorical. As subsequent thinkers have observed, Schmitt's later decisionistic theories are themselves the clearest examples of occasionalist thinking (Fraenkel 1941: 131), which carry no qualitative stipulations about the character of the political order which they affirm (see Krockow 1990: 85). Schmitt departs, therefore, from a substantive theory of order and natural law, but he ultimately reaches an argument which endorses all order, in the spirit of the occasionalism which he earlier reviles (Löwith 1960: 103). In his early writings, Schmitt defines legal execution by the state in neo-Kantian categories, as a mediation between pure law and legal validity (1914: 58). Yet, in his later works, he proposes a model of law which also claims absolute authority, although it has lost all ties to any conception of natural law.

In this respect, Schmitt, like Kelsen, moves very close to Hans Vaihinger's tradition of neo-Kantianism (see Heller 1971c: 529–30). In Schmitt's later works, the idea that political law might correspond to divine-natural law is clearly abandoned. But the *formal* process by which the state, in personal form, enacts the execution of absolute law remains intact. The state, which makes its decisions in varying figures – as absolute sovereign, as distinction between friend and foe, or as constitution of the collective will – acts *as if* it were enacting supra-positive law. However, the laws which it actually enforces are really only the technical prerogatives of everyday political life (economic laws, yearly budgets, spending cuts etc.). Vaihinger's brand of neo-Kantianism especially stresses the significance of fiction in the translation of general norms, cognitive or juridical, into the world of validity and appearances (Vaihinger 1911: 174; Kelsen 1919: 634). For Vaihinger (as for Kelsen), the norms of law have no genuinely binding normative legitimacy. However, they are purposively applied to the world as if they possessed this binding quality. The theory of law in Schmitt's works of the late-Weimar period thus closely reflects Vaihinger's theory of cognitive fiction. The sovereign decision, Schmitt asserts, creates legitimate order. But this legitimate order is legitimate only in symbolic form, only *as if* it were real order. Law is produced by a President who possesses the dignity of the law-giver. But the laws which he passes have only *formal* claims to authority. It is for this reason that Schmitt's theories are so appropriate to the bureaucracy. Schmitt, in essence, argues that law is entirely positivized, and that its validity is wholly contextual, or functional. At the same time, however, his theory of law confers an aesthetic gloss of absolute authority upon law (upon all law), simply in its quality as a legal decision, made by a particular political order. Schmitt's theory provides the perfect model for the fluid, non-substantive codes of an authoritarian bureaucracy. Vaihinger's norm and Schmitt's decision thus both mark shifts from substantial order to the symbolic representation of order.

The mixture of secularization-theory, decisionism, neo-Kantianism and ius-naturalism in Schmitt's ideas is by no means unique. Indeed, it is merely one position within a broad renaissance of natural-law theory in early twentieth-century Roman Catholic political thought. The significance of natural-law theory amongst German Catholics at this time can be traced to the encyclicals of Leo XIII (Pope 1878–1903), which set out a theory of politics which is full of implications for Schmitt's work. Leo XIII argued that it is the duty of all Roman Catholics to obey the state to which they are subject (E. Alexander 1953: 431), and that the state itself has a moral obligation to abide by the general terms of good politics (1953: 431). Most importantly, Leo XIII asserted that no Catholic is justified in rejecting a state on confessional grounds, and that obedience is due to the state simply because it is the state. This was especially important in the political context in which these encyclicals were issued, after the *Kulturkampf* in Germany, and the foundation of the Third Republic in France, in both of which situations Catholics openly rejected the temporal orders of the nation-states to which they were subject. Leo XIII's conciliatory approach towards Bismarck was a crucial factor in the subsequent integration of the German Catholics into the governmental system (Lambi 1963: 172).

These papal encyclicals show a dialectical attitude to the state which strongly anticipates that of Schmitt himself. Simply, Pope Leo XIII told the European Catholics that they must accept all order. Yet, he argued, they must accept it as something inferior to confessional order. The genuine order of the church, Leo XIII argued, exists outside the political order of the state, and cannot be circumscribed by this order (E. Alexander 1953: 431–2). The ideas of Leo XIII expressed thus a political attitude of dialectical indifference. They commanded obedience to any form of politically institutionalized law and order, in the knowledge that real law and real order remain unaffected by such institutes. As Hans Barion (1965: 147–8) and Ernst Wolfgang Böckenförde (1961: 234–5) have argued, it is precisely this attitude which informs Schmitt's own reflections on the polity. Schmitt's political fluctuations suggest that he was prepared to affirm any decision which sustains order, and that he was prepared to affirm such order, as order – *as if* it were a representation of natural law and natural order. The vacillations and shifts in Schmitt's political alliance show, however, that his genuine commitment to any form of temporal order was very limited. At the heart of Schmitt's decisionistic theory is the conviction that temporal order is by nature fleeting and always temporary. Order is, therefore, a necessary fiction.

Schmitt's reflections on the nature of politics can, in this regard, be linked directly to political developments within the Catholic community during the Weimar Republic. Indeed, Schmitt's thought refers to certain paradoxes and problems in the political organization of the Zentrum. Unlike the SPD, the Zentrum was not by original design a constitutional party. Although under Matthias Erzberger the party had supported the move towards constitutionalization before 1918 (H. Mommsen 1990: 76), the Zentrum had been a beneficiary of the old three-class electoral system. Its flexibility in economic issues had enabled it to enter an almost limitless number of coalition options, and thereby to secure a long-term position of influence in the Wilhelmine state. The Zentrum, partly for this reason, and partly because of its fundamental preference for monarchical systems, never formally acknowledged the Weimar Constitution as the legitimate foundation of government,[5] although influential theologians such as Joseph Mausbach and Peter Tischleder did their best to foster an atmosphere of republican loyalty within the party (see Mausbach 1920: 12; Tischleder 1927: 137; Lutz 1963: 99). At the same time, however, like the SPD, the Zentrum also drew great benefit from the Weimar coalition system (see Evans 1981: 241). The Zentrum was the only party involved in government from the beginning to the end of the Republic. The composition of the German executive was strongly marked by Catholic interests during this time – an astonishing position of power given the semi-ghettoized status of German Catholics only fifty years earlier (Knight 1952: 31). The German Catholic church was guaranteed parity with the Lutheran church under the terms of Article 137 of the Weimar Constitution. Broadly, therefore, the 1920s was a period of German history which offered unprecedented sociological advantages to the German Catholics.

Nonetheless, despite (or because of) these changes, the Zentrum was often perceived as a party in crisis during the years of the Weimar Republic. Before the First World War the climate of anti-clericalism in Germany had integrated almost all Catholics into the party, whereas after 1919 the Catholic vote was spread over a number of parties (Kühne 1994: 107). The cohesion of the party as a political body was therefore undermined by its status of relative privilege and new-found confessional parity (J. Becker 1963: 163). Indeed, the party repeatedly sought to reform itself as a cross-confessional Christian Social party, a feat not achieved until the formation of the Christian Democratic Union (CDU) in 1945 (Pridham 1977: 21–6).

---

5 Kaas 1919: 5. See also 'Richtlinien der Deutschen Zentrumspartei' 1960: 487. For the historical background to this, see Buchheim 1953: 329; also Morsey, 1977: 23.

Against this background, by the end of the Weimar Republic the only integrating issue in the Zentrum was the protection of the interests of the Catholic church in Germany – the motive for its initial foundation as a party (Nipperdey 1961: 282). Partly for this reason, the party retained an attitude of distance towards the Weimar state-system, for its investment in the system was essentially limited to a one-issue, confessional mandate (Lepsius 1993: 17). As a party of government, the Zentrum had abandoned its pre-1918 indifferentism in economic matters. However, attempts within the party to develop a cogent set of economic policies had not been entirely successful (Rapport 1992: 414), and it was broadly perceived that non-ecclesiastical interests were represented more effectively by other parties. Indeed, the party moved constantly further to the right after the relatively liberal cabinets of Josef Wirth in 1921. The Zentrum thus assumed the peculiar role of a party whose stability was of the most fundamental significance to the cross-class axis of the Weimar coalition system, but whose commitment to this system was limited to only one real issue, an issue in fact peripheral to the republic, and one which could be fulfilled outside the parliamentary framework (Morsey 1966: 618).

This paradoxical situation is underlined most particularly by the position of Brüning himself, the economics expert of the Zentrum, who was clearly no real adherent to the system of parliamentary democracy (Oberreuter 1978: 65–6). However, the political and economic agnosticism of organized Catholicism is reflected through the whole of the late-Weimar Zentrum. In fact, although the caucus of the party was for a short time, during Hitler's emergence, outspoken in its criticism of the NSDAP, Ludwig Kaas, leader of the Zentrum in 1933, was quick to accede to Hitler's Enabling Laws (see Aretin 1966: 256; Repgen 1976: 26), in return for certain guarantees regarding the property of the church and liberty of worship for Catholics (Morsey 1969: 630). Thus, although most Catholics would doubtless have preferred to see the Weimar Republic replaced by a benign monarchy than by a violently populist dictator (see Hörster-Philipps 1982: 233), the Zentrum notably wasted no time at all in endorsing its own dissolution as a party. Schmitt's own combination of grudging support for the Republic, his endorsement of Brüning's strong bureaucratic executive (Koenen 1995: 132) and his ultimate willingness to fall into line behind the NSDAP show therefore an attitude to the Republic which reflects the sociological and political ambiguities of the Weimar Catholics. Although Schmitt himself was often the object of criticism from the higher ranks of the Zentrum (including Brüning himself) during this time (Koenen 1995: 218; 'Schreiben des Vorsitzenden der Zentrumpartei' 1991: 649; Patch 1998: 53), his dilemmas were exaggerated manifestations of those of the party. As early as 1931, Walter Dirks had observed how the apparent antithesis between National Socialism and Catholicism actually disguised a deep affinity between the two movements, and that Catholics whose confessional loyalties had been undermined were highly susceptible to the nationalist preachings of the NSDAP (cit. Lepsius 1993: 76). In the Weimar state, the

Zentrum was the key parliamentary party and the most important cross-class and cross-confessional hinge for democratic consensus. But the Zentrum sustained its pragmatic attitude only as long as the parliamentary system itself held (Hönig 1979: 282). The Zentrum was also the first party to agree to its own termination, and thus to the termination of democracy (see Matthias and Morsey 1979: 395).

It is striking, in this respect, that Schmitt's pro-Hitler writings mark a shift away from the decisionistic tone of his reflections on the Weimar state. These writings, the most infamous of Schmitt's theoretical contributions, actually mark a regression to the post-historicist content of his very earliest works (see J. H. Kaiser 1988: 321). This neo-historicist aspect to Schmitt's post-1933 writings is usually termed 'concrete-order-thinking'. In these works, Schmitt puts foward a theory based on the 'normativity of facticity' – that is, on the conviction that law possesses normative legitimacy simply as an expression of the national will at one particular moment in history. The supreme executive expression and representation of this will is, in Schmitt's writings of the early 1930s, Hitler himself. After Hitler's accession to power, therefore, Schmitt retains his earlier hostility to the rigidity of legal norms, and his predilection for the strong executive, but his earlier decisionistic sense that law can be ceaselessly created and recreated slips into an enthusism for Hitler, as the sole source of executive legitimacy.

This transformation is shown most clearly in the short essay 'The Führer Protects the Law' (1934), written shortly after the Night of the Long Knives, when Hitler organized the assassinations of his former accomplices amongst representatives of the late-Weimar conservatives. This essay marks one of the crucial transitional moments in Schmitt's career – for Schmitt had been closely attached (as legal adviser) to Kurt von Schleicher (Koenen 1995: 206–7), last Chancellor of the Weimar Republic, and one of those murdered by the Gestapo at this point. In this essay, Schmitt explains Hitler's methods of administering justice as follows:

> In truth the action of the Führer was genuinely judicial. It was not subject to the judiciary – it itself was the pinnacle of the judiciary. It was not the action of a republican dictator creating new order in a legal vacuum, whilst the law closed its eyes for a moment, only then to let the fictions of flawless legality take over again on the basis of this new order. The status of the *Führer* as judge results from the same legal source from which all popular law arises. . . . All law comes from the vital law of the people. Each law of state, each judicial verdict, contains only as much law as it receives from this source. (1940: 202)

Despite Schmitt's initial support for Hitler's regime, however, it has been widely documented that Schmitt's attempt to establish himself as the leading juridical theorist of the National Socialist state did not meet with prolonged success. Even during the very early years of Hitler's regime, during which time Schmitt worked under Göring in Berlin, Schmitt was attacked by theorists more closely connected with the most powerful members of the NSDAP (Koenen 1995: 427). The legal theorist Otto Koellreuter was the major figure in this assault, which in itself throws significant light on the peculiarities of Schmitt's political theory. Nazi thinkers such as Koellreuter generally put forward a model for totalitarian government which saw the function of the party as the key integrative organ in Hitler's system. Koellreuter viewed the party as the axis which chan-nelled the popular will of the *Volk* into the executive organs of government, thus enabling the enactment of the collective will through the *Führer*. Schmitt's responses to the take-over of power by Hitler, in contrast, under-line the incompatibility of his thinking with the party-based system of Hitler's state.

In 1933, immediately prior to the nomination of Hitler as Chancellor, Schmitt wrote a short essay which endorsed the emergence of the 'total state', and the strengthening of the executive in the late-Weimar system. 'Every genuine state', he argues here, 'is a total state. It has always been such, as a *societas perfecta* of the mortal world. Theorists of state have known for a long time that the political is the total, and what is new is just the technical means' (1958a: 361). Thus, Schmitt argues here that the real state is always total, because it embodies a total and durable vision of how political life should be ordered, and it is capable of subordinating technical devices to its own functional needs. Schmitt admits here that, despite his anti-technical rhetoric, his theory of state hinges upon the exploitation of technology. Of greatest historical relevance, however, is the fact that Schmitt distinguishes between one form of the total state, based upon a totalizing idea, and a different form of the total state, which possesses totalizing character because it ceaselessly intervenes in the mat-ters of the civil sphere. 'This kind of total state', Schmitt says of the latter, 'is a state which moves indiscriminately into all subject areas, into all spheres of human existence, which does not recognize areas which are free of the state' (1958a: 361). This second form of total state, Schmitt indicates, is a state which has grown directly out of the liberal party-political system. The total interventionist state has been produced, Schmitt argues, by the fact that the technical interests of the civil sphere have taken control of the state and that these interests consequently expect the state to resolve issues specific to this sphere. For Schmitt, therefore, a direct thread connects the modern total state to the interest-based conception of politics in classical liberalism. Liberalism, Schmitt argues, is the movement which originally blurred the proper distinctions between state-representation, administration and society. Most especially, he suggests, the totalization of the political order can be imputed to the technical and mediatizing function of political parties. The political landscape in Germany is domin-ated, he argues, by a 'plurality of total parties, each of which seeks to realize totality *in itself*, and to incorporate its members totally within itself' (1958a: 362). The totalizing party is itself, therefore, a complex product of liberalism. It is an organization, Schmitt implies, which gives particular interests supremacy over the total ethic of the state. It is an organization which seeks to recast the private-technical logic of interest as the dominant – totalizing – ethic of the state.

Schmitt's positive model of the total state is of a strong executive, informed by a strong political ethic, which is capable of resolving all issues which fall properly into the political sphere. It is not a state which assumes entire responsibility for the social sphere. His distinction between two forms of political totality – one ideal, one interventionist – is quite emphatically intended as a critique of the integration-parties of late-Weimar politics (S. Neumann 1965: 105), including, most obviously, the NSDAP. Schmitt claims that genuine political order is sustained only by an ethic of representation, in either a party or an executive, but not by the annexation of the state by technical interests – not, certainly, by the annexation of the state by a party. The NSDAP is for Schmitt, therefore, the key example of a party driven by a totalizing principle of integration, not by a representative ethic. The NSDAP is, Schmitt indicates, therefore a belated outcrop of liberalism.

In the immediate aftermath of Hitler's take-over, Schmitt was happy to make accommodations with the National Socialist state. However, even in his emphatically pro-Hitler writings, his ideas have little symmetry with the party-orthodoxy. In *State, Movement, People* (1935), for example, Schmitt argues that Hitler's state reproduces the ancient model of the *Ständestaat* (see Lousse 1980: 292–3), and that Hitler has created an order which reinstates the proper division between society (people), administration (party) and representation (state). Schmitt thus imagines that under Hitler the civil sphere will be organized by professional councils as a distinct socio-economic order, that the party will support the state, and that the representative body of the state will be situated at the top of this estate-like pyramid, as the 'precondition of the successful autonomy of its various members' (1935: 33). Schmitt intended such observations as an appreciation of the end of governmental pluralism under Hitler. However, these ideas reflect spectacularly his inability to comprehend the actual nature of National Socialist government. Contrary to Schmitt's fond projections, by 1935 the state, in the traditional sense of the word, had ceased to exist. Although Hitler did experiment with an estate-based organization of the economy (Esenwein-Roth 1965: 30), the formal apparatus of state itself was replaced by a fluid party-executive and an amorphous bureaucracy (F. Neumann 1966: 467). Moreover, Schmitt's estate-based ideas were unlikely to find favour for very long with the functionaries of the NSDAP. The suggestion that the state retained representative distinction from party and people clearly ran counter to the ideas upon which Hitler's party-regime was based.

These contradictions between Schmitt's theory of politics and the party-based orthodoxy of the NSDAP were soon reflected in reality. Once the NSDAP was firmly established in power, Schmitt's theories of the strong executive quickly lost their ideological usefulness, and by 1936 Schmitt's theory of the strong state had already been overtaken by alternative doctrines.[6] The institutional thinkers attached to the National Socialist party had, in fact, little time for theories of the state at all. The state, they argued, had already been superseded by the party as the organ of judicial execution (Koenen 1995: 523). The suggestion that a strong executive should be required to enforce unpopular or controversial political decisions naturally contradicted the proclamation of the NSDAP that the decisions made by the *Führer* could not be unpopular, for the *Führer* perfectly united and expressed the general will of the *Volk*. In 1935 Koellreuter (the most theoretically sophisticated of the genuine National Socialists) described Schmitt's theory as 'the philosophical counterposition to the world-view of National Socialism' (Koellreuter 1935: 11; see also Heinck 1978: 134) 'There is no place', Koellreuter explained, 'for a political theology in National Socialism. It falsifies the essence of National Socialism.... Religious and political activity are situated in different areas and have to be strictly separated from each other' (1935: 11). Schmitt's transcendent theory of the executive came therefore, in the eyes of the NSDAP, to assume the mantle of an outmoded form of statism, or even of strong-state liberalism (Koenen 1995: 530). The form of authoritarian (total) government which Schmitt endorses is very different from the party-based (total) dictatorship of the National Socialists. It is also very different from the order-conceptions amongst conservative Protestants in the early 1930s (see esp. Gerber 1932: 32; Tanner 1989: 266). Despite Schmitt's flirtation with concrete-order thinking during the first years of the Nazi regime, Koellreuter's diagnosis of the incompatibility of Schmitt's theories with National Socialist reflections on the state is correct. The defining feature in all Schmitt's work is the conviction that the state should be different from society. In this respect, Schmitt must necessarily remain a conservative adversary of the NSDAP. Schmitt sees genuinely representative politics as a system in which the functions of the state rely on a strict hierarchical gradation between state and society. This idea is articulated not only by Schmitt, but by the younger members of the so-called Schmitt School, who emerged in his wake (Forsthoff 1933: 24–5).

Schmitt's critique of democracy therefore also contains a critique of party-based systems of authoritarianism. Schmitt criticizes democracy because, he argues, it is not possible. Genuine democratic legitimacy, he suggests, can only reside in the absolute identity of governors and governed. As soon as any component which is not immanent to the will of the people is added to the political decision-making process, Schmitt argues, democracy ceases to exist (1928: 238). When the popular will is diluted by acts of representation (p. 262), of deputation, or of party-political mediatization, the immanence of the popular will is undermined (p. 239), and government is no longer democratic. As soon as the people are confronted with complex decisions whose resolution requires deputation and delegation, they are no longer democratically present in the decision

---

6 For the historical background to this, see Gotto 1992: 720.

(p. 277). These arguments explain, Schmitt argues, why democracy is not successful – because such democratic identity can no longer be upheld (pp. 234–5). In modern society, Schmitt asserts, the people are precisely those who do not assume offices of government (p. 241), who are outside the governmental apparatus (p. 242), and who do not make decisions. For this reason, Schmitt argues, the will of the people is best constituted via processes of representation (p. 277), which react neutrally to the particular inclinations of the people, certainly not as their 'functionary' or 'agent' (p. 212).

The primary function of the state, Schmitt therefore argues, is representation, not the fulfilment of specific demands. Representation itself instigates democratic unity in the people (see Mehring 1991: 211). As in Hegel's philosophy of law, or indeed in the old estate-system, representation is intended by Schmitt as a value-neutral term, which certainly does not mean the representation of the particular and technical interests which are located in the civil sphere (see H. Brandt 1968: 8; Beyme 1980: 401). The state, Schmitt asserts, has the task of representing the general will – the pure political quality – of the people. However, it can only fulfil this task if it is distinct from the particular components of this will (1928: 210). The state represents the 'political unity' of the people as 'a higher form of being' (1928: 210). 'Representation', Schmitt explains, 'is not a normative institute, not a process, and not a procedure, but something *existential*. To represent means to make an invisible being visible and present through a publicly existing being' (1928: 209). The political unity of the people, therefore, only exists in its representation by the state (Maschke 1988: 215). It is not prior to its representation. It is expressed only from above – through symbolizations of political grandeur, and through the absolute difference between the sphere of political representation and all particular, or non-political considerations (C. Schmitt 1928: 210). A system which aspires to full particular representation – the representation of all civil needs – is inevitably, therefore, less representative than a system which represents the will of the people in its pure political quality (1928: 207). Particular representation necessarily fragments and mediatizes the general will of the people, and it thus dismembers precisely what it is supposed to represent. Democratic representation is, in Schmitt's perspective, a contradiction in terms. Government is either representative, or democratic. As modern government can no longer be democratic, it is most democratic when it is representative. This means, paradoxically, that government is most democratic when it is least democratic.

Schmitt's hierarchical model of the state–society relation is at the base of a theory of politics which, despite Schmitt's activities in the period 1933–6, remains finally critical of the National Socialist state. Precisely the fact that the National Socialists themselves sought to deny the representative distinction between state and society forms the ground for Schmitt's ultimate (albeit heavily coded) critique of Hitler's state, put forward in *The Leviathan* (1938), Schmitt's homage to Hobbes. In this work, Schmitt,

like Hermann Heller before him, explains that National Socialism is interpretable as an advanced form of liberalism, which has assumed totalitarian
traits. He argues that the economization of the state effected by nineteenth-
century liberalism actually provides a clearer model for modern-style dictatorship than do the old forms of absolutism. Liberalism, Schmitt argues
(like Weber before him), leads to the total pervasion of society by interest-
based and exploitative forms of rationality. Against this, Schmitt argues
that genuine politics, or genuine total politics, relies on the exclusion of
non-political concerns from the highest decisions of state – hence his
attachment to the model of the old estates, or late absolutism. Because
liberalism seeks to erase the boundary between state and society, he argues,
it leads to a totalizing political system, in which the state has full control of
every sphere of activity. Schmitt explains this in one of his most profound
and impenetrable pronouncements (clearly obscured to prevent easy interpretation in 1938):

> The institutions and concepts of liberalism, upon which the positivistic legal
> state (*Gesetzesstaat*) rested, became weapons and positions of power for
> extremely illiberal forces. In this way, party-pluralism has completed the
> method of destroying the state ascribed to the liberal legal state. The
> Leviathan, in the sense meant by the myth of the state as the 'great machine',
> was shattered by the distinction between the state and individual freedom, in
> an age in which the organizations of this individual freedom were merely the
> knives with which anti-individual forces shredded the Leviathan and dis-
> tributed its flesh amongst themselves. Thus the mortal God died a second
> time. (1982: 118)

Although, clearly, the strong-state government which Schmitt proposes as
a check against the (so-defined) authoritarian liberalism of National Socialism is not the most effective way to counter the threat of authoritarian
populism, Schmitt's reflections on representation and identity resist easy
appropriation by modern totalitarianism (J. H. Kaiser 1959: 72). His ultimate opposition – albeit late and highly circumspect – to National Socialism was motivated by the fact that the crucial political moment of non-
identity between the governing and the governed, which Schmitt sets at the
heart of good politics, is not respected by Hitler's fusion of the party and
the state (Koenen 1995: 380). This itself becomes the substantive grounds
of Schmitt's critique. As seen above, even his most adulatory writings on
Hitler contain the delicately worded rejection of the subsumption of the
state by the party (1940: 202). The party, Schmitt asserts, is always
different from the state, and it always pertains to an inferior level of
human organization.

Schmitt's works of the last Weimar years are guided by related principles. Although in his works of the early-Weimar period Schmitt is relentlessly critical of the parliamentary system, in the early 1930s he puts
forward a defence of the Weimar governmental apparatus which is much
overlooked in the critical literature on his thought. Between 1930 and 1933,

Schmitt was intimately connected with the authoritarian, but non-Nazi, presidial cabinets which both temporarily checked and ultimately supported Hitler's rise to power (Noack 1993: 147). Central to this period of Schmitt's work is the belief (outlined above) that the second part of the Weimar Constitution contains moments of supra-positive law, of *political law*, in which the broad and decisive will of the people is represented. This is argued most coherently in *Legality and Legitimacy* (1932). The subsidiary constitutional laws (*Verfassungsgesetze*) pertaining to administrative institutes should, Schmitt argues here, be subordinated to those constitutional provisions (*Verfassungsrecht*) which frame the underlying ethics of political life. The basic components of political order should not, he explains, be formal rights *against* the state, or subordinate components of the technical institutes of administration. They should be principles of order which are enacted through, and enforced by, the state and the state-administration (Koenen 1995: 468–9). In such a system of positive order, Schmitt implies, the President would be at liberty to interpret the basic laws of the constitution (1931b: 186; see also Preuß 1993: 18), and to protect and secure the supremacy of the second part of the constitution (*Verfassungsrecht*) over provisions relating to inferior issues (*Verfassungsgesetze*). This would ensure that genuine constitutional laws, not inferior institutes, form the basis of the administration (see Jasper 1963: 13). Schmitt explains:

> The core of the second main part of the Weimar Constitution deserves to be stripped of its self-contradictions and weak compromises and developed in accordance with its inner logic. If this succeeds, the idea of a German constitution will be saved. Alternatively, the fictions of a majority functionalism, which is neutral towards value and truth, will soon be over. Then the truth will take revenge. (1932c: 91)

The final sentence is a warning against the National Socialists, a warning against the favouring of anti-democratic groupings by the apparatus of majority-democracy itself.

Thus, in summary, Schmitt believes that legitimate government is government from above. This conviction is unlikely to lead to an advocacy of the party-system of National Socialism. To avert the danger of National Socialism in the late-Weimar interim, Schmitt therefore (like many contemporaries amongst the non-Nazi conservatives) espoused a continuation and reinforcement of what was by this time already existing governmental practice under, firstly, Heinrich Brüning, secondly, Franz von Papen and, lastly, Kurt von Schleicher. This was a system of government by special decree, under Article 48 of the constitution,[7] through awesome executive authorization, coupled with the superlegal transfer of power to the bureaucracy, as suggested in *Guardian of the Constitution* (C. Schmitt 1931a: 156). The period 1930–3 provides the best historical context for understanding

---

7 See Grimm 1992: 195. See also: E. R. Huber 1975b: 34–5; Revermann 1959: 44; Jasper 1986: 80.

Schmitt's ideas. He can be regarded most accurately as the 'theorist of the interim' (Noack 1993: 128), whose writings validate the non-National Socialist authoritarianism of the late-Weimar regimes, especially that of Schleicher. Schmitt's personal trauma after the collapse of Schleicher's attempt at a 'third-way' social dictatorship is revealed by his diaries (Noack 1993: 159).

This does not, however, imply that Schmitt has any intrinsic investment in the plebiscitary system, although his writings have been enthusiastically received by proponents of direct democracy. On the contrary, Schmitt is committed merely to the idea of a government with a strong executive. His conception of the good polity reaches back into the pre-liberal era before the separation of powers, before the inscription of private needs in the system of public authority. For this reason, however, he has a dislike for the dictatorial populism of the NSDAP (as for Marxism), and he is willing to defend even democracy against the assumption of power by such a move-ment. His immediate (but short-lived) willingness to endorse Hitler after he attained power can, apart from reasons of personal opportunism and ambi-tion (see Rüthers 1990: 107), be interpreted in terms of the dialectics of order which always underpin his thinking. Above all else, the insistence on the transcendent, ethical character of state-government remains central to Schmitt's thought. Precisely what transcendent government might inte-grally be is, however, left unexplained. All the forms of order experienced by Schmitt in his lifetime receive, to some extent, the accolade of genuine politicality. The endorsement of a plebiscitary system in the period 1930–3 is itself merely a compromise in Schmitt's elaboraton of this theory, suited to the daily reality of executive rule under Article 48.

Throughout all Schmitt's writing he insists on the close interplay between the supra-positive quality of law and the coercive function of the executive. The legislative body is unimportant for Schmitt. Law, Schmitt argues, is an expression of the supra-positive political will, which itself is anterior to both law and state (1932a: 20). However, law is positivized contextually – transformed from fiction to fact – by the executive. The positive political will is thus *present* in the executive. The true relation between people and government is therefore located by Schmitt in the mere fact of popular *acclamation* for the personal symbols of executive power (C. Schmitt 1927: 49). Despite all Schmitt's fondness for authoritarian governments, however, his thought retains its attachment to the neo-Kantian explanation of supra-positive law to the very end. The executive, at least, can be viewed *as if* it were in possession of supra-positive dignity.

The shifts in Schmitt's thinking mark him out from any simple orthodoxy. The real Nazis reviled him as a Catholic, for he favoured the strong personal executive. Yet to an orthodox Roman Catholic Schmitt must appear as a liberal, for he is willing to approve a great number of political forms. In each of its guises, Schmitt's thought, as Derrida recognizes, charts a metaphysic of politics in its last collapse (Balke 1996: 21). Despite his repeated efforts to draw out a theory of truly *political* legitimacy, the quality of real politics is traceable only in its absence. In most aspects of his work, Schmitt can be compared to Weber. Weber, as a liberal, tried (and failed) to ground a pure theory of politics in the collective will. Schmitt, as a conservative, tried (and failed) to overcome the antinomies of Weber's thought by grounding a pure theory of politics in the principle of representation. Both Weber and Schmitt, most centrally, endeavoured to overcome the formal limitations of private (capitalist) law by attempting to introduce an adjunct of substantive law to the public sphere. Both failed. Schmitt's solution to the de-substantialization of law is to eliminate all elements of private law – in which he includes political parties, basic rights, separation of powers – from the political order. Far from overcoming the technical quality of modern law, however, he simply recreates the political order of the executive around the formal legal codes which he so reviles in the sphere of civil law. In Schmitt's political theory, most notably, the executive bureaucracy – beneath the symbolic figure of the President – becomes the centre of decision-making legitimacy. Schmitt, as a theorist of the interim, develops his pure theory of politics not (contrary to his own assertion) in order to expand the political moment in modern society, but to restrict it.

Perhaps Schmitt might be interpreted most justly as a cautionary example of a figure who advocates a return to pre-modern political order, but who, owing to the impossibility of this return, arrives at an endorsement of the most modern form of domination – namely, by the planned rules of the administration. In complex societies, it might be observed, the attempt to imagine personal sovereignty must necessarily collapse into government by an apersonal executive. Certainly, Schmitt's strongest influence has not been on pure theories of the state. Rather, Schmitt's truest legacy is found in the post-1945 technocratic theorists of political order, from Forsthoff, to Gehlen, to Schelsky, to Luhmann, who have interpreted political institutions not as internally legitimizable constructs, but as technical means for circumventing the consensual dimension of political organization.

## Selected further reading

Bendersky, Joseph W. (1983) *Carl Schmitt: Theorist for the Reich* (Princeton: Princeton UP, 1983).

Kennedy, Ellen (1987) 'Carl Schmitt and the Frankfurt School', *Telos* 71.

McCormick, John (1997) *Carl Schmitt's Critique of Liberalism: Against Politics as Technology* (Cambridge: CUP).

Preuß, Ulrich K. (1993) 'Political Order and Democracy: Carl Schmitt and his Influence', in: Leszek Nowak and Marcia Paprzcki (eds), *Social System, Rationality and Revolution* (Amsterdam/Atlanta: Rodopi), pp. 15–40.

Schwab, George (1989) *The Challenge of the Exception: An Introduction to the Political Ideas of Carl Schmitt between 1921 and 1936* (New York/London: Greenwood).

*Telos* 72 (1987) *Special Issue on Carl Schmitt*.

# 3

# Franz Neumann and Otto Kirchheimer

This chapter focuses on Franz Neumann and Otto Kirchheimer. Neumann and Kirchheimer are best known in the Anglo-Saxon world as the political thinkers connected with the Institute of Social Research in Frankfurt am Main, and later in New York, whose members are commonly grouped together as the Frankfurt School.

Neumann and Kirchheimer belonged, to use Axel Honneth's term, to the 'periphery' of the Frankfurt School (see Honneth 1990: esp. 56). Neither was a member of the 'inner circle' around Horkheimer, Pollock, Adorno and Löwenthal, and both entered their association with the Institute at a relatively late stage – owing to their displacement after the take-over of power by the NSPAD. Although both, like other exponents of Critical Theory, have their origins in the neo-Marxist debates of the Weimar period, Neumann and Kirchheimer are distinct from others attached to the Institute. The Weimar works of Neumann and Kirchheimer in fact show the strong influence of legal and political reflections which are very distant from the Marx–Hegel–Weber–Lukács axis of much early work of the Frankfurt School. Not without justification, both are often termed 'left-wing Schmittians', owing to the clear influence of Carl Schmitt (who supervised Kirchheimer's doctorate) on their thinking. Both are also strongly influenced by the leading Austro-Marxist theorists, Max Adler and Karl Renner. It is only in their diagnostic social-psychological works on the nature of National Socialism that their ideas can be closely (but not unambiguously) linked with the mainstream tradition of Critical Theory. Neumann and Kirchheimer are also distinct from the other members of the Institute because they, especially Neumann, were closely involved in general politics. Neumann played a senior legal advisory role in the Weimar

SPD and he was later (like Kirchheimer and Herbert Marcuse also) employed by the Office of Strategic Services in Washington during the period 1942–5, ultimately as Deputy Chief of the European Section (Wiggershaus 1986: 338). In the post-war period, Neumann, by this time an American citizen, assumed an advisory role in the de-nazification process in Germany. This also moved him closer to direct political involvement than other thinkers at the Institute.

The writings of Neumann and Kirchheimer constitute, in short, a body of work which connects the left wing of the SPD in the Weimar Republic, Schmitt's critique of parliamentary democracy, the Marxist-Hegelian political economy of the Institute of Social Research in its emigration period, and the redevelopment of political theory in Germany after 1945. Both Neumann and Kirchheimer prefigure theories of late capitalism which are central to the later thinking of Habermas. Neumann's theories of totalitarianism are also echoed by Hannah Arendt, and more recently in important historical studies (see esp. Bracher 1969: 5). The greatest theoretical importance of Neumann and Kirchheimer lies, however, in their attempt to develop a category of political action which is serviceable to the left. As will be seen, Neumann and Kirchheimer differ from conventional traditions of Marxism because they, like Weber and Schmitt, maintain a belief in the specific dignity of political action, as a sphere of interaction and freedom which is not determined by the strategies and compromises of economic or instrumental reason.

All Franz Neumann's writings are based, directly or indirectly, on his experience of the failure of the Weimar system of democracy. Essentially, Neumann argues that the failure of democracy in inter-war Germany was due to the ideological character of the parliamentary system itself. He sets out this argument most clearly in his essay of 1937, 'The Transformation of the Function of Law in the Law of Bourgeois Society'. This essay is actually a German abstract of his second doctoral thesis, which is strongly influenced by Karl Renner's juridico-political thinking. Neumann wrote this thesis at the London School of Economics under the supervision of Harold Laski. Like Marx (1981), Neumann interprets the modern state and modern law as ideological devices which obscure the relations of exploitation in civil society. The institutes of modern law, especially private and contract law, he explains, merely codify the organizational requirements of capitalism (F. Neumann 1967a: 40). The most essential premises of liberal law are, Neumann argues, superstructural fictions. They are merely 'the economic mask of the property-relation', which 'hides the fact that property is . . . the foundation of relations of domination and slavery' (1967a: 69). Like Marx, therefore, Neumann argues that the formal equality which is guaranteed by liberal democracy is merely a rational means of facilitating the domination of capital.

This has clear implications for Neumann's theory of politics and his explanation of the weaknesses of democracy. Law in liberal-capitalist democracy, Neumann asserts, is the distillation of property-relations.

Therefore, the formality of political law in liberal democracy is inextricable from its ideological base in the economy. Following both Marx and Weber, Neumann argues that the formal universality of law, which is the precondition for modern democracy, is really only the fulfilment of the quest of the bourgeoisie to create a legal order which is rationally adjusted to the contractual system of capitalism. 'The primary objective of the state resides', he argues, 'in the creation of a legal order which guarantees the fulfilment of contracts' (1967a: 48). Both Neumann and Kirchheimer argue, therefore, that democracy and capitalism are structurally incompatible (Blanke 1984: 166). The formal mode of equality which is represented by liberal-democratic law merely serves to disguise the relations of inequality and exploitation in the social sphere. Both Neumann and Kirchheimer explain liberal democracy as a system in which the sphere of public law is gradually pervaded by private law, and in which, consequently, the state becomes the guarantor for the private-legal relations of capitalism. The development of modern capitalism is reflected by the erosion of public authority through the system of private law. The triumph of liberal democracy is thus not the triumph of a democratic political order, but of the private-legal sphere over the sphere of public law.

However, Neumann's critique of the ideological quality of universal democratic law is not without ambiguity. Neumann examines the course of modern history as a transition from competitive capitalism to monopoly capitalism – thus, as a process through which private law annexes the public sphere. Like Marx, however, Neumann recognizes the positive aspects of capitalist law against earlier forms of personal law. Most especially, he ascribes positive qualities to liberal-capitalist law in contrast with the legal order of monopoly capitalism, the advent of which Neumann identifies with the beginning of the Weimar Republic. In the age of monopoly capitalism, Neumann argues, the legal system forfeits its quality of formal generality and is supplemented with legal additions which enable the direct influence of monopoly bodies on the ordering of the economy. He sees the emergence of the authoritarian state under Brüning and Hindenburg at the end of the Weimar Republic as the consummation of the development, which marks the whole of recent Prussian history, towards the creation of a state which is perfectly adapted to the needs of cartels and monopoly enterprises (see also Kehr 1965a: 44). The law of the monopoly state, Neumann explains, abandons the rational universality of positive liberal law and replaces it with context-specific edicts, especially in the sphere of labour law (1967a: 65). The late-Weimar system of government by decree, Neumann outlines, perfectly represents the elimination of the universal quality of law in favour of occasional measures which are suited especially to specific interest-groups. Carl Schmitt's decisionistic model of politics symbolizes most perfectly, Neumann argues, the supplantation of universal law by particular edict. Despite Schmitt's lofty endorsement of pure politics, Neumann views Schmitt's decisionism as a formal, or aesthetic, apology for a state which is in fact finely tuned to the interests of big business: 'In monopoly capitalism, the private ownership of the means of production remains unaltered as the unifying legal figure of the whole bourgeois epoque, but general law and contract disappear and are replaced by individual prerogatives of the sovereign' (p. 75). Neumann's examination of monopoly capitalism directly parallels the theory of the 'prerogative state', which is developed by Ernst Fraenkel (a close friend and colleague of Neumann).

Neumann's critique of the formal universality of law is therefore tempered by an awareness of the ambiguities of the bourgeois period. The conviction that bourgeois categories of freedom and equality can contain the hope of genuine emancipation is never wholly absent from his thinking. Like all thinkers associated with the Frankfurt School, Neumann seeks to realize the original promises of enlightened liberalism, and to give substance to the formal emancipatory claims of liberal thought. This can be seen most clearly in his reception and critique of the concept of freedom in liberalism. The guarantees of liberty and equality in capitalist democracy are, he argues, merely negative formulations of property rights against the intrusion and interference of the state. The history of liberal legal theory (especially in Germany), he asserts, is the history of a purely negative interest in liberty, of a lazy compromise between the bourgeoisie and the authoritarian state (p. 38). However, Neumann does not endorse the Marxist rejection of politics as a means of emancipation. Some real progress has been made in the development of modern law, he explains – especially in the 'recognition of rights of coalition for employees' (p. 39). Progress has been made where public law prevails over private law. Even the 'limited, formal and negative generality of law in liberalism' offers, Neumann argues, some formal resistance to the prerogatives of monopoly capitalism (pp. 74–5). Neumann's early thinking centres thus on the question how liberal law itself might be augmented to include stricter substantive provisions for social relations.

Neumann's theory of democracy thus combines aspects of Marxism and liberalism. Like Marx, he argues that modern law reflects, obscures and cements the relations of civil society. However, Neumann resists Marx's strict differentiation between the social and the political spheres. In contrast to Marx, he sets out a strongly volitional theory of the social state, which argues that the democratic ideal of equality and justice must actively encompass the terms of the social. In addition to formal stipulations regarding personal, juridical and political equality, he asserts, democracy must also contain an active realization of social equality. Social equality gives content to the otherwise formal liberties of political democracy (1978h: 218). Like Marx again, therefore, Neumann asserts that human liberty cannot be negatively enshrined in law. True liberty is only possible in the absence of property, for only outside property-relations can liberty be defined interactively and positively. Equality is thus the precondition of liberty. However, Neumann does not intend these ideas exclusively as a critique of liberal, or political, theories of law. Rather, he argues that, for all its negativity and formality, the universality of law which is inscribed in democratic liberalism is a key component of true, positive liberty. Without a democratic political order, with strong protection for individual liberty, active social equality cannot be realized. Social democracy therefore depends upon political democracy (1978c: 132). In his later work, Neumann again stresses the volitional nature of genuine political freedom, and he criticizes the restrictive (property-based) concepts of liberty in classical liberalism (1967b). However, positive liberty is not, for Neumann, absolutely at odds with the spirit of liberalism.

The salient aspects of Neumann's social ontology and his theory of positive liberty therefore concur broadly with Marx's reflections on the relation between politics and the economy. However, Neumann differs from classical Marxist theory in his explanation of the processes through which the political sphere can be extended to incorporate the social sphere. He is repeatedly critical of Marxist theory, which insists on the absolute primacy of the economy over the polity. In this respect, his ideas connect closely with the Austro-Marxism of Max Adler (Könke 1987: 130), whose own anti-pluralist theory of the class-state possesses strong Schmittian traits (Adler 1973: esp. 196). 'Marxist theory', Neumann argues,

> suffers from a misunderstanding – namely, it confuses political analysis with social theory, which is misinterpreted as a theory of action. In Marx's sociological theory politics appears as a function of the economy.... The function of the state is thus decisively determined by the economy. But does Marx conclude that the action of the proletariat has to be predominantly economic and not political? For Marx the answer is unquestionable. It is political action which is decisive, not economic action. The result of his sociological analysis – the state as class-state – is that the class-state has to be overthrown.... Revolution as a political means is only necessary for him in the struggle for democracy or in the defence of democracy. (1967c: 253–4).

Thus, Neumann outlines an interpretation of Marx which, although questionable as exegesis, foregrounds the political sphere as an area of operation in which socio-economic conflict can be resolved by democratic, political means. At the base of this explication of Marx is a critique of the history of social democracy in Germany, throughout which, Neumann implies, party officials have placed exaggerated faith in the power of technical dialectics to bring about the political emancipation of the proletariat (1967c: 254).

Still more fundamentally, however, Neumann also argues here – like Kirchheimer after him – that genuine democracy cannot be conceived as a separation of human life into distinct categories of political and economic existence. Political democracy on its own is not truly democratic, he explains. Genuine democracy must include a disposition over the means of technical reproduction (economic relations). Otherwise these means will gain power of disposition over the political sphere. However, Neumann also indicates that democracy is not exhausted in the administration of economic needs. The satisfaction of material demands is certainly a component of real democracy, but it is not its sole objective. In this respect, Neumann's theory of social democracy represents a new position in the general political anthropology of the German tradition. Social democracy, he intimates, is not a multitude of economic actions (contracts) through which the state fulfils specific needs. It is, rather, a political life-form, which is made possible by material equality, and which maintains material equality as its own precondition. Democracy *begins* with the establishment of material equality and the detachment of human life and liberty from the defence of property. Democracy, however, does not have its end and purpose in the technical securing of a social balance. Neumann's theory of social democracy therefore has a strongly dialectical character. The social component of democracy (equality) is not possible without its political component (liberty). But the social aspect of social democracy serves, lastly, to facilitate real *political* democracy, in which freedom can be positively structured.

For these reasons, Neumann asserts that genuine democracy can only be effected by sovereign, central state-organization. The crucial development in modern politics is, he asserts, the transition from competitive to monopoly capitalism. The latter phase is characterized by the unmediated translation of the interests of monopoly enterprises into political prerogatives (1978d: 80–1), a process which extracts legislative power from popular control. Because of this development, Neumann, like Weber and Hermann Heller before him, argues strongly in favour of a unified, central, sovereign state which is equipped with strong powers of economic co-ordination. Only such a state, he explains, is capable of resisting the powerful bodies which threaten democracy (1978e: 71). Only a strong state which can assert the primacy of public law over private law – which concentrates rights of disposition in the state – can provide the precondition for genuine democracy (1978d: 97). Social democracy thus depends upon a *political* decision over social conditions.

For Neumann, in sum, the central prerequisite of real democracy is the existence of a strong political order, in which supreme legislative power is secured. In this regard, Neumann's ideas reflect the influence of Schmitt (Schäfer 1984: 28). Neumann's model of democracy is a powerful parliamentary system, in which the elected legislature is the supreme source of decision-making authority, with constitutional authority to regulate the sphere of private production. In late capitalism, Neumann indicates, the political power of parliament is constantly under attack from potent economic bodies, especially cartels. Only 'the expansion of state-sovereignty' by means of legislation to curb the power of cartels and monopolies can, Neumann argues, act as a corrective to this process (1978d: 96). Political corporatism, he thus asserts, inevitably augments the influence of conservative bodies on parliament (1967a: 57). Any attempt to divide power between various organizations which are not directly subject to parliamentary control undermines the state and stabilizes these organizations against the state, so that they utilize the state for the protection of their own vested interests. Above all, Neumann argues, wherever the sovereignty of the parliamentary legislature is weakened by concessions to extra-parliamentary interests, the bureaucracy assumes a mediating role between the various sources of power,[1] and it thus detaches itself from governmental control. Neumann defines the 'transformation of the legislative state into an administrative state' as one of the key problems in the Weimar experiment with mass-democracy (1978c: 130). In pluralist, or corporate, modes of organization, he explains, the bureaucracy circumvents parliament and surreptitiously fuses the organs of legislature and judiciary in a suspended prerogative system (1978c: 131). Democracy, therefore, can only be instituted by a political order which reserves all legislative power for itself.

These central dimensions of Neumann's theory of democracy were issues of general discussion in the Weimar era. The status and function of the bureaucracy, most especially, was a crucial area of political debate amongst Social Democrats in the 1920s. Similarly, the power of cartels and monopoly groups was also much discussed in the theories of the left. There are strong historical explanations for both these debates. It has been explained briefly above that through the nineteenth century, after the acquisition of power by the Prussian bureaucracy during the reforms of Stein and Hardenberg (Kehr 1965a: 35), the critique of the administration became a common aspect of liberal political theory in Germany. The importance of this critique for socialist thinkers in the 1920s was, however, still more pronounced. This can be directly linked to the historical foundations of the Weimar Republic. The state-bureaucracy of the late-Wilhelmine period had acted as a major component in the overall conservative composition of the post-Bismarckian governmental system. Civil servants in the state-administration were recruited largely from affluent sectors of society, and offices were allocated as much on the basis of personal connections as on individual ability. Bethmann-Hollweg (Chancellor 1909–17) himself stressed the importance of conservative attitudes amongst those appointed to the administration of state (Frenske 1985: 13). After the end of the Hohenzollern dynasty, however, the SPD-led government of the early-Weimar period remained reliant on the bureaucracy of the old regime, as it had not had time to train new civil servants during the drafting of the Weimar Constitution (Runge 1965: 47). In 1919, conservative political parties (especially the DNVP, but also the DVP) attached particular weight to securing the privileges of the Hohenzollern bureaucracy in the new republic. These rights included, crucially, protection against dismissal. The old administration was therefore transported wholesale into the new republic. The rights and privileges of the civil service were expressly protected by Article 129 of the constitution. Article 130 even went as far as to guarantee liberty of political opinion for the civil service (Frenske 1985: 29), thereby legally sanctioning conservative opposition to the republic at its very administrative heart. In 1922, after the murders of Erzberger and Rathenau, legislation was introduced to democratize the civil service

---

1 This conviction was widely held in the Weimar SPD. See Kehr 1965b: 250. Kehr also develops a theory of state-capitalism. See also Witt 1983a: 147.

(Grottkopp 1963: 212). The Prussian parliament under Severing sought especially to appoint civil servants with good republican credentials, and it partially altered the composition of the Prussian bureaucracy (Müller 1983: 151). However, such measures had only limited effect. The civil service retained its conservative, anti-SPD character throughout the 1920s, and it ultimately proved a more than adequate foundation for the prerogative system instituted by Brüning. In this respect, therefore, Neumann's advocacy of the reinforcement of the parliamentary legislature against the bureaucratic executive refers to the special character of the imperial civil service in the 1920s. Indeed, Neumann's reflections in this respect mark a continuation and radicalization of the earlier anti-bureaucratic theories of the liberals.

Neumann's argument that governmental pluralism (or corporatism) strengthens monopoly-bodies can also be assessed as a response to the special configuration of economic and political management in early twentieth-century Germany. It has been outlined above that through the latter period of Bismarck's rule a particular brand of corporate government was created in Germany. Although this issue is the object of much controversy in historical literature,[2] it can be argued with some conviction that Bismarck created a system which gave strong economic bodies direct access to the executive, and in which, therefore, political legislation was tailored to the interests of such bodies. In this system, the interaction between the state and economic associations was a crucial component in the decision-making process, and the state assumed the function of regulator in the distribution of capital, and of co-ordinator in the process of economic expansion. Caprivi's trade-agreements of the early 1890s are usually identified as a key moment in the process of increasing interrelation between state and economy, as these represent the assumption of authority by the state for the co-ordination of expansion overseas (Ullmann 1976: 234). The power of the German bureaucracy in the early twentieth century can also in part be attributed to the corporate nature of the German system, which allowed the bureaucracy to mediate between extra-parliamentary economic groupings and the executive, thus bypassing the parliamentary legislature (Nipperdey 1979: 419). Significantly, this mode of government also went hand in hand with the increasingly systematic organization of economic interests in the form of employers' deputations (W. Fischer 1973: 142). In the years after 1900 an increasing number of employers' organizations formed united associations, which represented their collective interests to the government (Grübler 1982: 16). Significantly also, such organization of economic interest in structured groups was coupled with the increasing cartelization of the German economy. By 1907 25 per cent of the German economy was organized in cartels (Pohl 1977: 221). Thus, in short, the political landscape of early twentieth-century Germany was marked by a situation in which relatively few industrial companies possessed both very

2 For a conflicting position, see Hentschel 1978: 123.

high levels of economic power, and organizational access (via the bureaucracy) to the state-executive (Petzina 1985: 51). Neumann's plea for a reinforced legislature is – like that of Weber before him – an attempt to redress the erosion of parliamentary authority by the Prussian system of corporate deals.

Of greatest relevance to Neumann and Kirchheimer, however, is the fact that these corporate structures were not dismantled in the course of the 1914–18 war and the establishment of the Weimar parliamentary system. In fact, they were reinforced. Superficially, the war gave unprecedented power to the political organizations of the working class. The management of the economy in the war was characterized by a high degree of collaboration between different civil associations, such as unions, employers' groups and cartels. The bodies of organized labour used this collaboration as a means of securing new rights and powers. During the war and in its aftermath both parliament and the labour-force obtained a new degree of influence. As discussed above, in 1917 representatives of pro-reform parties formed the inter-party committee for electoral reform. Shortly beforehand, legal rights of unions were acknowledged as the unions agreed to their co-optation into the war-effort. However, it was not only the unions which obtained an increased level of influence and independence through the system of wartime collaboration. Cartels and monopolies also gained direct impact on economic and political administration. A variety of different civil associations therefore obtained a high degree of structural autonomy and political influence during the war (Feldman and Steinisch 1985: 19–20).

The wartime mode of organization also had consequences which went far beyond the war. The arrangements between employers and unions also extended into the Weimar Republic itself. It was from the personal relations and contacts forged during this period of cross-class collaboration that the early Weimar coalitions – and even the terms of the constitution itself – were derived (Lepsius 1993: 81). At the very foundation of the Weimar Republic was the agreement (November 1918) between the leading industrialist, Hugo Stinnes (Wulf 1979: 121), and the leading union delegate, Carl Legien. Stinnes and Legien agreed that policies of long-term co-operation would be developed between unions and management, and that a forum would be created for the regulation of labour- and wage-disputes. This, the Central Community of Labour (*Zentralarbeitsgemeinschaft*), existed until 1924 (Feldman and Steinisch 1985: 23–5). Stinnes and Legien also agreed that a system of local and national collective bargaining would be instituted between workforce and management (Braunthal 1978: 150). As a direct result of the Stinnes–Legien Pact, a Tariff-Agreement Order (December 1918) was introduced, which gave tariff-agreements binding legal status (Bohle 1990: 14, 23, 34). Provisions for the partial syndicalization of the mining industry (March 1919) were also introduced (1990: 14).

The system of labour law was thus given an unusual status in the Weimar period. After the Stinnes–Legien Pact, collective wage-agreements could be accorded legal authority without parliamentary ratification. Both unions and employers' associations were consequently endowed with quasi-legis-lative power. Notably, neither Stinnes nor Legien had great faith in the SPD as a party of government, and both sought to secure their own advantages outside the emerging parliamentary order (see Feldman 1993: 107; Bender 1988: 209). After 1923 a system of mandatory state-mediation in wage-disputes was introduced, by means of which the state assumed partial responsibility for setting wage-levels (Horn 1983: 330–1). This, however, did not greatly alter the guiding principle of Weimar labour law. Throughout the 1920s this remained, namely, that labour law should be positioned precisely on the juncture between private and public law and that certain private associations should have public power in the organiza-tion of industrial relations (Preller 1949: 260). The Stinnes–Legien Pact was in principle a deal in which Stinnes offered rights of co-determination to the unions, and Legien promised to secure the support of the unions for corporate capitalism, and to work against radical transformations of the economic order (Albertin 1974: 660). Both parties in this deal gained a high degree of extra-parliamentary influence because of it. Subsequent parlia-mentary legislation, which provided for the socialization of certain indus-tries, was, notably, not systematically implemented (Meister 1991: 15). The Weimar Republic, thus, rested on a brand of left-oriented societal corpor-atism, in which earlier agreements between government and economic associations were replaced by agreements between labour and management, based on the principle of social partnership and collective bargaining. Whole areas of legislative competence were thus devolved to bodies outside parliament.

Of equal importance for Neumann and Kirchheimer, however, is that the process of capital-concentration and cartelization also continued in an accelerated manner throughout the Weimar period. After the years of hyper-inflation in the early 1920s, the German economy was characterized by an extremely high level of cartelization (H. Mommsen 1990: 229). Stresemann (Chancellor 1923) attempted to introduce anti-cartel legislation in 1923, but this did not prohibit cartels (Leuschen-Seppel 1981: 198), and in fact did little to obstruct the concentration of power in a decreasing number of companies (Lehnich 1928: 118–19). After 1926 the SPD repeat-edly attempted to reinforce the existing anti-cartel measures (Naphtali 1931: 43). German industry had already been heavily cartelized at the beginning of the century. In 1890 there were 106 cartels. In 1905 there were 400. As a consequence of the hyper-inflation, however, there were 3,000 cartels by 1926 (Timm 1952: 72). Indeed, many larger firms profited directly from the inflationary period, and resisted attempts to stabilize the mark, as the cheap labour-costs made German commodities especially competitive abroad (Czada 1973: 37). This, in turn, gave larger firms the opportunity to buy up smaller firms which did not have access to foreign currency (Wulf 1979: 470). The period of hyper-inflation therefore greatly accelerated the tendency towards capital-concentration which was already a key characteristic of the German economy (see Timm 1953: 72; Petzina

1985: 54; Feldman 1993: 272). By 1930 40 per cent of industrial production was organized in cartelized branches (Bechtold 1986: 242).

These processes have direct significance for Neumann's theory of democracy. The rapid cartelization of the economy was to have chronic consequences for German political life after the economic downturn of 1928. The process of cartelization, coupled with the devolution of power to civil associations via systems of collective bargaining, meant that in the crisis-years after 1929 powerful economic groups already possessed entrenched positions at the fringe of government, from which they could exert direct influence on governmental decisions. This had a destabilizing effect on the parliamentary system (Petzina 1985: 63). By 1929 the character of the bargains entered into in 1918–19 had changed markedly. The relative weakness of organized management in 1918–19 was very different from its great strength in the late 1920s. Similarly, the relative strength of organized labour in 1919 was soon depleted by hyper-inflation and recession. The shift in the power-relation between these groups was reflected in the increasingly aggressive nature of industrial relations through the 1920s, and the ultimate abandonment of the agreements of 1918–19.

Brüning's anti-welfare policies after 1930 can also be interpreted against this background. Although major industrial associations were initially hostile to Brüning's presidial cabinet (Meister 1991: 177–9), his policies were ultimately endorsed by representatives of industry, including the Imperial Association of German Industry (A. Schmidt 1981: 39; Krohn 1978: 119; Meister 1991: 248), and the banks (Grübler 1982: 189). Arguably, moreover, the industrial organizations used Brüning's tenure on power to limit their obligations within the Weimar corporate system (Grübler 1982: 101; Petzina 1985: 63). Industrialists' associations had urged Hindenburg as early as 1925 to use Article 48 to limit parliament and protect the interests of business and cartels (Weisbrod 1978: 243–4). Major representatives of industrial associations notably refused to support measures to stimulate the economy after the collapse of 1929 (Grübler 1982: 353), and they utilized Brüning's cabinet as an instrument to rescind the wage-agreements which they had earlier entered through the compulsory mediation-process (1982: 168–9). Although Brüning attempted to introduce anti-monopoly legislation, his reduction of social spending and his limitation of state-activity in the economy, have been widely interpreted, at least in part, as a response to the promptings of influential business-groups. The Grand Coalition which Brüning replaced was notoriously sensitive to lobbying activities (see Böhret 1966: 104, 109, 125).

Therefore, in sum, the Weimar Republic was anchored in a set of compromises between parties, unions, business and the military, which were based on their co-operation during the war. These agreements ensured that the terms of Weimar democracy were pre-formed by corporate considerations. The power of parliament was limited before it was even established. It is for these reasons that the issue of cartel-legislation, and the threat posed to the parliamentary legislative by cartels and strong economic bodies, so dominated the political thinking of the Weimar left. Most particularly, these issues are reflected in the political theory of the SPD in the 1920s (especially that of Neumann) as a problem of governmental pluralism. The pluralist system of government, Neumann argues, creates a system in which power is amorphously distributed, and in which, therefore, power is open to usurpation – hence Neumann's insistence on the reinforcement of the parliamentary legislature. Advanced capitalism, Neumann explains, is inevitably marked by the usurpation of public power by private-legal bodies. If such bodies are installed at the edge of government, this process will simply be accelerated.

However, attitudes to governmental pluralism in the ranks of the SPD in the 1920s were necessarily complex. The broader problem of governmental pluralism was, for historical reasons, close to the heart of the Weimar SPD. The SPD was never a majority-party, and even in its strongest period in 1919 it never obtained more than 37.8 per cent of the vote. It therefore depended on collaboration with bourgeois parties. It depended, in short, upon a pluralist coalition-system. The compromise-form of the Weimar state was, moreover, the upshot of years of political debate and dissent within the SPD itself after 1890 – throughout the revisionist period of its history. The division of the SPD and the foundation of the USPD in 1917 had resulted from the determination of Friedrich Ebert and Philipp Scheidemann to strengthen the position of the working class through constitutional reform and economic negotiation (rather than revolutionary action). This moderate course steered by the SPD-leadership finally culminated in the constitutional foundation of the republic itself (Albertin 1974: 660). Ebert was himself a symbolic transitional figure, connecting the new order of the SPD with the old, and he was strongly identified with the conventions of monarchical government (Böckenförde 1987: 29). The SPD itself was thus, by the time it assumed power in 1919, the party of the non-revolutionary working class. The pluralist nature of government in the Weimar system therefore reflects the pluralist ideological composition of the SPD. As it was never a majority-party, the SPD sought from the beginning of the Weimar period to create a corporate state-structure, based on the compromise of interests between business and labour, in order to ensure its smooth co-operation at governmental level with the forces – and parties – of big business (Grübler 1982: 18).

Increasingly, also, through the later years of the Weimar Republic the SPD constantly became more reliant on its position in the system of corporate collaboration. The initial compromises which the SPD formed with its coalition-partners (the Zentrum and the DDP) lasted only until 1923, when the SPD withdrew from government. The SPD entered government again, as the main party in the Grand Coalition, in 1928. After 1923, however, the SPD moved away from its early plans for the gradual socialization of the economy, and it became exclusively a compromise party, whose chief goal was to soften the budgetary policies of the parties of the mid-Weimar bourgeois bloc (particularly the DVP), and to negotiate acceptable social provisions for the working class (Turner 1985: 101). Indeed, the SPD was not unsuccessful in this regard. The Weimar legal state provided an unprecedented organ for the reallocation of finance to the workforce. During the middle-period of the republic (1924–9), state investments in social provisions increased threefold (Preller 1949: 463), and Germany invested far more than other European countries in welfare-arrangements (Turner 1985: 38). The average wage of industrial labourers increased by almost 100 per cent in this period (Preller 1949: 155). During the whole Weimar period, advanced labour- and welfare-packages were passed by parliament, most notably the shop-council law of 1920, the partial recognition of the eight-hour day (Preller 1949: 210; Weisbrod 1978: 309), the institution of labour-tribunals in 1926 (Bohle 1990: 85) and legislation providing for compulsory unemployment- insurance in 1927.

During the crises of late-Weimar politics, therefore, even after the installation of Brüning (Fromme 1960: 118; Timm 1952: 188; Helbing 1962: 45), leading intellectuals of the SPD did not distance themselves categorically from the Weimar state. After March 1930, the official policy of the SPD was that the party should support Brüning, in order to prevent a further shift to the right (Schaefer 1990: 72). Many SPD-theorists (including Neumann, Rudolf Hilferding and Hermann Heller) supported the official SPD-policy of tolerance towards the presidial system, and they continued to argue that a strong state would restrict economic influence on politics (see esp. Heller 1971c: 608–9). In return for their grudging support, Brüning held out the promise that the residual substance of democracy would be kept intact, in case normal economic conditions were to return (Meister 1991: 211). Although the strategy of the SPD now seems strikingly naive, it must be remembered that of all Weimar parties only the SPD relied absolutely on the corporate-parliamentary system. All other parties had a mandate which did not depend on the existence of a parliamentary-democratic apparatus (Jasper 1986: 26).

Ultimately, however, the pluralist basis of the SPD's hold on power undermined the very object of its political quest. The innermost motivation behind the policies of Ebert and his apostles – the establishment of a democratic parliament – was severely compromised by the pluralist system which they employed to realize this goal. Brüning's policies, in fact, systematically exploited the central institutions of the republic – the bureaucracy and the constitution – to undo the welfare provisions and the collective wage-agreements which had been negotiated by the SPD (Hartwich 1967: 162), both as a party of government and in opposition (see Weisbrod 1982: 196). In the last months of the Grand Coalition, Hilferding (SPD Minister of Finance in 1923 and 1928–9) was replaced by Moldenhauer (DVP). This was due in no small part to the interventions of Hjalmar Schacht (Head of the Imperial Bank, and later Hitler's banker), who refused to sanction Hilferding's fiscal policies. The replacement of Hilferding began a move (initially orchestrated by Moldenhauer) towards a deflationary fiscal programme of price- and wage-sinking (Meister 1991: 78–80; Patch 1998:

56–8). Brüning continued this policy, ultimately employing Article 48 to cancel the unemployment-insurance rates, which had been agreed with the unions in 1927. In the period 1930–3, social spending fell from nearly 16 to 12 billion marks (Alber 1986: 9). Thus, after the SPD had created the framework for its governmental collaboration with the forces of business and industry, the forces of business and industry ultimately decided they could govern without the SPD (Abraham 1986: 270). The foremost goal of Brüning's deflationary measures was to secure Germany's yearly export-surplus (Golla 1994: 96). The SPD-state was lastly, therefore, turned against the SPD itself (see Ehni 1975: 171; Timm 1952: 193; Butterwegge 1979: 319). The plural system of corporate government was (as Neumann, Kirchheimer and Schmitt diversely explain) ultimately utilized to further the interests of anti-pluralist groups (see Megerle 1993: 218; Blaich 1979: 64; Preller 1949: 196). The complex attitude to pluralism in SPD-theory of the 1920s, in sum, derives from the fact that plural governmental forms were both pioneered by the SPD and, in part, responsible for its ultimate weakness.

The problem of pluralism for the Weimar SPD, however, does not relate exclusively to aspects of day-to-day government. It also relates to the terms of the Weimar Constitution itself. The Weimar Constitution strongly reflected the conditions of its historical genesis in the revolutionary winter of 1918–19 (Leuschen-Seppel 1981: 194). It was a formalized compromise between the various parties represented in the constitutional assembly of early 1919, namely the SPD, the Zentrum and the Liberal Democrats. It was a balance, therefore, between antagonistic classes, and between antagonistic visions of the conditions of good political order. The balance of these class-interests was expressed especially in the second part of the Weimar Constitution, drafted primarily by Friedrich Naumann (DDP) and Hugo Sinzheimer (SPD). Although the constitution expressly protected freedom of property and contract, it stated also that the economic order must 'conform to the principles of justice with the goal of guaranteeing the human dignity of all' (Article 151). This guarantee of property coupled with the recommendation for its use in the common interest also reflects Roman Catholic (proto-solidaristic) conceptions of private property. Konrad Beyerle, the constitutional expert of the Zentrum (1919: 4), was also involved in drafting this section of the document. Similarly, the constitution guaranteed union-rights, as 'freedom of coalition for the preservation and furthering of the conditions of employment and the economy' (Article 159). Most importantly, the constitution made provision for the socialization of key industries (Article 156). It also foresaw the establishment of workers' councils to regulate wage-payments, to participate in the organization of private enterprises, and to oversee the socialization-process (Article 165). These provisions – formulated by Sinzheimer – also included the creation of an economic council (*Reichswirtschaftsrat*), in which 'all important professional groups are represented according to their economic and social importance' (see Völtzer 1992: 148). Such paragraphs demonstrate the impact of the corporate agreement between Stinnes and Legien at the beginning of the republic. Two entirely conflicting conceptions of economic management – one based on state-regulation, one based on private property – are, in sum, roughly fused in the terms of the constitution. The Weimar Constitution, thus, drafted in the aftermath of the political upheaval of 1918–19, represents an uneasy accord struck between radically divergent, but temporarily coexistent concepts of social order. For this reason, Neumann, like Schmitt, says that: 'it is justifiable to call the Weimar Constitution a constitution without a decision' (1967a: 58).

Nonetheless, the compromise between the SPD and the Liberal Democrats in the inception of the Weimar Republic produced an early form of social state. In the system of government foreseen by the constitution, the order of state combined both universal liberal law and rights of state-intervention in the social sphere. Friedrich Naumann himself expressly advocated the creation of a 'national-social peoples' state' (Vestring 1987: 265). The Weimar Constitution can therefore be assessed, at least in its conception, as a 'post-traditional' constitution (see Scheuermann 1996: 5), which sought to provide mediating terms between different classes and economic interest groups (see Kurtze 1931: 73). At the heart of the constitution was the belief that class-interests could be balanced by provisions for economic organization in the common interest. It marked a significant departure from the classical liberal constitutions of the late eighteenth century and the nineteenth century (Naumann 1919b: 105). Even Otto Kirchheimer argued that the spirit of 'laissez-faire' is 'definitively removed' by the constitution of the Weimar state (1972a: 251). In his role in the constitutional commission, Naumann, particularly, opposed both purely socialist and purely individual-negative ideas of legal order (Kurtze 1931: 291). Instead, he imagined the constitution as an elastic social programme of action – 'not as freedom from the state, but freedom in and towards the state' (E. R. Huber et al. 1978: 398).

The compromise nature of the Weimar Constitution did not result only from the inter-party agreements at the origin of the Weimar Republic. The ambiguities in the regulations for property administration which remain in the constitution are the traces of earlier divisions within the SPD itself, and they can be dated back to the conflict between revisionist, social-reformist and dictatorial conceptions of socialist government (Schorske 1965: 17). During the winter of 1918–19, government by revolutionary workers' councils was, at least in some sectors of the SPD and the USPD, seen as a serious alternative, or at least addition, to parliamentary-democratic rule. This, clearly, was not realized. As the period of revolutionary fervour waned, especially after the murder of Rosa Luxemburg and Karl Liebknecht and the suppression of the councils in early 1919, the political influence of the council-model declined rapidly (Heinrich Potthoff 1972: 469). The idea of council rule had been abandoned long before the constitution was ratified in August 1919 (see Heidegger 1956: 240). Nonetheless, in 1919 important (although not all) representatives of the USPD saw the creation of council-based political organization as a means of consolidating the power of the proletariat in the revolutionary period – indeed, as the very 'incorporation of state-power' (*Allgemeiner Kongreß* 1919: 8). The executive of the SPD, in contrast, had little sympathy for the council-style order envisaged by the USPD and the far left of the SPD (Matthias 1969: xxix). Ebert himself argued simply that 'socialist experiments in individual firms can only damage and discredit socialism' (quoted in von Oertzen 1976: 256), and he clearly preferred social reform to genuine socialist economic policies (Schieck 1972: 155; Bermbach 1967: 73–4). Similarly, Scheidemann dismissed Sinzheimer's proposals for partial government by councils as 'spirited word-play' (see S. Miller 1978: 308). Broadly, therefore, the Majority SPD, in coalition with the DDP, firmly rejected council government and urged the creation of a parliamentary democracy (Apelt 1964: 199–200). The 'council-clause' (Article 165) in the constitution remains only as a signal of muted recognition for the promptings from the far left of the SPD and some former members of the SPD in the ranks of the USPD (see Kolb 1978: 169).

Notwithstanding these qualifications, however, the second part of the Weimar Constitution still contains a complex model for the administration of property. For all its limitations, Article 165 provided for a system of council-based deputation in which workers had certain powers to determine the conditions of their employment (Heinrich Potthoff 1974a: 343). Although these councils had no binding authority, they existed as forums of collective bargaining in the sphere of public law (Berlau 1949: 261–2). The social provisions of the constitution, reflected in the council-clause, had a discernible influence on the subsequent development of early-Weimar social and labour-law (see Günther 1920: 12). Although a definite post-traditional social order was not instituted by the Weimar Constitution, it made crucial legal provisions for the corporate limitation of private law (Wieacker 1967: 545), and these were subsequently expanded throughout the 1920s, although not to the extent initially envisaged by both parliament and unions at the beginning of the Weimar period (see Preller 1949: 251; Song 1966: 70–1).

The political position of Franz Neumann, and especially his critique of pluralism, can be understood against this background. Neumann acknowledges the ambivalent nature of the provisions made by the constitution. Unlike Schmitt, however, he rejects the idea that the constitution can only be truly protected by a strong executive. He argues instead that the second part of the constitution contains a submerged vision of socialist politics. It is the task of socialist political theory, Neumann argues, to develop and present the 'social content' of these provisions (1978e: 74). The most pressing obligation of socialist legal activity, Neumann asserts, is to devise legal means to limit the power of the monopoly enterprises in politics, and thereby to defend the social conception of property in the constitution. Above all, Neumann (like Sinzheimer) especially advocates the establishment of an economic constitution, which he sees as a means of regulating the activities of the cartels. An economic constitution, he argues, would act as a social adjunct to the sovereignty of state, as 'direct control of the market by the state' (1978d: 94–6). 'Thus,' he explains, 'if an economic constitution is developed, the last decision in all essential political and economic matters will be reserved for the state – that means the Imperial Minister of Economics' (p. 97). Neumann pleads thus for an expansion of state-authority over the economic sphere, especially in respect of the regulation of relations between wage-labour and management. The reinforcement of the state, he indicates, permits the state to exert control over the economy. A strong parliament, with codified legal control of the economy, therefore protects the citizen from the economy. The pluralist dissolution of parliamentary power, Neumann argues, leads by a direct path to the domination of the political arena by the forces of the economy.

In this respect, Neumann's thought links closely, but critically, with the varying forms of revisionist Marxism which formed the ideological core of the Weimar SPD. All major thinkers of the SPD in the 1920s attempted to explain the nature of social democracy, and above all to justify their own involvement in the administration of capitalism and their collaboration with bourgeois parties. Neumann's anti-pluralism is therefore part of a complex series of debates regarding the relation between capitalism and democracy and the possibility of democratic transition to socialism.

The seminal ideological position of the Weimar SPD is found in the state-theories of the Austro-Marxist Otto Bauer. Bauer claimed that the modern state (in his own case, the Austrian Republic) is no longer formally capitalist, but rather based on a balance of class-forces. The modern state, consequently, he argued, is not structurally opposed to the proletariat, but can be used to realize proletarian interests (Bauer 1923: 243; 1980). The theory of the balance of class-forces was ultimately a crucial theoretical tool for the inter-war Social Democratic parties. Bauer's theory of the balance of class-forces is a left-pluralist model of democracy which argues that socialist parties can legitimately participate in the government of non-socialist states, and that their involvement in such states can steer the state towards the realization of socialism. This argument was widely employed to justify the political activities of the SPD throughout the 1920s.

The model of revisionism which most strongly influenced Neumann was that contained in the legal-political writings of Hugo Sinzheimer, Neumann's mentor in the study of private and labour law. Sinzheimer claimed that the tariff-agreement (*Tarifvertrag*) should be used as a means of stabilizing conflict between social organizations and social classes by transposing this conflict into the system of public law (Sinzheimer 1916: 49). He concurs thus with Karl Renner's famous treatise on private law, which also argues that the tariff-contract will gradually assert its primacy over bourgeois private law (Renner 1965: 202). The outcome of negotiations between workforce and management, Sinzheimer argues, should stand as objective law, and this law should be ceaselessly recreated and restabilized through ongoing corporate bargaining. Sinzheimer claims therefore that class-struggle can be incorporated by such means into processes of collective juridification, and thus resolved (1916: 202). For Sinzheimer, the tariff-agreement represents and codifies the existing point of tension in the relation between the classes. This tension, he argues, is ordinarily articulated (and reinforced) through the system of private law – in relations of property. It can, however, be gradually eliminated through its assimilation into the system of public law, via the tariff-agreement. Sinzheimer's theory is a legal variant on Bauer's model of left-leaning social pluralism. He claims that the recognition of the tariff-agreement as the binding contract between the classes gives to the workforce greater influence on the relations of production, and thus leads to increased public control of the economy. Indeed, his definition of the collective tariff as a formal compromise between the classes closely parallels the terms of the Stinnes–Legien Pact.

Sinzheimer's theories of labour law also contain a more radical sketch for a mode of economic constitutionalism which influenced (as outlined above) Article 165 of the Weimar Constitution (see G. A. Ritter 1989: 119), but which filtered only marginally into political practice (see esp. Oertzen 1976: 203). During the revolutionary period, before the constitution was written, Sinzheimer advocated the creation of a special constitution, distinct from the political constitution, designed to set the terms for 'social, especially economic interests' (1976a: 327). Unlike the council communists, he did not think that workers' organizations should act as the sole source of legal authority. Rather, he favoured the creation of an economic constitution, 'which would stand beside the constitution of state' (p. 327), and facilitate the movement towards the socialization of property (Hartwich 1967: 18–19). Sinzheimer thus rejected the complete devolution of legislative power to economic bodies (1976a: 343). However, he suggested that a portion of state sovereignty should be delegated to a 'new body of economic self-administration' (p. 345). Although Sinzheimer's ideas are not without inconsistencies (see Berlau 1949: 265), he imagined essentially that a legal order might be instituted in which the state would retain final authority in political and social legislation, but would cede certain legislative powers to self-administrating institutions (especially the councils). Sinzheimer envisaged, therefore, that the councils (albeit under political command) might organically produce a socialist order out of the heart of the civil sphere. Fundamental to such a process, Sinzheimer argued, would be the ultimate restriction of private law in the public economy: the 'removal of private autonomy in the economic sphere' (1976a: 339–40). Sinzheimer's ideas, like those of Bauer, also remained influential throughout the 1920s (see Heinz Potthoff 1925: 24; Sinzheimer 1976b: 125–6).

Sinzheimer's reformist theories on labour law and private law were situated some distance to the left of both constitutional and socio-economic practice in the Weimar Republic, and in the SPD itself (Heinrich Potthoff 1974b: 91–2). Two facts are, however, especially notable in Sinzheimer's thinking. Firstly, his theories envision a legal system in which the state possesses organic-democratic control over private property (see Oertzen 1976: 67). He proposes, in social-reformist spirit, a legal order in which the Marxist demand for the regulation of property is identical with the democratic insistence on the universality of law (see Perels 1973: 49). Secondly, Sinzheimer also maintains that the Weimar Constitution itself contains provisions which legalize the socialization of the economic order, which overrule liberal conceptions of private law and thus serve the progress, within the confines of objective law, towards a socialist order.

A further major example of revisionist SPD-theory in the 1920s is found in the ideas of Rudolf Hilferding. Hilferding's brand of Marxism vacillates between an orthodox theory which asserts that modern government has been taken over by monopolies and general cartels, and a doctrine of organized capitalism, which argues that the modern state can itself resolve the contradictions between labour and capital (see Schimkowsky 1974: 286). Such theories closely parallel Werner Sombart's syndicalist theories of planned state-capitalism (Sombart 1927: 882, 1013; 1925: 64). Like Kautsky (see Blaich 1973: 210), Hilferding argues that liberal capitalism has been superseded by a quasi-collectivist system of economic control (Bechtold 1986: 187). The increasing organization of the economy by monopoly bodies, he asserts, can itself, however, provide a means by which the state, as a class-neutral subject, can gain power over the credit supply, and ultimately guide the economy towards socialism (Hilferding 1927: 5). Hilferding's doctrine of organized capitalism represents, on one level, the last trace of the council-democratic conceptions of 1919 (see Brigl-Matthiaß 1926: 246). At the same time, however, it gives to parliament a hinge role in the steering of pluralist, finance-capitalist organizations towards socialism (see Euchner 1982: 103). Hilferding sees in the conditions of monopoly capitalism great opportunities for the strengthening of state-power, for the economic-democratic representation of the interests of labour in the state (see Naphtali et al. 1929: 33) and for the consequent triumph of socialism through the introduction of anti-systemic reforms (see Thum 1991: 45). Hilferding's doctrine of organized capitalism, or the model of economic democracy derived from it, was adopted as orthodoxy by the representatives of the Weimar unions after 1925 (Thum 1991: 36), and formalized as such in 1928. Underlying Hilferding's theory are two assumptions: first, that the state exists above the economic sphere and can always steer the economy; second, that the pluralist organization of economic interests can be co-ordinated by the state itself, and that the emergence of powerful organizations ultimately reinforces state-power.

In addition to Bauer, Hilferding and Sinzheimer, the other outstanding political theorist attached to the Weimar SPD was Hermann Heller. Heller is famous, above all, for his theory of the social-legal state, which argues that the formal precepts of political democracy must also contain the terms of social emancipation. Heller's political theory is essentially based upon cultural assumptions about the relation between society, law and state-power. The representative body of the sovereign state, Heller argues (like

Schmitt), founds the political unity of the people. It founds this unity by interpreting the will of the people and by concretizing this will in appropriate institutions (Pasquino 1988). All organizations, including parties, unions and civil associations, he asserts, contribute to the creation of the state as a unified centre of action, which engages all citizens in social and political will-formation (Heller 1971a: 344). All such associations are themselves ultimately subordinate to, and integrated into, the highest organization of the state. Heller thus outlines a theory of integrative democracy, in which citizens attain rights of co-possession of the state through the organizational forms of civil and political activity.

In Heller's political theory, the underlying guarantee of democratic and political unity is constituted by the cultural community itself. The community, Heller implies, guarantees the ultimate success of democracy. Socialism, Heller indicates, is a political order in which the processes of socialization, redistribution and reorganization of production are carried out in the name of the community (1971b: 462). For this reason, Heller stresses the necessity of the strong state. He sees the strong state not merely as the expression of the general will of the national community, but as a means by which the community can be protected against the corrosive, contractual influence of the economy: private law (1971a: 211). The central danger to modern society, Heller argues, lies in the attempts of economic interest-groups to take hold of the administrative apparatus. Heller's most famous quotation illustrates this perfectly:

> In the long term indirect and anonymous influence is not sufficient for the leaders of the economy. They are, after all, constantly threatened in their influence by the provisions of the democratically governed legislator. This division between political and socio-economic power is a state which cannot last for long. Either the state must create the opportunity, by founding its own economic power, to constitute itself politically without dependence on private economic influences, or the struggle of the leaders of the economy will at least have the provisional success of removing the democratic legislature in order to serve their own interests. (1971a: 235–6)

Heller states in outline therefore, in the tradition of left-Hegelian thinking, that the state is an autonomous political body, in which the interests of the people, in distilled form, can be best expressed and realized. The task which confronts contemporary legislative processes, he argues, is the protection of the state from annexation by the economy. Heller is committed, in essence, to a mixture of corporate pluralism and strong state-organization. He views the state as a body which synthesizes the plural organizations in society, but which has the strength to prevent any particular one of these (especially employers' bodies) gaining political primacy. Heller's theories depend on an ethical-dialectical concept of national history, in which the *Volk* naturally produces forms of political order which resist the contractual basis of the economy.

Heller's thought reflects the very heart of SPD-orthodoxy in the 1920s.[3] The argument that the executive of state might provide a bastion against the economy was one of the key ideological aspects of the Weimar SPD (Blau 1980: 138; Hilferding 1925: 23; Naphtali et al. 1929: 33). Such conceptions of strong-state socialism have their origins in the economic interventionism of the Bismarck period (G. A. Ritter 1989: 11; Feldman 1974: 166). Historically, however, such theories also underline the defensive position of the SPD in the Weimar system. Heller's references to the importance of cultural homogeneity in the constitution of the state illustrate the attempts made by the party to appeal to middle-class voters (Butterwegge 1979: 307). Heller's thought also reflects the desperate struggle of the SPD in the last years of the Republic, during which time the party was prepared to justify even dictatorship as a means of preserving the institutions of the Weimar state (Heller 1971c: 607). His faith in the state as the expression of the community remained long after the German state had abandoned all interest in protecting the citizen from the economy. Even after Brüning was installed in power, Heller continued to advocate the strengthening of the state-executive in order to restrict economic influence on politics (1971d: 413). Like many influential SPD theorists, Heller was ultimately not concerned whether the national community existed in a socialist or capitalist economy, but merely that it existed at all. As late as 1931 he describes the state as an 'organized life-form' (1971d: 414), and he adds: 'We wish for an authoritarian state, not a total one' (p. 415).

Franz Neumann's passionate defence of parliamentary government in the late-Weimar period can thus be associated with the varying forms of revisionism, by means of which the SPD defined and justified its role in the Weimar state. However, unlike other SPD-theorists (including Fraenkel), Neumann does not assume that parliament can fully resolve social conflicts, or that it can sit as a neutral organ above the agreements formed between social bodies (1967d: 91). The very balance of class-forces upon which parliamentary agreements are based, he argues, restricts parliamentary power. The compromises negotiated in parliament are ultimately limited, he explains, by the simple fact that they are compromises. Therefore, like Schmitt, Neumann ultimately denies the legitimacy of democracy which is solely based upon class-compromise or the balance of class-interests. Neumann in fact imagines genuine democracy in clearly Schmittian terms – as the absolute identity between the people and the state (cit. Erd 1985: 79). He claims repeatedly that democracy can only be salvaged if the parliamentary legislature is secured as the only source of power, and if this body is given rights of political and constitutional sovereignty over the economic sphere.

For these reasons, all through his work Neumann resists the left-corporate model of pluralism. He condemns the modes of economic deputation, collective bargaining and extra-parliamentary negotiation which, for

3 For further examples of such thought, see Landauer 1925: 190. See also Luthardt 1986: 48.

conflicting reasons, were supported by most of the Weimar parties, especially the SPD. Notably, many conservative parties, including the DNVP, were not hostile to the council component in Weimar government, as they saw in this a partial return to the estate-based system (Winkler 1973: 229; see also Spann 1921: 270–1). Instead of this, Neumann argues that political legitimacy can only be constituted in the legislative assembly, and that pluralist government immediately adds a moment of compromise to this legitimacy. Like other significant left-leaning theorists around him, most particularly Carl Landauer (1923: 133) and Otto Kahn-Freund (1932: 168–9), Neumann argues that even professional councils can ultimately weaken the position of the workforce at legislative level (see Landauer 1972: 101; H. Mommsen 1978: 27–8). Neumann warns that in periods of economic crisis left-corporate politics can easily lapse into the form of a modern *Ständestaat*, in which workers' delegations are given token influence beneath the steering-directives of the executive (see also Gutmann 1922: 123–4). Generally, Neumann endorses the function of workers' deputations and economic councils because he sees such institutions as means of extending public authority to the private sphere. However, he also senses that such bodies can blur the boundary between public and private law, and thus, possibly, facilitate private influence on the political (public-legal) sphere. Unlike other theorists of the Weimar left, therefore, Neumann does not endorse social legislation because it gives power to interest-groups in civil society. Rather, he endorses social law as the imposition of binding political norms on the economic order (see Könke 1987: 169; F. Neumann 1967b: 131). It is for this reason that Neumann insists on the strong political component to social democracy. Neumann's proposal for an economic constitution demands, therefore, that the provisions of this constitution should never be placed above the normative frame of the political constitution (1978d: 86), and that real power should be left in parliament.

However, despite his reservations about the legal order of the 1920s, there remains a tone of great pathos in Neumann's interpretation of the decline of the Weimar experiment. Like Heller and Hilferding (Könke 1987: 64), Neumann ultimately also supported the SPD's 'policy of toleration' towards Brüning (see Luthardt 1984: 83). In this respect, Neumann's work mirrors the equivocating state-fidelity of the Weimar SPD in general. Otto Wels, President of the SPD during and after the Nazi take-over in 1933, illuminates the whole climate of political thinking within the ranks of the SPD during the last period of the republic. After the accession to power of the NSPAD, Wels stated simply: 'The constitution of Weimar is not a socialist constitution. But we abide by the principles of the legal state, of equality, and of social law, which are grounded in it' (*Stenographische Berichte des Reichstages* 1934: 33). For the Weimar SPD, as for Neumann himself, political law is, manifestly, not socialist law. But in its universality it carries a vanishing trace of socialist justice (Adolph 1971: 264).

In this respect, Neumann's position reflects not only the nature of the state-centred Marxism which arose in the SPD of the 1920s, but also the survival of natural-law thinking in such discourses. This tendency is illustrated most notably by Ernst Fraenkel, who defines 'proletarian natural law' as the foundation of socialist legal method (1927: 30). On one hand, Neumann himself rejects any suggestion that natural law can have any positive influence on legislation. However, he, like other thinkers attached to the SPD, ultimately (re)introduces a strong concept of natural law in his political theory. In his later writings, he argues expressly in favour of iusnatural legal assumptions (1967e: 203–4). Even in his early works, Neumann evidently retains a belief in the power of law to transcend its status as the formal abstraction of property-relations. The legal person is, he implies lastly, not reducible to an ideological mask for the labour–capital relation. Similarly, the state, as the collective embodiment of personal dignity, is also not reducible to the apparatic representation of the interests of capital. If law had no dignity it could not decline.

In certain respects, therefore, Neumann's ideas still recall those of Sinzheimer, Heller and Hilferding. In essence, Neumann implies that the transposition of matters of private-legal jurisdiction into the sphere of public law will facilitate the development of a socialist economy. In his explanation of late capitalism, he argues that powerful economic organizations have expanded the sphere of private law to monopolize the state. This culminates in National Socialism, in which, he explains, bodies situated in the sphere of private law finally take control of the system of public authority. As a corrective to this, he envisages the employment of an extended system of public law to limit the influence of private bodies. Unlike Hilferding, Neumann does not affirm the increasing organization of the economy in powerful blocs. He asserts, however, that the increase in the power of public law will strengthen parliamentary regulation of the economy. Moreover, he asserts (not unlike Hilferding), that the expansion of the domain of public law necessarily reinforces the power of the state and the power of popular sovereignty. Like Sinzheimer also, Neumann underlines the crucial function fulfilled by wage-agreements as the manifestations of 'communal self-help organizations in the sphere of private law' (1929: 22–3). Neumann accepts the widespread reformist belief that the establishment of an economic constitution, to limit the power of the monopolies, would itself automatically generate the preconditions for a social economy (Ramm 1980: 243). Likewise, Neumann accords great weight to the unions as institutions which mediate between the state and civil society (1929: 30), as labour-associations in the sphere of public law (1978b: 218). Like Sinzheimer again, therefore, Neumann advocates a genuinely integrative form of institutional pluralism. He describes this as 'collective democracy' or 'collective self-administration' (1929: 39).

Nonetheless, unlike Sinzheimer and others, Neumann ultimately resists the social-reformist belief that institutional pluralism, mediated through labour law, can on its own guarantee democratic government (Fraenkel 1973: 56). For Neumann, the economic constitution can never be the grounds of citizenship. Neumann repeatedly intimates that the benefits of collectivist theories of law can easily be outweighed by their drawbacks (1967b: 130–1). This clearly precludes full agreement with Sinzheimer's theory, or any reformist theory. The political sphere possesses, Neumann argues (like Schmitt), an inalienable dignity over and against the economy (Hennis 1973: 47). Real social democracy, he implies, is not the triumph of civil society over the political apparatus, but rather the political *transmutation* of civil society. Social democracy enables the production of a political society in which human liberty arises from human equality, and in which, as a result, liberty is not bound defensively to the preservation of property and privilege. Social democracy therefore *becomes* political democracy. It is the precondition of real politics.

Neumann's interpretation of the demise of the Weimar state is an early theory of late capitalism. Parliament, Neumann argues, no longer functions as the central arena in which the decisions of democratic order are made. It has, he asserts, been transformed into an organ which is dependent both on the bureaucracy and on extra-governmental economic organizations, and it therefore relinquishes power to these. Like Schmitt, therefore, Neumann tries to develop a constitutional theory in which the constitution sets finally binding terms for all aspects of political and social life. Above all, he explains, it is not legitimate for the state to equivocate in its decision for or against a particular economic order. Like Schmitt, Neumann also claims that the political law of the Weimar Constitution, although deeply compromised, still contains the traces of lost sovereign decisions. The clear assertion of these decisions in itself, Neumann indicates, is an anti-pluralist undertaking.

Neumann emerges in this light as an anti-Schmittian Schmittian. He is a thinker who seeks to give Schmitt's conception of unified sovereignty something other than merely formal, aesthetic or symbolic character. Whilst Schmitt attempts to secure the unity of the state by separating the system of private law from the state, Neumann argues that the state can only be genuinely sovereign if it *subordinates* the system of private law, if the terms of political citizenship integrate both private needs and public identity. Simultaneously, however, Neumann is also an anti-Marxist Marxist. Political and constitutional sovereignty is, for Neumann, something very different from the mere 'constitution of private property' which Marx describes in his early writings on state-theory (Marx 1956: 303). Like Schmitt (and Kirchheimer), Neumann implicitly suggests – against Marx – that the political sphere has its own particular dignity which places it above the social sphere. The underlying sense in Neumann's theory of the constitution is that the univocal political decision for a socialist socio-economic order *elevates* human interaction above the level of unreconciled antagonism and above the unresolved balance of technical interests. Social democracy is therefore, strictly, no longer social.

In this dual critique and reception of Marx and Schmitt, Neumann's ideas strongly anticipate the works of the early Habermas. The decisions of law, Neumann argues, are part of the systemic armoury of capitalist and bureaucratic domination. However, these decisions, equally, form the structure which transforms social needs into legitimate political power, and, moreover, which distinguishes political interaction from the technical resources of exchange and violence. Therefore, like Habermas after him, Neumann sees in law both the possibility of an integrally political sphere – popular sovereignty – and a technical device used to obscure the very character of this sphere.

The early writings of Otto Kirchheimer also show strong similarities to those of Neumann, although in the 1920s Kirchheimer was situated some distance to the left of Neumann (V. Neumann 1981: 242). Like Neumann, Kirchheimer interprets the crises of modern democracy through Marx's opposition between social and political democracy. Modern democracy, he argues, has always been only political democracy, and its social content is inevitably undermined by the bourgeoisie (1964: 19). Political law in modern democracies, he argues, is of exclusively formal character. Its provisions, he outlines, are applied only in accordance with the relative strength of the social bodies which profit from them. This, he claims, is symptomatic especially of the constitutional developments in the late-Weimar period, in which the social promises of the constitution have been ignored (1964: 33). Kirchheimer also argues that the conflict between economic and political order is most manifest in the original constitution of Weimar, especially in the conflicting proposals of Naumann and Sinzheimer for the social state. 'The basic rights of Weimar', he explains, 'are in their decisive points not a compromise, but a counterposition and recognition of the most different value systems, such as is unprecedented and unique in constitutional history' (p. 32). Like Neumann and Schmitt, Kirchheimer ascribes to the confused value-system of the Weimar Constitution the 'lack of ability to make political decisions which characterizes the agony of our present political life' (p. 40).

Kirchheimer argues that modern capitalist law possesses a double character (U. K. Preuß 1973: 10–11). It represents, on one level, a series of formal political or democratic stipulations. However, the enforcement of these is rarely identical with their content. This is seen most clearly in the case of Weimar. The democratic provisions of the Weimar Constitution, especially in their relation to property law and socialization, have, Kirchheimer argues, fallen victim to the structural manipulations which are inevitable components of bourgeois jurisdiction (1976a: 73). Whatever its formal content, Kirchheimer explains, in the capitalist order law is systematically brought into the service of property-interests. Bourgeois jurisdiction, he argues, always produces structures of non-legitimate legality in order to protect the interests of property. Brüning's mode of presidial superlegality, he asserts, is the key example of this (1932: 26). Like Schmitt, thus, Kirchheimer underlines the distinction between legitimacy and legality in modern pluralist democracies. The decisive public ground of the constitutional order, he argues, is always eroded by the acts of the judiciary, and its compulsion to protect private property-interests. Bourgeois jurisdiction, he states, invariably permits the triumph of the legal over the legitimate. Kirchheimer thus transposes Schmitt's theory of the relation between constitutional law (*Verfassungsrecht*) and subsidiary legal institutes (*Verfassungsgesetz*) into the relation between public law and private law. Public law (legitimacy) is always systematically undermined by private law (legality). Although the Weimar Constitution was conceived as a set of economic and political alternatives to the simple hegemony of the bour- geoisie, Kirchheimer concludes, the bourgeoisie has safely monopolized the constitution in order to preserve its own position (1964: 54).

More emphatically even than Marx or Neumann, Kirchheimer thus insists that capitalism and democracy are formally incompatible (1964: 17). In his critique of the double function of modern law, Kirchheimer argues that bourgeois jurisdiction will always retain its double character unless the system of private law is modified. The constitutional law of the Weimar Republic, he explains, entitles the state to restrict private property, and the social provisions of the constitution expressly limit the private ownership of public property – that is, of the means of industrial produc- tion (1972a: 265). The move away from the traditional concept of property- based democracy which was the intention of the Weimar Constitution, Kirchheimer argues, expressly prohibits the lapse into the high-liberal insistence on the universal sanctity of property. 'The pillars of the capitalist economic order, freedom of contract, private property and inheritance law,' he states, 'have had to renounce their former inviolability' (1972a: 252). Kirchheimer argues thus that the legitimacy of the social-legal state created in Weimar is debased if it is aligned simply to the terms of nineteenth- century political democracy. If the constitution is compelled to recognize the capitalist mode of property law, he indicates, the constitution itself is reduced to a variable in the system of bourgeois private law (Perels 1973: 64), and the legal edicts which are passed by the judiciary lose their foundation of legitimacy in the constitution.

In this respect, therefore, Kirchheimer argues that democracy and pri- vate law cannot coexist. Wherever the system of private law exists alongside the constitution, the terms of the constitution will inevitably be adjusted to this system, and the political order will be shifted from its legitimate foundation in the constitution. The constitution, Kirchheimer thus asserts, must prevail over private law. The double function of law, he suggests, can only be eliminated if the political and the social terms of the constitution are made identical. This is only possible if the system of private law is directly regulated by the terms of the constitution. Kirchheimer, therefore, clearly goes considerably further than Neumann in his critique of Weimar political economy. What Kirchheimer outlines here is not a technical theory for constitutional organization of the economy, but a proposed restructuration of the entire base of private law and private ownership. The political decisions of the constitution, Kirchheimer outlines, should have priority over all other legal forms. The social provisions in the constitution of the Weimar system should, therefore, preclude the formal autonomy of private law. If, however, private law is recognized as a formally autonomous system, the legitimacy of the constitutional decisions will immediately be replaced by a non-legitimate legal system, whose function is to protect property, and which thus prevails over the constitution. Like Schmitt, therefore, Kirchheimer argues that the lack of clarity in the terms of the constitution produces a polycratic governmental form, in which the fundamental decisions of the polity are undermined by forms of contract which it cannot regulate.

Kirchheimer's theory of law and state is also a seminal theory of late capitalism. In contrast to the nineteenth century, he argues, in the post-1919 era the bourgeoisie has been subject to a series of restrictions, due to the (partial) political emancipation of the proletariat (1964: 53). These restrictions are exemplified by the thwarted attempts to create a social state in the basic rights of the Weimar Constitution. The German bourgeoisie, he argues, has (more or less) successfully driven constitutional reality back into the terms of nineteenth-century legal rule. However, despite this, the bourgeoisie no longer exists as a wholly independent class, and the bourgeois state is forced to legitimize its power in new ways. Externally, Kirchheimer argues, the state is driven by the capitalist economy. However, internally, the capitalist state is also forced to legislate for the economic interests of the varying factions which it incorporates. The state, therefore, Kirchheimer asserts, is divided into a 'sphere of direction' and a 'sphere of distribution':

> Whereas within the 'sphere of direction' the government has to adjust more or less willingly to the autonomy of the capitalist economic order, it has increasingly become a clearing-house within the 'sphere of distribution'.... Its task is to balance the conflicting desires of economic organizations, represented by the highest associations, whilst constantly considering the existing balance of power of the individual groups, so that the prescribed overarching political course will not be jeopardized. (1964: 42–3)

In the second period of bourgeois rule, Kirchheimer thus argues, the state assumes a Janus-faced character. It does not have the power to make decisions about its compliance with the broad terms of the capitalist economic order. However, it is required to legitimize its decisions internally to the distinct classes and interest-groups which have a stake in it. It can only acquire this legitimation by acts of economic allocation or by the distribution of resources, undertaken through alterations in the balance of social legislation.

The modern (late-capitalist) state therefore, Kirchheimer explains, has no real legitimacy outside the economy. It cannot make a decision about its economic orientation. It can only justify this orientation through internal programmes of economic redistribution. Kirchheimer implies, therefore, like Habermas over forty years later, that the decision-making processes of the polity have been made over to the interest-groups of big business.

The modern state can only (at best), he alleges, generate partial or local legitimacy for its actions. Genuine legitimacy is not possible in advanced capitalism. Real legitimacy could only be produced by a state which had sufficient power to decide over its economic orientation and to organize its internal policies in accordance with this decision. In the modern capitalist state, Kirchheimer argues, the lack of fundamental legitimacy is demonstrated by the fact that the internal policies of the state are intended only to soften the effects of its external orientation. The only corrective to such a condition is, Kirchheimer suggests, a socialist democracy, which makes the spheres both of direction and of distribution subordinate to its own decisions.

Although Kirchheimer is clearly an opponent of Schmitt's integral decisionism, his theory of late capitalism evidently contains a Schmittian critique of polycratic forms of order. Like Schmitt, Kirchheimer recognizes that in the conditions of late capitalism the original decisive quality of government has been dissolved (1976c: 62). Manifestly, he claims, decisions are now made outside parliament by social organizations. These, at best, use the governmental apparatus to stabilize their own economic domination (1972d: 105). He sees parliament as a 'simplified and relatively peaceful means of class-struggle' in which 'economic powers, clothed in the form of political parties', pursue their interests (1964: 29). More fundamentally, however, Kirchheimer's theory shares with Schmitt the assumption that true legitimacy is only possible in government which is not determined by the sphere of material reproduction (the economy). The late-capitalist state, Kirchheimer argues, cannot legitimize itself, because it cannot make final decisions about its material orientation. Parliamentary government is, he implies, merely a means of palliating conflicts in the sphere of distribution without affecting the sphere of direction (V. Neumann 1981: 235). Legitimate government, Kirchheimer therefore argues (following Schmitt), is a mode of order which can freely state the terms of its own engagement with the technical-material sphere. Like Schmitt, he insists that the political constitution should mark a univocal decision for a specific political order (1976a: 71). The constitution is, ideally, he argues, a 'programme of action', which sets the terms for the 'organization of a new social order' (1964: 54). Underlying Kirchheimer's thought, therefore, is a quasi-Schmittian anthropology, which asserts that political legitimacy cannot be grounded in the mere administration of material needs. Legitimacy is guaranteed only when material needs are transformed into a collective will.

Both Neumann and Kirchheimer argue, like Schmitt, that the linkage of politics to the technical sphere can only be overcome by decisions, in the form of constitutional law. Unlike Schmitt, Neumann and Kirchheimer see the legitimate decision not as the decision of presidial power, but of popular solidarity, and corresponding modes of political action. Behind Kirchheimer's reflections, especially, is a theory of the executive which strongly recalls Max Adler's idea of the socialist state as a united coercive order (1973: 49), in which the legitimacy of the polity is anchored in the unified solidarity of the labour-force. Both Adler and Kirchheimer claim that real political legitimacy is only engendered if the state is produced directly from the social sphere. This does not imply, however, that the state should merely act as a broker for social interests. It means, rather, that the political will of the state should transform collective needs into positive order, through binding decisions (see Krumbein 1986: 169–70). Through this process of transformation, Kirchheimer implies, the state is able both to represent the material sphere, and to free itself from subordination to it. In short, Kirchheimer argues that a political order which does not from the outset harness the material sphere to its own decisions, and which does not neutralize the antagonisms in this sphere, will ultimately fall victim to the material sphere, and the antagonisms in it. The legal state, therefore, must eventually be superseded by a genuine workers' democracy (1976c: 63).

Kirchheimer, therefore, turns radically against the gradualism and pluralist reformism of the more orthodox thinkers of the SPD, and he moves strongly towards a theoretical fusion of Marx and Schmitt. He argues simply that substantive political decisions must be anterior to law. The corporate-pluralist system of the Weimar Republic, he implies, naively assumes that law itself will reconcile conflict in the form of positive order, as a balance between class-interests. However, Kirchheimer argues that conflicts (especially between classes) must be settled before the law is established. Law, he explains, emanates from concrete conflictual decisions, and it is as the expression of such decisions that it has its legitimacy. The attempt to devolve to law itself the autonomous power to reconcile conflicts invariably produces a situation in which stronger economic bodies will deploy the legislative system for their own interests. This, Kirchheimer argues, is the chronic shortcoming of the Weimar system.

Like Schmitt, therefore, Kirchheimer asserts that law is legitimate only if made in accordance with decisive principles of positive order, which elevate the political order above the material level of technical compromise. This calls implicitly on Schmitt's theory of the friend–foe relation. The state, Kirchheimer intimates, has to decide which class it wishes to represent, and it must be prepared to represent this class to the exclusion of all others. Technical systems of legality, Kirchheimer argues, fudge the decision between classes (between friend and foe) which all forms of political order must make. More fundamentally still, Kirchheimer argues that the conflicts between classes cannot be legitimately resolved under the conditions of capitalism. As soon as the labour-force is integrated into the legal state through universal franchise, the legitimacy of the legal order cannot be guaranteed, for the homogeneous value-system upon which democratic legitimacy is based cannot be sustained. The worker's substantive concept of social democracy, he explains, cannot be harmonized with the formal bourgeois concept of democracy (1976g: 34). Thus the radical differentiation between these two conceptions cannot be balanced out by the legal order. Under the conditions of capitalism, consequently the legal order can only be legal – it cannot be legitimate. Other, extra-juridical, activities are therefore necessary to constitute a decisive political legitimacy which runs through all classes (V. Neumann 1981: 250).

Kirchheimer concludes, in sum, that the salvation of democracy depends on increased mass-participation in political will-formation (1976b: 134; Scheuermann 1994: 72). Socialist parties, he argues, must use democracy itself, not merely its formal techniques, to attack the bourgeois mode of production (1972d: 113). It is only through the assault on the mode of production that political legitimacy can be created and that the substance of the proletarian concept of democracy can be elaborated. The severe separation of legality and legitimacy in the capitalist legal state is for Kirchheimer, thus, the space of radical political activity. Revolutionary struggle is the attempt to create an abiding basis of legitimacy for a proletarian state. In historical contrast to Neumann, Heller and other SPD-theorists, Kirchheimer rejected the policy of the SPD in the last years of the Weimar period, and he refused purely technical-juridical solutions to the class-antagonisms of this time (V. Neumann 1981: 249).

Kirchheimer, clearly, takes Marxism more seriously than Neumann. He rejects the suggestion that mere administrative reform can transform social relations. However, like Neumann, Kirchheimer also outlines a peculiarly state-centred form of Marxism. It is notable that Kirchheimer, unlike Neumann, is unremittingly hostile to calls from the ranks of the SPD for greater economic representation, or even for economic reform of the constitution. He argues: 'The theoretical speculation with which the necessity of a particular economic representation is supposed to be justified (as if the human being could be divided into the citizen of the state and the citizen of the economy) is mistaken.' Even more than Neumann, Kirchheimer thus argues that power should be restricted to political organs of representation (1972b: 107). The component of Schmittian anthropology in Kirchheimer's writings is also more pronounced than in Neumann's thought. For politics to be more than technical compromise, Kirchheimer asserts, the political will must suffuse all areas of activity. The creation of economic constitutions, he implies, merely enchains the citizen to purely material processes.

On its most fundamental theoretical level, Kirchheimer's thought links Schmittian anthropology to Marxist materialism. Human political action, he intimates (with Schmitt, and against Marx), is not merely a reflection of the process of material reproduction. In its political dimension, he suggests, human society has the potential to be self-creating and autonomous. This, however, he argues (with Marx, and against Schmitt), cannot be accomplished through political symbolism. Rather, it depends on the decisive subordination of material, or class-based, antagonisms by means of political programmes (decisions). Like Max Adler, Kirchheimer insists that political democracy and economic democracy must be simultaneous, and that economic democracy should not be extrapolated undialectically from the categories of political being (Adler 1926: 115–16). The detachment of the economic constitution from the political constitution, he suggests, would ultimately play into the hands of those who obstruct both political and economic liberation. The 'rule of the collective over the economy' (1972b: 98) can only be guaranteed, Kirchheimer argues, by a political constitution committed to socialism. Thus, again like Max Adler, he argues against all pluralistic variants on the theory of organized capitalism, and he states firmly that socialism (political legitimacy) can only be created after its economic programme, coupled with the abolition of the class-state, has already been realized – after the material sphere has been neutralized (1972b: 98). Like Neumann, Kirchheimer is not without respect for the formal-universal quality of state-law, and he shows grudging respect for democratic procedure, even in revolutionary party activity (1972d: 112). During Brüning's chancellorship, he came close to recognizing an irreducible moment of universality in bourgeois law (1976f: 106). However, he grasps law as something finally transparent to its sociological basis in economic interest (1976f: 112). For this reason, he (again following Schmitt) presents a pragmatic and volitional conception of law, in which legality only becomes legitimacy if it transposes social needs into a homogeneous political will-formation (1964: 21).

The theoretical examinations undertaken by Neumann and Kirchheimer into the relation between economy, state, law and society culminate in their inquiries into the structure and organization of National Socialism. During this period of their work, Neumann and Kirchheimer were closely connected with the Institute of Social Research in New York. Kirchheimer joined the Institute in 1934, Neumann in 1936. The complex, and often fractious, nature of their relations with other members of the Institute has been much discussed (see Erd 1985: 145). However, both Kirchheimer and Neumann worked in broad collaboration with Horkheimer, Pollock and Marcuse during this time, and their reflections on National Socialism bear the traces of theoretical debate with these, and other, associates of the Institute.

The prevailing interpretation of National Socialism amongst the proponents of Critical Theory in the late 1930s was that it marked a qualitatively new period of capitalism. Friedrich Pollock, most significantly, argued that National Socialism should be interpreted as state-capitalism, which has replaced private capitalism. In state-capitalism, Pollock claims, the state takes on functions previously held by independent entrepreneurs, and private forms of distribution are replaced by state-administered distribution (see Postone and Brick 1993: 250). Like Neumann and Kirchheimer, Pollock sees National Socialism as the product of monopoly capitalism, but he argues that in Hitler's system the function of the monopolies is appropriated by the state itself. In his works of the early 1930s, Pollock integrates this explanation into a theory of the crisis of capitalism. He claims at this point that the productive forces will ultimately overthrow the political and the economic order, as their own liberties are progressively restricted owing to the organization of the economy by the state (1975a: 67). In his later theorization of National Socialism, after his emigration to the USA, Pollock argues that inter-state military conflict is the most likely cause of political crisis (1975b: 26; see also Pollock 1941: 454), and that the conflictual dynamics of capitalism no longer contain the potential for radical upheaval.

Pollock's theory of state-capitalism is an attack on orthodox Marxist explanations of the primacy of economic factors over the political sphere. He asserts that in state-capitalism the political apparatus takes primacy over the economy and the state becomes the chief (if not sole) proprietor of the means of production (see Gangl 1987: 217–18). National Socialism is thus, Pollock argues, the culmination of a process of concentration, through the Weimar period, in which the state has assumed a steering capacity in economic regulation (Brick and Postone 1994: 255). Pollock's theory thus extends Hilferding's earlier structural analysis of organized capitalism. Organized capitalism, however, Pollock argues, has not led to socialism, but to state-capitalism – to National Socialism. Max Horkheimer, analogously, also draws on a theory of state-capitalism in his analysis of National Socialism. The National Socialist state-apparatus, Horkheimer argues, effectively integrates both economic and political bodies in one relatively unified political order (1987a: 283–5; Scheuermann 1994: 157).

The interpretation of National Socialism put forward by Neumann and Kirchheimer differs significantly from such claims for the primacy of the political in Hitler's system. Both Neumann and Kirchheimer, like others at the Institute of Social Research (most notably Marcuse and Alfred Sohn-Rethel), offer a more orthodox Marxist explanation of National Socialism, whose origins they trace to the cartelized organization of Weimar capitalism. In an early essay on National Socialism (1932), Sohn-Rethel anticipated these later debates by describing fascism as the antithesis of state-capitalism (1973: 171). Kirchheimer himself accepts that National Socialism has reformed certain aspects of the capitalist economy, especially in the socialization of the credit supply (the central banks). However, he rejects the suggestion that this is a structural move away from monopoly capitalism. He argues in fact that the economic policies of National Socialism constitute an 'active encouragement of the process of monopolization and cartelization' (1941a: 275). Indeed, the development of National Socialism is, Kirchheimer asserts, simply one phenomenon in the broader historical development from classical liberalism, through mass-democracy, to late capitalism.

In outline, therefore, Kirchheimer argues that government in the conditions of capitalism is always based upon negotiated compromises between economic (private-legal) power-groups and the political executive. These compromises serve to create the political conditions which facilitate the optimal production of excess capital. He explains the governmental conditions of classical liberalism as a 'complex of working agreements among parliamentary representatives and between themselves and the government' (1941a: 264). He defines the pacts underlying mass-democracy as 'agreements between voluntary organizations' – between unions, cartels and syndicates (p. 264). National Socialism, he argues, is based upon 'pacts by which the heads of the compulsory estates distribute power and duty'

(p. 264). The political history of capitalism – and also of National Socialism – is therefore a history of increasingly exclusive economic compromises, through which economic organizations enter bargains with the political apparatus. However, Kirchheimer explains, 'the form and structure of the compromise' on which National Socialism is based is not qualitatively distinct from earlier forms of capitalist compromise (p. 272). Political power under the conditions of capitalism, Kirchheimer indicates, has never really been truly *political*. All formations of capitalist-democratic order prefigure National Socialism through the simple fact that all are based upon a technical balance of economic interests. All previous modes of capitalist government have merely been bargains between private-legal groupings and national executives. No capitalist order, Kirchheimer argues, has ever possessed sovereign political legitimacy.

In Kirchheimer's historical sketch for a political economy of fascism, the compromise of government incorporates an increasingly reduced sphere of society. The liberal compromise, according to which economic freedom is exempted from state-regulation, is replaced by a fluid system of deals by means of which the economic freedom of the most powerful monopolies is guaranteed by the state, to the exclusion of all other social organizations. The government becomes thus 'the largest customer of industry' (1941a: 271), and it is empowered to allocate financial resources according to the promptings of the cartels. National Socialism is, Kirchheimer argues, therefore the last, logical position in the accelerated concentration of capital and cartelization which characterized the Weimar period (1941b: 462). Most importantly, the National Socialist system, Kirchheimer asserts, still contains pluralistic and conflictual elements, the contradictions between which are not yet resolved. The competitive mechanisms in capitalism are not suspended by National Socialism, but are worked out in the sphere of imperialist expansion, of which the state is the appointed instrument and co-ordinator. National Socialism, manifestly therefore, is not state-capitalism. The state does not regulate the economy.

The major work on the theory of National Socialism which emerged during this period is Neumann's *Behemoth*. This work, which contains a wealth of empirical detail, was designed primarily to explain to non-German readers what National Socialism actually was. Neumann wrote it when he was in the employment of the American Strategic Services. Therefore, it is cleansed largely of terminologies particular to Marxist examinations of fascism. At its base, however, is a compelling theory of the relation between monopoly capitalism and Hitler's government, a theory in fact some distance to the left of his earlier reformist positions (Butterwegge 1979: 308).

Neumann, like Kirchheimer, argues strongly against Pollock's suggestion that National Socialism constitutes an economic order which is qualitatively distinct from advanced capitalism.[4] For this reason, it is often alleged that

4 For details of the debates between Neumann and fellow members of the Institute, see Horkheimer 1985: 407.

*Behemoth* cannot be seamlessly linked with the theories of the Institute of Social Research (see Erd 1985: 145; Jay 1973: 163–5; Jarvis 1997: 61–4). Neumann argues, in fact, that the very term 'state-capitalism' is a contradiction in terms (1966: 224). National Socialism, for Neumann, is totalitarian monopoly capitalism. If the state, he argues, has truly arrogated to itself the exclusive ownership of the means of production, the economy can no longer be seen as a capitalist economy, for in such economic conditions the state necessarily destroys the mechanisms which make it possible for capitalism to function. In Hitler's Germany, therefore, Neumann claims that mechanisms of antagonism and compromise which characterize capitalism have not been eliminated. Instead, they have been transferred into the level of the party-executive, where they are 'covered up by a bureaucratic apparatus and by the ideology of the people's community' (1966: 227). However, the semblance of state-regulated order is, Neumann explains, merely an ideological device to obscure the increased power of monopoly bodies which support the government. These bodies use the state as a hinge in their bid to dedicate the economy to imperialist expansion, through war (p. 34). Like Kirchheimer, Neumann sees National Socialism as a direct continuation of the earlier organization of the economy in cartels (p. 266). He also pays special attention to the government's monopoly of the central banks, often cited as the hallmark of state-capitalism. In reference to Hilferding's much earlier treatise on the role of the banks in monopoly capitalism (1910: 231), however, Neumann does not view the fusion of the banks and the political system as a symptom of state-capitalism. Rather, he sees it as proof that 'the short-term interests of the banks and of the government have become almost identical' (1966: 326), and that the integration of the banks into the governmental apparatus is of use to the monopolies. Credit-control through systemic regulation of the banks finally strengthens the monopolies, Neumann argues, for the firms which depend on credit are liquidated, and absorbed by the cartels. Both the economic and political power of the cartels increases by consequence. In this regard, Neumann's rejection of Pollock's theory of state-capitalism merely repeats his earlier rejection of Hilferding's theory of organized capitalism.

Neumann interprets the state-apparatus of National Socialism as a broad hegemonic bloc, consisting of heavy industry, the party, bureaucracy and the armed forces (1966: 361). Government is therefore a 'small group of powerful industrial, financial and agrarian monopolists tending to coalesce with a group of party hierarchs into one single bloc disposing of the means of production and the means of violence' (p. 634). This, most especially, illuminates Neumann's hostility to the concept of state-capitalism. In his representation of the National Socialist elite as a broad bloc of conflicting but hegemonic interest-groups, Neumann implies that the National Socialist state is not, in fact, a state at all (p. 467). The system of coercion under Hitler's rule is instead, he argues, a structure of direct and institutionally fluid compulsion, which lacks both the sovereign authority of universal law and the unified character of a rational state (p. 470).

Like Pollock, therefore, Neumann also argues that certain political characteristics have emerged in National Socialism which mark it out from other systems. However, Neumann interprets the particular forms of the direction-sphere in National Socialism as the 'systemically inevitable product of the development of capitalist economic society' (Söllner 1979: 212). Neumann thus inverts Pollock's theory of the primacy of political factors as the determining trait of state-capitalism. He views the National Socialist government as an agglomerate of shifting economic interests which compete for power over the executive. In totalitarian monopoly capitalism, the party executive merely translates structures of previously extra-political domination into governmental edict, in both internal and external politics.

It is in this regard that the fundamental distinction between Neumann and other associates of the Institute of Social Research becomes most manifest. Common to all thinkers connected with the Frankfurt School is the argument that the systems of technical reason in mass-capitalism have attained a level of such dominance that all social interaction is pre-formed by them. Neumann and Kirchheimer are no exceptions to this. However, each exponent of Critical Theory also outlines modes of praxis in which human consciousness is able, at least in part, to evade the compulsion of technical reason. Adorno links this possibility to certain forms of cultural production, which indicate the possible conditions of life not dominated by economic rationality (1976: 12). Horkheimer argues that genuine social critique is always motivated by the demand for life not wholly determined by pure need (1987b: 257). Walter Benjamin argues that all cultural praxis exists simultaneously both inside and outside the processes of technical-capitalist domination (1974: 702). Neumann and Kirchheimer, however, argue (like Arendt after them) that it is political action itself which indicates the opportunity for liberation from compulsory obligation to the technical sphere. In this respect, Neumann and Kirchheimer carry an aspect of Schmitt's theory of politics into their version of Critical Theory. Schmitt himself argues that human action can be broken into two components: the material or technical, which is subordinate to natural reproduction, and the political, which is guided by ideas or ethics, and therefore separate from the life-process. Neumann and Kirchheimer argue accordingly that the production of binding, universal norms elevates political praxis above the systems of material reproduction. In this respect, they invest a degree of importance in political action which is foreign to the general cultural and socio-psychological theories of the Institute of Social Research.

Fundamental to the thinking of Neumann and Kirchheimer, therefore, is a faith in the sovereign power of the state to order the economy (V. Neumann 1984: 76), to limit the impact of the technical sphere on human life, and thereby to create the preconditions of real – political – liberty. Precisely for this reason, Neumann understands the National Socialist 'state' as a mere instrument of the material sphere, without the dignity of political status. Neumann's rejection of Pollock's theory of the primacy of the political in National Socialism revolves around a strong category of politics. The strength of this category is in fact at the base of the disagreement between Neumann and Pollock. For Neumann, the very fact that the moment of genuine politics has been attenuated by technical and pluralist (private-legal) modes of coercion is responsible for the triumph of Hitler's party. Hitler's system, Neumann argues, is not *political* at all, but a mere sporadic refraction of economic interests. It has triumphed because of the absence, not the primacy, of the political. Pollock's suggestion that National Socialism marks the primacy of the political is, for Neumann and Kirchheimer, not only empirically incorrect. It is a most spectacular mis-interpretation of the conditions of human freedom.

It is, lastly, a measure of Neumann's significance that his reflections on law, economy and politics came to set the terms for the body of left-oriented constitutional thinking after 1945. After his return to Germany, Neumann's earlier theories on the necessity of a social constitution fed into the broad discussion of the terms of the Basic Law of 1949, the founding document of the Federal Republic. Concepts developed in the Weimar SPD generally regained currency-value during this time. Heller's theory of the social-legal state, most especially, was cemented in Article 20 of the Basic Law (U. K. Preuß 1973: 94). In this last period of his political involvement, before his death in 1954, Neumann again advocated the creation of a strong central state, equipped with powers to control industry and to redistribute national income. However, by this stage Neumann had moved to a position which partially modified the economic-constitutional aspects of his earlier thought. After 1945, he argued decisively against the quasi-syndicalist integration of unions in governmental administration (1978i: 395). Despite his positive evaluation of the constitutional rights of professional councils (1978j: 345), he saw the projected co-determination laws – which drew directly from earlier economic-democratic theory (see E. Schmidt 1970: 62) – as a means of securing the political compliance of the unions (1978: 396). He thus insisted again that parliament itself should be the sole location for the resolution of social antagonism. The influence of Neumann on constitutional debate on the left of the SPD during the early years of the Federal Republic is most evident in the works of Wolfgang Abendroth (1967a: 122), who applied Neumann's theories to issues of anti-monopoly legislation and the latent threat of National Socialism in post-1945 Germany (1967b: 286–7).

Neumann's last word is contained in his great essay 'The Concept of Political Freedom' (1953), which is in many regards a short-hand summary of all his primary concerns. Neumann returns here to his preoccupation with the division between state and economy, between citizen and bour-geois, in the writings of Schmitt and the early Marx. In doing so, however, he turns vehemently against both his precursors (Scheuermann 1994: 192). Implementing both a legal-theoretical and a psychological methodology, he argues that democratic-political participation is the sole means by which to overcome the economic alienation of labour in capitalism and the political-psychological alienation of the subject from the seat of power (1967b: 124). Democracy can, he thus argues, only be understood as a unity of political and economic liberation. Whilst in Neumann's earlier writings his thought relies on clear, but half-suppressed, ius-natural preconditions, here his association of genuine integrative democracy and political morality is made most explicit. 'Democracy', he argues, 'is not simply a political system like any other. Its essence resides in the execution of great social changes, which maximize the freedom of the person. . . . Its integrating element is of moral character, either freedom or justice' (1967b: 133). At the core of his post-war evaluation of democracy is therefore the familiar argument that the participatory dimension to democracy offers to citizens the opportunity to be more than what they are in the economy. Participatory democracy facilitates, Neumann argues, both the reconciliation of antagonisms in the material sphere and, through this, the self-realization of citizens in the political sphere. Active democracy is, therefore, the only possible mediation of freedom and power (1967b: 104). In this last essay, Neumann thus returns to the great preoccupation of German political theory. He – like Weber and Hegel before him, and Habermas after him – reflects on the preconditions for the creation of a public political society in which the political liberty of public citizens is co-original with their social liberty as private individuals. The establishment of such a society depends, Neumann argues, on the active component of democracy, by means of which the private needs of citizens are drawn into public, active discourse, and thus reconciled. Neumann, a decade before Habermas, thus argues that the *vita activa* in the public sphere is the basis of democracy – and the answer to the anti-democratic tradition in Germany.

These last observations can, of course, be interpreted as an overly optimistic endorsement of democracy, expressed after the twelve-year ordeal of National Socialism (Söllner 1982a: 288). Ultimately, however, Neumann's last writings remain a tellingly inconclusive lament. Like Arendt, Neumann argues that political liberty is only possible within the terms of popular sovereignty, but that these terms presuppose a ceaseless active refiguration of political life, which is hardly possible in modern mass-democracies. Indeed, Neumann's recourse to an ethical foundation for law in his last writings can be interpreted as an index of the ambiguity which runs through all his writings. Neumann always asserts that democratic law is both the technical means by which the bourgeoisie stabilizes its position and a structure through which state-power can be constituted as popular sovereignty. His ultimate description of genuine political and economic democracy, however, relies on an almost despairing shift to an ethical discourse, which claims that democracy is only sustainable on the basis of moral motivations. The lamenting tone of the reflection on power in his last work is no coincidence. The challenge of popular sovereignty, obtained only by the mediation of private needs and public existence, remains, for Neumann, a necessary but impossible challenge.

## Selected further reading

Alway, Joan (1995) *Critical Theory and Political Possibilities: Conceptions of Emancipatory Politics in the Works of Horkheimer, Adorno, Marcuse, and Habermas* (London/Westport: Greenwood Press).

Brick, Barbara and Postone, Moishe (1994) 'Friedrich Pollock and the "Primacy of the Political": A Critical Reexamination', in: Jay Bernstein (ed.), *The Frankfurt School: Critical Assessment*, vol. 1 (London/New York: Routledge) pp. 249–63.

Jay, Martin (1973) *The Dialectical Imagination: A History of the Frankfurt School and the Institute of Social Research, 1923–1950* (Berkeley/Los Angeles: University of California Press.)

Postone, Moishe and Brick, Barbara (1993) 'Critical Theory and Political Economy', in: Seyla Benhabib et al. (eds), *On Max Horkheimer: New Perspectives* (Cambridge, Mass.: MIT Press), pp. 215–57.

Scheuermann, William E. (1994) *Between the Norm and the Exception: The Frankfurt School and the Rule of Law* (Cambridge, Mass./London: MIT Press).

Scheuermann, William E. (1996) 'Introduction', in: *The Rule of Law under Siege: Selected Essays of Franz L. Neumann and Otto Kirchheimer* (Berkeley/Los Angeles/London: University of California Press), pp. 1–25.

Söllner, Alfons (1987) 'Beyond Carl Schmitt: Political Theory in the Frankfurt School', *Telos* 71.

# 4

# *Jürgen Habermas*

The most influential figure to have emerged from the second generation of the Frankfurt School, and indeed the most influential thinker in the history of post-war Germany, is Jürgen Habermas. Naturally, it is not possible here to give an all-embracing critical account of Habermas's highly diverse and voluminous writings, which range from the 1950s to the present. This chapter will therefore attempt solely to draw out Habermas's theory of politics, and to illuminate its historical context in the overall development of German politics.

Habermas's first major work, *Structural Transformation of the Public Sphere* (1962), shows clear traces of the influence of the first generation of the Frankfurt School. This work, a significant milestone in the reflection on governmental legitimacy in the early years of the Federal Republic (see Ebbighausen 1973: 27), combines aspects of Adorno's critical-sociological inquiries into the role of the media in modern society with the critique of modern democracy put forward by Neumann and Kirchheimer. However, in many respects the key antecedent for this work is Max Weber's sociology of law and politics. In *Structural Transformation*, Habermas argues that the basic principles of Western democracy have been betrayed by the political order of modern society. Like Weber, he argues that this betrayal is due to the division of the political order into a formal sphere of private interest and a sphere of administrative operation, with no link between them. Like Weber, Habermas also attempts to outline a means of overcoming this separation. Whereas Weber, to this end, puts forward a theory of political integration, Habermas argues that only the existence of a strong public sphere, situated above the private-economic sphere, but below the political apparatus, can guarantee genuine democracy.

*Structural Transformation of the Public Sphere* contains a history of modern democracy. Habermas outlines how in the classical-bourgeois period of democracy, after the differentation of the political system as an organ of control separate from economy, the state operated as a body with genuinely representative functions. In classical-bourgeois democracy, Habermas argues, the private needs of property-owners – the franchise – constituted a more or less homogeneous set of interests. These were mediated with the state in the public sphere (1990e: 142). In classical-bourgeois society, Habermas argues, there existed a variety of literary forms (such as journals, reading-circles, debating arenas), which acted as instruments of public will-formation, through which public issues were subject to general scrutiny, and thus mediated through common discussion (1990e: 223). Habermas, therefore, identifies the emergence of modern political democracy, in the form of the legal state, with the self-constitution of the bourgeoisie as a class which could assert its needs through the public sphere, and which could thereby obtain direct impact on the legislative functions of government. Owing to its strong public sphere, classical-bourgeois democracy, Habermas argues, created a legislative order anchored in 'public opinion'. Its political order was not interpretable simply as 'domination' (*Herrschaft*; 1990e: 152).

The public sphere has special status in Habermas's thought for two reasons. Firstly, it is the space which emerges when state and economy are separated after the erosion of the absolutist system. It is therefore the space of Enlightenment. Secondly, however, it is also the location of discourse, which emerges when human rationality is separated from theological presuppositions, when human rationality tests its own potentials, freed from either pure need or pure (theological) certainty. In this respect, also, the public sphere is the space of Enlightenment. Contrary to interpretations of Habermas as an anti-institutional theorist (Schelsky 1980b: 87), Habermas is at heart a utopian theorist of institutions. In the public sphere, the institution of law, especially, acquires elevated significance. In the emergence of a public sphere, situated above material needs, detached from pre-secular conviction, and vertically open to the state, Habermas imagines – like Kant before him – that law can provide a bridge between the political sphere and the private sphere, and that in law citizens can recognize themselves as both privately and publicly autonomous (1976a: 265). In the public sphere, therefore, law – at least potentially – takes the place of theology, as a set of references in which the terms of secular political identity can be established (1976a: 263–4).

In this stylized representation of classical political democracy, Habermas outlines a consensual theory of legitimacy, according to which genuinely legitimate government is secured only when private needs are mediated through the discursive channels of the public sphere, and in which public opinion plays a regulatory role in the legislative. However, Habermas also argues that the bourgeois vision of the collective rule of law is ultimately ideological. Private interests, Habermas argues, are unified in bourgeois democracy only to the extent that early democracy is based upon 'the fictional identity of private persons, assembled as a public, in their dual role as property-owners and people' (1990e: 121). The unified nature of bourgeois democracy is, consequently, tenable only as long as the unity of private interest is maintained – until private interests are admitted to the franchise which contradict the general interest in the maintenance of existing property-relations. The link between Habermas and Neumann is rarely treated extensively in receptions of his work, but his early thought is clearly continuous with Neumann's own ambiguous commitment to the legal state. Both Neumann and Habermas imply that democratic liberty in the constitution of power ultimately presupposes equality in the material sphere. Both, however, also recognize the worth of political democracy as a value in itself.

In these early works, moreover, Habermas's thought revolves in part around a complex reception and critique of Kant and Aristotle. On one hand, Habermas follows Kant's argument that private and public life can be reconciled through law. On the other hand, however, he makes a crucial Aristotelian addition to Kant's philosophy. Habermas does not believe that the public arena can be based upon the representation of private-legal interests (see Saage 1983: 255). Habermas – like Arendt, also, in the late 1950s (1958b: 32–3; see also Arendt 1982: 18) – thus draws out the substantial component of Kant's notion of public law, which indicates that public life, simply by virtue of its communicative nature, detaches interests from private obligations (Kant 1966a: 250; see also Saner 1982: 125). In his reception of Kant, in consequence, Habermas plays down the aspect of possessive contractarianism in Kant's legal theory. He supplements this with an anthropological argument (partly implied by Kant himself), which claims that the quality of public/political communication necessarily elevates interests above the level of private exclusivity (see Villa 1996: 4; Chambers 1996: 184–5), and that public life transforms interests into interactively elaborated, common commitments. Against Kant, but with Aristotle and Arendt, therefore, Habermas implies that public life cannot be grasped in terms of pre-public – or pre-political – rights or needs (F. D. Miller 1995: 122). In the good polity, public interaction itself sets, hermeneutically, the terms for rights and order. Nonetheless, against more conservative readings of Aristotle, Habermas's interactive model of political life still contains a strongly Kantian theory of law. Political institutions, Habermas insists, must correspond to norms of practical reason. They cannot be justified solely by common ethics.

Also at the base of Habermas's early work is a structuration of the private, the public and the political spheres which is strongly influenced by Hannah Arendt's brand of neo-Aristotelianism (Arendt 1958a: 38; see Villa 1996: 6). Habermas (like Arendt) argues that different forms of rationality correspond to different areas of human activity. Naturally, Habermas does not follow Arendt in arguing that the public sphere possesses an absolute dignity, separated absolutely from civil society. However, he explains that the political rationality of public will-formation is disrupted when the public sphere is determined and preoccupied by the development of technical strategies for the resolution of social issues. The integrity of the public sphere, and its normative impact on political organization, can only be sustained if the political apparatus itself is not forced to intervene in the private sphere in order to resolve private conflicts of interest (1990e: 225). Habermas (like Arendt) thus makes the distinction, crucial for his later work, between political interaction and social labour (see also Habermas 1963a: 46). The integrity of political will-formation is possible only if the public sphere is not wholly determined by the need to satisfy specific social interests – if (here Habermas follows Arendt) it is not chained to the life-process. In subsequent writings, Habermas expands this argument to develop the theory that human communication can draw on three resources – power, money and solidarity – and that the latter resource constitutes the medium of genuinely legitimate politics (1985a: 158). The legitimate political will, he indicates in his early work, cannot be formed through strategic action, planning or economic administration, but only through the free interaction of citizens. Non-technical interaction is thus the foundation of real politics (Zöller 1975: 182). Ideally, Habermas understands the state, in its classical-democratic conception, as an overarching integrative body whose normative base is anchored in the interactions of citizens, but which is elevated above private needs by the public sphere, where private needs are reconciled and unified (see Glaser 1972: 138).

Habermas sets out his theory of modern democracy partly as a general history of late capitalism. At the stage of late capitalism, he claims, the rationality of political interaction has been usurped by the technical rationality of administration, and the traditional resources of non-technical communication – especially in the public sphere – have been eroded (Zöller 1975: 232). Habermas sees the demise of the public sphere as a product of the onus placed upon the state (especially in late nineteenth-century Germany) to intervene in the private sphere, and to reconcile antagonisms between increasingly powerful social organizations. The state thus legitimizes its actions on the basis of its ability to reach into the private sphere and settle private conflicts, not because it represents a public consensus. Like Neumann and Kirchheimer, Habermas also argues that such socialization of state-activity coincides with the partial transfer of state-authority to private corporations, and it thus produces semi-private systems of authority which evade the need for legitimate will-formation. Habermas describes how 'the expansion of public authority over private spheres is connected with the contrary process of the substitution of state power by social power' (1990e: 226). The social sphere is itself politicized by this process, and the classical-democratic distinction between private, public and political is lost. The status of the public sphere as a locus in which social interests can be mediated by free discussion is rendered invalid by the politicization of the private sphere by governmental and quasi-governmental bodies. The public sphere thus becomes indivisible from the sphere of private conflict (and private law).

Habermas thus ascribes the collapse of classical-bourgeois democracy to a variety of factors. It is due, broadly, to the emergence of conflicting corporate interest-groups, each of which seeks a stake in the legislative body; to the intervention of the state in social conflicts; and to the demand that the state should balance the antagonisms in civil society (1990e: 230). Most of all, however, Habermas argues (like Neumann and Kirchheimer) that the dissolution of classical democracy is due to its own ideological character. As soon as the terms of democracy are even partially extended to the non-property-owning classes, the assumption that public will-formation can mediate private interests into the state loses its validity. In such conditions, the state itself must abdicate its representative function in order to maintain a balance of interests between the plural bodies which struggle for influence. As a result, in advanced capitalist societies the state cannot found itself upon norms produced and universally accepted in society. The basis of legitimacy in modern political society must therefore, Habermas argues, be artificially manufactured – for the state must ceaselessly attempt to produce the motivations for obedience which Habermas (like Weber) defines as legitimation. The political foundation of discursive legitimacy is therefore superseded by the technical endeavour to secure popular belief and commitment.

Habermas's earliest writings call upon very different aspects of Critical Theory. Like Neumann and Kirchheimer, Habermas argues that pluralist social bodies obstruct the formation of genuine democracy (1990e: 237). The welfare-state particularly, Habermas explains, cements a balance of interests between the classes and interest-groups, and thereby prevents real democratic will-formation (p. 294). The welfare-state locks the spheres of private and public law together as an 'indistinguishable functional connection' (p. 234), and it thus creates an order in which the genuine reconciliation of private and public life is impeded. However, Habermas's debt to later aspects of Critical Theory is also pronounced. Modern citizens, Habermas argues, are doomed to increasing passivity as the private sphere is invaded by television and other technical media of communication. This, Habermas (like Adorno) argues, is a crucial factor in the erosion of real democracy.[1] The spurious public sphere of mass-media is, for Habermas, the very antithesis of the active publicity of genuine democracy (1990e: 261). In late capitalism, in sum, the public sphere is dominated by techniques for administering class-compromise, and the integrity of the private sphere is dismantled in favour of the pseudo-intimacy of regulated leisure and manufactured liberty (p. 247). The private sphere, which in classical democracy is the genetic origin of the public will, is thus reduced to 'the inner regions of the nuclear family, largely stripped of function and weakened in its authority' (p. 247).

---

1 Habermas duplicates and criticizes simultaneously many aspects of the theories of technology put forward by Schelsky and Gehlen. See Schelsky 1965: 455.

However, Habermas's reflections on the political malaise of mass-democracy also refer to more general debates in the Federal Republic in the 1950s. Like many thinkers of this time (including figures on the right), Habermas reflects critically on the technicization of the political apparatus through the social control-mechanisms of the welfare-state. Certain aspects of his early work share common preoccupations with such conservative thinkers as Ernst Rudolf Huber (1965: 268), Ernst Forsthoff (1968a: 191–2) and Werner Weber (1951: 43), each of whom also claims, variously, that the modern state is overburdened by its social-pluralist functionalization. Habermas, naturally, does not subscribe to the statist convictions of such post-Schmittian theorists. However, he implies that true politics cannot be reduced to the establishment of plans, strategies or *techniques* for government (1963b: 244). Politics, strictly, is a mode of interaction – between state and economy – in which private autonomy and public liberty are mediated. For Habermas, politics, therefore, has (as for Schmitt, Neumann and Kirchheimer) a unique anthropological quality, as a mode of action in which citizens detach themselves from simple *needs*. Habermas also argues here against other conservative social theorists of the late 1950s and early 1960s, especially Arnold Gehlen (1957: 105) and Helmut Schelsky, who claim that democracy has lost its meaning through autonomous processes of technologization (see Outhwaite 1994: 21), and that the human-normative essence of law has been replaced by mere technical forms of administration (Schelsky 1965: 435; 1970: 23). Historically, the anti-normative dimension to the institutionalism of Gehlen and Schelsky provides a theoretical reflection of the general acquiescence in the process of political restoration after 1945. Against such post-normative conceptions of politics, however, Habermas articulates his own discursive project for the salvation of human practical reason in the public sphere.

Like earlier thinkers in the tradition of Critical Theory, Habermas asserts therefore that the anthropological foundations of political liberalism were, despite their subsequent ideological implications, not originally ideological in character. The sources of active politics, he suggests, can genuinely be found in the classical model of bourgeois democracy. Habermas states:

> Bourgeois culture was not only ideology. Only because the reasoning of private people in the salons, clubs and reading circles was not immediately subordinate to the cycle of production and consumption, the dictate of the necessities of life; only because, on the contrary, in this Greek sense of an emancipation from the necessities of life, it possessed 'political character' even in its merely literary form (self-expression through new experiences of subjectivity), could the idea, which was later reduced to ideology, be constituted at all – namely humanity. (1990e: 248)

Thus, like Arendt, Habermas argues that the classical-republican model of democratic interaction must be invoked, normatively, as the modality of good, active politics. At the very heart of Habermas's early work – like his most recent writings – is a universal-anthropological conception of popular sovereignty and good politics, which indicates that the interactive ethic of politics contains the latent possibility of good life – or even natural right (J. Ritter 1969b: 76). This has its origins in a fusion of Aristotelianism and classical republicanism, but it also contains a shot of Marx.

In contrast to this, however, Habermas argues that the functional role of the modern state, which is an organ designed to broker compromises between autonomous social bodies, and thus to circumvent the public sphere, has disastrous consequences for democratic political life. The functional aspect of the state, he argues, destroys the integrity of the politically sentient body of the citizenry (1990e: 266). It offers technical compromises as solutions for deep-lying social antagonisms, and it thus relieves citizens of the need to realize fully their own interests in the public sphere. Above all, it ensures that modern politics is always subordinate to the fulfilment of material interests. The balancing of material needs becomes the chief grounds for political engagement and the chief means by which the state justifies itself. Far from guaranteeing social equality, therefore, the materialization of the modern state, as the welfare-state, leads to a refeudalization of society. The political executive is transposed into the hands of a few representative – or quasi-plebiscitary – figures who rely on the more or less passive compliance of the population. The economy is resubjected to political command. The key attribute of Western democracy, namely the integrity of the legislature, is also subtly undermined in this de-politicization of power, for the democratic quality of law is eroded by the acquiescence of the citizens and by the deals made by non-parliamentary bodies (1990e: 277). The classical function of the public sphere as a locus which enables the mediation between state and society is thus replaced by a system in which both the public and the private sphere are themselves structurally annexed by the social organizations which compete for a share in the state (1990e: 273). The public sphere is juridified from above by a state which is forced constantly to balance social interests against each other.

Evidently, Habermas's critique of modern democracy is specific to Germany. Habermas's history of modern democracy assesses, in essence, the preconditions for the absence of democracy in Germany. The sphere of interaction between the private sphere and the political system, Habermas indicates, never developed fully in Germany. Private and public law remain complexly fused, but not mediated. The political sphere regulates the economy, but the political sphere is also open to organized coercion from the economy. The separation of state and economy which Habermas views as the precondition of modern democracy has, he argues, therefore never been finally achieved in Germany. Above all, he indicates, this influences the production of law. Legitimate democratic law can – according to Habermas – only be produced in a sphere which is dominated neither by the technical apparatus of the state nor by the interests of economic bodies.

Legitimate law, thus, relies on the existence of a sphere in which subjective rights and political obligations originate from each other, and are therefore neither strictly private nor strictly public. Like Weber, Habermas here seeks to outline a theory of politics in which private freedom and public power are integrally connected. His solution to this issue is, however, anti-Weberian. Legitimate law, Habermas argues (echoing Neumann, Kirchheimer and, distantly, Schmitt), overcomes the duality between the formality of economic law and the authority of state-law only if it is generated by the communicative power of the public sphere, which is situated above the system of needs (economy) but below the system of the executive. In this light, *Structural Transformation of the Political Sphere* is, historically, a lamenting commentary on the (alleged) absence of a democratic tradition in Germany.

However, *Structural Transformation* also includes a complex commentary on the failure of the opportunity for genuine political foundation in Germany, after 1945. It is a damning critique of the specific conditions of the Federal Republic under Adenauer's administration.

The economic and political orientation of the Federal Republic in its earliest years was, under the strong influence of American legislation, intended as a break with the corporate system of the Wilhelmine, Weimar and National Socialist eras. The model of the 'social market-economy' which Ludwig Erhard (Minister of Economics 1949–63) put forward as the CDU-manifesto for the first post-war elections in 1949, and which became economic orthodoxy through the 1950s, was in many respects a compromise between models of dirigistic and non-interventionist economic administration. Ordo-liberal economic theory, which argued that the state should set the parameters for the competitive market, and should co-ordinate industrial production in the name of national interest (Eucken 1951: 72), had a discernible influence on Erhard (see Blum 1969: 6). Nonetheless, the basic principles of the social market-economy determined that free competition would be the foundation of the new economic order (Nichols 1994: 240), and that state-planning would be limited to welfare-provisions (Blum 1969: 103). Although the first economic manifestos of the CDU, most notably the Aahlen Programme of 1947, had echoed aspects of Christian-socialist economic theory (Berg-Schlosser 1979: 103), such policies were soon abandoned. Erhard expressly sanctioned the autonomy of the market, and rejected state-control (Ambrosius 1979: 309–10). Similarly, the American occupying forces introduced military statutes to prevent the re-establishment of interventionist systems of economic administration (Robert 1976: 97–8). Other allies also introduced measures to de-couple industry from political control (Berghahn 1985: 98). The Parliamentary Council, responsible for the creation of the new constitution in 1948–9, voiced strong opposition to all collectivist forms of economic policy, including cartelization (Hüttenberger 1976: 288). Erhard's first proposals for the economic policy of the CDU (issued in June 1948) anticipated the passing of effective anti-cartel legislation (C. E. Fischer 1954: 426).

Throughout the late 1940s and the 1950s Erhard remained an advocate of anti-cartel legislation, at times insisting that he would continue to act as Minister of Economics only on condition that anti-cartel legislation were passed (Robert 1976: 245).

Despite Erhard's policies, however, it is striking that by the mid-1950s many traditional traits of the German economic and political system had begun to re-emerge in the Federal Republic. Notably, anti-cartel legislation was not finally passed by the Bundestag until July 1957. This legislation represented a diluted version of the initial proposals for anti-monopoly laws, and it did little to limit the concentration of economic power (Robert 1976: 245). Indeed, it has been widely, but not unanimously (Nichols 1994: 292), argued that the corporate structures of inter-war Germany were in fact reinforced in the West soon after the war. Adenauer was notably more enthusiastic than Erhard about the promotion of direct links between government and business (Hüttenberger 1976: 307; Baring 1972: 52–4). By 1950 the reformed Federation of German Industry (always opposed to the anti-cartel legislation) had forged close links with the political executive (Braunthal 1965: 230; Tornow 1979: 239). More significantly still, high-level business associations became increasingly influential in economic government during the Korean War (1950–3), when industrial products of the Federal Republic were required internationally for rearmament-programmes (Abelshauser 1983: 75). Werner Abelshauser has argued extensively that representatives of economic organizations assisted the government during the crisis by directing investment into the production of commodities required by the American military (1987: 22). This established a closer linkage between economic and political power than was foreseen by the original conception of the social market-economy (Abelshauser 1981: 312). Therefore, Erhard's plan for the renunciation of corporate politics lasted (arguably) only from 1948 until 1951 (Abelshauser 1983: 81). The subsequent structuring of the economy of the Federal Republic showed, at least in part, a return to an informal balancing of political and economic interests, through which executive power was placed in the hands of non-elected bodies. Even historians less hostile to corporate government have stressed the significance of extra-parliamentary interest-groups in the early years of the Federal Republic as a reaction against the state-control of the economy in the Hitler period (see Bracher 1964: 119). Habermas's critique of capitalist pluralism can clearly be situated in this context.

It is important to note, however, that the re-creation of the system of capitalist pluralism through the 1950s did not initially meet with un-animous support. In the immediate aftermath of the war, the German unions, encouraged especially by representatives of Attlee's government in the British occupation zone, hoped to cement statutory forms of economic democracy, including state investment-planning and rights of economic co-determination, in the Basic Law of the Federal Republic (Schönhoven 1987: 209). Kurt Schumacher, the post-war leader of the

SPD, sought to introduce economic chambers of co-determination, and to secure the representation of unions in supervisory councils in private companies (Fitting 1977: 376). Like the Weimar Constitution, the Basic Law was at its most ambiguous in its provisions for economic administration (see Doemming et al. 1951: 144, 154, 157), and it showed in this respect the traces of inter-fractional disagreements and pragmatic bargains.[2] Carlo Schmid (the SPD-deputy in the Parliamentary Council) had especially attempted to synthesize models of social and legal democracy in the Basic Law. The traces of Schmid's interventions remained manifest in Articles 20 and 28. In their own constitutions, before the composition of the Parliamentary Council, various federal regions (*Länder*) had also passed socialization-laws, which provided for the state-control of key industries (see Abendroth 1967a: 118), although these laws were not recognized by American occupying forces (Bernecker 1979: 277). Even the governmental policy of the CDU did not emphatically endorse capitalism. Erhard's model of the social-market economy was, in part, a strategic compromise between the demands of the labour-movement, the initial anti-capitalist programmes of the CDU itself and the pro-capitalist imperatives of American occupation-forces and German industry, which were influential in the CDU (Altvater et al. 1979: 83). The transition to the capitalist-democratic order was, in short, not the result of popular debate or demand. It was imposed, firstly by the Economic Council in Frankfurt (Antoni 1991: 150), and it was sanctioned, secondly, by the Basic Law (Berghahn 1985: 209). The demands of the unions were initially placated by the insistence of the SPD that the Basic Law was merely a provisional document, which would be subject to later modification – especially in respect of economic administration (Seifert 1967: 79). The right to strike was not anchored in the catalogue of rights in the Basic Law, although this right was given limited recognition in 1955 (Schönhoven 1987: 222–3). Despite the failure of union policies during the period of transition, in 1951 the unions achieved partial success by securing the implementation of co-determination laws in the coal and steel industries.

However, the mode of economic administration in the 1950s represented a far more successful – or at least more harmonious – brand of corporatism than the fraught agreements of the Weimar Republic. The development of union and labour law during the early years of the Federal Republic followed a course which was markedly different from the Weimar period. Wage-relations in the Federal Republic were located (by legislation of March 1949) outside the political order (Armingeon 1988: 119–20). The autonomy of wage-relations guaranteed by this legislation was endorsed by both employers and unions throughout the 1950s (Schönhoven 1987: 222). The first decade of the Federal Republic, characterized by extremely rapid

---

2 Discussions in the German unions during the interim government of the allied Control Council demonstrate the resistance to the imposition of the capitalist economic order, and in fact show similarities with the models of economic democracy of the 1920s. See E. Schmidt 1970: 62, 90, 157.

economic growth, was also marked by a model of relatively peaceful social partnership, in which negotiations between unions and employers were (unlike in the Weimar period) not directly politicized, in which wage-levels and welfare-provisions continued to rise steadily (Abelshauser 1987: 33), and in which the labour-force (at least after the federal elections of 1953) adjusted to a co-operative function in the market-economy (Schönhoven 1987: 219). Helmut Schmidt's later corporate ideal of the *Modell Deutschland*, based on industrial partnership, the social integration of the workforce and broad co-operation in the maintenance of the international competitiveness of export-goods, has its origins in this period (Esser and Fach 1981: 164). In the development of the liberal–conservative corporate system of the Federal Republic in the 1950s, it is also of great importance that the legal status of political parties had changed significantly since the Weimar period. The Basic Law expressly recognized parties as active components in the popular will-formation. Social organizations, although not given the same status, were also recognized in the catalogue of basic and civil rights (Berghahn 1985: 199). The legal status of the unions was also reinforced throughout the 1950s. The 1950s model of social partnership and collective co-operation – underpinned by loosely ordo-liberal economic concepts – thus depended on the existence of legally protected negotiating organs, each committed loosely to the corporate task of national stabilization.

In many respects, therefore, Habermas's historical inquiries into the structural weaknesses of the German democratic tradition are a response to the conditions of the 1950s, which outlines a critique of ordo-liberalism and corporate capitalism. During the 1950s, the system of government in the Federal Republic shifted once again towards a pluralist mode of balanced interests, in which parliament's power was structurally limited, in which political decisions accorded with macro-economic guidelines and were based upon technical or strategic consensus between organized bodies. Underlying Habermas's reflections in *Structural Transformation* is the fear that modern society (implicitly, the Federal Republic) is at once rendered both rigidly static and structurally fragile by the technical modes of governance which have emerged from corporate agreements. Habermas describes a society in which the active components of human reason, volition or even conflict have been eliminated in order to stabilize the collective interests of social groups and organizations (labour and capital) against each other. The political sphere, Habermas thus asserts, is no longer subject to 'rationalization in the medium of public reasoning of private persons', but merely 'to the reciprocal control of rival organizations' (1990e: 311). In the conditions of mass-democracy, he explains, the public sphere is a commodity which political and social organizations seek to dominate in order to legitimize their own claim to power. Through their technical administration by parties, unions and other organizations, Habermas implies, particular social interests remain merely private, annexed and unformed, and do not enter the stage of public mediation. Modern society is therefore coloured by a plurality of non-general interests, which are represented by collective organizations, and for the balancing of which the state takes on technical responsibility. This, Habermas suggests, is the reason for the fragility and the autocratic character of modern government. Because the political order cannot count upon generalizable interests at its core, it must constantly endeavour to produce artificial consensus, which empowers it to continue its balancing role. It is therefore open to destabilization whenever the economic means at its disposal are reduced. Notably, the writing of *Structural Transformation*, in the late 1950s, coincided with the 'deep caesura' in post-war economic growth, in which Adenauer's policy of social investment was curbed owing to protests at the overburdening of the state, and the conditions for the rapid economic expansion of the immediate post-war period were no longer guaranteed (Abelshauser 1987: 62). Habermas's *Structural Transformation* represents thus the first major theoretical reflection on the legitimacy of the Adenauer/Erhard-state, and on the limited possibility of consensual change which this state offered.

It is striking in this regard that, after Erhard himself became leader of the CDU and Chancellor of the Federal Republic in 1963, Adenauer's system of anti-conflictual, technical pluralism became yet more central to the economic policies of both government and unions. In 1963 the Federation of German Unions formally acknowledged the 'common good' as the guideline in all wage-negotiations (C. Schulz 1984: 105). In 1964 Erhard created an expert committee for economic planning, which was designed to limit public spending, to develop a long-term policy of financial reform and to strengthen the export-sector. Confronted with unpromising conditions for economic growth and a mounting public debt, Erhard and his advisers put forward the concept of the 'integrated society' as the guiding idea for politics in the Federal Republic (see Briefs 1968: 195). The ideological core of this plan for the 'integrated society' was a theory of 'interest-balance' between employers and unions (see Beyme 1979: 197), on the basis of which Erhard sought to integrate all important political and economic groups into a collective macro-economic planning-system (Opitz 1965: 753). Such ideas have their general origins in the ordo-liberal belief that the state can guide the spontaneous reactions of the market (Blum 1969: 58–9). The more immediate inspiration for Erhard's thinking at this juncture was Goetz Briefs's doctrine (initially developed during Brüning's period of office; Krohn 1978: 126) that the 'strengthened organizations' of modern pluralist democracy (especially the unions) have become too powerful. The unions, Briefs argued, force the government to implement inflationary budgetary policies, and should be obliged to orientate their demands more realistically around national growth (Briefs 1966: 127–8). Erhard's model of the 'integrated society' is thus almost the perfect reflection of Habermas's dystopian description of a technically and ideologically dominated society with minimal intrinsic capacity for change, balanced around the planned economic needs of a business-led executive situated above the political arena of parliament (Opitz 1965: 759).

The genuinely political alternative to such a society, Habermas argues, can only be derived from public discourse, from rational interaction. 'The neutralization of social power and the rationalization of political domination in the medium of public discussion', Habermas argues, 'always presupposes a possible consensus, an objective reconciliation of competing interests according to general and binding criteria' (1990e: 340). If this is not obtained, political life will be based merely on 'at best a fragile balance of interest, supported by temporary power-constellations, which is fundamentally lacking in the rationality of general interest' (1990e: 340). As an antidote to the technical-authoritarian state, Habermas thus holds up a strongly utopian category of the political, in which the state is formed by universal norms produced by social interaction.

Central to Habermas's critique of mass-democracy is that he sees modern government as a partial return to plebiscitary rule. He argues that parties, now stripped of their initial mediating function, have acquired a status of mere technical representation. Political decisions, he claims, are legitimized by the quasi-charismatic appeals of leaders, not through reference to concrete issues (1990e: 299). Accordingly, he argues that parliament has 'developed from a disputing to a demonstrating corporation' (1990e: 305). Public opinion in modern democracies, consequently, is constituted artificially by social organizations whose function is to annex and manipulate the public sphere. Democratic will-formation has become a technically controlled process of public communication, in which citizens are integrated into the political system as mere passive components in the procedures of formal approval which typify mass-democracy. Citizens can be mobilized for the purposes of public acclamation, but they lack even the most basic qualifications for active democracy.

In these respects, Habermas's thinking focuses on common political preoccupations in the Federal Republic of the 1950s, especially regarding Adenauer's brand of Chancellor Democracy (see Niclauß 1988: 51). Habermas was by no means alone in his anxiety about the undermining of political legitimacy in the 1950s (see Alber 1989: 107). Similar apprehensions (in differing political shades) mark the sociological works of most major political theorists in the period. A vast amount of sociological literature was produced in the 1950s on the relations between the state and economic organizations. Hans Huber, for example, saw in organizational pluralism the replacement of democratic institutions with structures of 'group-egoism' (see Huber 1985a: 61). Theodor Eschenburg (1955: 60) also put forward a similar argument (see also Breitling 1955: 93). Like Habermas, other theorists, of different political orientations, also saw the emergence of an authoritarian welfare-state as a product of organizational pluralism (W. Weber 1985: 71; see also Stammer 1957: 597). Thinkers on the moderate right, especially those close to Erhard, feared that the co-determination laws of 1951–2 could lead to the establishment of a quasi-syndicalist corporate state (Briefs 1952: 107), and they generally viewed the strength of social interest-groups as a factor which undermines the authority of the democratic state.[3] Arnold Gehlen, from his proto-functionalist position, claimed that the power of social interest-groups leads directly both to the personalization of political authority and to the functional neutralization of the state's power (1956: 346). The Schmittian element in the critique of the corporate system is clearest in Gehlen's work. Gehlen argued that the latent political threat of the state of exception is structurally palliated, but not eliminated, by the development of the welfare-state (1963: 271).

Analogously, Habermas was also not alone in his anxiety about the emergence of neo-plebiscitary political forms in the 1950s. Other comment-ators also interpreted Adenauer's elitist style of government as a neo-plebiscitary system, influenced by Adenauer's political education in the Zentrum, and bolstered by support from economic interest-organizations (see Thum 1991: 80; Heidenheimer 1960: 129–30). Gerhard Leibholz, a highly esteemed constitutional theorist in the early years of the Federal Republic, argued that the party-state is, in essence, a 'rationalized form of plebiscitary democracy (1967: 93). Wolfgang Abendroth, the major socialist legal theorist of the post-war period, interpreted the constitutional system of the Federal Republic as a 'plebiscitary democracy, which is mediated by institutions' (Greven 1977: 181). Abendroth's is also the most radical critique of social organizations (see esp. 1967b: 295–6). Ernst Fraenkel (1964: 67) also appropriated Arendt's Aristotelian categories in his exam-ination of the relation between manipulated communication and plebiscit-ary government. Naturally, Habermas's position is not simply identical with any one of these arguments. However, Habermas's ideas reflect the broad consternation – by no means specific to the left – that the developing corporate welfare-system of the Federal Republic in the 1950s was based on merely technical modes of mediation between the executive and the elector-ate, and that this system contributed greatly to the erosion of the legitimacy of parliament.

Apart from the immediate relevance of such theories to Adenauer's personal regime, however, Habermas's concern about the restoration of technical-plebiscitary modes of will-formation also relates to the wide-spread anxiety of the late 1950s and early 1960s that the CDU, in conjunc-tion with its Bavarian sister-party, the CSU (Christian Social Union), was, in one form or other, a permanent fixture at the head of the executive of the Federal Republic. Habermas interprets the political composition of the contemporary Federal Republic as a static political axis in which distinct bloc-interests are rigidly formed in relation to each other, and in which political parties lack both the active-democratic substance and the prox-imity to the electorate which might enable them to alter this configuration (see Lohmarr 1963: 99–100). Habermas's theory of politics therefore closely describes the 'party-cartel' which confronted political analysts in the Fed-eral Republic of the 1950s, in which the CDU/CSU union (in close

---

3 Hagemeyer 1973: 277. See also Altmann 1960: 34, 47, 130. Despite his closeness to Erhard, some of Altmann's analyses overlap with those of Habermas. See also Allemann 1956: 346.

working harmony with powerful economic groups; Lohmar 1963: 96) constituted an apparently immovable executive bloc, which submitted itself for public approval every few years. After the defeat of the SPD in the federal elections of 1961 (even after the SPD had disavowed any attachment to theoretical Marxism in the Godesberg programme of 1959) intellectuals on both left and right openly reflected on whether the existing coalition could ever be replaced (Knorr 1975: 19). Moreover, the Basic Law of the Federal Republic, which had initially been accepted by the unions and the SPD as a provisional working paper (Kaack 1971: 192), was interpreted widely as a document which merely formalized existing bloc-interests in the legislative heart of the republic, but which failed to provide a genuinely democratic mechanism to alter the representative cartel at the highest political level (Seifert 1977: 23–9).

The truth in such apprehensions is clearly demonstrated by the fact that the SPD ultimately assumed power only because it first entered a Grand Coalition with the CDU/CSU in late 1966, which enabled it gradually to demonstrate its reliability. Adenauer himself had considered the possibility of a Grand Coalition as early as 1961, as a means of extending his own tenure on power (Kaack 1971: 266). The plebiscitary nature of the 'party-cartel' was not, however, diminished by the Grand Coalition, but re-inforced. Not unlike the Weimar coalition-system, the Grand Coalition of the late 1960s had a quasi-plebiscitary character, for it relegated broad social differences to a contingent level. During the Grand Coalition, com-promises between members of the coalition-parties assumed crucial import-ance in everyday government, and the working dependence of government upon top-level deals between the parties detached the executive still further both from the grass-roots of the parties and from the general population (Knorr 1975: 265). Even when the SPD finally became the party of government under Brandt in 1969, this was itself not a genuine power-change, but merely an alteration within the party-bloc (Kaltefleiter et al. 1970: 13). Habermas's diagnoses in the 1950s regarding the immobile nature of the modern democratic order and its reliance on administered bargains were therefore highly prescient.

In his early works, in sum, Habermas puts forward a damning critique of modern parliamentary democracy, which, he argues, has become little more than a technical institution for managing economy and society, and whose claims to representative legitimacy are minimal. However, although much attention has been paid to the impact of Carl Schmitt on Habermas's early thought (see Jäger 1973: 6; Kennedy 1986: esp. 319–20; H. Becker 1994: 88), Habermas is not opposed to liberal concepts of democracy. His early arguments in the 1950s imply that he supported the state-form of the Federal Republic which had been imposed by the Western allies in 1949 (see Söllner 1986: 526). He was, however, insistent that this form required greater legitimacy than it actually possessed. Habermas's emphasis on the necessity of a committed public sphere for the legitimization of power echoes the widespread conviction throughout the early post-war period that the Basic Law of the Federal Republic was a compromise document (see Otto 1971: 21). It was commonly argued at this time that the Basic Law had been created by secret party negotiations and covert pacts between the Parliamentary Council, the allies and the parties, and that it merely refracted the interests of these groups as they then existed (see Merkl 1963: 128). In certain regards, Habermas's reflections are close to those of Wolfgang Abendroth, who argued in the 1950s that the social components of the Basic Law (Articles 20 and 28) should be grasped as the parameters for constitutional and political life in the Federal Republic (Abendroth 1967a: 138; Niclauß 1974: 35). Habermas, however, unlike Abendroth, does not accord to the state the technical or prerogative authority to intervene in economic distribution-processes (Habermas 1967a: 118), and he condemns the materialization of law in the administration of welfare-provisions. Rather, he suggests that the legitimacy of the political order cannot be statically derived from a constitutional document, especially one which has emerged through the mediatizing interventions of political parties. Long before Habermas, Werner Weber, the major conservative critic of the Basic Law, had also criticized the imposition of a new con-stitutional fabric without public debate, and had roundly condemned the mediatization of the people by the parties in such a crucial moment of foundation (Merkl 1963: 129).

An important undercurrent in Habermas's earliest writings is a nascent turn of perspective against the earlier theories of political rationality devel-oped by the first generation of the Frankfurt School. As shown above, the theory of state-capitalism, adopted with varying degrees of unanimity by Horkheimer, Pollock and Adorno, turns on the (rather elliptical) argument that the technical rationality of political economy and the power-monopoly of the state dominate all aspects of human action. Habermas, in contrast to this, argues that the techniques of capital-accumulation and political dom-ination do not infiltrate all society, and that government cannot be reduced apriori to technical rule. In *Structural Transformation of the Public Sphere* these distinctions are still somewhat inchoate. Habermas explains how modern democracy has developed neo-plebiscitary components precisely because the discursive, or non-instrumental integrity of public society has been invaded by systemic imperatives. The possibility of legitimate democ-racy, he explains, depends upon the protection of the non-instrumental spheres of human interaction from annexation by the systemic sphere. Habermas thus makes a plea for the establishment of counter-systemic structures (perhaps including direct democracy) which might facilitate popular discourse and co-determination (see Outhwaite 1994: 12). Throughout his subsequent development, however, the distinction between technical and non-instrumental rationality becomes Habermas's central preoccupation. This is given its first thorough theoretical treatment in *Knowledge and Human Interest* (1968). In this work, written at the height of the activities of the student-movement in the Federal Republic, Haber-mas attempts both to provide a foundation for the emancipatory content of philosophical reflection and to link his own philosophical projects with the radical organizations active in university politics at the time.

Habermas's continuing preoccupation with these themes, especially during the late 1960s, can also be partly interpreted in light of the systemic conditions of government in the Federal Republic. Throughout the 1950s, the Adenauer-executive developed an increasingly programmatic – or technical – style of government (Grube et al. 1976: 179). This process culminated in the administrations of the 1960s. For instance, the basic idea in Erhard's model of the integrated society was that the role of government should be defined in purely technical terms – as the co-ordination of social interests in the name of national economic growth. Erhard's governmental declaration of 1965 promised little more than a reduction of the budgetary deficit and the development of increased powers of state-intervention to reduce inflation (Hinz 1967: 307). However, notably, the policies of the Grand Coalition and later SPD-administrations were not substantially distinct from this. Indeed, the SPD-influenced policies of the Grand Coalition can in certain respects be understood as a continuation of earlier models of guaranteed growth. The incorporation of the SPD in the government of the Grand Coalition resulted from the short-lived economic crisis of 1966–7 (Schönhoven 1967: 314). It was recognized during this crisis that the official representatives of the labour-movement would have to be co-opted into government in order to overcome the structural problems (particularly the budgetary deficit) in the economy of the Federal Republic (Grube et al. 1976: 171; M. G. Schmidt 1978: 207). At the heart of the Grand Coalition – the SPD's first taste of power since 1930 – was therefore a technical plan for organizing a compromise government around the need for increased growth.

The Minister of Economics under Kiesinger's Grand Coalition was Karl Schiller (SPD), an economist with a long Keynesian history, who as early as the 1950s had propagated Keynesian rather than Marxist models of economic administration in the SPD (Nichols 1994: 304). In 1967, directly after the inception of the Grand Coalition, Schiller introduced a legislative package (the stability-law), which was designed to stabilize the economy by cutting inflation and increasing industrial production. This legislation provided the state with extensive instruments of financial administration (Aderhold 1973: 40). It foresaw the reduction of state-spending, the corporate integration of the unions into economic planning and policy-making (Kruppa 1986: 131), the reinforcement of the planning authority of the Chancellor in relation to the regions (Schatz 1974: 21–2) and the introduction of wage-policies based on levels of sustainable economic growth (Schiller 1973: 99). The general intention behind Schiller's plan was to develop a labour-friendly, but also anti-cyclical economic policy of strategic investment, with price- and wage-levels fixed against yearly guidelines, in order to limit inflation (Rossmann 146–7). Schiller's stability-law thus reflected a general move away from classical-liberal theories of economic administration towards a Keynesian theory of state-regulation (Altvater et al. 1983: 33), which supported the stimulation of demand (Kruppa 1986: 131). Schiller's laws (like Erhard's earlier declarations) envisaged that supply and demand could be perfectly balanced against each other, through willing co-operation between tariff-partners, in order to secure controlled expansion without inflation. However, although Schiller followed Erhard in recognizing the need to cut budgetary spending, he coupled the reduction of spending with the introduction of strategic 'structural policies'. These provided for the investment of public money in infrastructure, housing, agriculture and information-technology, in order to stimulate productive industrial innovation (Nahamowitz 1978: 179). In total, in the period 1967–9 181 pieces of economic legislation were passed by the Bundestag, including twenty-one laws for the correction of structural problems (Nahamowitz 1978: 258). Schiller's policies were avowedly union-friendly. However, the unions partially forfeited their autonomy in wage-negotiations as a result of their agreement to adhere to governmental guidelines for pay-settlements (Kern 1973: 94).

The Keynesian euphoria after the 1966–7 crisis produced in the Federal Republic, therefore, a markedly interventionist state-apparatus, which began to develop a technocratic mode of universal planning (Naschold and Väth 1973: 11), and which enthusiastically embraced regulatory policies as a means of stabilizing the political and economic system (Altvater et al. 1983: 33; Nahamowitz 1978: 54). It might also be observed in this respect that the Keynesian revolution in the Federal Republic carried slightly more authoritarian overtones than in other countries, as it was closely linked with the spirit of Erhard's original stabilization-programme, which itself looked back to the principles of post-1945 ordo-liberalism (Altvater et al. 1979: 304–6). One of the key motives behind Schiller's stability-law was to secure the position of the Federal Republic in international competition (Rossmann 1986: 157). Significantly, in this respect, Schiller's Keynesian planning-system also further reinforced the technical corporatism which had characterized the Federal Republic in the 1950s (Schiller 1973: 99). Schiller's assumptions, crucially, rested on the assertion of a universal 'economic reason' (Altvater et al. 1979: 305), which would successfully balance all interest-groups against each other in corporate unanimity, thereby limiting the possibility of structural conflict.

Especially important for Habermas's work is the fact that the economic ideas of Erhard and Schiller went hand in hand with a move towards strategic investment policies, which had a direct impact on university politics. Both Erhard and Schiller channelled state-funds into the development of new technologies likely to be used by industry. Between 1950 and 1970 state-investment in technological research increased threefold, and new legislation was introduced in 1964 and 1969 to encourage the pursuit of research likely to trigger industrial innovation (K. Schmitz et al. 1976: 183). Committees and ministries designed to discuss the industrial implementation of scientific research were set up in 1957, 1962 and 1963. In the early 1960s, Erhard arranged for regular exchanges between

representatives of universities and industry, in the context of which closer
co-ordination of scientific research with industrial innovation was encouraged (1976: 346). Under the economic guidance of Karl Schiller,
investment in science and technological research reached its zenith in
1971 (Fels and Schmidt 1980: 67; Nahamowitz 1978: 179). Schiller also
set about increasing the 'cognitive resources' of the state, by introducing
statistical documentation of economic sectors in need of technological
modernization (Fels and Schmidt 1980: 178). Schiller's steering state,
therefore, sought not only to correlate wages and overall growth. It also
attempted to organize the future relations of supply and demand by
sponsoring innovative scientific practice in order to ensure that the produc-
tion-industries of the Federal Republic remained in the international
vanguard. In short, Schiller's economic policies tried to effect a pre-
planned transformation of the economy of the Federal Republic (Altvater
et al. 1979: 310), by means of structural policies directed at modes of
production, structures of employment, regional problems, and levels
of qualification in the workforce (K. Schmitz et al. 1976: 508). The
ideological background for such technological policies was the widespread
discussion in the mid-1960s of the 'technological gap' between the industries of the Federal Republic and its international competitors, especially in
the USA (Kruppa 1986: 79). Willy Brandt himself openly pledged his
support for the 'prioritization of technological reasearch' (1983: 28).

Connected with these economic issues, the late 1960s also saw a rapid
increase in the level of extra-parliamentary political agitation, which was
centred primarily on student activism and renegade unions (E. Schmidt
1971: 7). The radicalization of student politics in the 1960s can be attributed to a number of factors. Externally, it was attached to general resent-
ment among the young for the Grand Coalition's support for the Vietnam
War. It was also brought about by the archaic and conservative quality of
the universities in the Federal Republic, and it therefore took the form of a
general demand for greater student influence on the content of seminars
and the organization of the universities (see Jacobsen and Dollinger 1968:
182). However, the SPD itself was also a highly significant factor in this
process of radicalization. The temporary absorption of the SPD into the
Grand Coalition with the CDU/CSU under Kiesinger was seen by the left
of the SPD as a betrayal of the party's true social function (Göbel 1978: 25).
Most especially – the willingness of the SPD to support emergency legislation (*Ausnahmegesetze*), which gave the state special authorizations to curb
subversive political activities, was the main focus of student and popular
unrest (see Fichter and Lönnendonker 1977: 84). In the late 1960s, this
legislation contributed greatly to a climate in which parliament was seen as
an apparatus rendered insensitive to protest by its functionalization for a
broad bloc of hegemonic interests (see Bauß 1977: 35; Euchner 1972: 109).
The emergency legislation, ultimately passed in June 1968, was the political
adjunct to the stability-law of 1967. Together they formed a legal package
which gave political licence to the state to regulate (if necessary by force)

any activities, either political or economic, which might threaten its stability.

Habermas's inquiries of the 1960s into the distinct quality and functions of human rationality can be addressed against the background of these processes of simultaneous social radicalization and political technologization. In the early 1960s, Habermas had already begun to argue that the sciences should be linked to broad social interests (1963b: 256). Later, in 1969, Habermas argued more emphatically for the 'politicization of the sciences' as part of the interactive relation between scientific and social interest (1981b: 196). With other academics at the University of Frankfurt am Main, he drew up a reform-document (Jacobsen and Dollinger 1968: 67), which advocated the increased participation of students in research (1981b: 194). In his writings of the mid-to late 1960s Habermas sought therefore to define and defend a conception of scientific rationality which is not absolutely subordinate to the dictates of economic innovation, and in which the technical processes of scientific inquiry are not detached from broader social commitments. Underlying Habermas's reflections on the function of the university, also, is the insistence that the university has a vital role, not only in the technical stabilization of the political system, but equally in the social integration of reflexive citizens. The university, he argues, is an arena where rational discourse can take place without being immediately subject to prior technical or political planning. For this reason, Habermas was not entirely in accord with the political demands of the student-movement. Despite his plans for the social integration of the universities at this time, Habermas condemned the idea of student control of lecture material (1981c: 214), and he protested at the occupation of universities by students for the purposes of radical agitation. He argued that the function of universities is to protect discussion from the invasion of political-technical strategy (1981d: 262–3). Indeed, Habermas made a specific distinction in these debates between the 'one-sided communication' of political agitation and the community of communicative research upon which scientific inquiry at universities depends (1981d: 263). Like other leading academics on the democratic left of the Federal Republic, Habermas even accused the radical protest-movements of adopting 'left-wing fascist' tactics in their demands for direct control of the universities (1990b: 25).

Broadly, Habermas sympathized with the protest-movements of the late 1960s to the extent that they attempted 'to make explicit the social functions of science in the consciousness of our political responsibility' (1981b: 194). He approvingly observed the attempts of student bodies to combat 'the depoliticized public sphere, on the basis of which the will-formation cannot assume democratic form' (1981e: 251). He also endorsed the moves within the protest-groups to make scientific research accountable to overarching general social interests. In his own project for pedagogic reform, Habermas argued in 1968 that 'the employment of technologically available potentials for the satisfaction of needs articulated without compulsion should, as far as pragmatically possible, adhere to maxims about which a consensus can be established in public discussion and political will-formation which is free of domination' (1981f: 243). In these respects, therefore, Habermas saw the student-movement both as a compensatory reaction against the manufactured public sphere of mass-democracy and, equally importantly, as an insistence that technical rationality should be practically and socially accountable.

However, Habermas's most eloquent response to the political contours of the 1960s is *Knowledge and Human Interest* itself. In this work, Habermas refines the theory of reason in *Structural Transformation of the Public Sphere* by explaining human rationality in terms of its motivation by differing forms of interest. Habermas's point of departure here is the anti-Marxist separation of interaction and labour as two typologically distinct forms of human activity (1968: 71). Labour, he outlines, is the technical-instrumental organization of natural resources. It is guided by the technical interests of human self-preservation. Interaction, in contrast, is the communicative sphere of human coexistence, the sphere of normative or hermeneutic socialization. It is guided by the practical interest in consensus, recognition and the possibility of agreement (1969a: 62). This basic distinction is part of a comparative methodological scrutiny of the sciences. The natural sciences, Habermas argues, are 'organized in the transcendental context of instrumental praxis', in which 'nature is necessarily the object of knowledge with regard to its possible technical disposition' (1968: 348). The interest which influences such sciences is the technical interest of labour. Contrary to this, 'the research-process of the human sciences operates on the transcendental level of communicative action in such a manner that sense-contexts are explicated with a view to the possible preservation of the intersubjectivity of communication' (1968: 348). The interest which motivates the human sciences is, therefore, the communicative interest of interaction. Technical rationality is monological reason, in which means are used for the attainment of self-imposed ends (1969b: 22). Communicative rationality is the rationality of dialogue, in which the explication of socially embedded experience necessarily entails a hermeneutic relation to the objects of inquiry. Most centrally, the experiences treated by the human sciences are symbolically embedded in language, and they can be meaningfully approached only insofar as their interpreters act as 'socialized fellow players and not as objective observers' (1968: 237).

Habermas thus puts forward a nuanced anthropological explanation of human thinking. The technical reason of the natural sciences, according to this model, is rooted transcendentally in the interest in objective goal-fulfilment. The human sciences, Habermas argues, however, are guided by a transcendental, practical interest in the preservation of intersubjective discourse. The human sciences are committed to revealing the symbolic or communicative norms according to which the actions of others are perpetrated. Significantly, this is also the precondition of practical coexistence between individuals (1968: 222). Habermas, like Karl-Otto Apel (1993), asserts therefore that the process of interpretation in the human sciences is a mode of human interaction which is entwined with the transcendental human interest in non-violent coexistence (McCarthy 1978: 325). The hermeneutic basis of the human sciences reflects, anthropologically, an interest which is not, like technical reason, monologically goal-determined, but rather oriented towards disclosing and interpreting the terms of practical agreement with others. This practical interest in human coexistence is ultimately redeemed, Habermas argues, in the critical social sciences. It is only through a degree of critical self-reflection, which is not possible in the hermeneutic medium of the human sciences, that human interest actually explains its transcendental character (1968: 350). The critical social sciences are thus motivated by the transcendental interest in the realization of human reason. They are interested in the possible conditions of social emancipation, and they reflect critically upon the conditions of distorted communication under which social labour and interaction are commonly organized. Unlike the human sciences, the critical social sciences are anchored in the interest in the overthrow of the social and institutional conditions which restrict the realization of free communication.

Habermas argues therefore that human interaction is transcendentally motivated by a rational interest in the abolition of violence (1968: 244). In a broad fusion of anthropology and epistemology, Habermas claims that human practical reason, or human practical interest, are manifestations of transcendental reason or transcendental interest, for they both contain an orientation towards the suspension of force. Even the human interest in self-preservation is part of the course of human emancipation (1968: 350). The human quest for self-preservation, Habermas indicates, is itself interested in the communicative preconditions of self-preservation – the preservation not of the solitary self, but of the interactive social agent. Most importantly, however, it is the critical social sciences which hold out the possibility of the realization of transcendental human interests. The critical social sciences combine processes of self-reflection, through which subjects interpret their own conditioning through social and institutional power-relations, and their interest in the termination of such relations. Knowledge and transcendental interest are therefore united in the critical social sciences. At this point, the critical reflection of the Frankfurt School turns full circle against Horkheimer's sceptical anthropological reflections on the dominatory nature of human interest (Horkheimer 1987a: 288). Habermas's ideas here mark an attempt to salvage neo-Aristotelian categories of non-instrumental reason and interaction from the socio-epistemological critiques put forward by Weber, Lukács and the early Frankfurt School (see Moritz 1992: 198). Although many interpreters (including Habermas himself) have viewed this communicative turn as a refiguring of Adorno's mimetic theory, Habermas's anthropological reflections at this point have only very limited connection with Critical Theory (Habermas 1985c: 219–20). Indeed, Habermas's early theory of communicative reason in some respects reproduces an Aristotelian concept of natural law, in which the terms of public virtue and human interaction are broadly co-productive.

Historically, Habermas's theory of scientific interest criticizes both the technical functionalization of the state which characterized the political landscape in the Federal Republic in the 1960s, and the resultant technicization of the sciences. These aspects are also central to Habermas's more general understanding of the social role of theory. Habermas implies that both theory and its location, the university, should be protected from the effects of planning- or steering-rationality. Theoretical reflection, he argues, should provide a basis for the discursive and normative reconciliation of particular interests (1985b: 212). This idea surfaces repeatedly in Habermas's advocacy of university reforms (1981f: 244), and in his observations on the need for scientific 'self-reflection' in university life (1981b: 194). Habermas's contribution to the redefinition of the social function of the university in the Federal Republic of the 1960s was, therefore, profound – although it was by no means universally approved by radical student bodies.[4] Habermas's altercations with the more radical protestors have been widely documented (Fichter and Lönnendorfer 1977: 139).

Of wider significance for the development of Habermas's thinking are the clear distinctions which he makes in his works of the late 1960s between technical and practical interests, and between the different life-contexts to which these correspond. Despite his involvement in public debate at this time, Habermas's reflections on human rationality actually have a markedly cautious and defensive character. Whilst setting out his quasi-hermeneutic, quasi-anthropological theory of social and scientific interaction, Habermas also reinforces his earlier recognition of the relative autonomy of the sphere of labour, strategy, instrumentalization and natural domination. Technical reason, he suggests, should certainly, where possible, be subject to practical and critical reflection. However, he also recognizes that practical control of systemic functions is unlikely to be realized. Habermas, therefore, although not unsympathetic to radical upheavals in the Federal Republic, ultimately does not go beyond a social-reformist position, which envisages at best the practical/critical adjustment of systemic conditions in line with the promptings of non-instrumental discourse.

These reflections on interest and systemic differentiation are given a rather different treatment in Habermas's most controversial and committed work of political philosophy, *The Legitimation Crisis of Late Capitalism* (1972). In this work the ideas of *Structural Transformation of the Public Sphere* and *Knowledge and Human Interest* are brought together in a significantly altered figuration. In *The Legitimation Crisis*, Habermas returns to his earlier preoccupation with the inability of modern societies to legitimize their governmental structures. By this time, however, Habermas has also entered into extensive debate with the functionalist theories of Niklas

---

4 See Fenner 1977: 52. Fenner argues that Habermas's thinking influenced Brandt's intended reform of the education system.

Luhmann. Although Habermas and Luhmann remain antipodes in many aspects of their social thinking, Habermas's work in the early 1970s begins to show the clear influence of Luhmann's brand of functionalism.

In *The Legitimation Crisis*, Habermas formulates the relationship between state and society, which he initially conceived as a relation between the political apparatus and the public sphere, as a relation between system and life-world. System and life-world are spheres of anthropologically and functionally distinct modes of interaction, each of which contains its own particular form of rationality. The systemic sphere is, Habermas explains, the steering- or planning-apparatus of society, which operates 'processes of socialization, in which the social system incorporates nature' (1973: 20). The systemic sphere is the organ of instrumental rationality, whose purpose is to stabilize society against nature, and to absorb nature, through production-processes, for its own expansion. The life-world, a term borrowed from Husserl's phenomenology, is the sphere in which the inner nature of social beings is socialized, the sphere of human interaction. In the life-world, inner nature is transformed by socialization-processes, through which social members become equipped with the power of speech and action. Through the differentiation and secularization of modern society, Habermas argues, the life-world is subject to processes of rationalization, through which the acceptance of the norms of social existence is no longer reliant upon theological or mythological symbolization, but upon demonstrable argument (p. 23). Social systems preserve themselves in the life-world via communicative actions, the validity of which can be critically called into question (p. 21). Socialization in the life-world, therefore, cannot be accomplished unless the norms of social coexistence and integration can be universally instituted. The entire social system of modern society, Habermas argues, must preserve itself simultaneously through the instrumental appropriation of external nature (resources), and through the communicative socialization of internal nature (human nature). Habermas represents these processes (in quasi-functionalist terms) as systemic integration and social integration, both of which are essential for the functional preservation of social integrity (p. 14). The latter process is accomplished by the transformation of individual needs into the symbolic intersubjective forms of language, and it is through these forms that the norms of social integration can be tried and affirmed (p. 21).

Habermas argues that the relation between social and systemic integration in late-capitalist societies contains a latent threat of crisis. Late capitalism, he asserts, contains an endemic crisis-potential because the integrating processes of the social sphere – 'the consensual foundation of normative structures' – can be disrupted by crises within the systemic sphere (p. 12). Disruptions to the successful functioning of the system, Habermas explains, also produce disruption in the integrating procedures of the social sphere. If the system loses its ability to integrate one area of systemic operation – for instance, the economy – this cannot be simply absorbed by the social sphere, for the integrity of the social sphere is

determined by the interwovenness of the social identity of its members with
the system itself (p. 13). Crises in the functions of systemic regulation
therefore lead directly to crises in the sphere of social integration.

In this regard, Habermas gives, in outline, a historical-systematic
account of the problem of legitimacy at different stages of Western historical development. The existence of crisis-potentials within social organization has its origins, he argues, in traditional societies, in which a
contradiction arises between systems of justification 'which do not explicitly
sanction exploitation' and the emergence of a class-structure which is based
upon 'the appropriation of socially produced wealth' (p. 35). Such potentials for contradiction between the norms of social integration and the
practice of the systemic sphere are intensified in liberal capitalism. At this
stage of development, the economy is granted formal autonomy, and the
political system is not answerable for economic processes and problems.
However, Habermas argues that the formal autonomization of the market
already contains the threat of systemic crisis, because the ideological principles of equality and liberty of exchange engendered by the capitalist
economy become components in the norms of social integration. Capitalist
principles of systemic organization in the economy are propagated, therefore, as principles of social integration, around which members of the social
sphere construct their identity (p. 39). Social integration, increasingly, is
based upon principles of systemic integration which contain latent and
irreconcilable contradictions, and which cannot be generalized to constitute
the legitimate basis of the social order (p. 39). In capitalist societies, in
short, the fundamental contradiction between labour and capital is internalized by social systems as aspects of their integrative processes. Whenever
systemic operations undergo periods of crisis, therefore, this latent conflict
becomes manifest on the levels of both social and systemic integration.
When the economy contracts, social legitimacy, metaphorically, contracts
also. 'The economic crisis', in such conditions, 'is transposed directly into a
social crisis. When it reveals the conflict between social classes it performs a
practical critique of the ideology by means of which the sphere of social
commerce spuriously presents itself as free of compulsion' (pp. 47–8).

Habermas's argument revolves here around a complex of post-Marxist,
functionalist and humanist anthropological assumptions about the character
of social systems. Unlike Marx, he sees the question of political legitimation
not as a mere technical device by which the systemic superstructure
engenders belief in its justification (Rockmore 1989: 35). Rather, his argument depends upon the assertion that systemic operations retain an attachment to social procedures. In Weberian-functionalist manner, he sees the
modern state as an apparatus which is historically produced through social
differentiation, but which, owing to the conditions of the genesis of bourgeois democracy, is not wholly severed from the social sphere. The operation of the state is therefore, in part, reliant on the congruence between
social norms and its own steering-capacities. The state, simply, must
legitimize itself to society (1976b: 271). Underlying Habermas's theory,

also, is the humanist belief that human interaction in the social sphere contains a utopian moment of genuine universal validity, and that the system of state can only legitimize itself truly if its norms comply with the universal norms of human practical interest – if the state is a representation of social-political norms. The hypothetical ideal of a 'discursively constituted system of norms' (1973: 156), he argues, must form the basis for a critical analysis of existing legitimation-structures. In similar post-Marxist vein, Habermas asserts that systemic crisis is produced not by a contradiction between the material-instrumental interests of labour and the exploitative operations of the system, but between the communicative norms of social interaction and the systemic sphere – between the life-world and the system. The normative correlation between system and life-world must be maintained, in order to generate the motivation (legitimacy) required for the continued acceptance of the system by social agents (see Alway 1995: 117).

At the stage of late capitalism, Habermas argues, the latent ideologies of bourgeois democracy have been finally installed at the heart of the social system. The formal autonomy of the economy has been abandoned in favour of a process in which the state assumes direct responsibility for the obviation of dysfunctional developments in the economy. The state therefore presides over the corporate compromise between business, unions and parties (1973: 82). Habermas (like Claus Offe at the same time; McCarthy 1978: 363–4) views this as a development through which both social relations and the administration are complexly politicized (Offe 1974: 336). The late-capitalist state, Habermas outlines, arrogates to itself partial regulatory responsibility for the means and mode of production. It accomplishes this through control of the infrastructure, through intensification of the productive force of human labour (technological innovation), through investment-regulation, and through maintenance of the class-compromise, or attenuation of the class-conflicts which are at all times latent in the capitalist system. The late-capitalist state is thus charged with softening the antagonisms within the capital economy, with mediating between classes and interested organizations in the allocation of resources and the guarantee of social welfare (Habermas 1973: 53), and, most obviously, with creating conditions for the utilization of excess capital (see Thompson 1981: 85). As a consequence of this 'open repoliticization of the class-relation' (Habermas 1973: 85), the state is subject to an inordinate number of legitimation-demands, as it is forced to intervene ceaselessly in social relations and to assume authority for issues external to the systemic sphere. Moreover, as it has internalized the economy as the basis of both systemic and social integration, the late-capitalist state can no longer call upon traditional patterns of integration to maintain social cohesion (1973: 54). Ultimately, Habermas asserts, the economy becomes the sole means of social integration. The maintenance of class-compromise becomes the exclusive foundation of the political apparatus. Consequently, wherever the state acts, it is forced not only to legitimize particular acts of intervention, but also to legitimize its own non-legitimizable core – the socialization of production for the service of non-generalizable needs. With every act of state-intervention the entire legitimacy of the system is called into question.

At the heart of Habermas's argument here is the claim that in the conditions of late capitalism the political system can never be legitimized according to universal-communicative rationality, for the late-capitalist state is structurally anchored in non-universal interest. Any crisis in the operative rationality of the system (due to economic crisis, or technical overburdening) leads therefore by a direct path to an identity-crisis for the whole social sphere (1973: 68–9). Rationality-crises of the system and the identity-crises of the social sphere are therefore coexistent. Habermas returns here to the earlier argument of *Structural Transformation of the Public Sphere*. The legitimacy required by the system, he argues, must now necessarily be engendered by ideological devices – by the proferring of material compensation to the members of the social sphere, by media-manipulation, by annexation of the social sphere through institutional organizations (parties), and by general depoliticization and (re)privatization of the public sphere. Such devices protect the administration of the system from the need to legitimize itself and they fend off the threat of rationality-crisis. These modes of 'colonization of the life-world' are the key technical mechanisms through which the system protects its precarious legitimacy (Habermas 1981g: 433). The systems of the economy and the administration reach back into the resources of the life-world and manipulate these in order to produce legitimacy for themselves. Members of the social sphere assume the status, merely, of 'passive citizens with the right to refuse acclamation' (1973: 55). Habermas therefore recentres his political theory on the basic problem of German history – the absence of a sphere which mediates between private and public life.

This argument, however, raises simple, but complex questions about Habermas's theory of politics, and his ambiguous understanding of the political apparatus. The political apparatus, Habermas indicates, in fact has two distinct functions of integration – both social and systemic. The modern state suffers from a precarious lack of legitimacy because it has been transformed into simple administration (a planning-apparatus) by the fact that it has internalized the coercive order of capitalism. Habermas thus laments the vertical closure of the political system to the life-world, and its resultant orientation around purely material needs, rather than universal processes of socialization. However, this theory of the state implies that the state is originally, or at least potentially, not exclusively a component of the systemic apparatus, and not functionally distinct from common socialization-processes. Despite his functional (and anthropological) separation of system and life-world, therefore, Habermas's argument is still underscored by the assumption that the system of political integration is a distinct system amongst other social systems, and that this system can receive information from other systems. The crisis of late capitalism is so acute precisely because the political system is – potentially – the central, public locus of social integration. In *Legitimation Crisis*, thus, Habermas deploys a two-sided concept of politics. In late capitalism, he indicates, the state is transformed into a set of technical reflexes (administration) for managing economic growth and limiting social tensions. Yet underlying this argument is still a strong notion of political action and integration, according to which the political system is, in origin, an integrative organ in the public energies of the social sphere. Indeed, up until the early 1980s Habermas's works continue to echo (albeit distantly) Kirchheimer's earlier argument that the political order cannot be legitimate unless it can freely state the terms of its interaction with the economy, and thus integrate citizens on that basis. The relation between system and life-world remains, in any case, a highly inconsistent aspect of Habermas's thought.

In this respect, Habermas also enters a number of debates relating directly to the contemporary conditions of the Federal Republic in the late 1960s and early 1970s. *Legitimation Crisis* turns, firstly, against the resuscitation of the integration-theories of Hermann Heller and Rudolf Smend amongst certain influential political theorists in the SPD at this time. Such thinkers, especially Horst Ehmke (1969: 57–63), argued that the state is a normative centre of action, with stable powers of social integration. Habermas clearly implies that such theories are simply naive, and that the powers of integration possessed by the state are increasingly artificial. Primarily, however, *Legitimation Crisis* is also a riposte to Luhmann's systemic-functionalist conviction (in which Luhmann follows Gehlen and Schelsky) that political systems no longer have to legitimize themselves at all. In *Legitimation Crisis*, Habermas clearly argues that the systemic sphere cannot lastly operate without a vertical, normative attachment to other social systems. Indeed, Habermas especially condemns the technocratic steering-state of the Federal Republic, for which Luhmann was the chief apologist. Habermas's own political nightmare is a society in which all traces of human value-orientations have been eroded by the functional operations of administrative systems (1969a: 91), and in which the political system acts as an organ of technical-scientific dictatorship, run by bureaucratic elites (1969c: 124). In certain respects, therefore, Habermas himself owes a pronounced debt to the tradition of integration-theory. His thinking at this juncture falls between purely normative-integrative and purely functionalist explanations of the political order. The modern political system, he implies, cannot be interpreted, in quasi-Aristotelian manner, as a unified focus of integration (see also Hesse 1959: 11; Scheuner 1978: 73). However, at the same time, Habermas suggests, it cannot be treated in exclusively functionalist terms. It is because the state *ought* to act as an integrative order amidst other social systems that its lack of legitimacy is so threatening. Habermas remains thus between two camps, recognizing both the realism of functionalism and the anthropological claims of integration-theory.

Habermas's theory of the late-capitalist state also links with the debate about the role of the welfare-state and the nature of social democracy in the

Federal Republic, after Schiller's budgetary reforms of 1967 (Oertzen 1974: 71; H. R. Kaiser 1977: 15). Habermas understands the welfare-state in its current form as a device through which an uneven class-compromise is secured in order to preserve the monopolizing interests of big business in the systemic sphere. He describes the Federal Republic as 'a social system organized as an authoritarian welfare-state' (1981h: 302). Like Offe (and Luhmann after him), he argues that the political apparatus is overburdened by the administration of the welfare-state – which creates rationality-deficits in the systemic sphere and legitimation-deficits in the social sphere (Thompson 1981: 86). Both Offe and Habermas stress particularly their conviction that social relations are excessively politicized through the welfare-state. Both also argue that the politicization of these relations throws light on the dubious legitimacy of the system itself. Like his mentor Wolfgang Abendroth, Habermas repeatedly argues that the 'transformation of the bourgeois class-state into a democratic social-legal state' (1981f: 244) is an accomplishment of only limited significance if it is not followed by more thorough systemic modifications. He proposes a programme of 'radical reformism' as the means by which the system should be structurally altered (1981h: 302). Elsewhere, he describes the policy of the 'social taming of capitalism' as mere 'resignation' (1985a: 156). The path to a humane society, initially projected by the welfare-state, has been blocked, he explains, by the administration of class-compromise which underpins the welfare-state – by the 'instrumental reason unleashed in the productive forces' and the 'functionalist reason emerging in the capacities for organization and planning' (1985a: 161). In such pronouncements, Habermas's ideas distantly echo Abendroth's constitutional insistence that the social provisions of the Basic Law should be interpreted not as an act of strategic or late-capitalist planning, but (in the sense implied earlier by Heller) as rights of co-possession (Abendroth 1967c: 492; Spieker 1986: 171), to be expanded and realized through non-technical social collaboration.

It is also tempting, in this respect, to draw a historical parallel between the theories of social democracy in Germany in the 1920s and those developed by Habermas and Offe in the 1970s. As shown above, much socialist thinking of the 1920s is marked by a conflict between the belief in social reformism and the anxiety that social reforms stabilize the influence of economic interests on the governmental executive. This dilemma is also at the heart of both Habermas's and Offe's thinking (Offe 1969: 171). Both Habermas and Offe trace the legitimation-crises of the modern state to the unmediated pluralism (class-conflict) at its core. Both imply, consequently, that the state can only legitimize itself by expanding its openness to the social sphere. Both argue, however, that the opening of the state to social interests also produces a non-consensual system of corporate welfarism, which enables economic bodies to regulate both social interation and the political apparatus. The warning that capitalist pluralism leads to authoritarian government is never far from Habermas's thinking. Habermas and Offe, therefore, like Neumann and Kirchheimer before them, are left to dream again the dream of redical social democracy – namely, that the state can open itself to the social sphere without immediate annexation by strong corportate groupings.

Such symmetries between social theory in the 1920s and the 1970s are no coincidence. Like the 1920s, the early 1970s was also a period of social-reformist experiment in the Federal Republic. Willy Brandt's administration of the early 1970s was the result of a long period of consolidation by the SPD, through the course of which it had distanced itself from its image as a radical class-party and defined itself as a social-reformist party (Klotzbach 1982: 311). Despite this, the first Brandt-administration – symbolically represented as a radical power-change (*Machtwechsel*) – was marked by a high degree of democratizing euphoria. Brandt's symbolic pledge in his election declaration of 1969 was that he would 'risk more democracy' (W. Brandt 1983: 10). Brandt, like his antecedents in the Weimar Republic, saw the political constitution as a dynamic framework, whose content could be realized only through the establishment of relative legal parity between capital and labour, and through the democratic organization of the economy and society (see Sarcinelli 1979: 87). He would, he proclaimed, make governmental procedures open and accessible, and ensure the primacy of humanist-socialist principles over forces of economic coercion (1983: 52).

Brandt's 'policy of internal reforms' envisaged, in fact, no less than a radical modernization of both state and society in the Federal Republic. He planned a reform of the taxation-system, of the laws of co-determination, of the system of social security, of the education system, and of criminal and family law (Borowsky 1980: 64). At the base of these reforms was a policy of redistribution, which foresaw a constant yearly increase in the social component of state-spending, and the ultimate elimination of class-divisions. The theoretical base of Brandt's administration was ultimately formulated in its major policy-document – the 'orientation-framework '85'. In this document, the SPD pledged itself to the introduction of 'structural reforms with a view to a long-term socialist goal' (Heimann 1973: 17). The document was submitted to the party in two drafts, in 1972 and 1975. The first version planned future reforms on a year-by-year basis, on the condition that a certain level of annual growth (4–6 per cent) could be guaranteed (Braunthal 1983: 147). This first document was condemned by the left of the SPD. Leading representatives of the party's left wing (especially the Young Socialists) saw the orientation-framework merely as a programmatic form of 'enlightened capitalism' (Hickel 1975: 188). They rejected it for its technocratic nature (Küpper 1977: 53), and its (alleged) policy of Keynesian 'crisis-management' (1977: 51). The second version, which was formally ratified by the party, expressly de-coupled promises of reform from yearly growth, and planned instead a brand of social corporatism, based on models of economic co-determination. This document set out theoretical guidelines for a mixed-economic system, in which, it was promised, the state would regulate investment, curb the power of big business and establish the conditions for redistribution (Braunthal 1983: 148–50).

Importantly, Brandt's 'system-overcoming reforms' were projected in a manner which strongly recalls the social democratic reform-policies of the 1920s. Like the senior figures of the Weimar SPD, Brandt – influenced by the Swedish corporatism which he had experienced whilst in exile (Hardes 1974: 17) – strongly advocated the move towards the incorporation of economic associations as partners in political dialogue (see Lompe 1987: 13). By the 1970s, corporate pluralism was broadly acknowledged in SPD-orthodoxy as the 'state-theory of reformism' (Fraenkel 1970: 269). Most significantly, Schiller's stability-law had included a provision for a Concerted Action, in which unions and employers' associations would establish cross-class consensus on issues of national priority (see Alemann 1987: 34–5), especially in the regulation of wages and prices (Mottl 1992: 187–8), and in which wage-demands would be tied to overall growth (Hinz 1967: 319–20). This Concerted Action was designed for renegotiating the relation between workforce and employers and for engineering a broad 'social dialogue' or 'social symmetry' (Hardes 1974: 33), in order to mollify the conflicts between antagonistic social interest-groups (Lompe 1987: 170–1, 188, 207). Schiller's policy of Concerted Action projected a harmonious democratization of labour-relations in the Federal Republic. It resulted in the passing (after repeated submission of draft bills to the Bundestag; Braunthal 1983: 116) of a new shop-constitution by Brandt's administration in late 1971 (Muszynski 1975: 83) and, ultimately, of a new co–determination law in 1976 by Helmut Schmidt's government (Thum 1991: 182).

In the spirit of a state-administered 'Keynesian class-compromise' (J. Hoffmann 1987: 346), therefore, the economic policies of the Brandt-era focused on the maintenance of economic growth and social stability by means of long-term planning and high levels of state-investment. The years 1970–2 saw the highest increase ever in wage-levels in the Federal Republic (1987: 347), and in the overall period 1965–75 social spending increased from 24.6 per cent to 32.4 per cent of the GNP. The increase was most rapid in the period 1970–3. However, Schiller's corporate model of wage- and income-policies was only in part motivated by democratizing interests. Its underlying strategy was that micro-economic bodies (including organized labour) could be integrated into the macro-economic projections of the state, and rewarded by means of social pay-offs (Hennig 1970: 512). Indeed, the policy of co-operation between unions and employers was not especially successful. It was not accepted by all members of the negotiating corporations (Kern 1973: 164). It remained effective only during the economic boom-period 1968–73 (Jacob: 1982a: 68–9), and it was disturbed by strikes even during this time, in 1969 and 1973. It was formally dissolved in 1977 (Rossmann 1986: 148–9). By the mid-1970s the SPD abandoned these policies, and attempted instead to establish 'structural councils', along quasi-syndicalist lines, which were intended to co-ordinate the interests of workforce and management (see W. Roth 1979: 545), and to distribute economic authority between the state and the private economy (Kruppa 1986: 203).

Habermas's theory of the late-capitalist state is therefore based directly on the neo-Keynesian developments in the Federal Republic after 1967 (C. Schulz 1984: 172). In contrast to the economic policies of the 1950s, in the late 1960s and 1970s the Federal Republic once again experienced a governmental system which partially internalized the antagonisms within the economy. Although, unlike the 1920s, in the late 1960s the state did not directly intervene in wage-settlements, and did not abandon the general policy of tariff-autonomy, this period was characterized both by the socie-talization of conflicts in the economic sphere and by the transposition of such conflicts onto the level of collective, state-regulated planning. The corporate committees which Brandt and Schiller created for the resolution of tariff-disputes installed the contradictions in the economy at the heart of the systemic sphere. They also forced the state to juridify and institution-alize class-relations, insofar as these were voiced through wage-conflicts (Rossmann 1986: 514). The rapid increase in taxation and social spending after 1967 was certainly tied to a policy of redistribution. But it was also designed both to maintain existing levels of economic growth (especially in the export-sector), and to prolong domestic stability (1986: 141). These are precisely the attributes of the late-capitalist state which Habermas discusses in his analysis of the repoliticization of class-relations (Scharpf 1978: 16).

Notably also, the Keynesian attempt to co-ordinate economic and social interests led directly to a highly technical and strategic form of government (Naschold 1973: 81). In the period 1967–72, in addition to the instruments for economic steering created by the stability-law, the technical facilities of the state were expanded in several significant ways. Each Federal ministry was allowed to appoint a planning-committee (Aderhold 1973: 146). The size and authority of the planning-staff of the Chancellor was significantly increased (Schatz 1974: 22). Expert committees were created to treat economic policy-planning (Grube et al. 1976: 161–73). Long-term commissions were created to rule over issues of policy (1976: 161). Individual ministries were given increased influence over their own budgets (thus increasing their planning-authority). The role of state- and quasi-state consultative bodies also increased dramatically (Rossmann 1986: 184), and a large commission (comprising members from politics, unions and employers' associations) was created to document and plan policies of 'economic and social transformation' (Besters 1979: 25). These develop-ments, which reflect the ethic of technical social planning in government circles, constitute, in short, a background to Habermas's thinking, in which political decisions were increasingly left to specialists and technical con-sultants, and thus removed from the influence of public will-formation. Despite notable attempts to democratize the planning-authorities under Brandt's administration (Scharpf 1973: 70), the increasing delegation of policy-decisions to trained advisers resulted in further usurpation of parlia-ment as the location of power.

It is also of great relevance to Habermas that the crux of Keynesian policy – namely the juggling of economic growth and welfare aims – was abandoned in the Federal Republic by the mid-1970s (Riemer 1982: 55). Owing to the economic crises of the early and mid-1970s, the SPD ultimately dropped its reformist dream of the structurally ensured equality of capital and labour in favour of much more defensive policies (see Narr et al. 1976: 17–18, 42–3; Mottl 1992: 226; Offe 1976: 101–2). Although in certain instances (notably the education system) Brandt's government did indeed introduce far-reaching reforms, other planned reforms (especially the tax-reform) were introduced belatedly, and in a form unlikely to alienate wealthier sectors of the electorate (Braunthal 1983: 246). During the recession of 1975, Helmut Schmidt implemented a far more restrictive budgetary policy, formalized in the Budget Structure Law (Altvater et al. 1979: 335). The chief purpose of this law, which initiated the austerity-period or the *Tendenzwende* of the late 1970s (Alber 1986: 85), was to reduce inflation by cutting public spending and to strengthen the export-sector by investing financial reserves in new technologies (Jacobi 1982a: 81; J. Hoffmann 1987: 353). This marked the end of the labour-friendly doctrines of the SPD of the 1960s and early 1970s.

Indeed, the defining economic problems of the early to mid-1970s – the period of stagflation – clearly revealed the limitations of Keynesian crisis-management. After the first oil-crisis of 1973–4, Western economies, especially the Federal Republic, entered a period of radically reduced growth and increased inflation owing to the increment in the cost of raw materials (Neuthinger 1982: 551). Confronted with a stagnatory economic climate, both the political executive and the employers' associations in the Federal Republic imposed restrictions on the bargaining syndicates which had been created through the late 1960s (C. Schulz 1984: 224). Schmidt, unlike Schiller, expressly refused to increase public spending during the 1975 recession (Riemer 1982: 64), and he deliberately attempted to reduce state-led stimulation of demand (Altvater et al. 1979: 245). After the first oil-crisis, the Schmidt-administration sought above all to stabilize the economic position of the Federal Republic by cutting welfare- and labour-costs, and thus maintaining an 'export-offensive' (Rupp 1976: 27). Arguably, therefore, the neo-corporate policies of the early 1970s (as in the 1920s) also consolidated the power of strong economic organizations at the executive level of government (Heinze 1981: 14), and engendered a set of close working relationships between government and business. Throughout the 1970s the CDU itself also became increasingly well-disposed to the idea of societal pluralism (see Beyme 1991b: 139), and it looked favourably upon the contribution of the corporate system to the maintenance of social order (see Groser 1979: 454).

The period of stagflation therefore showed up the deficiencies of political legitimacy based upon class-compromise, and it underlined the half-suppressed conflict in the Federal Republic between the interest-groups brought together in the name of 'social dialogue'. In this regard, at least, Habermas's suggestions in 1972 that Keynesian compromises are a poor replacement for genuine social agreement, and that systemic integration in late-capitalist societies depends structurally on economic growth, were borne out by subsequent developments. The antagonisms between work-force, government and management became increasingly manifest through the 1970s. Only Habermas's prognosis that the crisis of systemic integration can lead to a more genuine discursive mode of political legitimacy proved incorrect.

Habermas's *Legitimation Crisis* therefore closely reflects the political and economic symmetries between the 1920s and the 1970s. Habermas himself clearly diagnoses corporate pluralism as a means of 'activating the steering-potential of large associations, outside the state' (1985a: 154). Written at the beginning of the reforms of the 1970s, *Legitimation Crisis* is a warning to the Brandt-administration (to which Habermas was not wholly unsympathetic) that the SPD must not fall once again into the corporate traps of the 1920s. Habermas expressly argues against the institution of a pluralistic system which leaves the antagonisms between labour and capital unreconciled, and which results simply in the institution of an elite cartel at the decision-making level (see Alemann and Heinze 1981: 61). Similarly, he condemns from the outset the organization of society around individual interest-groups (see Raschke 1978: 14). Most significantly, Habermas is sceptical about the suggestion that the compromise between the workforce and management (the balance of class-forces) can constitute the basis of political legitimacy (see S. K. White 1988: 76). Such compromises depend, he argues, upon 'the ideological form of justification, which counterfac-tually asserts or imputes the generalizability of interests' (Habermas 1973: 155–6).

However, Habermas himself admits in his analysis of late-capitalist planning-systems that not all areas of cognitive-instrumental operation can be subjected to communicative or consensual discourse (1981i: 324). He accepts, broadly, the technical structures of the existing systemic apparatus and he argues that the internal alteration of these structures is the best hope of social utopia. He advocates the discursive democratization of the decision-making apparatuses of government, and he even endorses the use of direct-democratic techniques for guaranteeing greater democracy (1981c: 323). However, Habermas's own theory of rationality implies that communicative reason can only set the basic parameters of government. It cannot implement individual acts of planning or technical disposition. Habermas (like certain notable conservative figures) indicates that pre-determined reformist programmes (including those of Brandt) also corrupt the practical rationality of discourse, and subordinate the communicative essence of politics to technical strategy. Helmut Schelsky, at the same time, also derided the 'denaturation of action to a mere plan' and the 'ideologization of rationality' in technical steering-systems (1980a: 301; see also Hennis 1977a: 193). Furthermore, Habermas asserts, communicat-ive rationality cannot constitute the basis of spontaneous or radical political action, for it is bound to the stable conditions and procedures of discursive exchange.

Despite his thorough critique of the legitimacy structures of modern democracy, therefore, Habermas himself does not go far beyond a social-reformist plea for an open society, with plural centres of public debate. In his double-edged suggestion that state-law refracts economic interests, but that it can, potentially, also respond to the resources of solidarity in the life-world, Habermas moves very close indeed to Neumann's central argument (Söllner 1982b: 112). Although Habermas exposes the structural problems of a state based upon the balance of class-forces, the state, in his conception, is not driven solely by economic imperatives and it remains susceptible, as an integrative body, to impulses from the social sphere (see Butterwegge 1979: 40). Habermas, for this reason, rejects reform within the predeter-mined framework of class-balance. Reform within foreclosed horizons is counter to the spirit of public discourse free of compulsion which, for Habermas, must be the basis of genuine legitimacy (Rehg 1994: 29–30). 'We have to pursue reforms for the sake of clear and publicly debated goals,' he asserts, 'even and indeed most determinedly when their effects are not compatible with the mode of production of the existing system' (1981h: 302; 1990b: 503). Habermas thus favours a polycentric discursive reform policy, which is significantly distinct from the pre-charted technical reforms of the SPD government in the 1970s. The substantive content of Habermas's position, however, does not envisage radical modification either of the system of government or the mode of production (see Rockmore 1989: 124). Even in his critique of late capitalism, in sum, Habermas still argues that the state is produced out of social needs. With regard to the possibility of the 'total democratic restructuration of the economic system from top to bottom', he observes simply: 'I cannot really believe in it any more' (1990b: 503–4).

The major arguments of *Legitimation Crisis* are sustained in Habermas's works throughout the 1970s, and they culminate in *Theory of Communicative Action* (1981). In *Theory of Communicative Action* Habermas, in Parson-ian manner, explains how the possibility of emancipatory praxis in modern society has been neglected by his sociological precursors, most especially Weber, Lukács, Horkheimer and Adorno. These theorists, he alleges, have stressed the role of instrumental reason in the emergence of complex societies to the exclusion of all other forms of rationalization. Against such wholly pessimistic theories of rationalization, Habermas expands his theory of communicative action, or 'post-traditional everyday communica-tion', to argue that social rationalization, based upon practical interests and communicable norms, can contain the latent possibility of emancipated political praxis (1981j: 452), and can to some extent limit the power of semi-autonomous systems (p. 486).

However, in *Theory of Communicative Action* the claims which Habermas makes for social rationalization are developed through a further investment in functionalist social theory. In this work, Habermas continues to repres-ent the aspects of the systemic sphere – the state-administration and the economy – as steering-media which are de-coupled from the social sphere, and which conform to strategic (success-oriented) motivations (1981k: 460). The life-world continues to exist as a locus characterized by understanding, by the consensual co-ordination of action and socialization: 'the symbolic structures of the life-world reproduce themselves through the continuation of valid knowledge, the stabilization of group-solidarity and the development of responsible actors' (pp. 208–9). However, by this stage, the relation between the social sphere and the system has changed considerably from Habermas's earliest works. In *Structural Transformation of the Public Sphere*, Habermas puts forward a normative critique, which argues that the political arena should be grounded on a legitimate will-formation. This same argument, expressed in more functionalist terms, underpins *Legitimation Crisis*. In *Theory of Communicative Action*, however, his analysis is more descriptive and defensive in character, and the concept of political life at the heart of this work is much more tentative. Habermas maintains that the sphere of social integration has primacy over the sphere of systemic integration, and that the system begins to malfunction if it loses its 'foundation of trust' (legitimation) in the social sphere (pp. 404–5). Nonetheless, he implies that the media of money and power have now established themselves instrumentally against their normative environments. Little can be done directly to transpose these media into alternative functional structures. Prescriptively, Habermas still asserts that the life-world should be freed from systemic colonization and that liberty should be created for the communicative establishment of universal norms within this sphere. However, Habermas now sees greater resilience in the ability of the advanced capitalist state to obscure or compensate for legitimation-deficits (see S. K. White 1988: 118). He warns now with greater urgency about the 'colonization of the life-world' – about, that is: 'the penetration of forms of economic and administrative rationality into areas of action which resist adjustment to the media of money and power because they specialize in cultural tradition, social integration and education and are reliant on understanding as a mechanism for the co-ordination of action' (1981k: 488). The chief characteristic of modern capitalist democracies, Habermas now argues, is that the systems of money and power, which have properly differentiated themselves from the social sphere, have developed mechanisms for colonizing the social sphere in order to sustain their own operative basis. Habermas's interest in the life-world is at this stage more protective than assertive, and he does little more than suggest that the life-world possesses symbolic status as the last region of non-administered action, which must be kept distinct from the political and economic spheres.[5]

Important for a contextual evaluation of Habermas's work is the fact that in *Theory of Communicative Action* law is examined as a key mechanism by means of which technical systems infiltrate the life-world. Habermas argues here that objective law possesses a twofold character. It is both a technical 'means of organization' or 'steering-medium' which acts neutrally towards

5 1981k: 126. See also Joas 1986: 156; Honneth 1986: 333–4; S. K. White 1988: 126.

the contexts of the life-world (1981k: 507–8), and which is not obliged to justify its contents against the norms of the social sphere. Such law is intimately linked with the media of money and administrative power. It 'extends to the formally organized action-areas' which are constituted in the 'forms of bourgeois formal law' (p. 537). Therefore, Habermas sees formal or positive law as a technical medium, whose function is to create the optimal working conditions for the economic and administrative systems. However, Habermas argues that objective law, as a *legal institution*, also belongs to the 'social component of the life-world' (p. 537). The norms of constitutional and criminal law, for example, are not acceptable simply because they have the quality of legality. These are fundamental norms which have assumed a regulative function in everyday human action, which are closely connected with moral expectations, and which thus belong to the 'legitimate orders of the life-world' (p. 536). Such norms give determinate form to the moral agreements which already informally exist in communicatively structured areas of action, and they play a significant role in the articulation of shared moral identities.

However, in the era of advanced capitalism, Habermas argues, these norms are also transmuted into means by which the system of the economy guarantees its success. In the modern welfare-state, the legal institutions which are both embedded in the life-world and sanctioned by the political order – especially the expectation of social and material security – are applied in the medium of social law. In its application of social law, however, the administration unleashes a palliative device for the instrumental *juridification* of social relations, to ensure that social conflict does not impede the operations of the economy. Law, therefore, is deployed in the welfare-state not only as a technical medium for stabilizing particular systems, but also as an objective material technique for organizing spheres of social interaction in order to protect the system of the economy. The objective norms upon which the shared identities of citizens are based are thus transformed into the preconditions for the stability of the capitalist state. The legal order of the welfare-state, Habermas asserts, therefore revolves around the formal 'constitutionalization of the social relation of violence which is anchored in the class-structure' (p. 530). In these respects, Habermas's arguments directly connect again with the political conditions of the Federal Republic in the 1970s and 1980s. From a moderate left position, he asserts that the technical balancing-acts of the social state retract more liberty than they engender. The sphere of social integration, he argues, must be protected from 'the system-imperatives of the autonomously growing sub-systems of the economy and administration' (p. 547).

Such arguments, clearly, have a long tradition in German political thought. Habermas joins the history of opposition to both the formalization and the materialization of modern law. His chief interlocutor in this tradition is Weber. Unlike his precursors, however, Habermas implies that the legitimacy of law depends on its openness to moral input from social systems. Law can only be more than formal legality if it is sustained by discourse in the public sphere, if public law is extended to include moral discourse (1976a: 266). Only in this way can law overcome the strategic, exchange-based formality of modern civil or private law upon which the legal order is based (1976a: 263–4). This implies that legality can only be legitimacy if the subordination of public law to the administration of private interests is eliminated. Legal institutions are legitimate, Habermas indicates, if private legal subjects recognize themselves in law as public citizens – if law can transpose a plurality of private interests into commonly binding terms. In advanced capitalism, however, law is formalized as a steering-medium, and it is materialized as a device for administering compensation to the socially disavantaged. It thus remains a complex fusion of private and public law, in which private interests are protected by the media of public power.

*Theory of Communicative Action* describes therefore the relation between the citizen and the economy in modern society, in which the possibilities of political action are severely restricted. In this work, Habermas's earlier functionalist description of the non-normative autonomy of economic – and economically driven – systems prevails over his more anthropological reflections on the potentials of human interaction. Habermas explains here (in quasi-functionalist manner) that the systems of money, power and administration inevitably de-couple themselves from the life-world (1981k: 488). This development assumes socio-pathological features when these systems completely block their communication with the life-world. Under such conditions they are forced to extend back into the life-world in order to secure technically the normative legitimacy which they forfeit through differentiation. The systems of modern society suffer a chronic lack of legitimacy because they are placed in the service of the non-universal needs of the capitalist economy. Habermas argues clearly that the normative claims of democracy cannot be realized under the conditions of capitalism (p. 507). In late capitalism, the administrative and political system is reduced to the functional protection of the system of money. Politics, law and administration become devices for intercepting, palliating and juridify-ing the legitimatory demands arising from the social sphere. Habermas thus returns to Kirchheimer's earlier (more radical) distinction between the sphere of direction and the sphere of distribution. Modern law and modern politics become, for Habermas, formal, material and functional variables in the overarching system of private law. Law thus forfeits its utopian potential as mediator between private and public freedom.

It is notable, however, that through the 1980s the focus of Habermas's theory shifts significantly from such defensive reflections on the relation between citizen and economy, to more optimistic reflections on the rela-tion between citizen and state. In this respect, *Theory of Communicative Action* can be interpreted as an important transitional work in Habermas's overall opus. In subsequent works, culminating in his legal-theoretical writings of the 1990s, Habermas moves to a perspective which is more inclined to bracket out the economy, as a system of action which cannot be linked to communicatively established norms. Especially in his interventions in issues of everyday politics through the 1980s, Habermas staked out his position as that of a committed popular philosopher, contributing moral commentary on general aspects of German political and cultural life. The two issues which especially preoccupied Habermas in the 1980s were the problem of post-traditional political identity, especially in the Federal Republic, and the related issue of patriotism. Habermas's involvement in such discussions was initially triggered by the *Historikerstreit* of 1986, but these matters became, naturally, more central to his thinking after the reunification of Germany after 1989.

In these debates, Habermas argues in essence that the only form of collective identity possible for the citizens of Germany is 'constitutional patriotism' (1990c: 151). This formulation opposes, on one level, the apparent rehabilitation of German national identity proposed by the conservative participants in the *Historikerstreit*. More generally, however, Habermas's theory of constitutional patriotism argues that social identity (especially in Germany) can no longer be legitimately attached to the nation-state, because the nation-state is no longer a centre of power in global society (1995a: 187). The issue of collective identity is always close to the heart of Habermas's thinking, as the construction of social identity is a central function of social rationalization in the life-world (1976c: 116). As an alternative to the nation-state, Habermas proposes that collective identities should be developed which are based on the basic rights inscribed in democratic constitutions. Such identities are, by definition, transnational (1990c: 152).

After 1989, Habermas recommends constitutional patriotism especially as a means for integrating the citizens of the German Democratic Republic into an overarching normative, but post-traditional mode of citizenship (1990d: 216). The constitution, Habermas argues, provides the optimal post-conventional focus of political loyalty. It represents a set of terms in which public (collective) identity and private autonomy are not mutually restrictive. In the guarantee of basic rights offered by liberal constitutions, Habermas explains, the citizen is recognized both as a rational and autonomous private agent and as a component of a general political formation (1995b: 158). In this respect, Habermas's theory of constitutional patriotism is a contextual return to his earlier theory of legal-democratic identity as the realization of private–public unity. Moreover, Habermas argues that basic rights contain a guarantee of social pluralism which obstructs exclusive identity-formations. The basic rights in the constitutions of modern republics ensure that collective identities can be formed which are not detached – like national identities – from the plural normative bases of the life-world. Habermas thus recognizes the democratic constitution as a legal institution which is embedded in the varying and distinct structures of recognition which characterize the life-world. Through the constitution, the terms of public interaction can be set in a manner which accords with the distinct dignity of private subjects.

In the theory of constitutional patriotism, in short, Habermas goes back, in Kantian manner, to an old German debate. Popular sovereignty and human rights are, he asserts, co-original (1995b: 159). The collective (public) inscription of popular sovereignty in a democratic constitution is simultaneous with the recognition of the particular (private) dignity of each person. Although Habermas's theory of constitutional patriotism is a response to (alleged) attempts to resuscitate German national identity, it has its origins in his earlier reflections on the German lack of a connecting set of discourses between the political and private spheres. Habermas's championing of transnational republicanism represents a rejection of legal politics based either in the system of needs (the economy), in the state, or in the ideological devices which merge public and private into a false synthesis (national historicism). Indeed, in his vehement rejection of the exhumation of German national identity proposed by his adversaries in the *Historiker-streit*, Habermas directly calls upon the Kantian traditions of political reflection which were initially suppressed by historicism in the nineteenth century (1990c: 150) – namely rights-based republicanism and the legally circumscribed claim to popular sovereignty. Implicit in these observations is the argument that German historicism in the nineteenth century was in part responsible for obstructing the formation of a genuine political society – it should not, therefore, in its latter-day guise, do so again. In this regard, Habermas's interventions in political debates in the 1980s, although motivated by specific issues, are components in the long resistance to the fiction of the national community in Germany, and to the employment of this fiction to obstruct radical-liberal political forms.

In the overall development of Habermas's work, his observations on national identity crystallize a broad shift in his thinking, towards a positive theory of political action and citizenship (1995b: 144). Central to this shift is the belief that law can, after all, realize the promise of Enlightenment, which, as positive law, it originally carried. In this respect, it is striking, indeed, that Habermas ultimately abandons the rigid (although ambiguous) separation of system and life-world which is at the heart of his earlier critiques (Beyme 1996: 13). In his most recent major work, *Between Facts and Norms* (1992), Habermas relinquishes the strict division between social integration and systemic integration, and he argues instead that positive law is not, in fact, merely a systemic steering-medium. Law possesses, he argues here, a privileged status as 'transformer' between the solidarity of the life-world and the operations of the system (1992: 108). Positive law, Habermas thus explains, derives its legitimacy from its latent republican sense that the addressees of law can also consider themselves the authors of law. Modern law 'draws its strength from the solidarity which is concentrated in the role of the citizen' (p. 52). It provides a medium which, however imperfect its realization, reflects the normative claim that the systemic media of administrative power should (and can) be bound to the 'social-integrative process' of the 'self-determination of citizens' (p. 60). Indeed, contrary to his earlier works, Habermas indicates here that law can reconnect the system of administration to the system of social integration, in the form of genuine politics. Habermas thus argues that the constitution of positive law is always, at least potentially, open to the processes of intersubjective communication in the life-world (p. 60). It is able to ensure, by transforming the needs of the life-world into codes which are assimilable to systemic media, that the processes of systemic integration do not lose their legitimizing base in the life-world (p. 78). Here, Habermas argues not only against Luhmann's functionalist theory of communication, but against his own earlier scepticism regarding the possibility of positive politics (K. Roth 1994: 425). He elaborates a theory of radical or deliberative democracy, in which law provides a flexible medium for filtering the public will into the systemic media. The universal medium of law can transport the plural ethical discourses of the life-world into a mode of solidarity-based control of the system. He emphasizes thus, against both Weber and Luhmann, 'the particular social-integrative function of law' (1992: 98), and he argues even that the economy and the bureaucracy themselves 'only emerge in the medium of their legal institutionalization', and are thus, in principle, subject to legal control (p. 150).

This late work, therefore, marks a partial return to liberal-rational ideas of popular sovereignty. Habermas here ascribes to legality itself the power to create political legitimacy. Legality, he implies, cannot be viewed either functionistically or decisionistically, but should be construed rather as a structure which 'regenerates itself from traditions of freedom and preserves itself in the relations of association of a liberal political culture' (p. 165). The processes of system-integration, Habermas argues, can never dissolve the residues of ethical intersubjectivity in the life-world, from which universal law derives its substance. However, Habermas's version of liberalism also contains a strong component of active (Arendtian) republicanism. Habermas's liberalism does not seek to stabilize permanently the form of state, but rather to recast constantly and positively the terms of collective life. The public power of government is not a statically decided system, but always, lastly, a fluid, procedural organ of 'communicative power' (p. 200).

*Between Facts and Norms*, naturally, does not imply that there can occur a direct transposition of social needs into systemic integration. The title of the work itself indicates that the ethical potentials of interaction always exist in a relation of tension with the facticity of systemic organization (p. 124). However, Habermas sees law as a channel of imperfect but vital communication between system and life-world, which, by means of institutionalized procedures, can assert the will-formation of the spheres of public life against other integrative mechanisms (p. 363). At the base of this communicative theory of law and power is a demand for plural, discursive or radical-democratic procedures which are equipped to channel interactive norms into the legislative organs. Habermas now affirms the traditional role of associations, parties and parliamentary corporations, which link directly with the political public sphere. However, he argues most strongly in favour of the institution of plural, democratic procedures of public discourse. The state, thus, should be connected to society by a 'multi-level intersubjectivity of communication-processes, which takes place on one level in the institutionalized form of discussions in parliamentary corporations and on a different level in the communication-network of political public spheres' (1997: 288).

In terms of the overall development of his work, Habermas's most recent contributions to the theory of legality and legitimacy are a return to his earliest (pre-functionalist) concern with the realization of genuine democracy in highly complex societies (1990e: 43). The deliberative, radical-democratic theory of law and politics in his last works is a response to the problem addressed in *Structural Transformation* – which is, indeed, the recurrent concern of much modern German political thought. In *Between Facts and Norms*, namely, Habermas attempts to explain how the liberal foundation of democracy in the private-legal order can be overcome without asserting an absolute primacy of state-law. In *Structural Transformation*, Habermas asserts that the bourgeois public sphere produces universalizable norms, but that the conditions of advanced capitalism block the realization of these norms. In his latest works, however, he argues that the institution of plural deliberative procedures of public discourse can effectively open law to the moral discourses of the civil sphere (Rasmussen 1996: 42). Law, thus, can transpose the private interests of citizens into the public terms of citizenship (Habermas 1992: 492). In his deliberative theory of law, therefore, Habermas therefore finally develops a paradigm for explaining how the public sphere can act once again as a radical-progressive force for social change, between economy and state. The strong category of the political which is both present and suppressed in Habermas's earlier work is here, therefore, finally expanded.

Significantly, Habermas expressly defines this deliberative theory of law in opposition to Weber. Weber, he implies, was unsuccessful in his attempt to overcome the formalization of law because he rejected the status of law as a possible bearer of value-rationality (1992: 343–5). Habermas understands his own theory therefore as a corrective to Weber – as the solution to the key problem of German political theory. 'The internal connection between subjective and objective law on one hand and between private and public autonomy on the other', he argues, 'only discloses itself when we take seriously and explain appropriately the intersubjective structure of laws and the communicative structure of self-legislation' (1992: 135).

Habermas's optimistic theory of the possible deliberative democratization of law moves away, however, from a consideration of the economy. Some critics have argued that Habermas's discursive theory of democracy still carries the suggestion that citizens, if allowed to deliberate co-operatively with one another, will prefer deliberative interaction to market-based strategies (Chambers 1996: 192). This might, following this interpretation, be grasped as a residual element of Marxism in Habermas's late thought.

However, the economy is, to a very large extent, excluded from Habermas's late theory of democracy. Whereas in his earlier works Habermas suggests that material equality (or at least the absence of economic coercion) is the precondition of political liberty, here he substitutes *anthropological* equality for material equality. Indeed, Habermas intimates that capitalism is often the precondition for deliberative democracy. The deliberative openness of political and economic systems, he states, is only possible in *liberal* public spheres (1992: 462). More pointedly, the ideal outcome of deliberative democracy is not the regulation of economic life. The crucial point in Habermas's theory of deliberative law is, therefore, not the 'restructuration of socio-economic organization' but rather the 'rationalization of the execution of administrative power' by means of the 'reconstruction of the normative content which is peculiar to law and the legal state' (1997: 379). The shift of Habermas's focus between 1981 and 1992 involves therefore a more positive reappraisal not only of the capitalist state, but also of the capitalist economy.

In these later examples, Habermas's thinking falls into line with a broad theoretical move in German politics, instigated by the collapse of the GDR, towards a 'post-ideological' theory of politics (Beyme 1996: 10), which breaks with economically differentiated reflections on citizenship. Habermas's earlier emphasis upon 'constitutional patriotism' also underlines his move towards anthropological ( K. Roth 1994: 427; Narr 1994: 94), radical-liberal explanations of the conditions of human coexistence (Habermas 1990c: 151). Like, diversely, Ulrich K. Preuß (1994b: 29) and Axel Honneth (1992: 178), Habermas represents the political constitution of the legal state as a framing semantic in which the terms of legal-social *recognition* of others, and, consequently, recognition of the laws themselves (Habermas 1985d: 85), are always given.

Habermas's trajectory, in sum, moves from his earliest radicalization of popular sovereignty, through a critique of technocratic reason, a critical reception of functionalism, a discussion of national identity-formation, and back to a theory of the legal state. His thinking shadows, as its left-liberal conscience, the shifts in the history of post-war Germany itself, from the uncertain legitimacy of the Basic Law and the new republic, through the radical movements of the 1960s, the reforms of the 1970s, the *Tendenz-wende*, and the altered ideological figures after 1989. Through their universalist turn, his last major works move Habermas towards a radical-democratic variant on a classical-liberal political position. The latent discursive possibility of universal justice which Habermas finds in the *Rechtsstaat*, with its structures of recognition, mirrors the core of this latter period of history itself. The uniformity of political contours in post-1989 Europe is translated easily and often into a new anthropological universalism. Habermas's early thought can be interpreted as a fusion of Kant, Marx and Arendt (or Arendt's Aristotelian component), which saw the possibility of communicative power and interactive political legitimacy always obstructed by the systemic apparatuses of late capitalism. The real heart of

Habermas's work, however, has been drawn out more closely since he (more or less) abandoned Marx. The utopia of civil interaction was, from the outset, Habermas's own utopia, not invariably (or necessarily) bound to material equality (1969b: 36). In this respect, *Between Facts and Norms*, although it moves surprisingly and decisively away from the defining premises of Critical Theory, can be viewed as a more perfect statement of the key preconditions of Habermas's thought than *Theory of Communicative Action* or *Legitimation Crisis*. Significantly, Habermas's very late work continues the fusion of Kantian legal theory and radical Aristotelian anthropology which informed his earliest works. The broad contours of Habermas's thought can, in sum, be seen as a move from the postulated identity of the social and the political, through a despairing retreat into the social, back to his earliest conception – now less cautiously stated – that the social sphere can be actively mediated into political life.

## Selected further reading

Bernstein, J. M. (1995) *Recovering Ethical Life: Jürgen Habermas and the Future of Critical Theory* (London: Routledge).

Bernstein, Richard J. (ed.) (1985) *Habermas and Modernity* (Cambridge: Polity Press).

Brand, Arie (1990) *The Force of Reason: An Introduction to Habermas' Theory of Communicative Action* (London: Allen & Unwin).

Chambers, Simone (1996) *Reasonable Democracy: Jürgen Habermas and the Politics of Discourse* (Ithaca, NY/London: Cornell UP).

Deflem, Mathieu (ed.) (1996) *Habermas, Modernity and Law* (London: Sage).

Held, David and Thompson, John (1982) *Habermas: Critical Debates* (London: Macmillan).

Ingram, D. (1987) *Habermas and the Dialectic of Reason* (New Haven: Yale UP).

Kellner, Douglas (1989) *Critical Theory, Marxism and Modernity* (Baltimore: Johns Hopkins UP).

McCarthy, Thomas (1978) *The Critical Theory of Jürgen Habermas* (Cambridge, Mass./London: MIT Press).

Outhwaite, William (1994) *Habermas: A Critical Introduction* (Cambridge: Polity Press).

Rehg, William (1994) *Insight and Solidarity: A Study in the Discourse Ethics of Jürgen Habermas* (Berkeley/Los Angeles/London: University of California Press).

Rockmore, Tom (1989) *Habermas on Historical Materialism* (Bloomington/Indianapolis: Indiana University Press).

Thompson, John B. (1981) *Critical Hermeneutics: A Study in the Thought of Paul Ricoeur and Jürgen Habermas* (Cambridge: CUP).

White, Stephen K. (1988) *The Recent Work of Jürgen Habermas: Reason, Justice and Modernity* (Cambridge: CUP).

# 5

# *Niklas Luhmann*

As in the above chapters on Habermas and Weber, this chapter will focus on a very selected area of Luhmann's works, namely on those directly connected with his theory of politics. Luhmann's entire opus covers issues as diverse as aesthetics, the sociology of religion, the sociology of knowledge, the sociology of law and economic theory. Although there is as yet no thorough treatment of Luhmann's work which might make his ideas accessible to readers of English, a discussion of the whole range of his works is beyond the scope of this chapter.

Luhmann, who spent the bulk of his academic career as Professor of Sociology at the University of Bielefeld, is renowned in modern sociology as the most prominent exponent of systems-theory, or radical functionalist sociology. His political writings, although they have had relatively little impact outside of Germany, have been extremely important and influential in German political debate. These writings set out striking refigurations of conventional political questions, treating issues such as the separation of powers, the relation between government and administration, the role of social movements and the impact of ecological questions on government. Luhmann's political position is broadly neo-conservative, although recently his ideas have been more sympathetically received on the left. He has worked in conjunction with the CDU at various stages in his career, but his activities as a legal theorist have also brought him into contact with the SPD. The historical background to Luhmann's considerable influence can be broadly traced, however, to the wholesale shift to the right (*Tendenz-wende*) in the second half of the 1970s, after Helmut Schmidt's assumption of power. During this time Luhmann's thought provided important perspectives in the debates on governability, deregulation and state-intervention. His technocratic theory of government closely echoes the swing during the 1970s towards the reduction of state-activities, and the transfer of power to the bureaucracy. Equally significantly, Luhmann's pronouncements on issues of general political importance have usually been hostile (or mocking) towards grass-roots movements in German society – especially the Green party and the student movement. As will be illustrated below, his ironic distance towards anti-systemic formations within German society is inscribed in the innermost logic of his theoretical sociology.

Luhmann's brand of systems theory is an amalgam of diverse influences. His legal positivism echoes the ideas of both Carl Schmitt and Hans Kelsen. His functionalist anthropology is coloured both by Bronislaw Malinowski and by the conservative institutionalism of Arnold Gehlen. Gehlen's theory that social institutions obviate the need for individual political response underlies all Luhmann's reflections. Luhmann's most direct influence is Talcott Parsons, under whom he studied at Harvard in the early 1960s. A further influence on his thought is Edmund Husserl, to whose phenomeno-logical conception of social being he is much indebted. In his more recent works, after his shift in the early 1980s towards a biological paradigm for explaining social systems, the Chilean biologists Humberto Maturana and Francisco Varela have strongly influenced his thought (see Lipp 1987: 452). Although Luhmann's antecedents are often complex and obscure, it is surprising that little critical attention has been paid to the foreshadowing of his ideas in the sociology of Georg Simmel (Simmel 1989: 304).

Luhmann's theory of modern society is a theory of differentiation and complexity. He argues that the key attribute of modern society is its composition through the differentiation of social functions – or through its differentiation into individual systems, which fulfil specific social func-tions. The functional systems of modern society include, for instance, the legal system, the political system, the administration, and the system of money (the economy). The differentiation of modern society into functional systems is distinct from the segmentary or stratificatory forms of differ-entiation (especially class- or estate-based hierarchies) which characterize pre-modern society. The strict segregation of the economic and the political system is, for example, an attribute of modern society which distinguishes it from the personal centration of both economic and political power in pre-modern societies.

The institutional contours of modern society are produced, Luhmann thus argues, according to a logic of functional complexity and specificity. As the environment becomes increasingly complex, Luhmann explains, more systems – and more functionally specific systems – are required to organize this complexity. The fundamental function of systems is to reduce com-plexity and to create operations which manage complexity. In the develop-ment of modern society, therefore, differentiated systems emerge as distinct spheres of human activity. Economy, polity, administration and law are all gradually separated out from each other. Each system creates the mechan-isms appropriate to solving the problems produced by its own mode of activity. Systems therefore also generate sub-systems which allow them to absorb increasing pressures in the environment. This subsidiary differentiation of social systems is the production of institutions. Institutions form the secondary dimension in the systemic evolution of modern society. Courts, universities, bureaucracies, banks, governments etc., Luhmann asserts, produce themselves in order to catch the spiralling complexity of the environment, as it impacts on the broader systems of law, pedagogics, finance etc. By means of the production of such institutions, overarching social systems generate a degree of internal complexity which enables them to hold themselves at the level of the escalating complexity of their environment.

In their purest conception, Luhmann explains, systems create themselves through the principle of 'double contingency'. This means that systems create a code through which the components of the system order their operations, both functionally and temporally (Thome 1973: 23). For example, the code right/wrong, around which the legal system operates, means that A has an expectation of what B will do if A commits a certain action, and B has an expectation of what A will do in response. The actions of B are contingent on those of A, as are those of A on those of B. The systems thus stabilize themselves by creating an internal self-referential code which must be ceaselessly extended as the complexity of both the system and the environment increases (Luhmann 1980: 103). The creation of an 'expectation-expectation' is therefore at the heart of modern systems. A's expectation of B's expectation constitutes a trust in the codes and the communications of the system itself. Systems, therefore, have no external definition or rationalization. They seek to stabilize their own operations, and to ensure that the unstable horizon of the world can be made, to some extent, predictable, through the expectation-expectations which connect their components. 'Systems are rational', Luhmann explains, 'to the extent that they can grasp and reduce complexity, and they can do this only when they make use of trust and mistrust, without overburdening those who, in the final analysis, show trust and mistrust – people themselves' (1973c: 105).

It is in this context that Luhmann outlines the significance of modern law. The modern legal system, he argues, constitutes itself through the positivization of law. Through the creation of structures of positive law, which are not anchored in substantive value-conceptions, the legal order creates a code which stabilizes it – as order – against the disordered environment, and through which it represents information to itself about the environment (Kleinknecht 1992: 246–7). The positivization of law is, Luhmann argues, the decisive moment in the production of modern systems, as it marks the point where systems begin to interact functionally and autonomously with their environment (1981a: 150). This means, essentially, that systems acquire in positive law an independent code which enables them to represent and formalize their own internal expectation-expectations. The code right/wrong of the legal system, for instance, creates a binary sequence of options, according to which the legal system can represent to itself impulses from outside it, as these affect the system's own expectations. The fluidity of positive law means also that the expectations of the system can be adjusted – however gradually – to the information which it gathers from the environment.

The conditions of modern politics are, Luhmann therefore argues, linked very closely to the positivization of law. Positive law allows the political and the administrative systems to register problems in their environment and to adjust their operations accordingly. Democracy itself, Luhmann argues, is merely an administrative order in which positive law enables the political and the administrative systems to pick up problems in their relation to the environment (1980: 34). These problems are then registered by alterations in positive law. Owing to the positivization of law, the political and administrative systems possess a changeable relation to their environment, and they can alter this relation wherever they encounter systemic obstacles. Positive law is therefore the precondition of democracy. In democracy, Luhmann argues, the interests of the social sphere (the people) are detected as hindrances to organizational systems. These systems then negotiate with these hindrances through positive law. Perfect democracy, Luhmann implies, would be a system in which the codes of administration and politics would encounter no obstacles in their relation to the environment. Perfect democracy, thus, would be a smooth-running set of social systems, each tuned perfectly to the others.

At the base of Luhmann's theory of systems, like Gehlen's theory of institutions, is the idea that the world is too complicated for people to understand. Therefore, they must establish collective sense-orientations, through which they interpret and simplify the world. These sense-orientations form the fabric of institutions. Like Habermas, Luhmann works with a loosely phenomenological notion of human understanding. The unity of each social system resides, Luhmann argues, in its creation of internal sense – in its creation of stable codes of understanding, through which it can represent its own functions to itself. 'Sense', Luhmann explains, 'is the form of order of human experience, the form of the premises through which information is absorbed and consciously processed' (1975a: 61). The creation of sense is the process by means of which systems reduce the external complexity of their environment and maintain the internal complexity of their own institutions (1975a: 37). If a system creates sense, it can explain its own operations and it can produce directives which regulate these operations. The production of sense, Luhmann thus explains, provides an internal series of systemic references by means of which the system can select how it should react to the environment and to other systems. The administration of state, Luhmann argues, is the perfect model of systemic operation (1966a: 115). The administration of state has its own 'sense', constructed around its own internal administrative codes, which is not directly responsive to demands articulated from outside these codes.

Broadly, Luhmann's theory of social systems falls into two periods, although these cannot be finally distinguished from each other. His early work contains a theory of open systems. This theory argues that social systems develop by interacting with their environment and by processing information which they draw from their environment. His later work, influenced by the autopoietic theory of systems developed by the Chilean biologists, states that social systems are closed units (autopoietic systems), which comply exclusively with their own internal codes, and which are capable of processing information solely in accordance with these codes. In his early theory of systems, Luhmann asserts that systems attempt to represent to themselves a perfect (isomorphic) copy of their environment in order to respond to it appropriately. In the early period of his work, Luhmann thus implies that social systems attempt to react directly to the actual character of the impulses – needs – which they encounter (Schmid 1970: 200). Through his later autopoietic turn, however, he argues against the openness of social systems, and he states rather that a system is a closed circuit of self-referential codes and procedures. The legal system, for example, he argues, revolves around the binary code right/wrong. The code of the economy is the code payment/non-payment. When confronted with a case to be decided, the procedures of a system produce a decision according to the data which they have stored. The decision made within a system refers therefore only to the inner codes of the system, not to the substantive nature of the issue or problem which confronts it in its relation to the environment. This is especially significant for Luhmann's theories of democracy and politics. His autopoietic theory of social systems rejects normative proposals that state and society are bound together by contractual or reasoned motivations. Politics, he argues, operates by a code which has no correspondence with the social sphere. 'Society' can have no meaningful input in the operations of the self-referential system of politics. Indeed, in this theory of society, 'society', in the traditional sense, does not exist, or at least it exists only as the broad category which incorporates all social systems (Metzner 1993: 155). In his last work, *The Society of Society* (1997), Luhmann argues that, as all modern societies are systemically interlinked (1971b: 9), society is merely the environment of universal systems, which is not bound to geographical or physical essence (1997: 89–90).

Not surprisingly, therefore, Luhmann's theory has been received as the political theorization of 'postmodernity' (see Beyme 1991a: 17). His depiction of the internal rationality of systems as an 'expectation-expectation' implies that rationality has an exclusively functional status (see Schelsky 1980b: 91). In this relation, Luhmann questions definitions of rationality inherited from the Enlightenment, and from the canon of sociological theory. Like Helmut Schelsky (1980c: 68), he argues that each operative system has its own rationality which cannot be reduced to a collective or anthropological foundation. His ideas represent a movement away from humanistic conceptions of political action, liability and responsibility. They suggest a vision of a de-centred society, in which actions cannot be imputed (or can only be symbolically imputed) to specific agents. Like Kelsen and Schmitt before him, Luhmann argues that systems revolve around the maintenance of fictions, or paradoxes, and that the imputation of personal agency to roles within the system is just one fiction upon which systems reside. In this respect, Luhmann moves very close indeed to Carl Schmitt. Both Schmitt and Luhmann see the systemic decision, within the high executive or the administration, as a means by which systems define themselves against the environment (1984a: 400). When a system makes a decision, both Luhmann and Schmitt argue, it defines itself as order against the disordered environment. By doing so, it legitimizes itself as order. Schmitt's theory of the friend–foe relation can itself be interpreted as a crude formulation of the binary code through which the political system stabilizes itself against the obstacles in the environment (Beyme 1991b: 97).

Central to Luhmann's sociology is the assertion that the bureaucracy plays a key role in modern political order (1983: 34). The status of the bureaucracy is especially important, Luhmann argues, in modern democracies. In modern democracies, he explains, the political system divides itself into two separate but connected systems – government and administration. The administration has primacy in the relation between these systems. The function of the political system – government – is merely to set the premises for the decisions made within the administration, and to establish the programmes within which administrative decisions can be made – therefore, to decide over decisions (1966b: 272). Yet, Luhmann explains, the government is itself not directly responsible for political decisions. The political system must allow the administration to develop its own processes for the reduction of complexity (1966b: 284). It is fictitious to imagine, Luhmann thus implies, that the political sphere has measurable control over the operations of the administration. At most, the government can create purposive programmes, designed to absorb environ-mental complexity, which then provide the guidelines for the bureaucracy. However, Luhmann emphasizes that most planning activities are already located in the administration (1966b: 294). Implicitly, therefore, Luhmann asserts that in differentiated societies the government cannot project or propose a notion of public, collective or even 'political' interest, which it might claim to represent. Common ideas of particular, representation-based legitimacy are not appropriate to modern society. The most fundamental interest of the public (as far as it can be registered by the administrative system) is, Luhmann suggests, that everything should run smoothly – that uniform sense-orientations should be established, to which some level of compliance can be guaranteed. Governments are legitimate, he therefore states, only insofar as they create sense and reduce complexity. By doing this, they comply with their own rationality. The legitimation of political decisions is, he explains, nothing more than an institutional learning process, in which political institutions adjust systemic expectations to the realities of the environment (1983: 119), as positive law

(Weiß 1977: 76). A decision – a legal edict, for example – is legitimate if it successfully stabilizes the political system by demonstrating that the political system can learn enough about the environment to hold itself on a level of adequacy, or equivalence, to it. The political core of Luhmann's thought can thus be grasped as the transformation of political rationality into administrative rationality. Political decisions, he implies, can no longer create political legitimacy. Society is too complex to be regulated by individual decisions. It is also too complex for all interests to be registered by the political system. The political system, he therefore argues, is legitimate only if the administration can ensure that it operates properly.

Luhmann thus transports the basis of political legitimacy from the political to the administrative system. The administration, he indicates, is the point where the political system traces its relation to the environment and where it seeks to address issues presented to it through this relation. The political system, Luhmann claims, is ascribed far too much importance in popular understandings of politics. This is a residue from archaic, hierarchical conceptions of power and 'rule'. Government, he suggests, is merely the province of administrators. Good government is a process of 'functional equivalence', in which the relation between systems is adequately drawn. Good government passes laws exclusively in order to stabilize itself. Luhmann's theory is therefore intended as technocratic advice to the government in its quest for self-stabilization (see Bubner 1973: 122).

Luhmann's theories of government and administration relate most directly to the political conditions of the Federal Republic after 1967. Most especially, his theories are a response to the technical development of the state-apparatus in the Federal Republic throughout the 1960s. This period, as outlined above, was characterized by the gradual supplanting of consensual decision-making organs by planning-apparatuses, and by the hierarchicization of government around elite-cadres (see Naschold and Väth 1973: 11; Narr 1969: 180). The mode of systemic rationalization which Luhmann outlines corresponds perfectly to the shift away from government as a legally justified and enshrined set of practices towards plan-based concepts, which define government as an amalgam of technical responses to technical problems (H. Adam 1972: 22).

Moreover, Luhmann's theories at this time refer directly to the ideological incongruities of the Brandt/Schiller era. As outlined above, the reformist period of the late 1960s and early 1970s was marked by two apparently contradictory political tendencies – namely, by the move towards social-reformist policies and, equally, by the move towards technical modes of administration. Brandt stated in his governmental declaration of 1969 that administrative processes should be more open to public scrutiny and participation (Aderhold 1973: 302). At the same time, however, the planning-systems and resources at the disposal of his government expanded with striking rapidity, and became constantly less penetrable to those outside the executive.

Luhmann's thought touches therefore, indirectly, on the ideological discrepancy between the planning-euphoria of the SPD-government of the early 1970s and its proclamations in favour of basis-democracy. The basic suggestion in Luhmann's theory of the political system is that governments do not make decisions in accordance with pre-established or debated plans. They make decisions, he argues, in order to keep the political system at the pace of the developments in its environment. The real decisions are made beneath the highest level of the executive – in the bureaucracy. Therefore, Luhmann argues that the cognitive and dispositional resources (bureaucracy) of the state are always and inevitably in a process of expansion, because the environment itself is always becoming more complex. The expansion of these resources is accelerated still further when the state becomes an agent in the social sphere, and wilfully confronts itself with wider areas of complexity. The expansion of the bureaucracy is, therefore, Luhmann explains, the unavoidable technical side-effect of social reform. The claim, however, that such expansion might be legitimized by a collective or social commitment to reform is, for Luhmann, risible. In fact, Luhmann intimates, the attempt to create more democracy by means of social reform-programmes actually creates less democracy, and more diffuse and impenetrable bureaucratic apparatuses.

Historically, Luhmann's theory has serious implications for the reformist policies after 1967. Luhmann argues that the actual efficacy of reform-programmes is extremely limited. In modern society, he suggests, political legitimacy is devolved to, and produced by, the bureaucracy. He intimates, therefore, that the attempts of the Brandt administration to introduce wholesale social and economic reforms drastically misinterpret the conditions of the modern political system. In modern society, Luhmann explains, the political system cannot arrogate to itself responsibility for the co-ordination of areas of operation which fall properly outside its own codes. The conviction that the political system can assume a steering-position in the economic and social spheres marks, in fact, a regression to pre-modern conceptions of society. The functional stability of each social system, Luhmann argues, depends on its differentiation from other systems. A system can pick up information from a different system only if it is properly distinct from it. Wherever the political and the economic systems tend to coalesce (i.e. in the Eastern bloc), this, Luhmann claims (1997: 160–1), inevitably leads to the collapse of both. If the state attempts to steer the economy, it makes its own legitimacy dependent upon a sphere over which it has no authority, and it therefore undermines this legitimacy. Wherever social and political systems are fused together, the political system is destabilized by the fact that it cannot properly regulate activities in the social sphere. The legitimacy of any system is therefore functionally dependent upon its own differentiation from other systems. This means that each system must trace its own codes accurately and must not conflate its objectives with those of other systems. Luhmann thereby implies that Brandt's programme of social and economic reforms actually threatens the substance of political democracy.

Luhmann's thought at this juncture falls into a broad climate of neo-liberal and neo-conservative debate, in both the Federal Republic and the USA, about the function and objectives of the modern state. Such debates reached a crescendo in the late 1970s. His thinking in this respect is especially close to Helmut Schelsky's. Schelsky also argued that Brandt's reform policies, especially his promise to 'risk more democracy', actually jeopardized the stability of the democratic order (1973: 78). Like Luhmann after him, Schelsky warned that excessive socialization of the procedures of political democracy undermines the liberties which are guaranteed by the technical fabric of modern constitutions and bureaucracies (1973: 63–4). Amongst Luhmann's other conservative contemporaries, Wilhelm Hennis, especially, also reflected critically upon the expansion of the objectives of the political system under Brandt. The transformation of the political system into an 'existence-shaping power' (Hennis 1977c: 192) leads to a situation, Hennis argued, in which the substantial and ethical foundations of the social sphere are eroded (1977c: 196). Hennis thus spoke out against the 'teleocratic' and 'programmatic' nature of the modern state created by the SPD (1977d: 268). He argued particularly, also, that the modern planning-state was in the process of plotting its own downfall. Because the state seeks to plan and regulate the entire social sphere, he explained, the state weakens the regenerative faculties of society itself. This, in turn, makes the planning activities of the state too numerous, and impossible to accomplish. A successful political system, Hennis asserted, relies on the integrity and autonomy of the social sphere. In varying ways, therefore, Schelsky and Hennis (like Luhmann) argued that the political system should be kept distinct from the civil sphere, and that the success of democracy depends on the limitation of its social component. The anxiety underlying Hennis's thought, in particular (in this regard he is similar to Habermas), is that politics itself will ultimately become impossible, owing to the technical expansion of political objectives. Hennis eventually became a major contributor to the 'ungovernability-debate' of the late 1970s (Hennis 1977b: 233).

Luhmann's position is, in some respects, clearly distinct from such conservative anxiety about the functionalization of the state for social objectives. In fact, Luhmann might easily be viewed as an opponent of this form of conservatism, as he clearly approves the transformation of the political apparatus into a functional planning-executive (see Seibel 1982: i). However, Luhmann's thought also overlaps significantly with such positions. He too describes the death of politics, the end of substantial legitimacy, and the factual overburdening of the political system in the name of social reforms.

Most specifically, however, Luhmann's technocratic theory relates to political circumstances in the Federal Republic during the latter part of the 1970s. It has been described above how the Brandt-administration of the early 1970s failed in its attempts to develop a broad mode of social democracy through its reform policies. The political implications of

Luhmann's thinking can be located in the direct aftermath of these developments – namely, in the ensuing mood-swing towards the reduction of the role of social organizations (especially the unions) in political decision-making (Raschke 1978: 177), and the ascription of a more limited role to the state in the ordering of society and economy (Mottl 1992: 243). Luhmann's theory of social systems contains the clear implication that the boundaries of politics should not be excessively extended, and that politicians and parties should recognize the restricted powers which they possess to alter conditions outside the bureaucracy (Beyme 1996: 22). This directly reflects the changes in governmental praxis after the end of Brandt's government, through the latter part of Helmut Schmidt's rule, and on to the electoral triumph of Helmut Kohl's CDU (see Narr et al. 1976: 42–3). After the 1975 recession, Helmut Schmidt introduced a series of economic laws designed to reduce public spending, and to move decisively away from the left-leaning Keynesianism of the Brandt-era. This tendency was declared emphatically in Schmidt's Budget Structure Law of 1975, which was followed by other cuts in social spending, notably in 1977 and 1978 (Spieker 1986: 35–7). The policy-statements issued by Schmidt's government in the late 1970s also demonstrated this reduction of the role of the welfare-state (1986: 13). Social spending, calculated as a proportion of the GDP of the Federal Republic, reached its peak in 1975 ( J. Hoffmann 1987: 353; Alber 1986: 85), and it declined steadily thereafter.

Schmidt's economic and social policies, however, did not wholly abandon the model of state-investment propagated by his predecessors. Although Schmidt refused to sustain the full-employment policies pursued by Schiller, he developed a strategy for pump-priming selected areas of the economy, which promised the most rapid growth. After the economic traumas of stagflation and the oil-crisis, Schmidt set out to modernize spheres of production likely to sustain the position of the Federal Republic in international exports (Fels and Schmidt 1980: 166). Volker Hauff, Minister for Research in the late 1970s, actively encouraged the transformation of the economy by concentrating state-resources in sectors characterized by a high level of technological advancement and international competitiveness (Hauff 1976: 111). Hauff also urged the implementation of structural policies to connect the state, the unions and the universities. Such policies were designed to identify crisis-threatened employment-sectors, and to ensure that technological innovation could be stimulated in such areas (Altvater et al. 1979: 338–40). To this end, Hauff introduced a system of financial allocation and distribution, through which the state offered risk-capital for technological development, sponsored investment (generally by 7.55 per cent) in technological innovation (K. Schmitz et al. 1976: 35), supported joint ventures, co-ordinated links between business and research institutions (Hauff 1976: 112) and gave support to private research bodies (Hübl and Schepers 1983: 96). In addition to these policies, Hauff also promoted the investment of state funds in educational sectors which seemed likely to serve the modernization of industry, and he introduced measures for regional economic growth-stimulation (Kunst-mann 1983: 7–8). The economic policies of Schmidt's administration thus also contained a very strong element of social planning. They envisaged and ordained a structural alteration of the employment- and qualification-patterns of the workforce (K. Schmitz et al. 1976: 508). They also foresaw a policy of concerted investment-direction, which planned the macro-economic regulation of industrial supply in order to maintain the inter-national competitiveness of the major export industries of the Federal Republic. These policies were clearly distinct from the full-employment policies of Brandt and Schiller. They constituted, in effect, a system of right-leaning Keynesianism, which was prepared to maintain high levels of state-spending in areas where the long-term interests of industry might benefit, but which rejected the social component (demand-stimulation) of Brandt's economic regulations. Schmidt's policies, therefore, upheld the technocratic planning ethic which Brandt and Schiller had pioneered. However, Schmidt's economic programmes provided only for highly selective state-regulation of the economy (K. Schmitz et al. 1976: 79), in order to promote innovative areas of production. Such policies continued through the late 1970s, until the final rejection of Keynesian theory in the early 1980s (Roehl 1988: 101–3).

In sum, therefore, the recession of 1967 had produced a brand of left-Keynesianism in the Federal Republic, which continued through the boom-period until 1974. However, the far deeper recession of 1975, coupled with the oil-crisis, saw the endorsement of a system of right-Keynesianism, which sought to mobilize society around the interests of the export sector, and which was prepared to accept high levels of unemployment. These technocratic policies of the Schmidt-administration in fact originated (arguably) from the policies of Brandt and Schiller. Owing to the corporate regulation of the economy in the boom of the early 1970s, the cost of labour had increased significantly by 1975. As a reaction against this increase, less labour-intensive, more technically advanced modes of production were programmatically stimulated in the later 1970s (M. G. Schmidt 1978: 214; Altvater et al. 1983: 100). This, in turn, led to the increasing special-ization of the workforce (Esser and Fach 1981: 173), to the accelerated expansion of production, and to the decrease in the importance of hitherto influential social bodies (especially the unions, and labour-deputations). The tendency towards the technologization of politics, or the transfer of decision-making power from the social/political interface to the level of mere planning and finance, reached new heights under the Schmidt-administration (Ronge 1975: 330). Luhmann's thought stands both as a description and as a validation of this transfer.

It is also significant that Schmidt's technocratic brand of social-engineering also relied heavily on a corporate system of social regulation. Although union rights of co-determination were increased in 1976, the late 1970s saw a weakening of organized labour in the Federal Republic and a signific-ant reduction of industrial action (Rossmann 1986: 515). The late 1970s, therefore, in keeping with Schmidt's right-Keynesian policies, produced a system of corporatism which was more selective than that which had developed in the 1960s (Esser and Fach 1981: 178). This system relied upon the co-operation of the unions with employers' organizations, whose position had been reinforced during the 1974–5 recession, but it renounced Brandt's earlier ideal of full employment. Indeed, in the later 1970s the unions broadly fell into line with the modernization-strategies of the employers, even at the cost of increased unemployment. In the period 1975–80 there were no strikes in major industrial sectors (Jacobi 1982b: 238), although unemployment increased by over 100 per cent during the same period (Kisker 1985: 12). The technological policies of the government also led to a concentration of capital in large firms, especially those financed by the export-market. This in turn led to an increased level of cartelization, at the expense of smaller firms (Fels and Schmidt 1980: 245). The democratically expansive, and socially inclusive, welfare-aims of the Brandt era were thus replaced in the late 1970s by a semi-regulated corporate system which relied upon economic exclusivity, and which derived its legitimacy from technologically progressive sectors of the economy (the export-market).

Luhmann's theory of systems therefore provides a precise model for the description and legitimization of governmental methods during the *Tendenzwende*. Manifestly, the strong anti-social component to Luhmann's thinking clearly describes (and affirms) the reduction of state-involvement in the social sphere in the late 1970s. Moreover, Luhmann's systems-theory also describes and affirms the increasingly selective blocks which Schmidt's corporate system placed upon access to the political sphere. Schmidt's governmental system – *Modell Deutschland* – aimed at the installation of a technically sustained balance between economic prerogatives and social organizations (especially unions), in which the demands of the latter were linked exclusively to the former. This constituted a mode of technologically driven, non-consensual politics, resting on pragmatic, trilateral agreements between government, unions and employers (Jacobi 1982a: 81). This system of government naturally limited the extent to which social problems could be politicized, for the co-ordinates of the political sphere were subject to prior restrictions, in accordance with macro-economic guidelines. Luhmann's argument that consensus has no significance in political action, and that government is most effectively conducted via planned communication between decision-making units, fits this system perfectly. The theory of systems maps closely, therefore, onto the structure of the 'planning-state', in which real decisions are not open to discourse from below. It describes a mode of government in which effective politics relies merely on the balancing of the imperatives of one system against those of another. Systems-theory (not untypically for the 1970s) attempts to divest the state of direct responsibility for problems arising in the social sphere (see Lehner 1979: 2). Systems-theory, in short, restricts the code of politics to limited exchanges and responses between pre-stablized planning-elites.

However, there is a further, more determinate aspect of Luhmann's theory which overlaps with the emerging governmental models of the 1970s. The theory of systems also explains how social interests can be addressed by government at a subsidiary level, beneath the position of the executive. By stressing the role of the bureaucracy, Luhmann indicates that the interests of civil bodies can in fact – at least in part – be caught and registered in the administrative system before they approach the complex processes of politicization which mark the decision-making sphere (see Hammans 1987: 265). Luhmann is expressly sympathetic to the inclusion of deputations of organized interests in the administrative system, as long as this is accomplished at sub-executive level (1994a: 160). The theory of systems describes, therefore, a model of bureaucratic – or polyarchical (Lehner 1979: 113) – pluralism. This system combines the auspices of a strong planning government (see Heinze 1981: 110) with a fine network of administrative apparatuses which filter issues from the environment. Systems-theory outlines a mode of governance in which the highest level of government – the truly political sphere – would be hopelessly overtaxed if it were to accept accountability for all areas of jurisdiction. But it implies also that the specialization of bureaucratic and planning departments can, to a certain degree, facilitate the treatment of individual issues. Problems deriving from the social sphere can be referred to specific sub-systems of the bureaucracy, which are equipped to respond to them. From a systems-theoretical perspective, therefore, social and economic interest-groups *can* (to a limited extent) be assimilated into specific sections of the governmental bureaucracy, and thus be adequately addressed (Alemann 1987: 42). If the sub-systems of the bureaucracy are deployed to address individual issues, the state retains its primacy as a planning-instance above the bureaucracy – as the producer of decision-premises for the administration – and it remains broadly unaffected by whatever happens beneath its own level (Beyme 1991b: 131). Luhmann thus suggests that the rigid segregation of administrative bodies into closed units guarantees an effective form of pre- or quasi-political corporatism, in which corporate interests are intercepted by planning-organs before they disrupt the smooth operations of the decision-making executives.

In this light, Luhmann's thought can be interpreted as a model of semi-authoritarian, bureaucratic pluralism. Systems-theory, although it reflects on the demise of politics, political power and political legitimacy, insists that the integrity and the primacy of the political system should be acknowledged. Systems-theory has, in this respect, often been justifiably compared with the administrative dimension to the ideas of Carl Schmitt (Seibel 1982: 199). Most especially, however, Luhmann's theory is close in spirit to the governmental practice of Helmut Schmidt – although it overlaps in certain respects with the pluralistic politics of order set out by the economic experts of the CDU in the 1970s (see Groser 1979: 454). Luhmann's thought describes clearly how the administration can be used to limit the range of issues which are openly politicized. By doing so, the administration restricts the resources of legitimation which the state has to deploy in order to justify its policies. The smaller the number of issues which the political system has to address, the less it has to legitimize itself. The less it has to legitimize itself, the stronger it is. Gunther Teubner, after Luhmann the major legal-political exponent of systems-theory, describes accordingly how the positivization of law in the administration provides a code through which the government can adjust to the 'increase of conflict' in the social sphere (Teubner 1979: 300; Beyme 1981: 90). Thus, like Luhmann at the same time, Teubner uses the systems-theoretical approach to explain how social problems can be addressed at the level of the bureaucracy without diluting the proper functions of politics itself.

At the heart of Luhmann's inquiry into the procedural nature of political legitimacy is an investigation into the character of power. Luhmann's basic assumption in his discussion of power is that the state should be interpreted only as a semantic form of systemic self-description, through which society attempts to represent to itself the location of power. The particular semantic of politics is, he argues, the product of the differentiation of social systems. Through the separation of political from economic power, the political system has stabilized itself as a complex of codes which are distinct from those of any other system. This complex of codes is represented in a particular sematic – as the state. Luhmann locates the development of this semantic of state in the second half of the eighteenth century (1984c: 103). During this period – during the separation of the economy from the state – he explains that the political system became temporarily the most pronounced of all social systems (Willke 1996: 139). Today, however, this importance is, Luhmann asserts, archaic. The concept of sovereignty itself, he explains, is a temporary semantic representation of the autonomy of the political system, exaggerated for a brief historical period: 'The political system allows the paradoxical character of its code to culminate in the formula of sovereignty, lastly in the formula of popular sovereignty. . . . The concept of the state becomes an artificial peg for the self-propelling dynamic of the legal and the political system' (1993a: 418). The grandeur of the political system is, Luhmann thus explains, merely an anachronistic fiction. Owing to the differentiation of political and social systems, he argues, power in modern societies can no longer be imputed to one person, or to one set of political organs. The power of the political system, he claims, is invariably restricted by other systems (especially the system of the economy), which constitute its environment. Political sovereignty is therefore an outdated construct. Popular sovereignty, for Luhmann, is an even more ludicrous concept. Political systems can never be grounded upon voluntary agreement with their environment.

Despite this, Luhmann argues that in the inclusive structure of modern democracies power has not decreased. On the contrary, the fundamental precondition of democracy is that power always increases. In the democratic-constitutional state, Luhmann asserts, power does not lie in the hands of one or more persons. Rather, power is the code according to which politics operates. The political system is an autopoietic system, in which the bearers of power are not persons, but roles. Luhmann explains:

> The political system can now be construed as a self-regulative autopoietic system of power-application, in which power is applied to power and is subject to the application of power. It is a recursive, closed, therefore symmetrical and non-hierarchical system, which facilitates communication through the communication-code of power and which sees no application of power as an exception from this. (1984c: 108; see also Luhmann 1975c: 68)

Power in modern systems is, thus, a circuit which connects all parts of the political system. It is a series of codes and options by means of which the political system secures itself against the environment. The more power is present in a social system, the more options it can sustain, and the more flexibility it possesses in its responses to the environment: 'More complex systems, which permit more alternatives and therefore undertake greater acts of selection, have to activate more power' (1969a: 168). The more complex (de-centred and differentiated) society is, therefore, the more power it requires. Social liberty in modern society is itself, Luhman argues, the technical corollary of power. 'Money, power and truth', he explains, 'are social mechanisms which make it possible to postpone decisions and yet to have some certainty about them – therefore to live with a future of great, indeterminately complex occurrences' (1973c: 17). Above all, Luhmann suggests, decisions made within the power-code resemble the choices made in the code of money (1988: 142). The fluid generality of power in modern societies prevents the monopolization of the means of violence by one person or one party.

Luhmann does not confer upon himself the role of political adviser. Nonetheless, in his theory of power he implies that the differentiation of social systems is the functional precondition of democracy and personal freedom. Democracy and freedom are undermined, he argues, wherever two properly distinct systems interlock. These ideas are also central to Luhmann's writings on the constitution. The function of the constitution, Luhmann argues, is to act as a block which prevents the annexation of other social systems by the political system. The 'basic rights', he explains, 'protect the differentiating structure of modern society against tendencies towards simplifying de-differentiation, which can be triggered by the political system' (1965: 135). Unlike the classical liberal argument, however, which interprets constitutional rights as devices for protecting society from the state itself, Luhmann claims that rights are actually produced by the state. By generating codified rights, Luhmann asserts, the state creates a check between the political and other social systems, and it thus ensures that its administrative functions remain undisturbed: 'The fact that the basic rights are directed against the state has led dominant opinion to the conclusion that they cannot therefore be granted by the state. This conclusion . . . fails to recognize that in a differentiated social order the state develops its own interest in stabilizing its boundaries, because otherwise it cannot rationalize itself as a system' (1965: 182–3). The separation of powers, thus, codified by the constitution, is primarily a device for the preservation of the internal unity of different systems (legal and political) and, only secondly, for maintaining democracy (1993a: 416; 1984b: 39).

Analogous to this process of constitutional differentiation, the modern democratic system, Luhmann explains, has emerged as a 'threefold differentiation' (1981c: 164). Through the evolution of this system, *administration* (parliaments, governments and administrative bureaucracies), *politics*, based in political parties, and the *public* are formed as distinct sub-systems (1981c: 164). This produces a circular power-process: 'Politics can hardly operate without the plans of the administration. The public depends on the pre-selection of persons and programmes within the political sphere. The administration requires, as it expands into complex fields of operation, the voluntary collaboration of the public, and therefore has to concede influence to the public' (1981c: 164). Democracy, thus, Luhmann argues, is not based on the mediated unity of people, administration and state, but rather on the systemic differentiation of these. As one system differentiates itself from another, Luhmann explains, this system must also grant power to that system and accept its own limitation by that system in order to hold itself in a relation of functional equivalence to it (1981c: 166).

Thus, whilst it would be incorrect to confuse Luhmann's theory of evolution with a theory of normativity, or indeed teleology, the theory of social systems contains an important conception of democracy. The evolution of differentiated social systems is, Luhmann claims, a process of inclusion, through which ever greater areas of society are integrated into the operations of social systems and subject to decision-making codes of democratic power. Through the process of differentiation, inclusive democratic systems are secured against each other in the form of institutionally pluralist democracies, based on the separation of powers. Inclusive democracies therefore depend on the maintenance of the functional autonomy of each system.

Owing to its opposition to theories of mediated or consensual democracy, Luhmann's concept of democratic government is often categorized as neoconservative. His theory of power is customarily grasped as an 'extremely reduced concept of democracy' (Naschold 1968: 505). However, despite Luhmann's suggestion that popular democracy is impossible in modern society, the actual image of society which Luhmann puts forward (1974: 267) cannot be easily interpreted according to common political categories. In essence, Luhmann outlines a democracy without agency. 'Democracy', Luhmann argues, 'is not a form of rule, but rather a technique for steering the system, which becomes inevitable as a result of the positivization of law' (1971a: 49). The evolution of democracy, he argues, is not a series of teleological or rational choices about the conditions of good society (1973b: 342), but rather the gradual response of the social system to the complexity of the environment, and to its own ever-proliferating internal complexity (1969b: 319–20). Democracy develops because society becomes increasingly complex, and because fluid (positive) responses to this complexity are required if the systems of society are to sustain themselves. Democracy, based on positive law, is the total of these fluid decisions. Luhmann describes modern society, therefore, as a de-centred complex of political institutions, in which power is not anchored anywhere in particular – where power is everywhere, running through the codes and communications of each system, especially between politics, administration and people. 'It is', he states, 'only a slight exaggeration to say that today we are not ruled by persons, but by codes' (1984b: 44). In this respect, in fact, through a circuitous route, Luhmann actually outlines a system of democracy which is very similar in appearance (if not in spirit) to the checks and balances of classical liberalism. The codes of each institution, he argues, are checked by the codes of others. The code of power is checked by the code of law. The code of property is checked by the code of money. Most codes are therefore double-coded (1984b: 40). It is thus impossible for one system to colonize another (1984b: 43). For related reasons, Luhmann accords 'highest admiration' to the constitutional system of the nineteenth-century legal state. He views this as a realized system of double-coding, in which the constitutionally guaranteed separation of powers double-codes the authority of the political system (1984c: 112).

Above all, however, Luhmann argues that democracy and bureaucracy are mutually dependent (if not identical). In a democratic society, Luhmann explains, problems of external complexity are addressed through processes of bureaucratization, which make it possible to refer problems to institutions in a manner which equips them for response. The real hallmark of a good democracy is therefore not popular support for political edicts – but a functioning bureaucracy, empowered by positive (democratic) law to process issues addressed to it. In Luhmann's theory of democracy the administration assumes the position given to the legislature in classical liberalism. This, however, does not mean that Luhmann is opposed to democracy. It implies merely that he sees democracy as a set of systems which adjust themselves to environmental complexity. This, he indicates, can be better accomplished in the codes of the bureaucracy than by the conscious decisions of the legislature. Luhmann's model of systemic pluralism is therefore, in sum, a democracy without needs, interest, agency or volition. There is no longer a central representation, or a central political code, in Luhmann's description of modern society. Issues of social resistance and non-conformity can be treated only in bemused terms, for there is no determinate source of power which could be directly modified by acts of resistance. Luhmann states: 'Different decisions do not indicate a different order. They are nothing but different decisions' (1984b: 43). There is no space in this model for the democratic subject to (re)propose itself as a centre of action in protest, resistance, non-conformity – or even consent.

Luhmann's best-known intervention in discussions on issues of politics and democracy is *Political Theory in the Welfare State* (1981).

This work, widely received in German political debate, is uncharacteristic in Luhmann's opus, as it marks a partial departure from his role as a mere observer of political events. In fact, it offers a series of clear tips on how politics should be defined and ordered in modern society. In this work, Luhmann falls closely into line with the broad tendency towards neo-liberalism in Europe and the USA in the early 1980s. Although he remains aloof from the pure economism of his neo-liberal counterparts, Luhmann's position here is in clear sympathy with the programmes of economic non-interventionism and deregulation which gained credence at this time (Nahamowitz 1988: 36). *Political Theory in the Welfare State* proceeds from the argument that modern democracies rely on de-centred institutional pluralism for the integrity of their democracy. The key political question of the moment, Luhmann announces, is whether it is possible to accept a society without a centre. The de-centration of society, he explains, is the precondition of an efficient democracy (1981: 23), and any attempt to modify this weakens democracy itself. The principle of de-centration, however, is contradicted by the welfare-state. The principle of the welfare-state, he argues, is 'realized inclusion' (1981b: 27). Through the welfare-state, Luhmann argues, the entirety of society is admitted to the political sphere. Society, therefore, is fatally re-centred around the political system. This process of increasing inclusion poses various crucial problems. Most importantly, it creates a circular system in which all three parts of the political system are forced to rely on each other – the boundaries between people, administration and politics become fluid, and thereby threaten the operative integrity of the system. The political system of the welfare-state, Luhmann argues, which like all systems is required to reduce the complexity of the environment, is expected to maintain too many channels of communication with its environment(s). The politicization of all issues creates internal levels of complexity which the system cannot master. The administration, especially, is overburdened by the number of issues which it is required to treat.

Therefore, Luhmann concludes, whilst systemic differentiation has created the dynamic of inclusion upon which democracy is based, it has finally become too inclusive, and it now threatens the democracies which have evolved through it. Like other thinkers in the late 1970s, Luhmann's ideas show great respect for the liberal-constitutional democracies of the late nineteenth century, in which different systems – especially economy and state – were stabilized against each other and thereby maintained maximum efficiency. Indeed, as shown above, he sees in the constitutional state (as opposed to the welfare-state) an effective means of codifying the limitation of politics, and of preventing the absorption of economic problems by the political sphere (1984c: 110–12). In Luhmann's ideal model of democracy, the political and the administrative system check and limit each other and therefore sustain their own efficiency (and the institutionally pluralist basis of democracy). In the welfare-state, however, the expansion of issues which are understood as 'political' threatens the very separation of powers around which democracy has evolved. Here again, Luhmann's thought overlaps closely with Schelsky's theories (Schelsky 1973: 63).

Luhmann's theory, however, occupies a hybrid position in the neo-liberal/neo-conservative deregulation-theories of the 1970s and 1980s. Unlike the neo-liberal – economic – critique of the welfare-state in the 1970s, Luhmann's observations on the overburdening of the state are not premised in a faith in self-regulating dynamics of the economy. Unlike the conservative – political – critique of the welfare-state, equally, his ideas do not reflect a belief in the abstract dignity of the state (see Lehner 1979: 36). In his theory of the welfare-state, he insists simply that the border of the political system has been lowered too far, and that certain issues – for example economic equality – have been falsely introduced into political jurisdiction. In the welfare-state, Luhmann implies, all problems which have not been resolved in the system in which they were produced are transported into the political system. Luhmann thus advocates an altogether stricter segregation of political and economic imperatives. However, unlike the neo-liberals of the same period, Luhmann phrases this argument as a defence of the administrative system, not as a mere call for deregulation of the economy (Nahamowitz 1988: 47). Elsewhere (like Habermas), he explains that the absorption of economic factors by the political sphere creates additional legitimation-problems which the state cannot solve. Like Habermas, he also complains that 'the complexity of the developing economy is taken as measure and boundary for the requisite variety of the political system and the performance of politics is gauged by economic success' (1969b: 323). In other words, Luhmann endorses the limitation of state-power not in order to liberate economic interests, but to protect the rationality of the administration and the legitimacy of the state itself (see Heidorn 1982: 106–7). Politics, he argues, should return to its initial quality: 'A reduction of politics to its precise function, to the satisfaction of the need for collectively binding decisions, would fit better into the framework provided by functional differentiation' (1981b: 122).

Luhmann's indication that state-intervention should be restricted can, in fact, once more be closely linked with the modernization-programmes pursued by Schiller and Brandt in the 1960s and Schmidt in the 1970s. The technological modernization of selected industrial sectors, which had been deliberately engendered by the spending policies of the SPD in the early 1970s, led directly to a discrepancy between the steering-potential of the state and the complexity of the private economy. Owing to government-financed advances in technology, and the increased production in the private economy which resulted from these, the political apparatus of the Federal Republic in the late 1970s was quickly confronted with a complex set of new objectives and functions. It was forced to regulate new markets, to regulate educational and research-institutions, to provide financial back-up for developing sections of the economy, and to transfer finance to protect those made unemployed by technological innovations (there were 1.8 million unemployed by 1980; Bark and Gress 1989: 376). Most especially, the state was compelled to maintain increasing levels of investment in the areas of growth which it had stimulated, and, accordingly, to increase employment in the public sector, especially in the state bureaucracy (Wittmann 1982: 294). The state, therefore, was forced constantly to modernize its own administrative and cognitive resources, in order to hold itself on the same level as the new areas of production which it had nurtured (Fels and Schmidt 1980: 237). Although, as a proportion of the GDP, social and welfare provisions decreased in the late 1970s, the total sum of state-expenditure did not (Krupp 1982: 3). In 1981 the government of the Federal Republic had a budgetary deficit of 40 billion marks (M. G. Schmidt 1990: 54).

Luhmann's theory of politics is therefore a highly ironic description of the political predicaments of the Federal Republic in the late 1970s and early 1980s. In essence, Luhmann describes how the planning-state automatically produces unmanageable levels of complexity whenever it intervenes in the private economy. Wherever it acts as a private-economic planning agent, which commissions and performs economic functions, the state is forced into a spiral of administrative self-modernization, so that it can meet (or attempt to meet) the complex demands imposed upon it by the social systems whose development and modernization it accelerates. In the social-economic planning-state, in short, the plan acquires a dynamic of its own, which stimulates the need for more, and more diverse, planning. Luhmann's diagnosis of the problems of the 1970s is in fact strikingly similar to the law of economic growth set out in the late nineteenth century by Adolf Wagner. Wagner argued that the speed of modernization and production in the private economy always exceeds the flexibility of state-resources, and that, consequently, governmental organs are ceaselessly forced to modernize in order to absorb the demands from the private economy (Wagner 1967: 91; Bäuerle 1969: 5). Luhmann's theory of politics is therefore an ironic reflection upon the dialectic of technology. He, as a technocratic planner, argues that the political system must, for its own stability, necessarily maintain planned levels of technical innovation. Technology, however, develops more rapidly than the resources of the system itself. Wherever the system intentionally triggers or commissions technological development, it is rapidly threatened by what it produces. This threat can present itself either as an external factor in the form of environmental catastrophe – state-investment in atomic energy in the Federal Republic reached 1,616 million marks in 1977 (K. Schmitz et al. 1976: 280–3) – or as the over-production of economic and legitimatory demands upon the political apparatus. In each case, the political apparatus is – Luhmann describes – symbolically de-legitimized by its inability to process problems which have resulted from its own planning-functions.

In these respects, therefore, Luhmann makes a clear contribution to the theory of economic deregulation. The implication in such theories is that the sphere of public-political action should be strictly separated out from the private economy. Not all areas of social activity, Luhmann implies, can or should be planned. Most areas, if at all, should be addressed by the bureaucracy. If the state assumes a planning function in the private economy, it becomes overwhelmed by the demands which it attracts from this sphere. More importantly, however, as a planner himself, Luhmann asserts that the success of planning-systems depends in principle upon the preservation of difference and equivalence between different systems. Luhmann's theory means, therefore, that there must remain at all times a functional distinction between those who plan, those who perform and those who pay for a particular systemic performance. If the state itself plans, performs and pays for a particular task, Luhmann explains, the binary code of payment/performance by means of which economic operations differentiate themselves begins to malfunction (Scharpf 1988: 66). Wherever one agent is both executor and contractor of a particular performance, the systemic differentiation between execution and contraction becomes unstable. In the case of state-involvement in the private economy, this means, firstly, that if the state plans a performance, which it then buys from itself, the state has no means of ensuring (except through escalating bureaucratic resources) that this performance is executed correctly. Secondly, if this performance is not executed correctly, the state forfeits a share of its legitimacy. Thirdly, following Wagner's law, wherever the state is involved in the private economy it assumes accountability for more issues than it can process, and it enters necessarily a spiral of bureaucratization. The state, Luhmann thus explains, has a basic capacity for planning, but only if the execution and realization of its plans are left to others. What Luhmann ideally outlines therefore is a return to the classical-liberal separation of the public and private domains. The particular advantage of the legal state in its classical form, Luhmann explains, is precisely that the constitution contains provisions for the protection of private autonomy (private law) against the state. The functional limitations of public authority are thus constantly made present to the state (1984c). However, Luhmann continues, if the state is to be involved in the private economy, it must ensure that it transmits its resources to private companies which are functionally distinct from its own system. This is, in short, a theory of privatization. Luhmann's systems-theory thus touches the heart of the demands for the deregulation of the economy and the de-socialization of the state which were widespread in the early 1980s.

For such reasons, in the late 1970s and 1980s Luhmann's ideas were often utilized to describe the crisis or collapse of the modern state. His theories were especially called upon by different positions in the so-called 'ungovernability debate' of the late 1970s. By the late 1970s, the allegation that the modern state had become 'ungovernable' figured widely in a diffuse set of liberal and conservative arguments in the Federal Republic, and it was ultimately influential in the end of the SPD's hold on power in 1982. This argument derived, firstly, from the conservative conviction (already widespread in the 1950s) that the social-legal state was simply overburdened by the escalation of expectations in the social sphere (Offe 1979: 297).

Indeed, the entire debate had its origins in the technocratic theories of Carl Schmitt and Ernst Forsthoff. In the 1950s and 1960s Forsthoff had already argued that it is ridiculous to imagine that the modern industrial state can respond to all social needs (1965: 59). The state, he therefore asserted, should be viewed as a representative planning-apparatus, above the level of the civil-political sphere (1965: 21). However, the argument against the imposition of excessive social burdens on the state also drew on certain anti-Keynesian liberal positions, which were commonplace in the Free Democratic party (FDP) in the 1970s (Offe 1979: 300). Leading figures in the FDP argued that social expenditure and taxation-levels incurred by the systems of corporate arrangement in the Federal Republic discouraged foreign investment, and were detrimental to the competitiveness of German industrial products (see Süß 1991: 92; Bark and Gress 1989: 373). In liberal- monetarist circles, it was widely alleged at this time therefore that the high level of state-intervention in the private economy and in the infrastructure caused a 'crowding-out' of private investment and a willingness on the part of private investors to leave responsibility for structural regulation to the state.[1] Notably, the issue of 'ungovernability' constituted an important aspect of the earliest political declarations of the CDU/FDP coalition which replaced Helmut Schmidt. Schmidt's governmental coalition with the FDP was eventually brought down in October 1982 because of differences in fiscal policy between the grass-roots of the SPD (especially the unions) and the economic experts of the FDP (Bark and Gress 1989: 376–9). After the change of coalition in 1982, Kohl sought to legitimize the non-elected change of power by claiming a mandate to 'put the house in order' and to resolve budgetary problems (Süß 1983: 51). Kohl promised especially to 'reduce the state to the core of its responsibilities' (Webber 1989: 74). Lambsdorff, Kohl's coalition-partner in the FDP, also repeatedly claimed that the need to consolidate the public budget provided a justification for the change of government (Sturm 1993: 43). The chief fiscal component of Kohl's policies in the 1980s was the so-called reform-package which – albeit insubstantially – reduced the levels of contribution to the health, insurance and taxation systems (Webber 1991).

Both liberal and conservative contributors to the 'ungovernability' and deregulation debates of the 1970s and 1980s found use for Luhmann. Conservative theorists, who advocated a return to a simple separation of state and society (see esp. Hennis 1973: 46; 1977c: 196; 1977a: 189), saw in Luhmann's theory a model for furthering the de-socialization of politics and the liberation of the political superstructure (see Hammans 1987: 7). They also found in Luhmann's ideas a technical confirmation of their argument that the meticulous planning of the social sphere is not a condition of the legitimacy of state (Spieker 1986: 101). Neo-liberals saw in Luhmann's theory of systems a model which supported deregulation of the economy and the reprivatization of public responsibilities. Most

---

1 See Wittmann 1982: 306. Also: Neuthinger 1982: 570; Sturm 1993: 89; Böttger 1982: 74.

especially, Luhmann's thinking supported a move away from the neo-Keynesian stimulation of demand in the 1970s towards economic policies which favoured the supply-component – which reduced production-costs by limiting taxation and curtailing state-intervention. This move from demand-regulation to supply-oriented policies was at the very heart of the so-called *Tendenzwende* of the 1970s (Gabriel 1991: 114). The most significant legislative package in this context was Kohl's Law for the Promotion of Employment of 1985, which provided for the partial deregulation of the employment-market and the reduction of labour-costs (Boss et al. 1996: 341). In short, although Luhmann is neither, strictly, neo-conservative nor neo-liberal, his association with the debates on deregulation is no coincidence. Luhmann certainly suggests that the course of political inclusion should be decelerated and that political systems might profitably return to the limited mode of politics which characterized the democratic constitutional state.

Despite this, however, Luhmann argues that the issue of 'ungovernability' is itself merely part of the more general problem of modern politics. Anxiety about ungovernability, and especially the conservative suggestion that the state might retreat to its location of lost dignity, serve, Luhmann argues, merely artificially to inflate the state-semantic – they act as the 'negative self-reinforcement' of the excessive expansion of the state (1981b: 145). Luhmann supports the de-socialization of the state not because he wishes to see the state readorned in its transcendental grandeur (see Forst-hoff 1968b: 146), but because he does not think that the state in its current form can exist as an effective functional agent. Furthermore, the chief distinction between Luhmann and more conservative participants in the 'ungovernability debate' is that Luhmann is not opposed to planning as a central aspect of political life. The conservative critique of the welfare-state revolves around the conviction that the representative functions of the political apparatus (and the virtues of the civil sphere) are structurally undermined by the planning interventions of the state in social existence. From this conservative perspective (shared by Wilhelm Hennis, Werner Weber, Forsthoff and Schelsky), the political legitimacy of the modern state is eroded by the expansion of the state to a universal prerogative planning-organ (Spieker 1986: 58). According to the conservative critique of the welfare-state, excessive state-planning weakens the sovereign legitimacy of the state, the private-existential autonomy of citizens (Spieker 1986: 243), and – as Hermann Lübbe argued most pressingly (1981: 57) – the ethical value-systems upon which political integrity relies. Luhmann argues instead that the ascription to the political sphere of anything more than a mere planning-function is part of the semantic fiction by means of which the political system has differentiated itself from other systems. Luhmann simply suggests that the state cannot plan everything, and that most problems should be filtered by the bureaucracy before they touch the legitimation-resources of the political system. Therefore, whilst Luhmann's theory of systems opposes the concept of the state as a universally active planning-instance, it reinforces the position of specific planning- or administrative elites within the state.

Luhmann's thinking of the late 1970s and early 1980s also relates to other significant developments in the political and social life of the Federal Republic. It has been widely argued in German sociology that the period after the end of the Brandt-administration was characterized by a large-scale transformation of political values (see H. Schmitt 1987: 23; Klages 1985: 102). This was flanked by a tendency, particularly amongst younger voters, to seek political expression outside the conventional structures of party-political organization, and to turn towards social movements or citizens' initiatives as a means of political representation. It is against this background that the Green party emerged in the early 1980s.

Historically, it is not difficult to pin such trends to the systemic conditions of government in the Federal Republic. By the late 1970s, the SPD had effectively shifted towards political ground commonly occupied by the CDU. The corporate nature of Helmut Schmidt's government, with its ramified links with large-scale business associations and its anti-labour overtones, created manifest communication-blocks between government and society (Frankland and Schoonmaker 1992: 59–60). Most especially, the brand of selective corporatism developed by Schmidt left little room for political dissent within existing structures, and it excluded significant sectors of society from the bargaining system (Esser and Fach 1981: 176). Schmidt's legislative policies, especially his anti-terrorist laws of 1976, which legalized arrest on suspicion of terrorist involvement, reinforced the security of the corporate bloc and undermined further (at least symbolically) non-institutionalized modes of representation. For such reasons, the SPD alienated many younger voters during this time, after the failure of the heady promises of Brandt's reforms (Frankland and Schoonmaker 1992: 6). Owing to the increasing similarity between the SPD and the CDU, it can also be seen that the traditional models of class-affiliation began, at least temporarily, to lose their resonance as the legitimation for party-allegiance (Klages and Herbert 1983: 11). This, in turn, undermined the binary legitimation-models of the established parties, and therefore of parliament as a whole (Wiesendahl 1989: 91). Of all parties, Schmidt's SPD was most immediately disadvantaged by the broad move away from conventional politics. The social movements and movement-parties which began to emerge in the late 1970s, most especially the Greens, fulfilled the role of a 'left-wing corrective' to the SPD, and drew off a share of its normal electoral potential (Dräger and Hülsberg 1986: 15).

The Green party itself can be understood in its inception as a movement-party which grew out of diverse social formations, initially combining elements of the Peace Movement, anti-nuclear campaigns, the residual organizations of the New Left from the 1960s (Fogt 1989: 110) and the disparate ecological groups which had emerged through the 1970s (Rucht 1994: 244). After its foundation as a party in 1980, the Green party succeeded in tapping broad disenchantment with the governmental apparatus, and with the closed corporate bloc around the executive. It also profited from the growing frustration with the welfare-system of the Federal Republic, later reduced by Kohl's anti-welfare policies (Dräger and Hülsberg 1986: 24). Despite the rapid transformation of the Greens from a purely oppositional movement-party to a 'real-politically oriented competitive party' in the early 1980s (Stöss 1987: 298), the Greens, at least initially, maintained the support of sections of the Marxist left. They integrated elements of left theory by propagating policies of radical 'grass-roots democracy' (*Basisdemokratie*). They also rejected the party-based elitism of the representative system (Wiesendahl 1987: 374). It was initially envisaged that the Green party would function merely as a parliamentary arm for diverse and more important grass-roots activities (Frankland and Schoonmaker 1992: 153). However, the actual number of ecological protest-actions peaked in 1981 (Rucht 1994: 273). The development of the Green party can thus be summarized as an expression of a growing climate of extra-parliamentary protest in the 1970s. The chief ideological components of the Green movement were, firstly, an attempt to refocus political debate on a grass-roots level, thus to 'de-corporatize' politics, and to undermine the over-bureaucratized planning-systems of the welfare-state (Wiesendahl 1987: 381). This tendency, secondly, went hand in hand with a 'beyond-left-and-right' ideology, by means of which the Greens attempted to mobilize cross-class interest-groups, and to stimulate post-traditional modes of organization (Brand 1982: 116).

Importantly for the background to Luhmann's thinking, it can be seen in the case of the Greens that the common disaffection with the welfare-state on the political right was also reflected by those on the left. The political right of the 1970s and 1980s grasped the problem of the existing political apparatus as an excessive expansion of the state into areas properly outside its jurisdiction. However, the position of the extra-parliamentary movement-bodies on the left might be interpreted in similar terms. These movements condemned above all the failure of the state to deal with problems (especially environmental problems) which it had produced, and they insisted that the substance of the civil sphere should be released from annexation by the state. Luhmann's second major work on contemporary political issues, *Ecological Communication* (1986), contains his interventions in these debates on the left. This work is written as a broad response to the emergence of the Green party in Germany. Its guiding question is: 'Can modern society adapt to ecological dangers?'

At the heart of systems-theory is the assertion that each system is defined through its self-differentiation from its own environment. The system has no teleological rationality or purpose which guides it or which might enable it to attain a state of relative harmony with the systems with which it coexists. Systems exist by means of the negation of their environment. Accordingly, therefore, the 'environment' of the system does not exist in definable form. It is merely the environment which a system creates for itself and at the level of which it holds itself. 'Systems define their own boundaries,' Luhmann explains:

> They differentiate themselves from, and thereby constitute, their environment as that which exists beyond their boundaries. Environment in this sense is thus not a system in its own right, not even a unit of operation. It is only the totality of external circumstances which restricts the arbitrariness of the morphogenesis of systems and which subjects them to evolutionary selection. (1986: 23)

For this reason, Luhmann argues, it is not possible to observe the operative functions of the system from a privileged position outside it. Even the critical commentators on systems occupy a position inside the systems, and they relate to the system only through its own codes. This is a key moment in Luhmann's theory of environmental politics. No one, he implies, can speak for the environment. It is only possible to speak about it – and this speech can occur only through the codes of the system itself (1986: 218). The central communication-systems in human society, he argues, do not have a language with which to represent ecological dangers. The political system itself, predictably, only possesses a very limited capacity to respond effectively to ecological threats. This is only possible at all if these threats are represented to the system through pre-established codes of parliamentary debate (1986: 191).

Generally, therefore, Luhmann casts a more than half-ironic glance at the status of the politician in modern society. He implies that politicians are the people least capable of responding to ecological problems, as they can operate only within the restricted systemic logic of politics, and have little influence on economic or technological systems. Politics, as a system of problem-solving, is constituted only by the channelling of information in the code government/opposition, which is (since the nineteenth century) institutionally structured around political parties (1994b: 129). The system of politics works, therefore, only in those spheres which the economy leaves unoccupied, and all attempts to make unrealistic promises about the environment ultimately make the politicians look laughable (1986: 225–6). Luhmann claims, therefore, simply that the political system is overburdened by the politicization of ecological and technological problems. These are issues which cannot be solved through 'collectively binding decisions' (1996a: 173). Any attempt to counter ecological risks, which cannot be solved by the means internal to existing social systems, merely transforms risks into systemic risks. Systems, he explains, commonly respond to ecological risks by acting in a manner which is itself laden with risks – by passing laws without certainty, by making ill-informed political decisions, by making imprecise technological calculations, or by articulating apocalyptic ethical imperatives. Luhmann describes this as a semantic of 'risk-transformation' (1996a: 172), which allows disruptive forces to enter the smooth-running bureaucratic network, and to undermine the operations of the distinct social systems. Expansive technological-ecological definitions of politics, there-fore, ultimately erode the political institutions upon which systemically differentiated democracy is based (1996a: 174; see also Luhmann 1986: 220). Broadly, in short, Luhmann advocates, resignedly, an orientation of politics – even (or especially) in ecological matters – around the status quo. He implies that the only mechanisms for addressing ecological issues are provided by the functional codes which already exist. The consequences of ecological disaster should themselves, he explains, be addressed solely at the level of state-administration, not through the channels of civil politics or social movements. Clearly, he does not promise that the political system can do much about these ecological issues. But, he intimates, no one else can either.

Like his earlier theory of the welfare-state, therefore, Luhmann's atti-tude to the overstretching of social systems by protest-groups is not based on a normative defence of the state. Rather, it revolves around the assertion that anti-systemic action is pointless (or impossible). Social movements, Luhmann explains, can fulfil a genuine function in social organization, as partial systems within the general functional systems (1996b: 185). Protest movements are themselves, he indicates, components in the stabilization-mechanisms of the social systems (1996f: 205). Protest is a parasitic descrip-tion of problems which arise from the relation between the system and the environment (1996b: 194). Because a functional system cannot communi-cate directly with its environment, Luhmann explains, it communicates problems with the environment through its internal conflicts and resist-ances. These are communicated through protest (1996f: 214). One-issue political groups are therefore, for Luhmann, merely parasitic forms of communication which exist at the boundary of stable functional systems.

In his response to debates on the political left, therefore, the anti-social component to Luhmann's thought is expressed in slightly altered form. In *Political Theory in the Welfare State*, Luhmann argues against the excessive inclusion of social issues in the planning-operations of the state. In *Ecolo-gical Communication*, he explains that the attempts of protest-groups to seek inclusion in the political system are equally futile and self-deluding. Above all, Luhmann argues, protest presupposes that those who protest mobilize truth-claims against the existing social order. For Luhmann, however, this is not possible. Social systems cannot be made aware of truths about themselves from outside. Systems do not have truths. The 'truths' of systems are simply the codes which allow them to function (1970: 60). There is therefore, Luhmann asserts, no difference between truth and ideology. Both truth and ideology are part of the functional process of complexity-reduction. The transcendent claim implied in acts of anti-systemic protest – namely that protest shows the system its own untruth – is, Luhmann indicates, merely a component of the dynamic through which a system stabilizes itself. Protest describes weaknesses in the func-tional code of the system. This description, although administered as critique – or even ideological critique – is merely a functional constituent of the system itself (Narr and Runze 1974: 16–17). Luhmann's theory of protest stands therefore as a pointer to the nature of his theory of democracy. Protest-groups which seek to represent to the political system the interests of society or nature fail to recognize that it is the function of the political system to differentiate itself from society and nature – that these only exist for the political system as the indeterminate space from which it is functionally compelled to detach itself. 'Truths' projected against the system from society or nature do not demonstrate the untruth of the system. They show up at most its need for adjustment. In most cases, however, the system cannot adjust to its environment. There is, in any case, no normative position outside the system from which an observer might tell the system how to react and respond to either natural or social issues.

Luhmann's theory is widely reviled as a smug, neo-conservative pronouncement on environmental issues. Notably, however, it is striking that political theorists who are much more committed to environmental causes have found it difficult to overcome the debilitation of the political system which Luhmann mockingly describes. For example, Ulrich Beck (Professor of Sociology at the University of Munich) has attempted to put forward an ecological counter-theory to Luhmann's position. The central idea which runs through all of Beck's work is that modern industrial society is a 'risk-society'. His best-known work is entitled simply *Risk-Society* (1986). Beck uses this term to examine how industrial society produces environmental risks and dangers which its institutions cannot absorb or process, and which consequently undermine the legitimizing basis of these institutions. Most particularly, Beck (like Luhmann) argues that the global nature of risks dismantles the traditional political structures of the nation-state (see Giddens 1990: 52). The global 'world-society', he explains, is without a 'world-state or world-government'. It is the society of 'globally disorganized capitalism' (Beck 1997: 32), in which the concept of political sovereignty is 'obsolete' (p. 72), and in which 'publicly legitimized politics loses its binding qualities' (p. 174). Beck thus sees risk and globality as general social experiences which render unstable the fixed political horizons of national and representative democracy. 'How can political authority be sustained,' Beck asks, 'when it responds to the increasing consciousness of danger with passionate claims that everything is safe, but . . . risks its entire credibility with every accident or sign of an accident?' (1988: 112). The attempts made by public institutions to legitimize themselves in face of risk, through promises of security and attempted measures to prevent ecological crisis, condemn these institutions – Beck thus argues (again like Luhmann) – to ever greater loss of legitimacy.

Beck's ideas are ostensibly written in direct opposition to Luhmann, whose ideas he describes as an 'extreme counter-position to the atomistic challenges of democracy' (1988: 166). Whilst Luhmann affirms the stability of the political system in its relation to ecological risks, Beck argues that ecological threats show up the insufficiency of the institutional system (1997: 180). Owing to the resultant de-legitimization of political institutions, Beck claims, civil society itself acquires new importance as a sphere of extra-institutional, 'sub-political' agency. Owing to the demise of traditional institutions, Beck argues, new contexts for local and civil politics have been created, through which the traditional resources of political power are relocated into the civil sphere. The loss of legitimacy by political institutions naturally involves an atomization of political society, and therefore an increase in influence for civil associations. The process of political globalization is, Beck argues, a move towards a 'transnational civil society', or a 'society of citizens' (1997: 210), in which 'a new transnational space of the moral and the sub-political is opened' (p. 54). Society, for Beck, is therefore evidently far more than Luhmann's 'residual-category' (p. 181). Equally, whilst Luhmann argues that social and political systems are closed to external input (and therefore individual thought), Beck, in contrast, euphorically envisages the emergence of new forms of individual and collective political reflexivity, as the closed systems of politics are exposed to contradiction, debate and critical scrutiny. The entire utopian content of Beck's thought is invested in the idea that 'the process of modernization is becoming reflexive, its own subject and problem' (1988: 26).

Notwithstanding these great differences, however, there are certain very considerable overlaps between Beck and Luhmann, which indicate that their focus on the key problems of (post)modernity is not as distinct as their political orientations might suggest. Both Beck and Luhmann describe the pluralist de-centration of modern society. Both see modern democracy as a system in which no institution or body can claim power for itself (Beck 1986: 371). Both also argue that modern political systems are hopelessly overburdened by their confrontation with extra-political problems. Both Luhmann and Beck therefore diagnose both the lack of legitimacy of the modern political system, and the diffuseness of power as a result of this lack. Both, in sum, outline theories of post-political politics, and both see politics as a vanishing category of action. The last location of politics is, for Luhmann, the bureaucracy. In Beck's sociology, in contrast, the sphere of political responsibility is shifted into the loudly proclaimed, but ultimately impotent, sphere of civil-social (sub-political) action. The key issues of political life – whether the political sphere can influence the economy, and whether social interests can be absorbed into the state – are, however, not answered by either Luhmann or Beck. They are simply obscured, either in ironic brevity or in social euphoria.

For these reasons, therefore, the question might legitimately be raised whether ecological theory has progressed significantly beyond the cynical, anti-ecological positions marked out by Luhmann. Certainly, in the key respects of political action and organization, both Luhmann and Beck concur in describing a society without structured modes of agency and volition. For both Beck and Luhmann, the spaces of human authority and decisiveness are located only in those areas which no longer really matter, from which power has already departed. In these crucial respects, therefore,

Beck's brand of social ecologism is little more than an inexplicably jubilant variant on Luhmann's systemic nihilism.

In relation to this, the theories of agency, civil activity and social normativity which Luhmann elaborates in his critique of grass-roots and protest movements also encapsule the terms of his more protracted political-sociological debates with Habermas – the now famous Bielefeld–Frankfurt altercation. Although Habermas himself was notoriously uneasy in his dealings with radical protest-movements, Habermas remained, throughout the 1970s, a loosely anti-institutionalist theorist, for whom the normative potentials of the social sphere are the only truly legitimate foundation for government. In his debate with Luhmann, Habermas accuses Luhmann of representing a glossy version of the counter-Enlightenment. He rejects both Luhmann's anti-subjectivism and his orientation of politics around the status quo. He argues that Luhmann's sociology endorses social and political conformism through its bureaucratic gradualism: that it constitutes an 'apology for what already exists' (1975: 170). Naturally also, Habermas condemns the anti-normativity of Luhmann's thought and especially Luhmann's functional determination of truth and ideology (1975: 221). In opposition to Luhmann's functionalism, Habermas puts forward a non-institutionalist theory of discourse, in which the ethical claims of domination-free communication cannot be assimilated to systemic rationality. 'Discourse', he argues, 'is not an institution. It is the quintessential counter-institution. Therefore it cannot be grasped as a "system", for it only operates under the condition that the compulsion to adhere to functional imperatives is suspended' (p. 201). Luhmann, in his own reply to Habermas, observes simply: 'Rational consensus would be, if it can be secured through discourse at all, the removal of contingency' (1975b: 381). Habermas's utopia of discursive legitimacy would be, for Luhmann, merely a perfect adjustment of the system to its environment.

In general, therefore, the Bielefeld–Frankfurt discussion might be summarized as a critical exchange between two forms of communication-theory, one normative, hermeneutic and *social*, one autopoietic, de-centred and *asocial*. Luhmann's defence of bureaucratic rationality is based on his de-centred, post-ontological, post-humanist world-view. Instrumental action and interaction cannot be separated in Luhmann's thought. There is, for Luhmann, no non-technical space outside the systems where human beings can simply interact as rational communicative agents. Whilst Habermas argues that language contains an ethical, humanist rationality which sets the communication of the life-world apart from the administrative and economic systems, Luhmann uses a much broader category of communication to interpret the media of understanding. He is not willing to give one form of communication priority over another, as the receptacle of ethical norms. Luhmann's theory, especially, does not view communication as the intentional act of one consciousness, but as the codes in which individual consciousness is situated (see Nassehi 1992: 55). For Luhmann, all systems communicate – this is what constitutes them as systems. Habermas, therefore, focuses a notion of society, or 'life-world', as a zone of interactive understanding. Luhmann, in contrast, does not recognize the ethically graded separation of system and life-world. This separation, Luhmann argues, marks a crude over-simplification of the complex, interdependent structures of communication into which social agents are integrated (1996e: 71).

These differences are also reflected in the theories of politics put forward by Habermas and Luhmann. Luhmann argues that politics no longer exists. Certainly, he explains, there is no anthropologically unique set of practices which constitutes the political sphere. Politics, Luhmann argues, is merely a functionally limited system. Real political power is situated in the bureaucracy. Luhmann argues therefore that the state can no longer claim representative functions or status, and can no longer issue or support universal directives. In contrast to this, Habermas seeks to theorize politics – or political legitimacy – as a category of communicative praxis which cannot be reduced to technical, or economic processes. Habermas argues that legitimate politics arises from discursive interaction, which channels private needs into a political will-formation. Luhmann argues that political legitimacy is smooth-running administration.

There are also, however, strong similarities between Habermas and Luhmann in their theory of politics. These, as much as their differences, shed light on the relation between them. Both Habermas and Luhmann protect the political moment from overburdening, and both seek to separate the category of the political out from economic functions. Both argue that the efficacy (Luhmann) or legitimacy (Habermas) of political systems cannot be sustained if the political system is required to internalize issues outside its own orbit. Both also argue that the state forfeits its legitimacy (either as consensual foundation or as administrative rationality) if it absorbs economic problems and makes social promises which it cannot keep (Süß 1991: 92). In his depreciation of politics, however, Luhmann refuses to prioritize the political dimension over the technical processes of exchange and administration. He argues that politics must, if at all, be addressed in the same manner as all technical systems. There is, Luhmann explains, no liberal-anthropological primacy for the political moment. Habermas's theory of interactive legitimacy is, he therefore intimates, an archaic residue of classical republicanism which clings (against its own logical conclusions) to the sentiment that political order can be based upon its congruence with the environment. In this regard, Luhmann's thought stands – even to thought on the left – as an insistence that the recourse to universal-anthropological positions is foreclosed (see Jessop 1990: 331). In certain respects, in fact, Luhmann's theory of the relation between politics and economics is very close to Marx's theories of superstructure and political democracy. Both Marx and Luhmann argue simply that the steering-organizations of the economy are not permeable to normative stimuli from either the social sphere or the political body. Economic life and political life, both Marx and Luhmann therefore imply, cannot be reconciled under the conditions of modern systems. Most especially, both Marx and Luhmann assert that the invocation of humanist or anthropological values as a corrective to the autonomy of the economic system is illusory and pointless.

For all his opposition to concepts of sovereignty and political power, however, Luhmann's theory of systems remains a theory which gives especial weight to the executive. His idea of politics is based on a model of institutional pluralism. Democracy, he argues, is protected by the stabilization and autonomy of various systems against each other. Political subsystems – administrations, parties, and discussion-bodies – perform the real decision-making tasks of the political sphere. However, in Luhmann's mode of pluralism the political system is always defined as the original producer of decision-premises. 'In modern political systems,' Luhmann argues,

> we find throughout a primary functional differentiation in politics and administration . . . Politics concerns itself with the production of power, which enjoys political support, with the recruitment and testing of leading personalities, with the preservation of legitimizing symbols and ideologies, with the elaboration of themes and programmes likely to find agreement, with the forming and testing of consensus for particular projects. The administration (in the most extended sense, including parliaments and courts) accepts the authorization for binding decisions and concerns itself with the elaboration and execution of binding decisions. (1983: 183–4)

Luhmann thus explains the modern political system as a complex executive in which quasi-autonomous bureaucratic apparatuses operate within the decision-premises which are fed into them by the highest level of the planning-system. Here, Luhmann strikingly mirrors the thought of Carl Schmitt.

Indeed, the link between Luhmann and Schmitt is reflected in most aspects of Luhmann's work. Both Luhmann and Schmitt understand the basis of modern law as the *decision*, refined into planning-premises for the administration (Luhmann 1974: 260). Both Schmitt and Luhmann therefore represent varying configurations of decisionism (Luhmann 1993a: 38). Both Luhmann and Schmitt indicate that the terms of genuine political legitimacy can no longer be constituted in modern society, and they therefore endorse a bureaucratic executive, in which maximum power is devolved to the administration. The administration itself, in both instances, is the location where specific issues are addressed. The positive decisions at the peak of the executive are little more than symbolic legitimation-resources, which should not be overtaxed. Moreover, both Luhmann and Schmitt indicate that the positivization of law places law on fictitious ground. For both Luhmann and Schmitt, modern law is without substantive legitimacy. Both, in different ways, see the positivization of law as the decisive shift away from substantive order-concepts towards a system of law which adjusts to its environment by making decisions. Whilst Schmitt's

theory of the decision seeks to symbolize a chimeric form of legitimacy in
the figure of the personal sovereign, Luhmann's decisionism openly admits
that it has no claim to consensual or substantive justification. Luhmann
would, manifestly, reject Schmitt's attempts to confer a quasi-sacral gloss
on the decisions of the state. However, Schmitt's rhetorical (re)transcend-
entalization of the state actually enacts exactly the process which Luhmann's thought describes – namely, the transfer of power to the
bureaucracy, beneath the fictitious legitimacy of the post-political state.
Luhmann, like Schmitt, accords to the state the legitimizing capacity to
create ideologies and integrative mechanisms of identification. In direct
overlap with Schmitt, he also understands the state, not as the executor
of decisions, but as the projector of programmes within which decisions can
be made. Schmitt does not suggest that all decisions should be made by the
state. He only implies that the state should stand above the bureaucracy as
the defining structure of political form. This process leaves the actual
decisions of politics in the hands of the administration. If Schmitt, therefore, can be viewed as a thinker who attempts to refabricate the strong
central state after its demise, Luhmann might be viewed as a figure who,
finally, transposes the functions of Schmitt's state into the bureaucracy.
Indeed, Luhmann's thought also shows a striking similarity with Schmitt's
figuration of Vaihinger's philosophy of the as-if (Beyme 1991a: 6). Political
legitimacy, both Luhmann and Schmitt indicate, exists wherever executive
decisions can be treated *as if* they were legitimate.

   In recent essays, Luhmann has in fact paid special attention to the quality
of the political decision. The political decision, he argues, is a decision over
decision-premises – a decision which sets the parameters for subsequent
decisions. As such, it is the point of ultimate recourse which stabilizes the
codes, or fictions, which differentiate the political/administrative system
from its environment. The 'decision over decision-premises must', he
explains, 'take place on the level of observation in second order. Decision-premises are planned for deciders, with a view to how these observers
in first order observe their decision-premises' (1993b: 298). Unlike
Schmitt, Luhmann argues that political decisions are made by roles within
the party system, not by actual persons (1992: 8). The top-level decisions of
the political system are, however, Luhmann argues (like Schmitt), the
foremost differentiating moment of the system. The system engenders its
unity through the decisions which are made at its peak – at the highest
executive (Heidtmann 1974). It is through these decisions that the system
creates its own legitimacy. Indeed, both Schmitt and Luhmann imply that
the political decision has its greatest legitimacy as the moment in which the
system accepts its own contingency (Luhmann 1992: 11). The decision
becomes legitimate precisely in that moment when it is stripped of all
residual substance and interpreted simply as a functional necessity, by
means of which the system explains and represents its contingent relation
to its environment. Schmitt's theory of sovereign law in the state of
exception is itself little more than a glamorous variant on the functionalist

belief that law is not substantially validated, but produced as a positive, contextual response to the demands which the environment places on the system. In Schmitt's theory of the decision – in other words – the sovereign stabilizes the order of the system against the disorder of the exception. Luhmann (unlike Schmitt) asserts that the political parties are the authors of political decision-premises. However, both Luhmann and Schmitt argue that these decisions have no contact with any rationality which is external to their own structure. Decisions, as described by Schmitt and by Luhmann, are produced *ex nihilo*, and they set the functional programmes for all members of society (Giegel 1975: 55).

The paradox of Luhmann's thought can therefore be grasped in the tension between pluralism and monism, de-centration and centralism. Although Luhmann's democracy is built around a structure of institutional pluralism, the fact that it is a democracy which makes only technical concessions to the civil sphere re-centres it ultimately around the legitimizing programmes and plans of the political system, which orientate the functional codes of the bureaucracy. The common accusation that Luhmann is complicit in the 'refeudalization' of society must, therefore, be taken seriously (Maus 1994: 297). However, it is not strictly correct to argue that Luhmann's systems-theory recreates the model of the feudal state. Luhmann's post-subjective thinking certainly returns to a quasi-theological or, at least, pre-Enlightenment conception of authority, and of the relation of authority to needs, to rights, and to the civil sphere. Emphatically, however, unlike the feudal system, Luhmann argues that the state cannot regulate the economy. It is perhaps more appropriate to see Luhmann's theory as a hollow version of nineteenth-century liberalism, in which the operations of state, society and economy are strictly separated by the rigid codes of public and private law, and in which the entire system is governed by an intransigent bureaucracy. Whilst other theorists of the twentieth century have tried to infuse substantial or material value into positive law, for Luhmann the empty positivity of modern law and modern politics is precisely its virtue. Indeed, Luhmann evidently affirms precisely that separation of private and public law which other thinkers addressed here seek to overcome.

# Conclusion

In summary, all the major theorists of political life in modern Germany, except Luhmann, accord particular status to the dimension of *the political*. The historical reasons for this have been addressed in the introduction. Weber attempts to grasp political life as the integration of the collective in structures of rationality which are not exclusively produced out of technical (economic) reason. Schmitt argues that politics is a mode of existence in which human life is lifted out of the secular systems of strategic compromise and formal, private need-satisfaction. Neumann and Kirchheimer grasp true politics as free decision and interaction, which become possible through the suspension of material inequality and private antagonism. Habermas explains genuine political life as a process of deliberative integration, obstructed by systemic media, in which particular conflicts are resolved and public power is formed out of agreement. Although Habermas pays greater attention to the diversity and plurality of private needs than his precursors on the left, his concept of the political still depends on the assertion that political life is made possible by the transition from particular, private autonomy to collective, public interaction. Only Luhmann argues that politics cannot resolve formal differences of private interest. Luhmann's theory of politics leaves private spaces untouched. Indeed, his model political system is a system in which the diversity and the autonomy of the private is guaranteed, as long as private diversity places as few demands as possible on public operations.

In each case except Luhmann, therefore, political theory in modern Germany makes either an explicit or an implicit claim about the anthropological structuration of human life. In each case except Luhmann, a dual model of human existence is outlined, in which humanity exists both inside and outside the technical purposes of individual-material needs. This duality, foreshadowed by Kant's theory of first and second nature, is theorized theologically by Schmitt, and it remains a strong undercurrent in the works of Neumann and Kirchheimer, and even Habermas. In modern German political thought, the genuinely human element to human life commences at the moment where it is elevated above the private or technical system. This elevation is accomplished through identity, decision, discourse or common will. In each instance, human life is most determinately human where it is public and political.

At the origin of this tradition of thinking is a distinctive conceptualization of property-relations. The proper qualities of right, order and legitimacy in the German tradition do not depend on the stable representation of interests which are prior to politics itself. Rather, the key implication of post-Kantian political thought in Germany is that politics only becomes politics insofar as it detaches itself from the sphere of pre-political relations. This clearly does not imply that all the thinkers addressed above deny rights of economic liberty. It does mean, however, that such rights are not the sole justification for political power. Equally, this does not imply that each of these thinkers puts forward a theory of political liberty which does not acknowledge private needs. It does, however, mean that the acknowledgment of private needs (or plural autonomy) is reached through public ethics, not vice versa. The dimension of political life in each of these cases (except Luhmann) is a fluid, interpretive space where the justification for power is always under review, not fixed in advance.

Nonetheless, the major anthropological models of political action and power addressed in this work all contain insoluble problems. Weber, for instance, attempts to develop an integrating theory of politics. Politics, Weber implies, is a uniting ethic, which captures the heart of national interest, and which elevates citizens above material or class-based reflections. However, Weber is unable to represent the non-technical sphere of politics in terms which are not themselves technical. Weber's political system ultimately remains a formal variable of the private/material sphere. In fact, his entire theory might be grasped as a means of obscuring the fundamental lack of legitimacy of the modern political order, in the form in which he describes it. Schmitt, analogously, attempts to theorize politics in its representative, ethical purity, as the embodiment of non-technical nature. But he finally becomes a theorist for the bureaucracy, whose theory of politics is without substantive foundations. Schmitt's sovereign President, supposedly the supreme embodiment of non-technical interest, is little more than a high-ranking administrator. Schmitt's early theory of substantive law is ultimately retraced as a theory of superficially aestheticized, but absolutely fluid, positive law, which facilitates the transfer of power to the administration in the executive. Although Schmitt, of all thinkers discussed here, makes the most superlative claims for the dignity of *the political*, he actually (with Luhmann) gives to politics the most restricted place and status in his model of society. Habermas, linking with

Neumann and Kirchheimer, also accords to the political dimension of human life the unique status of a sphere of interaction in which private autonomy and public freedom can be reconciled, indeed co-original and co-constitutive. Despite this, Habermas's enthusiasm for active citizenship is developed by means of various functionalist compromises. In his works of the 1960s and 1970s, Habermas sees the sphere of human liberty as an increasingly endangered location, threatened on all sides by technical media. His theory of politics is therefore barely more than cautious protection for the residual spaces of public-political life. Ultimately, Habermas shifts the focus of his functionalist bargain. In his latest works, Habermas finally elaborates a model for explaining how public interaction can be channelled into political will-formation. However, the public freedom of citizens does not, in his latter works, include the citizen's freedom of disposition over his/her own labour. The economy is therefore (more or less) left out of his concept of political freedom. In each of these cases, in sum, the concept of the political carries a faintly fictitious or self-undermining gesture.

Luhmann (and Beck), finally, turn away from such debate. Luhmann's ideas fuse an anti-political version of liberalism with a post-political outline of human life, in which nothing matters more than anything else. This theory accords no priority to political interaction, and certainly no anthropological dignity to political rationality. For Luhmann, politics is a system, and systems are produced, neutrally, out of functional necessities. Above all, Luhmann implies, politics is a system which can only take very limited responsibility for private desires and operations. These are expressed and fulfilled in the economy.

Luhmann's theory might soon be viewed as little more than a historical curio, as a hybrid of 1980s conservatism and nineteenth-century liberalism. However, Luhmann's systemic functionalism raises a question of the most fundamental importance for his antecedents and interlocutors in the tradition of German political thought. Luhmann's functional limitation of politics to administration questions, namely, whether the anthropological recourse in political theory is anything more than a rhetorical conceit. It is striking, certainly, that such avowedly anti-functionalist theorists as Weber, Schmitt and Habermas should, in different ways, be forced to assimilate aspects of functionalist (or pre-functionalist) political theory in order to constitute even the most restricted models of autonomous political action. Indeed, in certain key respects, Weber, Schmitt and Habermas *are* functionalists – or their theories of politics, at least, are not tenable without heavy concessions to functional necessities. Weber is not successful in his attempt to base politics on collective action and interest. Instead of this, he devises technical symbols for integrating and neutralizing popular interests. Schmitt cannot crystallize his pure political ethics except as a symbolic code, situated above the administration. Habermas ultimately brackets out the system of the economy in his attempt to show how political interaction might feed into the constitution of power. Despite his lengthy, and at times acrimonious, debates with Luhmann, Habermas in many respects duplicates Luhmann's own moves. Where he does not do so, he makes recourse to a committed, but limited, form of philosophical anthropology. In each case, thus, Luhmann's cynically minimalist theory of politics reflects, ironically, the limitations of his precursors.

Of the thinkers addressed here, Neumann and Kirchheimer – at least in their writings of the 1920s – are the most naive. In their models for the political fusion of state and society, they understand real politics as the collective decision, which neutralizes the economy. This detaches human liberty from negative interests and makes possible the free constitution of public power. At the heart of their theory of democracy is Max Adler's model of the state as a united coercive order, corresponding perfectly to the needs of the proletariat. This model presupposes, in the optimistic manner of inter-war social democracy, that all members of society are fundamentally socialists – despite, at the time when Neumann and Kirchheimer were writing, the most palpable evidence to the contrary.

Despite their naivety, however, Neumann and Kirchheimer might also be viewed as the only thinkers here who genuinely resist the abandonment of political life to functional necessity. Neumann and Kirchheimer claim that politics will (in future) only be possible if human interaction is not anchored in the protection of interests already established in the pre-political system, and if, therefore, the constitution of public power can be made genuinely public (positive). Liberty, they explain, is structurally reliant on equality. Of the thinkers discussed in this work, therefore, Neumann and Kirchheimer take their political anthropology most seriously. Functional systems (especially the system of private law), they argue, must be ruthlessly eliminated from public life. Real democracy, they suggest, can only be produced (in Rousseauian manner) through the complete de-privatization of interest. The de-privatization of interest is, they thus indicate, identical with the de-functionalization of politics.

In certain respects, therefore, it might be argued that the German tradition of political thought confronts the reader with a stark either/or option between Luhmann, on the one hand, and Neumann and Kirchheimer, on the other. If the anthropological premises of the German tradition are to be taken at their word, they imply that political life and legitimacy are produced when the horizon of political constitution is self-creating and self-expanding – when the terms of good government are not restricted by prior limits. With various degrees of unwillingness, Weber, Schmitt and Habermas all admit that (or obscure their admission of the fact that) the terms of human political interaction cannot be separated from the pre-established systems of technical/material/economic interest. Only Neumann and Kirchheimer explain (however crudely and optimistically) what the real precondition of the liberation of political life might actually *be*. Politics is constituted as a free life-form, they argue, only when the impact of functional needs on human interaction is resolutely resisted – when the economy is subject to binding decisions. Only thus is human life at liberty to be *political*. If the anthropological premises of the German tradition are not taken seriously, however, politics is as Luhmann describes it. Luhmann says there is no such thing as political life. Politics, he states, is only an administrative system, which is always limited by the system of money.

Where attempts are made to square the circle between anthropological and functional conceptions of politics, the anthropological dimension usually acquires a rhetorical or apologetic quality. Arguably, for example, the claim to represent *political* interest in Weber and Schmitt is used to disguise the fact that their theories do not serve political interests at all, but in fact the most technical of interests – the export-economy and the bureaucracy. Habermas's entire work can be seen as an attempt to balance the claims of functionalist and anthropological theories of political life. At various junctures in his career, he gives priority to one or the other. Despite his inclination towards a strong theory of politics, however, his ideas always admit the power (and, arguably, the predominance) of functional systems over the political moment. The work of Ulrich Beck, latterly, also makes exuberant claims for the refiguring of politics as 'sub-politics', but this means little more than politics outside functional (or dysfunctional) systems – politics, therefore, where little is at stake.

In short, to conclude, it might be argued that the most extreme positions in both the depreciation and the radicalization of political life come closest to a coherent explanation of what politics is, or might be. On one hand, Luhmann's denial of autonomy to political action in many respects tells the stark truth which Weber, Schmitt and Habermas seek, in varying ways, to circumvent. On the other hand, the insistence of Neumann and Kirchheimer that politics can only be grasped as an autonomous mode of interaction if *all* prior restrictions on it are removed also tells the truth which is both recognized and disguised by Weber, Schmitt and Habermas. The either/or which emerges from the counterpoint between Luhmann's systemic functionalism and the political Marxism of Neumann and Kirchheimer is therefore a choice between a life in which politics has no claim to anthropological uniqueness, and in which private (economic) needs systematically limit human liberty, and a life in which private interests are decisively transformed into public commitments. In other words, the choice which emerges here is that between politics and the economy. For Luhmann, the economy (or at least the functional logic of equivalence) has primacy over politics. For Neumann and Kirchheimer, the political must prevail over the economy. The attempts of Weber, Schmitt and Habermas to derive politics from the economy, or to propose a coexistence of political and economic interest, ultimately leave politics as a variable in the economic system.

# References

Abelshauser, Werner (1981) 'Korea, die Ruhr und Erhards Marktwirtschaft. Die Energiekrise von 1950/51', *Rheinische Vierteljahrsblätter* 45, pp. 287–316.

—— (1983) *Wirtschaftsgeschichte der Bundesrepublik Deutschland 1945–1980* (Frankfurt a. M.: Suhrkamp).

—— (1987) *Die langen fünfziger Jahre. Wirtschaft und Gesellschaft der Bundesrepublik Deutschland 1949–1966* (Düsseldorf: Schwann).

Abendroth, Wolfgang (1967a) 'Zum Begriff des demokratischen und sozialen Rechtsstaates im Grundgesetz der Bundesrepublik Deutschland', in: *Antagonistische Gesellschaft und politische Demokratie: Aufsätze zur politischen Soziologie* (Neuwied: Luchterhand), pp. 109–38.

—— (1967b) 'Das Problem der innerparteilichen und innerverbandlichen Demokratie in der Bundesrepublik', in: *Antagonistische Gesellschaft und politische Demokratie* (see Abendroth 1967a), pp. 272–317.

—— (1967c) 'Die Alternativen der Planung: Planung zur Erhaltung des Spätkapitalismus oder Planung in Richtung auf eine klassenlose Gesellschaft? Einige marxistische Bemerkungen zum Problem der Planung', in: *Antagonistische Gesellschaft* (see Abendroth 1967a), pp. 463–93.

Ableitinger, Alfred (1983) 'Grundlegung der Verfassung', in: Erika Weinzierl and Kurt Skalnik (eds), *Österreich 1918–1938. Geschichte der ersten Republik* vol. 1 (Graz: Styria Verlag), pp. 147–94.

Abraham, David (1986) *The Collapse of the Weimar Republic: Political Economy and Crisis* (New York/London: Holmes & Meier).

Adam, Armin (1992) *Rekonstruktion des Politischen: Carl Schmitt und die Krise der Staatlichkeit* (Weinberg: VCR, Acta Humaniora).

Adam, Hermann (1972) *Die konzertierte Aktion in der Bundesrepublik* (Cologne: Bund-Verlag).

Aderhold, Dieter (1973) *Kybernetische Regierungstechnik in der Demokratie. Planung und Erfolgskontrolle* (Munich/Vienna: Günter Olzog).

Adler, Max (1918) *Die Sozialistische Idee der Befreiung bei Karl Marx* (Vienna: Verlag der Wiener Volksbuchhandlung Ignaz Brand).

——(1926) *Politische oder soziale Demokratie: Ein Beitrag zur sozialistischen Erziehung* (Berlin: E. Laub).

——(1973) *Die Staatsauffassung des Marxismus: Ein Beitrag zur Unterscheidung von soziologischer und juristischer Methode* (Darmstadt: Wissenschaftliche Buchgesellschaft).

Adolph, Hans J. L (1971) *Otto Wels und die Politik der deutschen Sozialdemokratie 1894–1939* (Berlin: de Gruyter).

Adorno, Theodor W. (1976) 'Kulturkritik und Gesellschaft', in: *Prismen* (Frankfurt a. M.: Suhrkamp), pp. 2–26.

Alber, Jens (1986) 'Germany', in: Peter Flora (ed.), *Growth to Limits: The Western European Welfare States since World War II*, vol. 2: *Germany, United Kingdom, Ireland, Italy* (Berlin: de Gruyter), pp. 1–154.

——(1989) *Der Sozialstaat in der Bundesrepublik 1950–1983* (Frankfurt a. M./New York: Campus).

Albertin, Lothar (1972) *Liberalismus und Demokratie am Anfang der Weimarer Republik. Eine vergleichende Analyse der Deutschen Demokratischen Partei und der Deutschen Volkspartei* (Düsseldorf: Droste).

——(1974) 'Faktoren eines Arrangements zwischen industriellem und politischem System in der Weimarer Republik 1918–1928', in: Hans Mommsen et al. (eds), *Industrielles System und politische Entwicklung in der Weimarer Republik. Verhandlungen des Internationalen Symposiums vom 12.–17. Juni 1973* (Düsseldorf: Droste), pp. 658–74.

Alemann, Ulrich von (1987) *Organisierte Interessen in der Bundesrepublik* (Opladen: Leske & Budrich).

Alemann, Ulrich von and Heinze, Rolf. G. (1981) 'Korporativer Staat und Korporatismus: Dimensionen der Neo-Korporatismusdiskussion', in: Ulrich von Alemann (ed.), *Neokorporatismus* (Frankfurt a. M./New York: Campus), pp. 43–61.

Alexander, Edgar (1953) *Church and Society in Germany: Social and Political Movements and Ideas in German and Austrian Catholicism (1789–1950)*, in: Joseph N. Moody (ed.), *Church and Society: Catholic Social and Political Thought and Movements* (New York: Arts Inc.), pp. 325–583.

Alexander, Jeffrey C. (1983) *The Classical Attempt at Theoretical Synthesis: Max Weber*. Theoretical Studies in Sociology, 3 (Berkeley/Los Angeles: University of California Press).

Allemann, Fritz René (1956) *Bonn ist nicht Weimar* (Cologne: Kiepenheuer & Witsch).

*Allgemeiner Kongreß der Arbeiter- und Soldatenräte Deutschlands. Vom 16. bis 21. Dezember 1918 im Abgeordnetenhaus zu Berlin. Stenographische Berichte* (1919).

Altmann, Rüdiger (1960) *Das Erbe Adenauers* (Stuttgart/Degerloch: Seewald).

Altvater, Elmar, Hoffmann, Jürgen and Semler, Willi (1979), *Vom Wirtschaftswunder zur Wirtschaftskrise. Ökonomie und Politik in der Bundesrepublik* (Berlin: Olle & Wolter).

Altvater, Elmar, Hübner, Kurt and Stanger, Michael (1983) *Alternative Wirtschaftspolitik jenseits des Kapitalismus. Wirtschaftspolitische Optionen der Gewerkschaften in Westeuropa* (Opladen: Westdeutscher Verlag).

Alway, Joan (1995) *Critical Theory and Political Possibilities: Conceptions of Emancipatory Politics in the Works of Horkheimer, Adorno, Marcuse, and Habermas* (London/Westport: Greenwood Press).

Ambrosius, Gerold (1977) *Die Durchsetzung der sozialen Marktwirtschaft in Westdeutschland 1945–1949* (Stuttgart: Deutsche Verlags-Anstalt).

Anter, Andreas (1994) *Max Webers Theorie des modernen Staates* (Berlin: Duncker & Humblot).

Antoni, Michael G. H. (1991) *Sozialdemokratie und Grundgesetz*, vol. 1: *Verfassungspolitische Vorstellungen der SPD von den Anfängen bis zur Konstituierung des Parlamentarischen Rates 1948* (Berlin: Berlin Verlag).

Apel, Karl-Otto (1993) 'Die Kommunikationsgemeinschaft als transzendentale Voraussetzung der Sozialwissenschaften', in: *Transformation der Philosophie*, vol. 2: *Das Apriori der Kommunikationsgemeinschaft* (Frankfurt a. M.: Suhrkamp), pp. 220–63.

Apelt, Willibald (1964) *Geschichte der Weimarer Verfassung* (Munich/Berlin: Beck).

Arendt, Hannah (1958a) *The Human Condition* (Chicago: University of Chicago Press).

——(1958b) 'Karl Jaspers', in: Karl Jaspers and Hannah Arendt, *Reden zur Verleihung des Friedenspreises des deutschen Buchhandels* (Munich: Piper), pp. 27–40.

——(1982) *Lectures on Kant's Political Philosophy*, ed. with an interpretive essay, Ronald Beiner (Brighton: Harvester).

Aretin, Karl Otmar Freiherr von (1966) 'Prälat Kaas, Franz von Papen und das Reichskonkordat von 1933', *Vierteljahreshefte für Zeitgeschichte* 14, pp. 252–79.

Armingeon, Klaus (1988) *Die Entwicklung der deutschen Gewerkschaften 1950–1985* (Frankfurt a. M.:/New York: Campus).

Aron, Raymond (1965) 'Max Weber und die Machtpolitik', in: Otto Stammer (ed.), *Max Weber und die Soziologie heute* (Tübingen: J. C. B. Mohr), pp. 103–20.

Atiyah, P. S. (1979) *The Rise and Fall of Freedom of Contract* (Oxford: OUP).

Balke, Friedrich (1996) *Der Staat nach seinem Ende: Die Versuchung Carl Schmitts* (Munich: Fink).

Ball, Hugo (1983) 'Carl Schmitts Politische Theologie', in: Jacob Taubes (ed.), *Religionstheorie und Politische Theologie*, vol. 1: *Der Fürst dieser Welt. Carl Schmitt und die Folgen* (Munich: Fink), pp. 100–15.

Baring, Arnulf (1972) *Außenpolitik in Adenauers Kanzlerdemokratie*, vol. 2: *Westdeutsche Innenpolitik im Zeichen der Europäischen Verteidigungsgemeinschaft* (Munich: DTV).

Barion, Hans (1965) 'Kirche oder Partei? Römischer Katholizismus und politische Form', *Der Staat* 4, pp. 131–76.

Bark, Dennis L. and Gress, David R. (1989) *A History of West Germany*, vol. 2: *Democracy and its Discontents 1963–1991* (Oxford: Basil Blackwell).

Bärsch, Claus-Ekkehard (1974) *Der Staatsbegriff in der neueren deutschen Staatslehre und seine theoretischen Implikationen* (Berlin: Duncker & Humblot).

Bauer, Otto (1923) *Die österreichische Revolution* (Vienna: Wiener Volksbuchhandlung).

——(1980) 'Das Gleichgewicht der Klassenkräfte', in: *Werkausgabe* edited by the Arbeitsgemeinschaft für die Geschichte der österreichischen Arbeiterbewegung, in 9 vols. (Vienna: Europaverlag) vol. 9, pp. 55–71.

Bäuerle, Bernd (1969) *Wachstum und Grenzen der Staatstätigkeit. Adolph Wagners Gesetz im Lichte neuerer Erkenntnisse* (Wiesbaden: dissertation).

Bauß, Gerhard (1977) *Die Studentenbewegung der sechziger Jahre in der Bundesrepublik und Westberlin* (Cologne: Pahl-Rugenstein).

Bechtold, Hartmut (1986) *Die Kartellierung der deutschen Volkswirtschaft und die sozialdemokratische Theorie-Diskussion vor 1933* (Frankfurt a. M.: Haag & Herchen).

Beck, Ulrich (1986) *Riskogesellschaft: Auf dem Weg in eine andere Moderne* (Frankfurt a. M.: Suhrkamp).

——(1988) *Gegengifte: Die organisierte Unverantwortlichkeit* (Frankfurt a. M.: Suhrkamp).

——(1997) *Was ist Globalisierung? Irrtümer des Globalismus – Antworten auf Globalisierung* (Frankfurt a. M.: Suhrkamp).

Becker, Hartmuth (1994) *Die Parlamentarismuskritik bei Carl Schmitt und Jürgen Habermas* (Berlin: Duncker & Humblot).

Becker, Josef (1963) 'Das Ende der Zentrumspartei und die Problematik des politischen Katholizismus in Deutschland', *Die Welt als Geschichte* 23, pp. 149–72.

Beetham, David (1985) *Max Weber and the Theory of Modern Politics* (Cambridge: Polity Press).

Bellamy, Richard (1992) *Liberalism and Modern Society: An Historical Argument* (University Park, Pennsylvania: Pennsylvania State University Press).

Bender, Gerd (1988) 'Vom Hilfsdienstgesetz zum Betriebsrätegesetz. Zur rechtlichen Regulierung des industriellen Verhandlungssystems zwischen Reform und Revolution', in: *Ius Commune*, spec. issue 37, *Revolution, Reform, Restauration. Formen der Veränderung von Recht und Gesellschaft*, pp. 191–210.

Bendix, Reinhard (1977) *Max Weber: An Intellectual Portrait*, intro. Günther Roth (Berkeley/Los Angeles: University of California Press).

——(1978) *Kings or People: Power and the Mandate to Rule* (Berkeley/Los Angeles: University of California Press).

Beneyto, José María (1988) *Apokalypse der Moderne: Die Diskurstheorie von Donoso Cortés* (Stuttgart: Klett-Cotta).

Benjamin, Walter (1974) 'Über den Begriff der Geschichte', in: *Gesammelte Schriften* ed. Rolf Tiedemann and Hermann Schweppenhäuser, 7 vols. (Frankfurt a. M.: Suhrkamp), vol. 1(2), pp. 691–704.

Berghahn, V. R. (1973) *Germany and the Approach of War in 1914* (New York: St Martin's Press).

——(1985) *Unternehmer und Politik in der Bundesrepublik* (Frankfurt a. M.: Suhrkamp).

Berg-Schlosser, Dirk (1979) 'Die Konstituierung des Wirtschaftssystems', in: Josef Becker, Theo Stammen and Peter Waldmann (eds), *Vorgeschichte der Bundesrepublik Deutschland. Zwischen Kapitulation und Grundgesetz* (Munich: Fink), pp. 93–121.

Berlau, Joseph (1949) *The German Social Democratic Party 1914–1920* (New York: Columbia University Press).

Berman, Harold J. (1983) *Law and Revolution: The Formation of the Western Legal Tradition* (Cambridge, Mass.: Harvard UP).

Bermbach, Udo (1967) *Vorformen parlamentarischer Kabinettsbildung in Deutschland. Der interfraktionelle Ausschuß und die Parlamentarisierung der Reichsregierung* (Opladen: Westdeutscher Verlag).

Bernecker, Walther L. (1979) 'Die Neugründung der Gewerkschaften in den Westzonen 1945–1949', in: Josef Becker, Theo Stammen and Peter Waldmann (eds), *Vorgeschichte der Bundesrepublik Deutschland. Zwischen Kapitulation und Grundgesetz* (Munich: Fink), pp. 261–92.

Bertram, Jürgen (1964) *Die Wahlen zum Deutschen Reichstag vom Jahre 1912. Parteien und Verbände in der Innenpolitik des Wilhelminischen Reiches* (Düsseldorf: Droste).

Besters, Hans (1979) *Neue Wirtschaftspolitik durch Angebotslenkung. Offene Fragen überbetrieblicher Investitionsplanung und vorausschauender Strukturpolitik* (Baden-Baden: Nomos).

Beyerle, Konrad (1919) *Die Bedeutung der neuen Reichsverfassung für Volk und Vaterland* (Berlin: Verlag der Reichszentrale für Heimatdienst).

Beyme, Klaus von (ed.) (1979) *Die großen Regierungserklärungen der deutschen Bundeskanzler von Adenauer bis Schmidt* (Munich/Vienna: Carl Hanser).

——(1980) 'Repräsentatives und parlamentarisches Regierungssystem. Eine begriffsgeschichtliche Analyse', in: Heinz Rausch (ed.), *Die geschichtlichen Grundlagen der modernen Volksvertretung. Die Entwicklung von den mittelalterlichen Korporationen zu den modernen Parlamenten* (Darmstadt: Wissenschaftliche Buchgesellschaft, 1980), pp. 396–417.

——(1981) 'Der liberale Korporatismus als Mittel gegen die Unregierbarkeit', in: Ulrich von Aleman (ed.), *Neokorporatismus* (Frankfurt a. M./New York: Campus), pp. 80–91.

——(1991a) 'Ein Paradigmenwechsel aus dem Geist der Naturwissenschaften: Die Theorien der Selbststeuerung von Systemen (Autopoiesis)', *Journal für Sozialforschung* 31, pp. 3–24.

——(1991b) *Theorie der Politik im 20. Jahrhundert: Von der Moderne zur Postmoderne* (Frankfurt a. M.: Suhrkamp).

——(1996) 'Theorie der Politik im Zeitalter der Transformation', in: Klaus von Beyme and Claus Offe (eds), *Politische Theorien in der Ära der Transformation* (Opladen: Westdeutscher Verlag), pp. 9–29.

Blackbourn, David and Eley, Geoff (1984) *The Peculiarities of German History: Bourgeois Society and Politics in Nineteenth-Century Germany* (Oxford: OUP).

Blaich, Fritz (1973) *Kartell- und Monopolpolitik im kaiserlichen Deutschland: Das Problem der Marktmacht im deutschen Reichstag zwischen 1879 und 1914* (Düsseldorf: Droste).

——(1979) *Staat und Verbände in Deutschland zwischen 1871 und 1945* (Wiesbaden: Franz Steiner).

Blanke, Thomas (1984) 'Kirchheimer, Neumann, Preuß: Die Radikalisierung der Rechtstheorie', in: Joachim Perels (ed.), *Aktualität und Probleme der Theorie Franz L. Neumanns* (Baden-Baden: Nomos), pp. 163–94.

Blasius, Dirk (1978) 'Bürgerliches Recht und bürgerliche Identität. Zu einem Problemzusammenhang in der deutschen Geschichte des 19. Jahrhunderts', in: Helmut Berding et al. (eds), *Vom Staat des Ancien Regime zum modernen Parteistaat. Festschrift für Theodor Schieder* (Munich: R. Oldenbourg), pp. 213–24.

Blau, Joachim (1980) *Sozialdemokratische Staatslehre in der Weimarer Republik: Darstellung und Untersuchung der staatstheoretischen Konzeptionen von Hermann Heller, Ernst Fraenkel und Otto Kirchheimer* (Marburg: Verlag Arbeiterbewegung und Gesellschaftswissenschaft).

Blum, Reinhard (1969) *Soziale Marktwirtschaft. Wirtschaftspolitik zwischen Neoliberalismus und Ordoliberalismus* (Tübingen: J. C. B. Mohr).

Boberach, Heinz (1959) *Wahlrechtsfragen im Vormärz. Die Wahlrechtsanschauung im Rheinland 1815–1849 und die Entstehung des Dreiklassenwahlrechts* (Düsseldorf: Droste).

Böckenförde, Ernst-Wolfgang (1961) 'Der deutsche Katholizismus im Jahre 1933', *Hochland* 53, pp. 215–39.

Böckenförde, Ernst-Wolfgang (1987) 'Der Zusammenbruch der Monarchie und die Entstehung der Weimarer Republik', in: Karl Dietrich Bracher et al. (eds), *Die Weimarer Republik 1918–1933: Politik, Wirtschaft, Verfassung* (Düsseldorf: Droste), pp. 17–44.

Boese, Franz (1939) *Geschichte des Vereins für Sozialpolitik 1872–1932* (Berlin: Duncker & Humblot).

Bogner, Artur (1989) *Zivilisation und Rationalisierung: Die Zivilisationstheorien Max Webers, Norbert Elias' und der Frankfurter Schule im Vergleich* (Opladen: Westdeutscher Verlag).

Bohle, Thomas (1990) *Einheitliches Arbeitsrecht in der Weimarer Republik: Bemühungen um ein deutsches Arbeitsrecht* (Tübingen: J. C. B. Mohr).

Böhret, Carl (1966) *Aktionen gegen die 'kalte Sozialisierung' 1926–1930. Ein Beitrag zum Wirken ökonomischer Einflußverbände in der Weimarer Republik* (Berlin: Duncker & Humblot).

Boldt, Hans (1972) 'Zum Strukturwandel des Ausnahmezustandes im 1. Weltkrieg', in: Ernst-Wolfgang Böckenförde (ed.), *Moderne deutsche Verfassungsgeschichte (1815–1918)* (Cologne: Kiepenheuer & Witsch), pp. 323–37.

——(1975) *Deutsche Staatslehre im Vormärz* (Düsseldorf: Droste).

——(1980) 'Der Artikel 48 der Weimarer Reichsverfassung. Sein historischer Hintergrund und seine politische Funktion', in: Michael Stürmer (ed.), *Die Weimarer Republik. Belagerte Civitas* (Königstein: Athenäum), pp. 288–309.

Borowsky, Peter (1980) *Deutschland 1970–1976* (Hanover: Fackelträger).

Boss, Alfred, Fischer, Claus-Friedrich and Schatz, Klaus-Werner et al. (1996) *Deregulierung in Deutschland. Eine empirische Analyse* (Tübingen: J. C. B. Mohr).

Böttger, Geert (1982) 'Anleihefinanzierte Politik der 'Crowding-out'-Hypothese', in: Bernd Rahmann and Johann Welsch (eds), *Wohlfahrtsstaat im Defizit. Sozialstaatliche Politik in der wirtschaftlichen Stagnation* (Cologne: Bund-Verlag), pp. 73–92.

Bowen, Ralph H. (1947) *German Theories of the Corporate State: With Special Reference to the Period 1870–1919* (New York/London: McGraw Hill).

Bracher, Karl Dietrich (1964) 'Die zweite Demokratie in Deutschland – von Weimar nach Bonn', in: *Deutschland zwischen Demokratie und Diktatur: Beiträge zur neueren Politik und Geschichte* (Berne/Munich/Vienna: Scherz), pp. 109–38.

——(1969) *Die deutsche Diktatur. Entstehung, Struktur, Folgen des Nationalsozialismus* (Cologne: Kiepenheuer & Witsch).

Brakemeyer, Heinz (1985) *Die sittliche Aufhebung des Staates in Kants Philosophie* (Frankfurt a. M.: Campus).

Brand, Karl-Werner (1982) *Neue soziale Bewegungen. Entstehung, Funktion und Perspektive neuer Protestpotentiale* (Opladen: Westdeutscher Verlag).

Brandt, Hartwig (1968) *Landständische Repräsentation im deutschen Vormärz. Politisches Denken im Einflußfeld des monarchischen Prinzips* (Neuwied: Luchterhand).

Brandt, Willy (1983) *Zum sozialen Rechtsstaat. Reden und Dokumente*, ed. Arnold Hartung (Berlin: Berlin Verlag).

Brauneder, Wilhelm (1976) *Österreichische Verfassungsgeschichte* (Vienna: Mainz).

Braunthal, Gerhard (1965) *The Federation of German Industry in Politics* (Ithaca, NY: Cornell UP).

——(1978) *Socialist Labor and Politics in Weimar Germany: The General Federation of German Trade Unions* (Hamden, Conn.: Archon Press).

——(1983) *The West German Social Democrats 1969–1982: Profile of a Party in Power* (Epping: Bowker).

Breger, Monika (1994) 'Der Anteil der deutschen Großindustriellen an der Konzeptualisierung der Bismarckschen Sozialgesetzgebung', in: Lothar Machtan (ed.), *Bismarcks Sozialstaat. Beiträge zur Geschichte der Sozialpolitik und zur sozialpolitischen Geschichtsschreibung* (Frankfurt a. M./New York: Campus), pp. 25–61.

Breitling, Rupert (1955) *Die Verbände in der Bundesrepublik. Ihre Arten und ihre politische Wirkungsweise* (Meisenheim am Glan: Anton Hain).

Breuer, Stefan (1994) *Bürokratie und Charisma: Zur politischen Soziologie Max Webers* (Darmstadt: Wissenschaftliche Buchgesellschaft).

Brick, Barbara and Postone, Moishe (1994) 'Friedrich Pollock and the "Primacy of the Political": A Critical Reexamination', in: Jay Bernstein (ed.), *The Frankfurt School: Critical Assessments*, vol. 1 (London/New York: Routledge), pp. 249–63.

Briefs, Goetz (1952) *Zwischen Kapitalismus und Syndikalismus. Die Gewerkschaften am Scheideweg* (Berne: A. Francke).

——(1966) 'Staat und Wirtschaft im Zeitalter der Interessenverbände', in: *Laissez-faire-Pluralismus. Demokratie und Wirtschaft des gegenwärtigen Zeitalters* (Berlin: Duncker & Humblot), pp. 1–317.

——(1968) 'Unternehmenswirtschaft und Gewerkschaft: Ein existentieller Zusammenhang', in: *Gewerkschaftsprobleme in unserer Zeit. Beiträge zur Standortsbestimmung* (Frankfurt a. M.: Fritz Knapp), pp. 178–96.

Brigl-Matthiaß, Kurt (1926) *Das Betriebsräteproblem in der Weimarer Republik* (Berlin: de Gruyter).

Bröckling, Ulrich (1993) *Katholische Intellektuelle in der Weimarer Republik: Zeitkritik und Gesellschaftstheorie bei Walter Dirks, Romano Guardini, Carl Schmitt, Ernst Michel und Heinrich Mertens* (Munich: Fink).

Brunner, Otto (1959) *Land und Herrschaft. Grundfragen der territorialen Verfassungsgeschichte Österreichs im Mittelalter* (Vienna/Wiesbaden: Rudolf M. Rohrer).

Bubner, Rüdiger (1973) 'Wissenschaftstheorie und Systembegriff: Zur Position von N. Luhmann und deren Herkunft', in: *Dialektik und Wissenschaft* (Frankfurt a. M.: Suhrkamp), pp. 112–28.

Buchheim, Karl (1953) *Geschichte der christlichen Parteien in Deutschland* (Munich: Kösel).

——(1963) *Ultramontanismus und Demokratie: Der Weg der deutschen Katholiken im 19. Jahrhundert* (Munich: Kösel).

Bürge, Alfons (1991) *Das französische Privatrecht im 19. Jahrhundert. Zwischen Tradition und Pandektenwissenschaft, Liberalismus und Etatismus* (Frankfurt a. M.: Klostermann).

Bussmann, Walter (1958) 'Zur Geschichte des deutschen Liberalismus im 19. Jahrhundert', *Historische Zeitschrift* 186, pp. 527–57.

Butterwegge, Christoph (1979) *SPD und Staat heute. Ein Beitrag zur Staatstheorie und zur Geschichte der westdeutschen Sozialdemokratie* (Berlin: Verlag des Europäischen Buches).

Canis, Konrad (1997) *Von Bismarck zur Weltpolitik: Deutsche Außenpolitik 1890 bis 1902* (Berlin: Akademie-Verlag).

Carsten, F. L. (1959) *Princes and Parliaments in Germany: From the Fifteenth to the Eighteenth Century* (Oxford: Clarendon Press).

Chambers, Simone (1996) *Reasonable Democracy: Jürgen Habermas and the Politics of Discourse* (Ithaca, NY/London: Cornell UP).

Clay, C. G. A. (1984) *Economic Expansion and Social Change: England 1500–1700*, vol. 2: *Industry, Trade and Government* (Cambridge: CUP).

Coing, Helmut (1985) *Europäisches Privatrecht*, vol. 1: *Älteres Gemeines Recht* (Munich: Beck).

——(1989) *Europäisches Privatrecht*, vol. 2: *19. Jahrhundert. Überblick über die Entwicklung des Privatrechts in den ehemals gemeinrechtlichen Ländern* (Munich: Beck).

Conze, Werner (1950) 'Friedrich Naumann. Grundlagen und Ansatz seiner Politik in der national-sozialen Zeit (1895 bis 1903)', in: Walter Hubatsch (ed.), *Schicksalswege deutscher Vergangenheit: Beiträge zur geschichtlichen Deutung der letzten hundertfünfzig Jahre* (Düsseldorf: Droste), pp. 355–87.

——(1967) 'Die politischen Entscheidungen in Deutschland 1929–1933', in: Werner Conze and Hans Raupach (eds), *Die Staats- und Wirtschaftskrise des Deutschen Reichs 1929/33* (Stuttgart: Klett Verlag), pp. 176–252.

——(1968) 'Die Krise des Parteienstaats in Deutschland 1929/30', in: Gotthard Jasper (ed.), *Von Weimar zu Hitler* (Cologne: Kiepenheuer & Witsch), pp. 27–57.

——(1978) 'Das Spannungsfeld von Staat und Gesellschaft im Vormärz', in: Werner Conze (ed.), *Staat und Gesellschaft im deutschen Vormärz* (Stuttgart: Klett-Cotta), pp. 207–70.

Czada, Peter (1973) 'Ursachen und Folgen der Inflation', in: Harald Winkel (ed.), *Finanz- und wirtschaftspolitische Fragen der Zwischenkriegszeit* (Berlin: Duncker & Humblot), pp. 9–42.

Dahrendorf, Ralf (1967) *Society and Democracy in Germany* (London: Weidenfeld & Nicolson).

Deggau, Hans-Georg (1983) *Die Aporien der Rechtslehre Kants* (Stuttgart/Bad Cannstadt: frommann-holzboog).

Diesselhorst, Malte (1988) *Naturzustand und Sozialvertrag bei Hobbes und Kant. Zugleich ein Beitrag zu den Ursprüngen des modernen Systemdenkens* (Göttingen: Otto Schwarz).

Dietz, Simone (1993) *Lebenswelt und System: Widerstreitende Ansätze in der Gesellschaftstheorie von Jürgen Habermas* (Würzburg: Königshausen & Neumann).

Dilcher, Gerhard (1977) 'Der rechtswissenschaftliche Positivismus. Wissenschaftliche Methode, Sozialphilosophie, Gesellschaftspolitik', in: Bruno Paradiso et al. (eds), *La formazione storica del diritto moderno in Europa*, vol. 1 (Florence: Leo S. Olschki), pp. 123–48.

Dilthey, Wilhelm (1883) *Einleitung in die Geiseswissenschaften* (Leipzig: Duncker & Humblot).

Doemming, Klaus-Berto von et al. (eds) (1951) *Entstehungsgeschichte der Artikel des Grundgesetzes im Auftrage des Parlamentarischen Rates und des Bundesministers des Inneren auf Grund der Verhandlungen des Parlamentarischen Rates*, in: *Jahrbuch des öffentlichen Rechts der Gegenwart*, NS, vol. 1.

Doyle, William (1980) *Origins of the French Revolution* (Oxford: OUP).

Dräger, Klaus and Hülsberg, Werner (1986) *Aus für Grün? Die grüne Orientierungskrise zwischen Anpassung und Systemopposition* (Frankfurt a. M.: isp-Verlag).

Dronberger, Ilse (1971) *The Political Thought of Max Weber: In Quest of Statesmanship* (New York: Appleton-Century-Crofts).

Düding, Dieter (1972) *Der Nationalsoziale Verein 1896–1903: Der gescheiterte Versuch einer parteipolitischen Synthese von Nationalismus, Sozialismus und Liberalismus* (Munich: R. Oldenbourg).

Dyson, Kenneth (1980) *The State Tradition in Western Europe: A Study in an Idea and an Institution* (Oxford: Martin Robertson).

Ebbighausen, Rolf (1973) 'Legitimationskrise der Parteiendemokratie und Forschungsstrategien der Parteiensoziologie, in: Jürgen Dittberner and Rolf Ebbighausen (eds), *Parteien und Materialien zur Soziologie der Parteien in der Bundesrepublik Deutschland* (Opladen: Westdeutscher Verlag), pp. 13–34.

Ehmke, Horst (1969) 'Staat und Gesellschaft als verfassungstheoretisches Problem', in: *Politik der praktischen Vernunft. Aufsätze und Referate* (Frankfurt a. M.: Fischer), pp. 38–63.

Ehni, Hans-Peter (1975) *Bollwerk Preußen? Preußen-Regierung, Reich-Länder-Problem und Sozialdemokratie 1928–1932* (Bonn: Neue Gesellschaft).

Elben, Wolfgang (1965) *Das Problem der Kontinuität in der deutschen Revolution. Die Politik der Staatssekretäre und der militärischen Führung vom November 1918 bis Februar 1919* (Düsseldorf: Droste).

Elert, Werner (1953) *Morphologie des Luthertums*, vol. 2: *Soziallehren und Sozialwirkungen des Luthertums* (Munich: Beck).

Ellwein, Thomas (1954) *Das Erbe der Monarchie in der deutschen Staatskrise. Zur Geschichte des Verfassungsstaates in Deutschland* (Munich: Isar Verlag).

Elm, Ludwig (1968) *Zwischen Fortschritt und Reaktion: Geschichte der Parteien der liberalen Bourgeoisie in Deutschland 1893–1918* (Berlin: Akademie-Verlag).

Erd, Rainer (ed.) (1985) *Reform und Resignation: Gespräche über Franz Neumann* (Frankfurt a. M.: Suhrkamp).

Ermacora, Felix (ed.) (1982) *Die österreichische Bundesverfassung und Hans Kelsen: Analysen und Materialien. Zum 100. Geburtstag von Hans Kelsen* (Vienna: Wilhelm Braumüller).

Eschenburg, Theodor (1929) *Das Kaiserreich am Scheideweg. Bassermann, Bülow und der Block* (Berlin: Verlag für Kulturpolitik).

——(1955) *Herrschaft der Verbände?* (Stuttgart: Deutsche Verlags-Anstalt).

Esenwein-Roth, Ingeborg (1965) *Die Wirtschaftsverbände von 1933 bis 1945* (Berlin: Duncker & Humblot).

Esser, Hartmut (1987) 'Theorien der Moderne und der Modernisierung: Buchbesprechung', *Kölner Zeitschrift für Soziologie und Sozialpsychologie* 39, pp. 806–11.

Esser, Josef and Fach, Wolfgang (1981) 'Korporatistische Krisenregulierung im "Modell Deutschland"', in: Ulrich von Alemann (ed.), *Neokorporatismus* (Frankfurt a. M./New York: Campus), pp. 158–79.

Euchner, Walter (1972) 'Zur Lage des Parlamentarismus', in: Gert Schäfer and Carl Nedelmann (eds), *Der CDU-Staat*, vol. 1: *Analysen zur Verfassungswirklichkeit der Bundesrepublik* (Frankfurt a. M.: Suhrkamp), pp. 105–32.

——(1982) 'Zum sozialdemokratischen Staatsverständnis zwischen den Weltkriegen. Einige Betrachtungen', in: Horst Heimann and Thomas Meyer (eds), *Reformsozialismus und Sozialdemokratie: Zur Theoriediskussion des Demokratischen Sozialismus in der Weimarer Republik. Bericht zum wissenschaftlichen Kongreß der Friedrich-Ebert-Stiftung 'Beträge zur reformistischen Sozialismustheorie in der Weimarer Republik' vom 9. bis 12. Oktober 1980* (Berlin/Bonn: Dietz), pp. 99–116.

Eucken, Walter (1951) 'Die Entwicklung des ökonomischen Denkens', in: *Unser Zeitalter der Misserfolge. Fünf Vorträge zur Wirtschaftspolitik* (Tübingen: J. C. B. Mohr), pp. 59–72.

Evans, Ellen Lovell (1981) *The German Center Party 1870–1933: A Study in Political Catholicism* (Carbondale/Edwardsville: Southern Illinois UP).

Fabert, Karl–Georg (1975) 'Strukturprobleme des deutschen Liberalismus im 19. Jahrhundert', *Der Staat* 14, pp. 201–27.

Fehrenbach, Elisabeth (1969) *Wandlungen des deutschen Kaisergedankens 1871–1918* (Munich: R. Oldenbourg).

——(1974) *Traditionelle Gesellschaft und revolutionäres Recht. Die Einführung des Code Napoléon in den Rheinbundstaaten* (Göttingen: Vandenhoeck & Ruprecht).

Feldman, Gerald D. (1966) *Army, Industry and Labor in Germany 1914–1918* (Princeton, NJ: Princeton UP).

——(1970) 'German Business Between War and Revolution: The Origins of the Stinnes–Legien-Agreement', in: Gerhard A. Ritter (ed.), *Entstehung und Wandel der modernen Gesellschaft. Festschrift für Hans Rosenberg zum 65. Geburtstag* (Berlin: de Gruyter), pp. 312–41.

——(1974) 'Der deutsche organisierte Kapitalismus während der Kriegs- und Inflationsjahre 1914–1923', in: Heinrich August Winkler (ed.), *Organisierter Kapitalismus. Voraussetzungen und Anfänge* (Göttingen: Vandenhoeck & Ruprecht), pp. 150–71.

——(1993) *The Geat Disorder: Politics, Economics and Society in the German Inflation, 1914–1924* (New York/Oxford: OUP).

Feldman, Gerald D. and Steinisch, Irmgard (1985) *Industrie und Gewerkschaften 1918–1924. Die überforderte Zentralarbeitsgemeinschaft* (Stuttgart: Deutsche Verlags-Anstalt).

Fels, Gerhard and Schmidt, Klaus–Dieter (1980) *Die deutsche Wirtschaft im Strukturwandel* (Tübingen: J. C. B. Mohr).

Fenner, Christian (1977) *Demokratischer Sozialismus und Sozialdemokratie. Realität und Rhetorik der Sozialismusdiskussion in Deutschland* (Frankfurt a. M./New York: Campus).

Ferber, Christian von (1970) *Die Gewalt in der Politik: Eine Auseinandersetzung mit Max Weber* (Stuttgart: W. Kohlhammer).

Fichter, Tilman (1988) *SDS und SPD: Parteilichkeit jenseits der Partei* (Opladen: Westdeutscher Verlag).

Fichter, Tilman and Lönnendorfer, Siegward (eds) (1977) *Kleine Geschichte des SDS. Der Sozialistische Deutsche Studentenbund von 1946 bis zur Selbstauflösung* (Berlin: Rotbuch).

Fischer, Curt Eduard (1954) 'Die Geschichte der deutschen Versuche zur Lösung des Kartell- und Monopol-Problems', *Zeitschrift für die gesamte Staatswissenschaft* 110, pp. 425–56.

Fischer, Wolfram (1973) 'Staatsverwaltung und Interessenverbände im Deutschen Reich 1871–1914', in: Heinz Josef Varain (ed.), *Interessenverbände in Deutschland* (Cologne: Kiepenheuer & Witsch), pp. 139–61.

Fitting, Karl (1977) 'Die Entwicklung der Mitbestimmung', in: Reinhart Bartholomäi, Wolfgang Bodenbender, Hardo Henkel and Renate Hüttel (eds), *Sozialpolitik nach 1945. Geschichte und Analysen* (Bonn/Bad Godesberg: Verlag Neue Gesellschaft), pp. 371–89.

Fogt, Helmut (1989) 'The Greens and the New Left: Influences of Left-Extremism on Green Party Organisations and Policies', in: Eva Kolinsky (ed.), *The Greens in West Germany: Organisation and Policy Making* (Oxford/New York/Munich: Berg), pp. 89–122.

Forsthoff, Ernst (1933) *Der totale Staat* (Hamburg: Hanseatische Verlagsanstalt).

——(1965) *Staat und Bürger in der modernen Industriegesellschaft* (Göttingen: Otto Schwarz).

——(1968a) 'Begriff und Wesen des sozialen Rechtsstaates', in: *Rechtsstaatlichkeit und Sozialstaatlichkeit: Aufsätze und Essays* (Darmstadt: Wissenschaftliche Buchgesellschaft), pp. 165–200.

——(1968b) 'Verfassungsprobleme des Sozialstaats', in: *Rechtsstaatlichkeit und Sozialstaatlichkeit* (see Forsthoff 1968a), pp. 145–64.

Fraenkel, Ernst (1927) *Zur Soziologie der Klassenjustiz* (Berlin: E. Laubsche Verlagsbuchhandlung).

——(1941) *The Dual State: A Contribution to the Theory of Dictatorship* (New York: OUP).

——(1964) *Deutschland und die westlichen Demokratien* (Stuttgart: W. Kohlhammer).

——(1970) 'Strukturanalyse der freiheitlich-rechtsstaatlichen Demokratie', in: Joachim Rohlfes and Hermann Körner (eds), *Historische Gegenwartskunde. Handbuch für den politischen Unterricht* (Göttingen: Vandenhoeck & Ruprecht), pp. 237–75.

——(1973) 'Die Gewerkschaften und das Arbeitsgerichtsgesetz', *Reformismus und Pluralismus: Materialien zu einer ungeschriebenen politischen Autobiographie*, ed. and compiled Falk Esche and Frank Grube (Hamburg: Hoffmann & Campe), pp. 56–9.

Frankland, E. Gene and Schoonmaker, Donald (1992) *Between Protest and Power: The Green Party in Germany* (Boulder, Colo.: Westview Press).

Frenske, Hans (1985) *Bürokratie in Deutschland. Vom späten Kaiserreich zur Gegenwart* (Berlin: Colloquium).

Freund, Julien (1968) *The Sociology of Max Weber*, trans. Mary Ilford (Harmondsworth: Penguin).

Freyer, Hans (1933) *Herrschaft und Planung. Zwei Grundbegriffe der politischen Ethik* (Hamburg: Hanseatische Verlagsanstalt).

Fromme, Friedrich Karl (1960) *Von der Weimarer Verfassung zum Bonner Grundgesetz. Die verfassungspolitischen Folgerungen des Parlamentarischen Rates aus Weimarer Republik und nationalsozialistischer Diktatur* (Tübingen: J. C. B. Mohr).

Frye, Bruce B. (1985) *Liberal Democrats in the Weimar Republic: The History of the German Democratic Party and the German State Party* (Carbondale/Edwardsville: Southern Illinois University Press).

Fulda, Hans Friedrich (1991) 'Rousseauische Probleme in Hegels Entwicklung', in: Hans Friedrich Fulda and Rolf-Peter Horstmann (eds), *Rousseau, die Revolution und der junge Hegel* (Stuttgart: Klett-Cotta), pp. 41–73.

Gabriel, Jürgen (1991) 'Das eingeschränkte Wirtschaftswunder. Zur Erklärung der wirtschaftlichen Entwicklung der Bundesrepublik in den 80er Jahren', in: Werner Süß (ed.), *Die Bundesrepublik in den achtziger Jahren. Innenpolitik, politische Kultur, Außenpolitik* (Opladen: Leske & Budrich, 1991), pp. 107–20.

Gadamer, Hans-Georg (1960) *Wahrheit und Methode: Grundzüge einer philosophischen Hermeneutik* (Tübingen: J. C. B. Mohr).

Gagel, Walter (1958) *Die Wahlrechtsfrage in der Geschichte der deutschen liberalen Parteien 1848–1918* (Düsseldorf: Droste).

Gall, Lothar (1975) 'Liberalismus und "bürgerliche Gesellschaft". Zu Charakter und Entwicklung der liberalen Bewegung in Deutschland', *Historische Zeitschrift* 220, pp. 324–56.

——(1993) *Von der ständischen zur bürgerlichen Gesellschaft* (Munich: R. Oldenbourg).

Gangl, Manfred (1987) *Politische Ökonomische und Kritische Theorie: Ein Beitrag zur theoretischen Entwicklung der Frankfurter Schule* (Frankfurt a. M./New York: Campus).

Gehlen, Arnold (1956) 'Industrielle Gesellschaft und Staat. Über einige Trieb-kräfte des politischen Lebens der Gegenwart', *Wort und Wahrheit* 11, pp. 665–74.

—— (1957) *Die Seele im technischen Zeitalter. Sozialpsychologische Probleme in der industriellen Gesellschaft* (Hamburg: Rowohlt).

—— (1963) 'Bürokratisierung. Macht und Ohnmacht des Apparates', in: *Studien zur Anthropologie und Soziologie* (Neuwied: Luchterhand), pp. 263–74.

Gerber, Hans (1932) *Freiheit und Bindung der Staatsgewalt* (Tübingen: J. C. B. Mohr).

Giddens, Anthony (1971) *Capitalism and Modern Social Theory: An Analysis of the Writings of Marx, Durkheim and Max Weber* (Cambridge: CUP).

—— (1972) *Politics and Sociology in the Thought of Max Weber* (London: Macmillan).

—— (1990) *The Consequences of Modernity* (Cambridge: Polity Press).

Giegel, Hans-Joachim (1975) *System und Krise: Kritik der Luhmannschen Gesellschaftstheorie* (Frankfurt a. M.: Suhrkamp).

Gierke, Otto von (1868) *Das deutsche Genossenschaftsrecht*, 4 vols (Berlin: Weidmann).

Gilg, Paul (1965) *Die Erneuerung des demokratischen Denkens im Wilhelminischen Deutschland: Eine ideengeschichtliche Studie zur Wende vom 19. zum 20. Jahrhundert* (Wiesbaden: Franz Steiner).

Glaser, Wilhelm (1972) *Soziales und Instrumentales Handeln. Probleme der Technologie bei Arnold Gehlen und Jürgen Habermas* (Stuttgart: W. Kohlhammer).

Gneist, Rudolf (1872) *Der Rechtsstaat* (Berlin: Julius Springer).

—— (1894) *Die nationale Rechtsidee von den Ständen und das preußische Dreiklassen-wahlsystem: Eine sozial-historische Studie* (Berlin: Julius Springer).

Göbel, Uwe (1978) *Die Studenten-Bewegung und ihre Folgen. Die politische Situation an den Hochschulen zwischen 1967 und 1977* (Cologne: Deutscher Instituts-Verlag).

Goldinger, Walter (1986) 'Der Staatsrat 1918/19', in: Isabella Ackerl and Rudolf Neck (eds), *Österreich im November 1918. Die Entstehung der Ersten Republik. Protokoll des Symposiums in Wien am 24. und 25. Oktober 1978* (Vienna: Verlag für Geschichte und Politik), pp. 55–65.

Golla, Guido (1994) *Zielvorstellungen und Auswirkungen der Brüningschen Spar-maßnahmen* (Cologne: Botermann & Botermann).

Gotto, Klaus (1992) 'Die historisch-politische Beurteilung des Zentrums aus nationalsozialistischer Sicht', in: Karl Dietrich Bracher et al. (eds), *Staat und Parteien: Festschrift für Rudolf Morsey zum 65. Geburtstag* (Berlin: Duncker & Humblot), pp. 711–26.

Gough, J. W. (1936) *The Social Contract: A Critical Study of its Development* (Oxford: Clarendon Press).

Grassmann, Siegfried (1965) *Hugo Preuß und die deutsche Selbstverwaltung* (Lübeck: Matthiesen).

Greenfield, Kent Roberts (1934) *Economics and Liberalism in the Risorgimento. A Study of Nationalism in Lombardy 1814–1848* (Baltimore: Johns Hopkins UP).

Greven, Michael T. (1977) *Parteien und politische Herrschaft: Zur Interdependenz von innerparteielicher Ordnung und Demokratie in der BRD* (Meisenheim am Glan: Anton Hain).

Grimm, Dieter (1977) 'Soziale, wirtschaftliche und politische Voraussetzungen der Vertragsfreiheit. Eine vergleichende Skizze', in: Bruno Paradisi et al. (eds), *La formazione storica del diritto moderno in Europa*, vol. 3 (Florence: Leo S. Olschki), pp. 1221–48.

——(1987) *Recht und Staat der bürgerlichen Gesellschaft* (Frankfurt a. M.: Suhrkamp).

——(1988) *Deutsche Verfassungsgeschichte 1776–1866* (Frankfurt a. M.: Suhrkamp).

——(1991) *Die Zukunft der Verfassung* (Frankfurt a. M.: Suhrkamp).

——(1992) 'Verfassungserfüllung – Verfassungsbewahrung – Verfassungsauflösung. Positionen der Staatsrechtslehre in der Staatskrise der Weimarer Republik', in: Heinrich August Winkler (ed.), *Die deutsche Staatskrise: Handlungsspielräume und Alternativen* (Munich: R. Oldenbourg), pp. 183–99.

Groh, Dieter (1973) *Negative Integration und revolutionärer Attentismus: Die deutsche Sozialdemokratie am Vorabend des Ersten Weltkriegs* (Frankfurt a. M.: Ullstein).

——(1986) '"Spuren der Vernunft in der Geschichte". Der Weg von Jürgen Habermas zur "Theorie des kommunikativen Handelns" im Schatten Max Webers', *Geschichte und Gesellschaft* 12, pp. 443–76.

Groser, Manfred (1979) 'Verbände und Staat: Positionen der CDU', *Zeitschrift für Parlamentsfragen* 10, pp. 451–8.

Grosser, Dieter (1970) *Vom monarchischen Konstitutionalismus zur parlamentarischen Demokratie: Die Verfassungspolitik der deutschen Parteien im letzten Jahrzehnt des Kaiserreichs* (The Hague: Martinus Nijhoff).

Grossfeld, Bernhard (1979) 'Zur Kartellrechtsdiskussion vor dem Ersten Weltkrieg', in: Helmut Coing and Walter Wilhelm (eds), *Wissenschaft und Kodifikationen des Privatrechts*, vol. 4: *Eigentum und industrielle Entwicklung und Wettbewerbsrecht* (Frankfurt a. M.: Klostermann), pp. 255–96.

Grottkopp, Jörg (1992) *Beamtentum und Staatsformwechsel. Die Auswirkungen der Staatsformwechsel von 1918, 1933 und 1945 auf das Beamtenrecht und die personelle Zusammensetzung der deutschen Beamtenschaft* (Frankfurt a. M.: Lang).

Grube, Frank, Richter, Gerhard and Thaysen, Uwe (1976) *Politische Planung und Parlamentsfraktionen* (Göttingen: Otto Schwartz).

Grübler, Michael (1982) *Die Spitzenverbände der Wirtschaft und das erste Kabinett Brüning: Vom Ende der Großen Koalition 1929/30 bis zum Vorabend der Bankenkrise 1931* (Düsseldorf: Droste).

Günther, Adolf (1920) *Arbeiterschutz und Arbeitsrecht. Die sozialrechtliche Gesetzgebung des Reiches seit 9. November 1918* (Berlin: de Gruyter).

Gutmann, Franz (1922) *Das Rätesystem: Seine Verfechter und seine Probleme* (Munich: Drei Masken Verlag).

Habermann, Norbert (1976) 'Die preußische Gesetzgebung zur Herstellung eines frei verfügbaren Grundeigentums', in: Helmut Coing and Walter Wilhelm (eds), *Wissenschaft und Kodifikationen des Privatrechts im 19. Jahrhundert*, vol 3: *Die rechtliche und wirtschaftliche Entwicklung des Grundeigentums und Grundkredits* (Frankfurt a. M.: Klostermann), pp. 3–43.

Habermas, Jürgen (1963a) 'Die klassische Lehre von der Politik in ihrem Verhältnis zur Sozialphilosophie', in: *Theorie und Praxis: Sozialphilosophische Studien* (Neuwied: Luchterhand), pp. 13–51.

——(1963b) 'Dogmatismus, Vernunft und Entscheidung – zu Theorie und Praxis in der verwissenschaftlichten Zivilisation', in: *Theorie und Praxis* (see Habermas 1963a), pp. 231–60.

——(1963c) 'Kritische und Konservative Aufgaben der Soziologie', in: *Theorie und Praxis* (see Habermas 1963a), pp. 215–30.

——(1968) *Erkenntnis und Interesse* (Frankfurt a. M.: Suhrkamp).

——(1969a) 'Technik und Wissenschaft als "Ideologie"', in: *Technik und Wissenschaft als Ideologie* (Frankfurt a. M.: Suhrkamp), pp. 48–103.

Habermas, Jürgen (1969b) 'Arbeit und Interaktion. Bemerkungen zu Hegels Jenenser Philosophie des Geistes', in: *Technik und Wissenschaft* (see Habermas 1969a), pp. 9–47.

——(1969c) 'Verwissenschaftlichte Politik und öffentliche Meinung', in: *Technik und Wissenschaft* (see Habermas 1969a), pp. 120–46.

——(1973) *Legitimationsprobleme im Spätkapitalismus* (Frankfurt a. M.: Suhrkamp).

——(1975) 'Theorie der Gesellschaft oder Sozialtechnologie? Eine Auseinandersetzung mit Niklas Luhmann', in: Jürgen Habermas and Niklas Luhmann, *Theorie der Gesellschaft oder Sozialtechnologie – Was leistet die Systemforschung?* (Frankfurt a. M.: Suhrkamp), pp. 142–290.

——(1976a) 'Überlegungen zum evolutionären Stellenwert des modernen Rechts', in: *Zur Rekonstruktion des historischen Materialismus* (Frankfurt a. M.: Suhrkamp), pp. 260–276.

——(1976b) 'Legitimitätsprobleme im modernen Staat', in: *Zur Rekonstruktion des historischen Materialismus* (see Habermas 1976a), pp. 271–303.

——(1976c) 'Können komplexe Gesellschaften eine vernünftige Identität ausbilden?', in: *Zur Rekonstruktion des historischen Materialismus* (see Habermas 1976a), pp. 92–125.

——(1981a) 'Vom sozialen Wandel akademischer Bildung', in: *Zur Kleine politische Schriften* vols 1–4 (Frankfurt a. M.: Suhrkamp), pp. 101–19.

——(1981b) 'Demokratisierung der Hochschule – Politisierung der Wissenschaft?' (1969), in: *Kleine politische Schriften* (see Habermas 1981a), pp. 186–98.

——(1981c) 'Diskussionbeiträge' (1967), in: *Kleine politische Schriften* (see Habermas 1981a), pp. 213–14.

——(1981d) 'Seminarthesen' (1968), in: *Kleine politische Schriften* (see Habermas 1981a), pp. 261–4.

——(1981e) 'Die Scheinrevolution und ihre Kinder' (1968), in: *Kleine politische Schriften* (see Habermas 1981a), pp. 249–60.

——(1981f) 'Einleitung einer Podiumsdiskussion' (1968), in: *Kleine politische Schriften* (see Habermas 1981a), pp. 239–44.

——(1981g) 'Einleitung zum Band 1000 der edition suhrkamp', in: *Kleine politische Schriften* (see Habermas 1981a), pp. 411–41.

——(1981h) 'Protestbewegung und Hochschulreform', in: *Kleine politische Schriften* (see Habermas 1981a), pp. 265–303.

——(1981i) 'Die Utopie des guten Herrschers', in: *Kleine politische Schriften* (see Habermas 1981a), pp. 318–27.

——(1981j) *Theorie des kommunikativen Handelns*, vol. 1: *Handlungsrationalität und gesellschaftliche Rationalität* (Frankfurt a. M.: Suhrkamp).

——(1981k) *Theorie des kommunikativen Handelns*, vol. 2: *Zur Kritik der funktionalistischen Vernunft* (Frankfurt a. M.: Suhrkamp).

——(1985a) 'Die Krise des Wohlfahrtsstaates und die Erschöpfung utopischer Energien', in: *Die neue Unübersichtlichkeit: Kleine politische Schriften*, vol. V (Frankfurt a. M.: Suhrkamp, 1985), pp. 141–66.

——(1985b) 'Bemerkungen zu Beginn einer Vorlesung', in: *Die neue Unübersichtlichkeit* (see Habermas 1985a), pp. 209–12.

——(1985c) 'Ein Interview mit der *New Left Review*', in: *Die neue Unübersichtlichkeit* (see Habermas 1985a), pp. 213–60.

——(1985d) 'Ziviler Ungehorsam – Testfall für den demokratischen Rechtsstaat', in: *Die neue Unübersichtlichkeit* (see Habermas 1985a), pp. 79–100.

——(1990a) 'Interview mit T. Hvid Nielsen', in: *Die nachholende Revolution. Kleine politische Schriften*, vol. 7 (Frankfurt a. M.: Suhrkamp, 1990), pp. 99–113.

——(1990b) 'Interview mit Angelo Bolaffi', in: *Die nachholende Revolution* (see Habermas 1990a), pp. 21–8.

——(1990c) 'Grenzen des Neohistorismus', in: *Die nachholende Revolution* (see Habermas 1990a), pp. 149–56.

——(1990d) 'Nochmals: Zur Identität der Deutschen', in: *Die nachholende Revolution* (see Habermas 1990a), pp. 205–24.

——(1990e) *Strukturwandel der Öffentlichkeit: Untersuchungen zu einer Kategorie der bürgerlichen Gesellschaft*, with an introduction (pp. 11–50) for the new edition (Frankfurt a. M.: Suhrkamp).

——(1992) *Faktizität und Geltung: Beiträge zur Diskurstheorie des Rechts und des demokratischen Rechtsstaates* (Frankfurt a. M.: Suhrkamp).

——(1995a) '1989 im Schatten von 1945. Zur Normalität einer künftigen Berliner Republik', in: *Die Normalität einer Berliner Republik. Kleine politische Schriften*, vol. 8 (Frankfurt a. M.: Suhrkamp).

——(1995b) 'Ein Gespräch über Fragen der politischen Theorie', in: *Die Normalität einer Berliner Republik* (see Habermas 1995a), pp. 135–64.

——(1997) *Die Einbeziehung des Anderen: Studien zur politischen Theorie* (Frankfurt a. M.: Suhrkamp).

Hagemeyer, Bernhard (1973) 'Sozialer Dialog – Konzertierte Aktion, gesellschaftspolitische Instrumente für eine wirtschaftsdemokratische Ordnung?', in: Ludwig Erhard, Kurt Brüß and Bernhard Hagemeyer (eds), *Grenzen der Demokratie? Probleme und Konsequenzen der Demokratisierung von Politik, Wirtschaft und Gesellschaft* (Vienna/Düsseldorf: Econ Verlag), pp. 261–82.

Hammans, Peter (1987) *Das politische Denken der neueren Staatslehre in der Bundesrepublik. Eine Studie zum politischen Konservatismus juristischer Gesellschaftstheorie* (Opladen: Westdeutscher Verlag).

Hardes, Heinz-Dieter (1974) *Einkommenspolitik in der BRD. Stabilität und Gruppeninteressen. Der Fall Konzertierte Aktion* (Frankfurt a. M./New York: Herder & Herder).

Harnack, Adolf von (1900) *Das Wesen des Christentums* (Leipzig: Hinrich).

Hartung, Fritz (1920) *Deutsche Geschichte von 1871 bis 1914* (Bonn/Leipzig, Schroeder).

Hartwich, Hans-Hermann (1967) *Arbeitsmarkt, Verbände und Staat: Die öffentliche Bindung unternehmerischer Funktionen in der Weimarer Republik* (Berlin: de Gruyter).

Hauff, Volker (1976) 'Modernisierung der Volkswirtschaft', in: *Politik als Zukunftsgestaltung. Reden und Aufsätze 1972–1976* (Karlsruhe: C. F. Müller), pp. 107–14.

Hautmann, Hans (1970) *Die Anfänge der linksradikalen Bewegung und der kommunistischen Partei Deutschösterreichs 1916–1919* (Vienna: Europa-Verlag).

Heckart, Beverly (1974) *From Bassermann to Bebel: The Grand Bloc's Quest for Reform in the Kaiserreich, 1900–14* (New Haven/London: Yale University Press).

Hegel, G. W. F. (1986) *Grundlinien der Philosophie des Rechts, oder Naturrecht und Staatswissenschaft im Grundrisse*, in: *Werke*, ed. Eva Moldenhauer and Karl Markus Michel, 20 vols (Frankfurt a. M.: Suhrkamp), vol. 7.

Hegselmann, Rainer (1976) 'Die Systemtheorie Luhmanns als technokratischer Institutionalismus und administrative Hilfswissenschaft', *Blätter für deutsche und internationale Politik* 11, pp. 38–57.

Heidegger, Hermann (1956) *Die deutsche Sozialdemokratie und der nationale Staat 1870–1920. Unter besonderer Berücksichtigung der Kriegs- und Revolutionsjahre* (Göttingen: Musterschmidt).

Heidenheimer, Arnold J. (1960) *Adenauer and the CDU: The Rise of the Leader and the Integration of the Party* (The Hague: Martinus Nijhoff).

Heidorn, Joachim (1982) *Legitimität und Regierbarkeit: Studien zu den Legitimitätstheorien von Max Weber, Niklas Luhmann, Jürgen Habermas und der Unregierbarkeitsforschung* (Berlin: Duncker & Humblot).

Heidtmann, Bernhard (1974) 'Traditionelle und ideologische Determinanten einer Theorie sozialer Systeme und ihrer Kritik', in: Franz Maciejewski (ed.), *Theorie der Gesellschaft oder Sozialtechnologie: Beiträge zur Habermas–Luhmann-Diskussion* (Frankfurt a. M.: Suhrkamp), pp. 154–85.

Heilfron, E. (ed.) (1919) *Die deutsche Nationalversammlung im Jahre 1919 in ihrer Arbeit für den Aufbau des neuen deutschen Volksstaates*, vol. 2 (Berlin: Nordeutsche Buchdruckerei und Verlagsanstalt).

Heimann, Horst (1973) 'Die Bedeutung der Strategie systemüberwindener Reformen und Langzeitprogramm für die sozialistische Theorie und Praxis', in: Rudolf Scharping and Friedhelm Wollner (eds), *Demokratischer Sozialismus und Langzeitprogramm. Diskussionsbeiträge zum Orientierungsrahmen '85 der SPD* (Hamburg: Rowohlt), pp. 12–35.

Heinck, Jürgen (1978) *Weimarer Staatslehre und Nationalsozialismus: Eine Studie zum Problem der Kontinuität im staatsrechtlichen Denken in Deutschland 1928 bis 1936* (Frankfurt a. M./New York: Campus).

Heinze, Rolf G. (1981) *Verbändepolitik und 'Neokorporatismus': Zur politischen Soziologie organisierter Interessen* (Opladen: Westdeutscher Verlag).

Helbing, Wolfgang J. (1962) *Die Reparationen in der Ära Brüning: Zur Bedeutung des Young-Plans für die deutsche Politik 1930 bis 1932* (Berlin: Colloquium).

Heller, Hermann (1971a) Staatslehre, in: *Gesammelte Schriften*, ed. M. Drath et al., 3 vols (Leiden: A. W. Sijthoff), vol. 3, pp. 79–413.

——(1971b) Die Bedeutung des nationalen Gedankens für den Sozialismus, in: *Gesammelte Schriften* (see Heller 1971a), vol. 1, pp. 460–526.

——(1971c) Europa und der Fascismus, in: *Gesammelte Schriften* (see Heller 1971a), vol. 2, pp. 463–610.

——(1971d) 'Ziele und Grenzen einer deutschen Verfassungsreform', in: *Gesammelte Schriften* (see Heller 1971a), vol. 2, pp. 411–20.

Hennig, Eike (1970) 'Zur Kritik der konzertierten Aktion', in: *Blätter für deutsche und internationale Politik* 5, pp. 508–18.

Hennis, Wilhelm (1973) 'Demokratisierung. Zur Problematik eines Begriffs', in: *Die mißverstandene Demokratie: Demokratie – Verfassung – Parlament. Studien zu deutschen Problemen* (Freiburg i. B.: Herder Verlag), pp. 26–51.

——(1977a) 'Parteienstruktur und Regierbarkeit', in: Wilhelm Hennis, Peter Graf Kielmansegg and Ulrich Matz (eds), *Regierbarkeit: Studien zu ihrer Problematisierung*, vol. 1 (Stuttgart: Klett-Cotta), pp. 150–95.

——(1977b) 'Legitimität. Zu einer Kategorie der bürgerlichen Gesellschaft', in: Wilhelm Hennis, *Politik und praktische Philosophie: Schriften zur politischen Theorie* (Stuttgart: Klett-Cotta), pp. 198–242.

——(1977c) 'Ende der Politik? Zur Krisis der Politik in der Neuzeit', in: *Politik und praktische Philosophie* (see Hennis 1977b), 176–97.

——(1977d) 'Vom gewaltenteilenden Rechtsstaat zum teleokratischen Programm-staat. Zur "lebenden Verfassung" der Bundesrepublik', in: *Politik und praktische Philosophie* (see Hennis 1977b), pp. 243–74.

——(1987) *Max Webers Fragestellung: Studien zur Biographie des Werks* (Tübingen: J. C. B. Mohr).

Hentschel, Volker (1978) *Wirtschaft und Wirtschaftspolitik im Wilhelminischen Deutschland. Organisierter Kapitalismus und Interventionsstaat?* (Stuttgart: Klett-Cotta).

Hesse, Konrad (1959) *Die normative Kraft der Verfassung* (Tübingen: J. C. B. Mohr).

Hickel, Rudolf (1975) 'Orientierung ohne Perspektive. Anmerkungen zum zweiten Orientierungsrahmen der SPD', *Leviathan* 3, pp. 170–206.

Hilferding, Rudolf (1910) *Das Finanzkapital: Eine Studie über die jüngste Entwick-lung des Kapitalismus*, in: *Marx-Studien*, vol. 3 (Vienna: Verlag der Wiener Volksbuchhandlung Ignaz Brand).

——(1925) *Die Schicksalsstunde der deutschen Wirtschaftspolitik* (Berlin: Dietz).

——(1927) *Die Aufgabe der Sozialdemokratie in der Republik* (Berlin: Dietz).

Hillgruber, Andreas (1977) *Deutsche Großmacht und Weltpolitik im 19. und 20. Jahrhundert* (Düsseldorf: Droste).

Hinrichs, Ernst (1972) 'Die Ablösung von Eigentumsrechten. Zur Diskussion über die droits féodaux in Frankreich am Ende des Ancien Régime und in der Revolution', in: Rudolf Vierhaus (ed.), *Eigentum und Verfassung. Zur Eigentums-diskussion im ausgehenden 18. Jahrhundert* (Göttingen: Vandenhoeck & Ruprecht), pp. 112–78.

Hintze, Otto (1962) 'Das monarchische Prinzip und die konstitutionelle Verfas-sung', in: *Staat und Verfassung. Gesammelte Abhandlungen zur allgemeinen Ver-fassungsgeschichte*, ed. Gerhard Oestreich, introduced by Fritz Hartung (Göttingen: Vandenhoeck & Ruprecht), pp. 359–89.

Hinz, Horst (1967) 'Konjunktur und Herrschaft. Zur politisch-ökonomischen Analyse des Stabilitätsgesetzes', *Konjunkturpolitik* 13, pp. 288–331.

Hock, Wolfgang (1957) *Liberales Denken im Zeitalter der Paulskirche: Droysen und die Frankfurter Mitte* (Münster: Aschendorffsche Verlagsbuchhandlung).

Hoffmann, Hasso (1964) *Legitimität gegen Legalität: Der Weg der politischen Philo-sophie Carl Schmitts* (Neuwied: Luchterhand).

——(1986) *Recht – Politik – Verfassung: Studien zur Geschichte der politischen Philosophie* (Frankfurt a. M.: Alfred Metzner Verlag).

Hoffmann, Jürgen (1987) 'Von der Vollbeschäftigungspolitik zur Politik der Dereg-ulierung. Ökonomische und soziale Strukturveränderungen in der Bundesrepub-lik 1967 bis 1988 und der sich daraus ableitende Korridor politischen Handelns', in: Heidrun Abromeit and Bernhard Blanke (eds), *Arbeitsmarkt, Arbeitsbeziehun-gen und Politik in den 80er Jahren*, in: *Leviathan*, spec. issue 8, pp. 344–63.

Hönig, Herbert (1979) *Das Preussische Zentrum in der Weimarer Republik* (Mainz: Matthias Grünewald).

Honneth, Axel (1986) *Kritik der Macht. Reflexionsstufen einer kritischen Gesellschaftstheorie* (Frankfurt a. M.: Suhrkamp).

——(1990) 'Kritische Theorie. Vom Zentrum zur Peripherie einer Denktradition', in: *Die zerrissene Welt des Sozialen: Sozialphilosophische Aufsätze* (Frankfurt a. M.: Suhrkamp), pp. 25–72.

Honneth, Axel (1992) *Der Kampf um Anerkennung: Zur moralischen Grammatik sozialer Konflikte* (Frankfurt a. M.: Suhrkamp).

Horkheimer, Max (1985) *Nachgelassene Schriften 1931–1949*, in: *Gesammelte Schriften*, 18 vols, ed. Alfred Schmidt and Gunzelin Schmidt Noerr (Frankfurt a. M.: Fischer), vol. 12.

——(1987a) 'Vernunft und Selbsterhaltung', in: *Traditionelle und kritische Theorie: Fünf Aufsätze* (Frankfurt a. M.: Fischer), pp. 271–301.

——(1987b) 'Traditionelle oder kritische Theorie?', in: *Traditionelle und kritische Theorie* (see Horkheimer 1987a), pp. 205–60.

Horn, Norbert (1983) 'Arbeitsrecht und soziale Beziehungen in der Bundesrepublik: in historischer Sicht', in: Werner Conze and M. Rainer Lepsius (eds), *Sozialgeschichte der Bundesrepublik Deutschland* (Stuttgart: Klett-Cotta), pp. 324–38.

Hörster-Philipps, Ulrike, (1982) *Konservative Politik in der Endphase der Weimarer Republik: Die Regierung Franz von Papen* (Cologne: Pahl-Rugenstein).

Huber, Ernst Rudolf (1927) *Die Garantie der kirchlichen Vermögensrechte in der Weimarer Verfassung. Zwei Abhandlungen zum Problem der Auseinandersetzung von Staat und Kirche* (Tübingen: J. C. B. Mohr).

——(1963) *Deutsche Verfassungsgeschichte seit 1789*, vol. 3: *Bismarck und das Reich* (Stuttgart: W. Kohlhammer).

——(1965) 'Rechtsstaat und Sozialstaat in der modernen Industriegesellschaft', in: *Nationalstaat und Verfassungsstaat: Studien zur Geschichte der modernen Staatsidee* (Stuttgart: W. Kohlhammer), pp. 249–72.

——(1975a) 'Zur Lehre vom Verfassungsnotstand in der Staatstheorie der Weimarer Zeit, in: *Bewahrung und Wandlung. Studien zur deutschen Staatstheorie und Verfassungsgeschichte* (Berlin: Duncker & Humblot), pp. 193–214.

——(1975b) 'Verfassung und Verfassungswirklichkeit bei Carl Schmitt', in: *Bewahrung und Wandlung* (see E. R. Huber 1975a), pp. 18–36.

——(1978) 'Friedrich Naumanns Weimarer Grundrechts-Entwurf: Der Versuch eines Modells der Grundwerte gegenwärtigen Daseins', in: Okko Behrends et al. (eds), *Festschrift für Franz Wieacker zum 70. Geburtstag* (Göttingen: Vandenhoeck & Ruprecht), pp. 384–98.

——(1981) *Deutsche Verfassungsgeschichte seit 1789*, vol. 6: *Die Weimarer Reichsverfassung* (Stuttgart: W. Kohlhammer).

Huber, Hans (1985) 'Die Umwälzungen im Staatsgefüge durch die Verbände', in: Rudolf Steinberg (ed.), *Staat und Verbände: Zur Theorie der Interessenverbände in der Industriegesellschaft* (Darmstadt: Wissenschaftliche Buchgesellschaft), pp. 58–63.

Hübinger, Gangolf (1994) *Kulturprotestantismus und Politik: Zum Verhältnis von Liberalismus und Protestantismus im Wilhelminischen Deutschland* (Tübingen: J. C. B. Mohr).

Hübl, Lothar and Schepers, Walter (1983) *Strukturwandel und Strukturpolitik* (Darmstadt: Wissenschaftliche Buchgesellschaft).

Hüttenberger, Peter (1976) 'Wirtschaftsordnung und Interessentenpolitik in der Kartellgesetzgebung der Bundesrepublik 1949–1957', *Vierteljahrshefte für Zeitgeschichte* 24, pp. 287–307.

Iggers, Georg G. (1969) *The German Conception of History: The National Tradition of Historical Thought from Herder to the Present* (Middletown, Conn.: Wesleyan University Press).

Ives, E. W. (1968) 'Social Change and the Law', in: E. W. Ives (ed.), *The English Revolution 1600–1660* (London: Edward Arnold), pp. 115–30.

Jacobi, Otto (1982a) 'Weltrezession und Strukturwandel', in: Gerhard Brandt, Otto Jacobi and Walther Müller-Jentsch, *Anpassung an die Krise: Gewerkschaften in den siebziger Jahren* (Frankfurt a. M./New York: Campus), pp. 58–82.

——(1982b) 'Industrielle Beziehungen, Korporatismus and Disziplinierung', in: Brandt et al., *Anpassung an die Krise* (see Jacobi 1982a), pp. 231–56.

Jacobsen, Hans-Adolf and Dollinger, Hans (eds) (1968) *Die deutschen Studenten. Der Kampf um die Hochschulreform. Eine Bestandsaufnahme* (Munich: Kurt Desch).

Jäger, Wolfgang (1973) *Öffentlichkeit und Parlamentarismus. Eine Kritik an Jürgen Habermas* (Stuttgart: W. Kohlhammer).

Jarvis, Simon (1997) *Adorno: A Critical Introduction* (Cambridge: Polity Press).

Jasper, Gotthard (1963) *Der Schutz der Republik. Studien zur staatlichen Sicherung der Demokratie in der Weimarer Republik* (Tübingen: J. C. B. Mohr), pp. 56–92.

——(1986) *Die gescheiterte Zähmung: Wege zur Machtergreifung Hitlers 1930–1934* (Frankfurt a. M.: Suhrkamp).

Jay, Martin (1973) *The Dialectical Imagination: A History of the Frankfurt School and the Institute of Social Research, 1923–1950* (Berkeley/Los Angeles: University of California Press).

Jessop, Bob (1990) 'Political Economy or Radical Autonomy? Regulation, Societalization and Autopoiesis', in: *State Theory: Putting the Capitalist State in its Place* (Cambridge: Polity Press), pp. 307–37.

Joas, Hans (1986) 'Die unglückliche Ehe von Hermeneutik und Funktionalismus', in: Axel Honneth and Hans Joas (eds), *Kommunikatives Handeln. Beiträge zu Jürgen Habermas' 'Theorie des kommunikativen Handelns'* (Frankfurt a. M.: Suhrkamp), pp. 144–76.

John, Michael (1989) *Politics and Law in Late Nineteenth-Century Germany* (Oxford: Clarendon Press).

Jones, Larry Eugene (1985) 'In the Shadow of Stabilization: German Liberalism and the Legitimacy Crisis of the Weimar Party System, 1924–30', in: Gerald D. Feldmann (ed.), *Die Nachwirkungen der Inflation auf die deutsche Geschichte* (Munich: R. Oldenbourg), pp. 21–41.

——(1998) *German Liberalism and the Dissolution of the Weimar Party System, 1918–1933* (Chapel Hill/London: University of North Carolina Press).

Kaack, Heino (1971) *Geschichte und Struktur des deutschen Parteiensystems* (Opladen: Westdeutscher Verlag).

Kaas, Ludwig (1919) *Staat und Kirche im neuen Deutschland* (Trier: Druck der Paulinus Druckerei).

Kahn-Freund, Otto (1932) 'Der Funktionswandel des Arbeitsrechts', *Archiv für Sozialwissenschaft und Sozialpolitik* 67, pp. 146–74.

Kaiser, Hans-Rainer (1977) *Staat und gesellschaftliche Integration: Zur Analyse und Kritik des Staatsbegriffs bei Jürgen Habermas und Claus Offe* (Marburg: Verlag Arbeiterbewegung und Gesellschaftswissenschaft).

Kaiser, Joseph H. (1959) 'Die Dialektik der Repräsentation', in: Hans Barion, Ernst Forsthoff and Werner Weber (eds), *Festschrift für Carl Schmitt zum 70. Geburtstag* (Berlin: Duncker & Humblot), pp. 71–80.

——(1988) 'Konkretes Ordnungsdenken', in: Helmut Quaritsch (ed.), *Complexio Oppositorum: Über Carl Schmitt* (Berlin: Duncker & Humblot), pp. 319–31.

Kaltefleiter, Werner et al. (1970) 'Im Wechselspiel der Koalitionen. Eine Analyse der Bundestagswahl', *Verfassung- und Verfassungswirklichkeit* 5, pp. 9–187.

Kant, Immanuel (1966a) *Zum ewigen Frieden*, in: *Werke*, Wilhelm Weischedel, 6 vols (Darmstadt: Wissenschaftliche Buchgesellschaft, 1966), vol. 6, pp. 195–251.

—— (1966b) *Die Metaphysik der Sitten*, in: *Werke* (see Kant 1966a), vol. 4, pp. 303–624.

—— (1966c) *Der Streit der Fakultäten*, in: *Werke* (see Kant 1966a), vol. 6, pp. 261–393.

Kaufmann, Erich (1960) 'Carl Schmitt und seine Schule', in: *Rechtsidee und Recht: Rechtsphilosophische und ideengeschichtliche Bemühungen aus fünf Jahrzehnten* (Göttingen: Otto Schwartz), pp. 375–77.

Kaufmann, Mathias (1988) *Recht ohne Regel? Die philosophischen Prinzipien in Carl Schmitts Staats- und Rechtslehre* (Freiburg/Munich: Karl Alber).

Kaulbach, Friedrich (1970) 'Moral und Recht in der Philosophie Kants', in: Jürgen Blühdorn and Joachim Ritter (eds), *Recht und Ethik. Zum Problem ihrer Beziehung im 19. Jahrhundert* (Frankfurt a. M.: Klostermann), pp. 43–58.

Kehr, Eckart (1965a) 'Zur Genesis der preußischen Bürokratie und des Rechtsstaats: Ein Beitrag zum Diktaturproblem', in: *Der Primat der Innenpolitik: Gesammelte Aufsätze zur preußisch-deutschen Sozialgeschichte im 19. und 20. Jahrhundert*, ed. and intro. Hans Ulrich Wehler (Berlin: de Gruyter), pp. 31–52.

—— (1965b) 'Die Diktatur der Bürokratie', in: *Der Primat der Innenpolitik* (see Kehr 1965a), pp. 244–53.

Kelsen, Hans (1919) 'Zur Theorie der juristischen Fiktionen', *Annalen der Philosophie. Mit besonderer Rücksicht auf die Probleme der Als-Ob-Betrachtung* 1, pp. 630–58.

—— (1922) *Der soziologische und der juristische Staatsbegriff: Kritische Untersuchung des Verhältnisses von Staat und Recht* (Tübingen: J. C. B. Mohr).

—— (1923) *Österreichisches Staatsrecht: Ein Grundriß entwicklungsgeschichtlich dargestellt* (Tübingen: J. C. B. Mohr).

—— (1929) *Vom Wesen und Wert der Demokratie* (Tübingen: J. C. B. Mohr).

—— (1934) *Reine Rechtslehre* (Leipzig/Vienna: Franz Denticki).

—— (1943) *Society and Nature: A Sociological Inquiry* (Chicago: University of Chicago Press).

Kennedy, Ellen (1986) 'Carl Schmitt und die Frankfurter Schule. Deutsche Liberalismuskritik im 20. Jahrhundert', *Geschichte und Gesellschaft* 12, pp. 380–419.

Kern, Manfred (1973) *Konzertierte Aktion als Versuch einer Verhaltensabstimmung zwischen Regierung und Wirtschaftsverbänden* (Cologne: Institut für Wirtschaftspolitik an der Universität zu Köln).

Kiefner, Hans (1969) 'Der Einfluß Kants auf Theorie und Praxis des Zivilrechts im 19. Jahrhundert', in: Jürgen Blühdorn and Joachim Ritter (eds), *Philosophie und Rechtswissenschaft. Zum Problem ihrer Beziehung im 19. Jahrhundert* (Frankfurt a. M.: Klostermann), pp. 3–25.

Kindermann, Harald (1981) 'Die Antwort des bürgerlichen Gesetzbuchs auf die soziale Frage', *Rechtstheorie* 12, pp. 209–25.

Kirchheimer, Otto (1932) 'Legalität und Legitimität', *Die Gesellschaft* 9, pp. 8–26.

—— (1941a) 'Changes in the Structure of Political Compromise', *Studies in Philosophy and Social Science* 9, pp. 264–89.

—— (1941b) 'The Legal Order of National Socialism', *Studies in Philosophy and Social Science* 9, pp. 456–75.

—— (1964) 'Weimar – und was dann? Analyse einer Verfassung', in: *Politik und Verfassung* (Frankfurt a. M.: Suhrkamp), pp. 9–56.

—— (1972a) 'Die Grenzen der Enteignung: Ein Beitrag zur Entwicklungsgeschichte des Enteignungsinstitutes und zur Auslegung des Art. 153 der Weimarer Verfassung', in: *Funktionen des Staats und der Verfassung. 10 Analysen* (Frankfurt a. M.: Suhrkamp), pp. 223–95.

—— (1972b) 'Verfassungsreform und Sozialdemokratie', in: *Funktionen des Staates* (see Kirchheimer 1972a), pp. 79–99.

——(1972c) 'Eigentumsgarantie in Reichsverfassung und Rechtsprechung', in: *Funktionen des Staates* (see Kirchheimer 1972a), pp. 7–27.

——(1972d) 'Marxismus, Diktatur und Organisationsform des Proletariats', in: *Funktionen des Staates* (see Kirchheimer 1972a), pp. 100–14.

——(1976a) 'Verfassungswirklichkeit und politische Zukunft der Arbeiterbewegung', in: *Von der Weimarer Republik zum Faschismus: Die Auflösung der demokratischen Rechtsordnung*, ed. Wolfgang Luthardt (Frankfurt a. M.: Suhrkamp), pp. 69–76.

——(1976b) 'Bemerkungen zu Carl Schmitt "Legalität und Legitimität"', in: *Von der Weimarer Republik zum Faschismus* (see Kirchheimer 1976a), pp. 113–51.

——(1976c) 'Bedeutungswandel des Parlamentarismus', in: *Von der Weimarer Republik zum Faschismus* (see Kirchheimer 1976a), pp. 58–63.

——(1976d) 'Das Problem der Verfassung', in: *Von der Weimarer Republik zum Faschismus* (see Kirchheimer 1976a), pp. 64–8.

——(1976e) 'Bedeutungswandel des Parlamentarismus', in: *Von der Weimarer Republik zum Faschismus* (see Kirchheimer 1967a), pp. 58–63.

——(1976f) 'Die Verfassungsreform', in: *Von der Weimarer Republik zum Faschismus* (see Kirchheimer 1976a), pp. 96–112.

——(1976g) 'Zur Staatslehre des Sozialismus und Bolschewismus', in: *Von der Weimarer Republik zum Faschismus* (see Kirchheimer 1976a), pp. 32–52.

——(1976h) 'Artikel 48 und die Wandlungen des Verfassungssystems. Auch ein Beitrag zum Verfassungstag', in: *Von der Weimarer Republik zum Faschismus* (see Kirchheimer 1976a), pp. 91–5.

Kisker, Klaus Peter (1985) 'Sozialabbau: Ein Mittel zur Bekämpfung der Wirtschaftskrise', in: Charlotte Niess-Mache and Joachim Schwammborn (eds), *Demontage des Sozialstaats. Verfassungsrechtliche Grenzen staatlicher Sparpolitik* (Cologne: Theuerer), pp. 9–16.

Klages, Helmut (1985) *Wertorientierungen im Wandel: Rückblick, Gegenwartsanalyse, Prognosen* (Frankfurt a. M./New York: Campus).

Klages, Helmut and Herbert, Willi (1983) *Wertorientierung und Staatsbezug. Untersuchungen zur politischen Kultur in der Bundesrepublik Deutschland* (Frankfurt a. M./New York: Campus).

Kleinknecht, Natascha (1992) *Positivität des Rechts bei Niklas Luhmann. Begriffsentstehung, Probleme und Lösungen in kritisch/konstruktiver Sicht, oder: Von der Welt der 'Natur' zur Welt der Unwahrscheinlichkeiten* (Florence: European University Institute).

Klotzbach, Kurt (1982) *Der Weg zur Staatspartei: Programmatik, praktische Politik und Organisation der deutschen Sozialdemokratie 1945 bis 1965* (Berlin/Bonn: Dietz).

Knight, Maxwell E. (1952) *The German Executive 1890–1933* (New York: Stanford UP).

Knorr, Heribert (1975) *Der parlamentarische Entscheidungsprozeß während der Großen Koalition 1966 bis 1969. Struktur und Einfluß der Koalitionsfraktionen und ihr Verhältnis zur Regierung der Großen Koalition* (Meisenheim am Glan: Anton Hain).

Kober, Heinz (1961) *Studien zur Rechtsanschauung Bismarcks* (Tübingen: J. C. B. Mohr).

Kocka, Jürgen (1973) *Klassengesellschaft im Krieg. Deutsche Sozialgeschichte 1914–1918* (Göttingen: Vandenhoeck & Ruprecht).

——(1986) 'Max Webers Bedeutung für die Geisteswissenschaft', in: Jürgen Kocka (ed.), *Max Weber, der Historiker* (Göttingen: Vandenhoeck & Ruprecht), pp. 13–27.

Koellreuter, Otto (1935) *Grundfragen des völkischen und staatlichen Lebens im deutschen Volksstaate* (Berlin: Pan-Verlagsgesellschaft).

Koenen, Andreas (1995) *Der Fall Carl Schmitt: Sein Aufstieg zum 'Kronjuristen des Dritten Reiches'* (Darmstadt: Wissenschaftliche Buchgesellschaft).

Kolb, Eberhard (1978) *Die Arbeiterräte in der deutschen Innenpolitik* (Frankfurt a. M.: Ullstein).

Könke, Günter (1987) *Organisierter Kapitalismus, Sozialdemokratie und Staat: Eine Studie zur Ideologie der sozialdemokratischen Arbeiterbewegung in der Weimarer Republik (1924–1932)* (Stuttgart: Franz Steiner).

Koselleck, Reinhart (1973) *Kritik und Krise. Eine Studie zur Pathogenese der bürgerlichen Welt* (Frankfurt a. M.: Suhrkamp).

——(1989) *Preußen zwischen Reform und Revolution: Allgemeines Landrecht, Verwaltung und soziale Bewegung von 1791 bis 1848* (Munich: DTV).

Koslowski, Peter (1982) *Gesellschaft und Staat. Ein unvermeidlicher Dualismus* (Stuttgart: Klett-Cotta).

Krieger, Leonard (1972) *The German Idea of Freedom: History of a Historical Tradition* (Chicago/London: University of Chicago Press).

Krockow, Christian Graf von (1990) *Die Entscheidung: Eine Untersuchung über Ernst Jünger, Carl Schmitt, Martin Heidegger* (Frankfurt a. M.: Campus).

Krohn, Claus-Dieter (1978) 'Autoritärer Kapitalismus. Wirtschaftskonzeptionen im Übergang von der Weimarer Republik zum Nationalsozialismus', in: Dirk Stegmann et al. (eds), *Industrielle Gesellschaft und politisches System. Beiträge zur politischen Sozialgeschichte. Festschrift für Fritz Fischer zum siebzigsten Geburtstag* (Bonn: Verlag Neue Gesellschaft), pp. 113–29.

Kronman, Anthony T. (1983) *Max Weber* (London: Edward Arnold).

Krumbein, Wolfgang (1986) 'Vorläufer eines "Dritten Weges zum Sozialismus"? Bemerkungen zu einigen theoretischen Konzepten der Weimarer Sozialdemokratie', in: Richard Saage (ed.), *Solidargemeinschaft und Klassenkampf. Politische Konzeptionen der Sozialdemokratie zwischen den Weltkriegen* (Frankfurt a. M.: Suhrkamp), pp. 167–90.

Krupp, Hans-Jürgen (1982) 'Möglichkeiten und Grenzen der Staatstätigkeit', in: Gottfried Bombach, Bernhard Gahlen and Alfred E. Ott (eds), *Möglichkeiten und Grenzen der Staatstätigkeit* (Tübingen: J. C. B. Mohr), pp. 1–51.

Kruppa, Adolf (1986) *Wachtumspolitik. Wachstumskrisen und die Möglichkeit stabiler Wirtschaftsentwicklung in der Bundesrepublik Deutschland* (Munich: R. Oldenbourg).

Kühne, Thomas (1994) *Dreiklassenwahlrecht und Wahlkultur in Preußen 1867–1914. Landtagswahlen zwischen korporativer Tradition und politischem Massenmarkt* (Düsseldorf: Droste).

Kunstmann, Wolfgang (1983) *Rechtsformen der staatlichen Strukturpolitik* (Erlangen: dissertation).

Küpper, Jost (1977) *Die SPD und der Orientierungsrahmen '85* (Bonn/Bad Godesberg: Verlag Neue Gesellschaft).

Kurtze, Eberhard (1931) *Die Nachwirkungen der Paulskirche und ihrer Verfassung in den Beratungen der Weimarer Nationalversammlung und in der Verfassung von 1919* (Berlin: Emil Ebering).

Küsters, Gerd-Walter (1988) *Kants Rechtsphilosophie* (Darmstadt: Wissenschaftliche Buchgesellschaft).

Lambi, Ivo Nikolai (1963) *Free Trade and Protection in Germany 1868–1879* (Wiesbaden: Franz Steiner).

Landauer, Carl (1923) 'Die Wege der Eroberung des demokratischen Staates durch die Wirtschaftsleiter', in: Melchior Palyi (ed.), *Hauptprobleme der Soziologie: Erinnerungsgabe für Max Weber*, vol. 2 (Munich/Leipzig: Duncker & Humblot), pp. 111–45.

——(1925) 'Die Ideologie des Wirtschaftsparlamentarismus', in: *Festgabe für Lujo Brentano. Die Wirtschaftswissenschaft nach dem Kriege*, vol. 1: *Wirtschaftspolitische Ideologien* (Munich/Leipzig: Duncker & Humblot), pp. 153–93.

——(1972) *Die Sozialdemokratie: Geschichtsabriß und Standortsbestimmung* (Hamburg: Weltarchiv).

Langewiesche, Dieter (1988) *Liberalismus in Deutschland* (Frankfurt a. M.: Suhrkamp).

Lehner, Franz (1979) *Grenzen des Regierens: Eine Studie zur Regierungsproblematik hochindustrialisierter Demokratien* (Königstein: Athenäum).

Lehnich, Oswald (1928) *Kartelle und Staat unter Berücksichtigung der Gesetzgebung des In- und Auslands* (Berlin: Reimar Hobbing).

Leibholz, Gerhard (1967) 'Der Strukturwandel der modernen Demokratie', in: *Strukturprobleme der modernen Demokratie* (Karlsruhe: C. F. Müller, 1967), pp. 78–131.

Lepsius, M. Rainer (1993) *Demokratie in Deutschland. Soziologisch-historische Konstellationsanalysen. Ausgewählte Aufsätze* (Göttingen: Vandenhoeck & Ruprecht).

Lerman, Katherine Anne (1990) *The Chancellor as Courtier: Bernhard von Bülow and the Governance of Germany, 1900–1909* (Cambridge: CUP), p. 242.

Leuschen-Seppel, Rosemarie (1981) *Zwischen Staatsverantwortung und Klasseninteresse: Die Wirtschafts- und Finanzpolitik der SPD zur Zeit der Weimarer Republik unter besonderer Berücksichtigung der Mittelphase 1924–1928/9* (Bonn: Verlag Neue Gesellschaft).

Liebersohn, Harry (1988) *Fate and Utopia in German Sociology, 1870–1923* (Cambridge, Mass.: MIT Press).

Lindt, Andreas (1973) *Friedrich Naumann und Max Weber: Theologie und Soziologie im Wilhelminischen Deutschland* (Munich: Chr. Kaiser).

Lipp, Wolfgang (1987) 'Autopoiesis biologisch, Autopoiesis soziologisch. Wohin führt Luhmanns Paradigmenwechsel', *Kölner Zeitschrift für Soziologie und Sozialpsychologie* 39, pp. 452–70.

Litt, Theodor (1919) *Individuum und Gemeinschaft: Grundfragen der sozialen Theorie und Ethik* (Leipzig/Berlin: Teubner).

Loewenstein, Karl (1965) *Max Webers staatspolitische Auffassungen in der Sicht unserer Zeit* (Bonn/Frankfurt a. M.: Athenäum).

Lohmar, Ulrich (1963) *Innerparteiliche Demokratie. Eine Untersuchung der Verfassungswirklichkeit politischer Parteien in der Bundesrepublik Deutschland* (Stuttgart: Ferdinand Enke).

Lompe, Klaus (1987) *Sozialstaat und Krise: Bundesrepublikanische Politikmuster der 70er und 80er Jahre* (Frankfurt a. M.: Lang).

Lousse, Emile (1980) 'Parlamentarismus oder Korporatismus? Die Ursprünge der Ständevertretungen', in: Heinz Rausch (ed.), *Die geschichtlichen Grundlagen der modernen Volksvertretung. Die Entwicklung von den mittelalterlichen Korporationen zu den modernen Parlamenten* (Darmstadt: Wissenschaftliche Buchgesellschaft, 1980), pp. 278–302.

Löwith, Karl (1960) 'Der okkasionelle Dezisionismus von Carl Schmitt', in: *Gesammelte Abhandlungen: Zur Kritik der geschichtlichen Existenz* (Stuttgart: W. Kohlhammer), pp. 93–126.

Lübbe, Hermann (1963) *Politische Philosophie in Deutschland: Studien zu ihrer Geschichte* (Basel/Stuttgart: Benno Schwabe).

——(1981) 'Staat und Zivilreligion. Ein Aspekt politischer Legitimität', in: Norbert Achterberg and Werner Krawietz (eds), *Legitimation des modernen Staates. Archiv für Rechts- und Sozialphilosophie*, spec. issue 15, pp. 40–64.

Luhmann, Niklas (1964) 'Zweck-Herrschaft-System: Grundbegriffe und Prämissen Max Webers', *Der Staat* 3, pp. 129–58.

——(1965) *Grundrechte als Institution: Ein Beitrag zur politischen Soziologie* (Berlin: Duncker & Humblot).

——(1966a) *Theorie der Verwaltungswissenschaft: Bestandsaufnahme und Entwurf* (Cologne/Berlin: Grote).

——(1966b) 'Politische Planung', *Jahrbuch für Sozialwissenschaft* 17, pp. 271–96.

——(1969a) 'Klassische Theorie der Macht: Kritik ihrer Prämissen', *Zeitschrift für Politik* 2, pp. 149–70.

——(1969b) 'Komplexität und Demokratie', *Politische Vierteljahresschrift* 1, pp. 314–25.

——(1970) 'Wahrheit und Ideologie: Vorschläge zur Wiederaufnahme der Diskussion', in: *Soziologische Aufklärung*, vol. 1: *Aufsätze zur Theorie sozialer Systeme* (Opladen: Westdeutscher Verlag), pp. 54–65.

——(1971a) 'Funktionen der Rechtssprechung im politischen System', in: *Politische Planung: Aufsätze zur Soziologie von Politik und Planung* (Opladen: Westdeutscher Verlag), pp. 46–53.

——(1971b) 'Die Weltgesellschaft', *Archiv für Rechts- und Sozialphilosophie* 57, pp. 1–35.

——(1973a) 'Politische Verfassungen im Kontext des Gesellschaftssystems', *Der Staat* 12, pp. 165–82.

——(1973b) *Zweckbegriff und Systemrationalität: Über die Funktion von Zwecken in sozialen Systemen* (Frankfurt a. M.: Suhrkamp).

——(1973c) *Vertrauen: Ein Mechanismus der Reduktion sozialer Komplexität* (Stuttgart: Enke).

——(1974) 'Der politische Code: Konservativ und progressiv in systemtheoretischer Sicht', *Zeitschrift für Politik* 5, pp. 253–71.

——(1975a) 'Sinn als Grundbegriff der Soziologie', in: Jürgen Habermas and Niklas Luhmann, *Theorie der Gesellschaft oder Sozialtechnologie – Was leistet die Systemforschung?* (Frankfurt a. M.: Suhrkamp), pp. 25–100.

——(1975b) 'Systemtheoretische Argumentation: Eine Entgegnung auf Jürgen Habermas', in: Habermas/Luhmann, *Theorie der Gesellschaft oder Sozialtechnologie* (see Luhmann 1975a),.

——(1975c) *Macht* (Stuttgart: Enke).

——(1980) *Rechtssoziologie* (Opladen: Westdeutscher Verlag).

——(1981a) *Ausdifferenzierung des Rechts: Beiträge zur Rechtssoziologie und Rechtstheorie* (Frankfurt a. M.: Suhrkamp).

——(1981b) *Politische Theorie im Wohlfahrtsstaat* (Munich/Vienna: Günter Olzog).

——(1981c) 'Machtkreislauf und Recht in Demokratien', *Zeitschrift für Rechtssoziologie* 2, pp. 158–67.

——(1981d) 'Selbstlegitimation des Staates', in: *Archiv für Rechts- und Sozialphilosophie*, spec. issue 15: *Legitimation des modernen Staates*, pp. 65–83.

——(1983) *Legitimation durch Verfahren* (Frankfurt a. M.: Suhrkamp).

——(1984a) *Soziale Systeme: Grundriß einer allgemeinen Theorie* (Frankfurt a. M.: Suhrkamp).

—— (1984b) 'Widerstandsrecht und politische Gewalt', *Zeitschrift für Rechtssoziologie* 5, pp. 36–45.

—— (1984c) 'Staat und Politik: Zur Semantik der Selbstbeschreibung politischer Systeme', in: Udo Bermbach (ed.), *Politische Theoriengeschichte: Probleme einer Teildisziplin der Politischen Wissenschaft*, in: *Politische Vierteljahresschrift*, spec. issue 15, pp. 99–125.

—— (1986) *Ökologische Kommunikation: Kann sich die moderne Gesellschaft auf ökologische Gefährdungen einstellen?* (Opladen: Westdeutscher Verlag).

—— (1988) *Die Wirtschaft der Gesellschaft* (Frankfurt a. M.: Suhrkamp).

—— (1992) 'Weizsäckers ungeliebte Parteien', *Die politische Meinung* 37, pp. 5–11.

—— (1993a) *Das Recht der Gesellschaft* (Frankfurt a. M.: Suhrkamp).

—— (1993b) 'Die Paradoxie des Entscheidens', *Verwaltungsarchiv* 84, pp. 287–310.

—— (1994a) 'Partizipation und Legitimation: Die Ideen und die Erfahrungen', in: *Soziologische Aufklärung*, vol. 4: *Beiträge zur funktionalen Differenzierung der Gesellschaft* (Opladen: Westdeutscher Verlag), pp. 152–60.

—— (1994b) 'Die Zukunft der Demokratie' in: *Soziologische Aufklärung* (see Luhmann 1994a), vol. 4, pp. 126–32.

—— (1996a) 'Umweltrisiko und Politik', in: *Protest: Systemtheorie und soziale Bewegungen*, ed. and intro. Kai-Uwe Hellmann (Frankfurt a. M.: Suhrkamp), pp. 160–74.

—— (1996b) 'Systemtheorie und Protestbewegungen. Ein Interview', in: *Protest* (see Luhmann 1996a), pp. 175–201.

—— (1996c) 'Tautologie und Paradoxie in den Selbstbeschreibungen der modernen Gesellschaft', in: *Protest* (see Luhmann 1996a), pp. 79–107.

—— (1996d) 'Frauen, Männer und George Spencer Brown', in: *Protest* (see Luhmann 1996a), pp. 107–56.

—— (1996e) 'Alternative ohne Alternative. Die Paradoxie der "der neuen sozialen Bewegungen" ', in: *Protest* (see Luhmann 1996a), pp. 64–75.

—— (1996f) 'Protestbewegungen' in: *Protest* (see Luhmann 1996a), pp. 201–16.

—— (1997) *Die Gesellschaft der Gesellschaft* (Frankfurt a. M.: Suhrkamp).

Lütge, Friedrich (1966) *Deutsche Sozial- und Wirtschaftsgeschichte* (Berlin/Heidelberg/New York: Springer).

Luthardt, Wolfgang (1976) 'Bemerkungen zu Otto Kirchheimers Arbeiten bis 1933', in: Otto Kirchheimer, *Von der Weimarer Republik zum Faschismus* (see Kirchenheimer 1976a), pp. 7–31.

—— (1984) 'Arbeiterbewegung und Weimarer Republik: Kritische Bemerkungen zu Franz L. Neumanns Interpretation nach 1933', in: Joachim Perels (ed.), *Aktualität und Probleme der Theorie Franz L. Neumanns* (Baden-Baden: Nomos), pp. 79–95.

—— (1986) *Sozialdemokratische Verfassungstheorie in der Weimarer Republik* (Opladen: Westdeutscher Verlag).

Lutz, Heinrich (1963) *Demokratie im Zwielicht: Der Weg der deutschen Katholiken aus dem Kaiserreich in die Republik 1914–1925* (Munich: Kösel).

McCarthy, Thomas (1978) *The Critical Theory of Jürgen Habermas* (Cambridge, Mass./London: MIT Press).

McCormick, John (1997) *Carl Schmitt's Critique of Liberalism: Against Politics as Technology* (Cambridge: CUP).

Mack Smith, Denis (1997) *Modern Italy: A Political History* (New Haven: Yale UP).

Marcic, Réné (1966) 'Verfassungsgerichtsbarkeit als Sinn der reinen Rechtslehre', in: Karl Dietrich Bracher et al. (eds), *Die moderne Demokratie und ihr Recht.*

*Festschrift für Gerhard Leibholz zum 65. Geburtstag*, vol. 2: *Staats- und Verfassungsrecht* (Tübingen: J. C. B. Mohr), pp. 481–511.

Marx, Karl (1956) *Zur Kritik der Hegelschen Rechtsphilosophie*, in: Karl Marx and Friedrich Engels, *Werke*, vol. 1 (Berlin: Dietz), pp. 203–333.

——(1962) *Das Kapital*, I, in: Karl Marx and Friedrich Engels, *Werke*, vol. 23 (Berlin: Dietz).

——(1981) *Zur Judenfrage*, in: Karl Marx and Friedrich Engels, *Werke*, vol. 1 (Berlin: Dietz), pp. 347–77.

Maschke, Günther (1988) 'Die Zweideutigkeit der Entscheidung', in: Helmut Quaritsch (ed.), *Complexio Oppositorum: Über Carl Schmitt* (Berlin: Duncker & Humblot), pp. 193–221.

Maser, Werner (1987) *Friedrich Ebert: Der erste deutsche Reichspräsident* (Munich: Droemer Knaur).

Matthias, Erich (1969) 'Einleitung', in: Matthias et al. (eds), *Die Regierung der Volksbeauftragten 1918/19*, pt 1 (Düsseldorf: Droste).

Matthias, Erich and Morsey, Rudolf (eds) (1979) *Das Ende der Parteien 1933. Darstellungen und Dokumente* (Düsseldorf: Droste).

Maus, Ingeborg (1994) *Zur Aufklärung der Demokratietheorie: Rechts- und demokratietheoretische Überlegungen im Anschluß an Kant* (Frankfurt a. M.: Suhrkamp).

Mausbach, Joseph (1920) *Kulturfragen in der deutschen Verfassung: Eine Erklärung wichtiger Verfassungsartikel* (Mönchengladbach: Volksvereins-Verlag).

Megerle, Klaus (1993) 'Verhaltensdispositionen und politische Orientierungen bei gesellschaftlichen Führungsgruppen: Richter und Großunternehmer in der Weimarer Republik', in: Detlev Lehnert and Klaus Megerle (eds), *Pluralismus als Verfassungs- und Gesellschaftsmodell. Zur politischen Kultur in der Weimarer Republik* (Opladen: Westdeutscher Verlag), pp. 215–70.

Mehring, Reinhard (1989) *Pathetisches Denken: Carl Schmitts Denkweg am Leitfaden Hegels: Katholische Grundstellung und anti-marxistische Hegelstrategie* (Berlin: Duncker & Humblot).

——(1991) 'Carl Schmitts Lehre von der Auflösung des Liberalismus: Das Sinngefüge der "Verfassungslehre" als historisches Urteil', *Zeitschrift für Politik* 38, pp. 200–16.

Meier, Heinrich (1994) *Die Lehre Carl Schmitts: Vier Kapitel zur Unterscheidung Politischer Theologie und Politischer Philosophie* (Stuttgart/Weimar: Metzler).

Meinecke, Friedrich (1963) *Die Idee der Staatsräson in der neueren Geschichte*, ed. W. Hofer (Munich: R. Oldenbourg).

Meister, Rainer (1991) *Die große Depression. Zwangslagen und Handlungsspielräume der Wirtschafts- und Finanzpolitik in Deutschland 1929–1932* (Regensburg: transfer Verlag).

Merkl, Peter H. (1963) *The Origin of the West German Republic* (New York: OUP).

Metzner, Andreas (1993) *Probleme sozio-ökonomischer Systemtheorie: Natur und Gesellschaft in der Soziologie Niklas Luhmanns* (Opladen: Westdeutscher Verlag).

Meuter, Günter (1994) *Der Katechon: Zu Carl Schmitts fundamentalistischer Kritik der Zeit* (Berlin: Duncker & Humblot).

Michels, Robert (1911) *Zur Soziologie des Parteiwesens in der modernen Demokratie: Untersuchungen über die oligarchischen Tendenzen des Gruppenlebens* (Leipzig: Werner Klinkhardt).

Millbank, John (1990) *Theology and Social Theory: Beyond Secular Reason* (Oxford: Basil Blackwell).

Miller, Fred D., Jr. (1995) *Nature, Justice, and Rights in Aristotle's Politics* (Oxford: OUP).

Miller, Susanne (1964) *Das Problem der Freiheit im Sozialismus: Freiheit, Staat und Revolution in der Programmatik der Sozialdemokratie von Lassalle bis zum Revisionismusstreit* (Frankfurt a. M.: Europäische Verlagsanstalt).

——(1978) *Die Bürde der Macht: Die deutsche Sozialdemokratie 1918–1920* (Düsseldorf: Droste).

Mommsen, Hans (1978) *Klassenkampf oder Mitbestimmung. Zum Problem der Kontrolle wirtschaftlicher Macht in der Weimarer Republik* (Frankfurt a. M.: Europäische Verlagsanstalt).

——(1990) *Die verspielte Freiheit: Der Weg der Republik von Weimar in den Untergang 1918 bis 1933* (Frankfurt a. M.: Propyläen).

Mommsen, Wolfgang J. (1959) *Max Weber und die deutsche Politik 1890–1920* (Tübingen: J. C. B. Mohr).

——(1963) 'Zum Begriff der "plebiszitären Führerdemokratie" bei Max Weber', *Kölner Zeitschrift für Soziologie und Sozialpsychologie* 15, pp. 295–322.

——(1965) 'Universalgeschichtliches und politisches Denken bei Max Weber', *Historische Zeitschrift* 202, pp. 557–612.

——(1974) *The Age of Bureaucracy: Perspectives on the Political Sociology of Max Weber* (Oxford: Basil Blackwell).

——(1975) 'Wandlungen der liberalen Idee im Zeitalter des Imperialismus', in: Karl Holl and Günther List (eds), *Liberalismus und imperialistischer Staat. Der Imperialismus als Problem liberaler Parteien 1890–1914* (Göttingen: Vandenhoeck & Ruprecht), pp. 109–47.

——(1990a) 'Das deutsche Kaiserreich als System umgangener Entscheidungen', in: *Der autoritäre Nationalstaat. Verfassung, Gesellschaft und Kultur im deutschen Kaiserreich* (Frankfurt a. M.: Fischer), pp. 11–38.

——(1990b) 'Die Verfassung des deutschen Reiches von 1871 als dilatorischer Formelkompromiß', in: *Der autoritäre Nationalstaat* (see W. J. Mommsen 1990a), pp. 39–65.

——(1993) *Großmachtstellung und Weltpolitik: Die Außenpolitik des Deutschen Reiches 1870 bis 1914* (Frankfurt a. M.: Ullstein).

Mooers, Colin (1991) *The Making of Bourgeois Europe: Absolutism, Revolution and the Rise of Capitalism in England, France and Germany* (London/New York: Verso).

Moore, Ronald (1978) *Legal Norms and Legal Science: A Critical Study of Kelsen's Pure Theory of Law* (Honolulu: University Press of Hawaii).

Morgan, Robert (1965) *The German Social Democrats and the First International 1864–1872* (Cambridge: CUP).

Moritz, Peter (1992) *Kritik des Paradigmenwechsels: Mit Horkheimer gegen Habermas* (Lüneburg: zu Klampen).

Morsey, Rudolf (1966) *Die Deutsche Zentrumspartei, 1917–1923* (Düsseldorf: Droste).

——(ed.) (1969) *Die Protokolle der Reichstagsfraktion und des Fraktionsvorstands der deutschen Zentrumspartei, 1926–1933* (Mainz: Matthias-Grünewald-Verlag).

——(1977) *Der Untergang des politischen Katholizismus: Die Zentrumspartei zwischen christlichem Selbstverständnis und 'Nationaler Erhebung' 1932/3* (Zürich/Stuttgart: Belser).

Mottl, Rüdiger (1992) *Politisches System und politische Innovation. Determinanten der Reformpolitik in der Bundesrepublik Deutschland* (Frankfurt a. M.: Lang).

Müller, Horst (1983) 'Verwaltungsstaat und parlamentarische Demokratie: Preußen 1919–1932', in: Gerhard A. Ritter (ed.), *Regierung, Bürokratie und Parlament in Preußen und Deutschland von 1848 bis zur Gegenwart* (Düsseldorf: Droste), pp. 149–80.

Mußgnug, Reinhard (1984) 'Die rechtlichen und pragmatischen Beziehungen zwischen Regierung, Parlament und Verwaltung', in: Kurt G. A. Jeserich et al. (eds), *Deutsche Verwaltungsgeschichte*, vol. 3: *Das deutsche Reich bis zum Ende der Monarchie* (Stuttgart: Deutsche Verlagsanstalt), pp. 109–27.

Muszynski, Bernhard (1975) *Wirtschaftliche Mitbestimmung zwischen Konflikt- und Harmoniekonzeptionen. Theoretische Voraussetzungen, geschichtliche Grundlagen und Hauptprobleme der Mitbestimmungsdiskussion der BRD* (Meisenheim am Glan: Anton Hain).

Nahamowitz, Peter (1978) *Gesetzgebung in den kritischen Systemjahren 1967–1969. Eine Rekonstruktion spätkapitalistischen Handelns* (Frankfurt a. M./New York: Campus).

—— (1988) 'Autopoiesis oder ökonomischer Staatsinterventionismus?', *Zeitschrift für Rechtssoziologie* 9, pp. 36–73.

Naphtali, Fritz (1931) 'Die Kontrolle der Kartelle und Trusts', *Die Gesellschaft* 8, pp. 43–53.

Naphtali, Fritz et al. (1929) *Wirtschaftsdemokratie. Ihr Wesen, Weg und Ziel* (Berlin: Verlagsgesellschaft des Allgemeinen Deutschen Gewerkschaftsbundes).

Narr, Wolf-Dieter (1969) *Theoriebegriffe und Systemtheorie*, in: Wolf-Dieter Narr and Frieder Naschold, *Einführung in die politische Theorie*, vol. 1 (Stuttgart: W. Kohlhammer).

—— (1994) 'Recht – Demokratie – Weltgesellschaft. Überlegungen anläßlich der rechtstheoretischen Werke von Jürgen Habermas und Niklas Luhmann (Teil I)', *Prokla* 94, pp. 87–112.

Narr, Wolf-Dieter and Runze, Dieter H. (1974) 'Zur Kritik der politischen Soziologie', in: Franz Maciejewski (ed.), *Theorie der Gesellschaft oder Sozialtechnologie: Beiträge zur Habermas–Luhmann-Diskussion*, pp. 7–91.

Narr, Wolf-Dieter and Schubert, Alexander (1994) *Weltökonomie: Die Misere der Politik* (Frankfurt a. M.: Suhrkamp).

Narr, Wolf-Dieter, Scheer, Hermann and Söri, Dieter (1976) *SPD – Staatspartie oder Reformpartei?* (Munich: Piper).

Naschold, Frieder (1968) 'Demokratie und Komplexität: Thesen und Illustrationen zur Theoriediskussion in der Politikwissenschaft', *Politische Vierteljahresschrift* 9, pp. 494–519.

—— (1973) 'Gesellschaftsreform', in: Frieder Naschold and Werner Väth (eds), *Politische Planungssysteme* (Opladen: Westdeutscher Verlag), pp. 59–98.

Naschold, Frieder and Väth, Werner (1973) 'Politische Planungssysteme im entwickleten Kapitalismus', in: Naschold and Väth (eds), *Politische Planungssysteme* (see Naschold 1973), pp. 7–42.

Nassehi, Armin (1992) 'Wie wirklich sind Systeme? Zum ontologischen und epistemologischen Status von Luhmanns Theorie selbstreferentieller Systeme', in: Werner Krawietz and Michael Welker (eds), *Kritik der Theorie sozialer Systeme: Auseinandersetzungen mit Luhmanns Hauptwerk* (Frankfurt a. M.: Suhrkamp), pp. 43–70.

Naumann, Friedrich (1900) *Demokratie und Kaisertum: Ein Handbuch für innere Politik* (Berlin: Buchverlag der 'Hilfe').

—— (1911) *Neudeutsche Wirtschaftspolitik* (Berlin: Buchverlag der 'Hilfe').

——(1919a) 'Versuch volksverständlicher Grundrechte', *Die Hilfe* 13, pp. 156–7.

——(1919b) 'Rede in der Nationalversammlung', *Die Hilfe* 9, p. 105.

——(1919c) 'Deutsche Grundrechte', *Die Hilfe* 11, pp. 141–2.

——(1919d) *Demokratie als Staatsgrundlage* (Berlin: Buchverlag der 'Hilfe').

Neumann, Franz (1929) *Die politische und soziale Bedeutung der arbeitsgreichtlichen Rechtssprechung* (Berlin: E. Laub).

——(1966) *Behemoth: The Structure and Practice of National Socialism, 1933–1944* (New York: Harper Torchbooks).

——(1967a) 'Der Funktionswandel des Gesetzes im Recht der bürgerlichen Gesellschaft', in: *Demokratischer und autoritärer Staat: Studien zur politischen Theorie*, ed. Herbert Marcuse, intro. Helge Pross (Frankfurt a. M.: Fischer), pp. 31–81.

——(1967b) 'Zum Begriff der politischen Freiheit', in: *Demokratischer und autoritärer Staat* (see F. Neumann 1967a), pp. 100–41.

——(1967c) 'Ökonomie und Politik im zwanzigsten Jahrhundert', in: *Demokratischer und autoritärer Staat* (see F. Neumann 1967a), pp. 248–60.

——(1967d) 'Ansätze zur Untersuchung politischer Macht', in: *Demokratischer und autoritärer Staat* (see F. Neumann 1967a), pp. 82–99.

——(1967e) 'Über die Grenzen bürgerlichen Ungenaisams', in : *Demokratischer und autoritärer Staat* (see F. Neumann 1967a), pp. 195–206.

——(1978a) 'Der Niedergang der deutschen Demokratie' in: *Wirtschaft, Staat, Demokratie*, ed. Alfons Söllner (Frankfurt a. M.: Suhrkamp), pp. 103–23.

——(1978b) 'Die Gewerkschaften in der Demokratie und in der Diktatur', in: *Wirtschaft, Staat, Demokratie* (see F. Neumann 1978a), pp. 145–222.

——(1978c) 'Rechtsstaat, Gewaltenteilung und Sozialismus', in: *Wirtschaft, Staat, Demokratie* (see F. Neumann 1978a), pp. 124–33.

——(1978d) 'Über die Voraussetzungen und den Rechtsbegriff einer Wirtschaftsverfassung', in: *Wirtschaft, Staat, Demokratie* (see F. Neumann 1978a), pp. 76–102.

——(1978e) 'Die soziale Bedeutung der Grundrechte in der Weimarer Verfassung', in: *Wirtschaft, Staat, Demokratie* (see F. Neumann 1978a), pp. 57–76.

——(1978f) 'Der Niedergang der deutschen Demokratie', in: *Wirtschaft, Staat, Demokratie* (see F. Neumann 1978a), pp. 103–23.

——(1978g) 'Zur Marxistischen Staatslehre', in: *Wirtschaft, Staat, Demokratie* (see F. Neumann 1978a), pp. 134–44.

——(1978h) 'Die Gewerkschaften in der Demokratie und in der Diktatur', in: *Wirtschaft, Staat, Demokratie* (see F. Neumann 1978a), pp. 145–222.

——(1978i) 'Die Arbeiterbewegung in Westdeutschland', in: *Wirtschaft, Staat, Demokratie* (see F. Neumann 1978a), pp. 393–401.

——(1978j) 'Deutsche Demokratie', in: *Wirtschaft, Staat, Demokratie* (see F. Neumann 1978a), pp. 327–72.

Neumann, Sigmund (1965) *Die Parteien der Weimarer Republik* (Stuttgart: W. Kohlhammer).

Neumann, Volker (1981) 'Verfassungstheorien politischer Antipoden: Otto Kirchheimer und Carl Schmitt', *Kritische Justiz* 14, pp. 235–54.

——(1984) 'Kompromiß oder Entscheidung? Zur Rezeption der Theorie Carl Schmitts in den Weimarer Arbeiten Franz L. Neumanns', in: Joachim Perels (ed.), *Aktualität und Probleme der Theorie Franz L. Neumanns* (Baden-Baden: Nomos), pp. 65–78.

Neuthinger, Egon (1982) 'Zum finanzpolitischen Planungskonzept in der Bundesrepublik Deutschland – Seine gesamtwirtschaftlichen Zielsetzungen und ihre

Realisierung bei erhöhter ökonomischer Unsicherheit', in: Gottfried Bombach, Bernhard Gahlen and Alfred E. Ott (eds), *Möglichkeiten und Grenzen wachsender Staatsaufgaben* (Tübingen: J. C. B. Mohr), pp. 548–98.

Nichols, A. J. (1994) *Freedom with Responsibility: The Social Market Economy in Germany 1918–1963* (Oxford: Clarendon Press).

Niclauß, Karlheinz (1974) 'Der Parlamentarische Rat und das Sozialstaatspostulat', *Politische Vierteljahresschrift* 15, pp. 33–52.

——(1988) *Kanzlerdemokratie: Bonner Regierungspraxis von Konrad Adenauer bis Helmut Kohl* (Stuttgart: W. Kohlhammer).

Nicoletti, Michele (1988) 'Die Ursprünge von Carl Schmitts "Politischer Theologie" ', in: Helmut Quaritsch (ed.), *Complexio Oppositorum: Über Carl Schmitt* (Berlin: Duncker & Humblot), pp. 109–28.

Nietzsche, Friedrich (1968) *Zur Genealogie der Moral*, in: *Werke*, ed. Giorgio Colli and Mazzino Montinari, 8 sections (Berlin: de Gruyter), section 6, vol. 2, pp. 257–430.

Nippel, Wilfried (1994) 'Max Weber: Nationalökonom und Politiker', *Geschichte und Gesellschaft* 20, pp. 274–98.

Nipperdey, Thomas (1961) *Die Organisation der deutschen Parteien vor 1918* (Düsseldorf: Droste).

——(1979) 'Organisierter Kapitalismus, Verbände und die Krise des Kaiserreichs: Literaturbericht', *Geschichte und Gesellschaft* 5, pp. 418–33.

——(1983) *Deutsche Geschichte 1800–1866: Bürgerwelt und starker Staat* (Munich: Beck).

Noack, Paul (1993) *Carl Schmitt: Eine Biographie* (Berlin/Frankfurt a. M.: Propyläen).

Nocken, Ulrich (1978) 'Corporatism and Pluralism im Modern German History', in: Dirk Stegman, Bernd-Jürgen Wendt and Peter-Christian Witt (eds), *Industrielle Gesellschaft und politisches System. Beiträge zur politischen Sozialgeschichte. Festschrift für Fritz Fischer zum siebzigsten Geburtstag* (Bonn: Verlag Neue Gesellschaft), pp. 37–56.

Nolte, Ernst (1963) 'Max Weber vor dem Faschismus', *Der Staat* 2, pp. 1–24.

Obenaus, Herbert (1984) *Anfänge des Parlamentarismus in Preußen bis 1848* (Düsseldorf: Droste).

Oberreuter, Heinrich (1978) *Notstand und Demokratie. Vom monarchischen Obrigkeits- zum demokratischen Rechtsstaat* (Munich: Ernst Vogel).

Oertzen, Peter von (1974) 'Schwerpunkte der innerparteilichen Diskussion um den Orientierungsrahmen '85', in: *Die Aufgaben der Partei. Reden und Aufsätze aus den letzten vier Jahren zur Arbeit der SPD und zur Entwicklung ihrer programmatischen Grundlagen* (Bonn/Bad Godesberg: Verlag Neue Gesellschaft), pp. 57–72.

——(1976) *Betriebsräte in der Novemberrevolution: Eine politikwissenschaftliche Untersuchung über Ideengehalt und Struktur der betrieblichen und wirtschaftlichen Arbeiterräte in der deutschen Revolution 1918/19* (Berlin: Dietz).

Oestreich, Gerhard (1969) 'Ständetum und Ständebildung in Deutschland', in: *Geist und Gestalt des frühmodernen Staates. Ausgewählte Aufsätze* (Berlin: Duncker & Humblot), pp. 277–89.

Offe, Claus (1969) 'Politische Herrschaft und Klassenstrukturen. Zur Analyse spätkapitalistischer Gesellschaftssysteme', in: Gisela Kress and Dieter Senghaas (eds), *Politikwissenschaft: Eine Einführung in ihre Probleme* (Frankfurt a. M.: Europäische Verlagsanstalt), pp. 155–89.

——(1974) 'Rationalitätskriterien der Administration', *Leviathan. Zeitschrift für Sozialwissenschaft* 3, pp. 333–45.

——(1976) 'Überlegungen und Hypothesen zum Problem politischer Legitimation', in: Rolf Ebbighausen (ed.), *Bürgerlicher Staat und politische Legitimation* (Frankfurt a. M.: Suhrkamp), pp. 80–105.

——(1979) ' "Unregierbarkeit. Zur Renaissance konservativer Krisentheorien" ', in: Jürgen Habermas (ed.), *Stichworte zur geistigen Situation der Zeit*, vol. 1: *Nation und Republik* (Frankfurt a. M.: Suhrkamp), pp. 294–318.

Optiz, Reinhard (1965) 'Der große Plan der CDU: die "Formierte Gesellschaft"', *Blätter für deutsche und internationale Politik* 10, pp. 750–77.

Otto, Volker (1971) *Das Staatsverständnis des Parlamentarischen Rates. Ein Beitrag zur Entstehungsgeschichte des Grundgesetzes für die Bundesrepublik Deutschland* (Bonn/Bad Godesberg: Rheinisch-Bergische Druckerei und Verlagsgesellschaft).

Outhwaite, William (1994) *Habermas: A Critical Introduction* (Cambridge: Polity Press).

Overdieck, Richard (1987) *Parteien und Verfassungsfragen in Österreich. Die Entstehung des Verfassungsprivisoriums in der Ersten Republik 1918–1920* (Munich: R. Oldenbourg).

Pack, Wolfgang (1961) *Das parlamentarische Ringen um das Sozialistengesetz Bismarcks 1878–1890* (Düsseldorf: Droste).

Pasquino, Pasquale (1988) 'Souveränität und Repräsentation bei Hermann Heller', in: Hans Maier et al. (eds), *Politik, Philosophie, Praxis – Festschrift für Wilhelm Hennis zum 65. Geburtstag* (Stuttgart: Klett-Cotta), pp. 189–201.

Patch, William, Jr. (1998) *Heinrich Brüning and the Dissolution of the Weimar Republic* (Cambridge: CUP).

Patemann, Reinhard (1964) *Der Kampf um die preußische Reform im Ersten Weltkrieg* (Düsseldorf: Droste).

Perels, Joachim (1973) *Kapitalismus und politische Demokratie: Privatrechtssystem und Gesellschaftsstruktur in der Weimarer Republik* (Frankfurt a. M.: Europäische Verlagsanstalt).

Petzina, Dietmar (1985) 'Soziale und wirtschaftliche Entwicklung', in: Kurt G. A. Jeserich et al. (eds), *Deutsche Verwaltungsgeschichte*, vol. 4: *Das Reich als Republik und in der Zeit des Nationalsozialismus* (Stuttgart: Deutsche Verlagsanstalt), pp. 39–66.

Pickart, Eberhard (1972) 'Die Rolle der Parteien im deutschen konstitutionellen System vor 1914', in: Ernst-Wolfgang Böckenförde (ed.), *Moderne deutsche Verfassungsgeschichte* (Cologne: Kiepenheuer & Witsch), pp. 258–81.

Pilch, Martin (1994) *System des transcendentalen Etatismus: Staat und Verfassung bei Carl Schmitt* (Vienna/Leipzig: Karolinger).

Plessner, Helmuth, (1969) *Die verspätete Nation: Über die politische Verführbarkeit bürgerlichen Geistes* (Stuttgart: W. Kohlhammer).

Plum, Günther (1972) *Gesellschaftsstruktur und politisches Bewußtsein in einer katholischen Region 1928–1933. Untersuchung am Beispiel des Regierungsbezirks Aachen* (Stuttgart: Deutsche Verlagsanstalt), p. 29.

Pocock, J. G. A. (1957) *The Ancient Constitution and the Feudal Law: A Study of English Thought in the Seventeenth Century* (Bath: Cedric Chivers).

Pohl, Hans (1977) 'Die Entwicklung der deutschen Volkswirtschaft (1830–1880)', in: Helmut Coing and Walter Wilhelm (eds), *Wissenschaft und Kodifikation des Privatrechts im 19. Jahrhundert*, vol. 2: *Die rechtliche Verselbständigung der Austauschverhältnisse vor dem Hintergrund der wirtschaftlichen Entwicklung und Doktrin* (Frankfurt a. M.: Klostermann), pp. 1–26.

——(1979) 'Die Entwicklung der Kartelle in Deutschland und die Diskussionen im Verein für Sozialpolitik', in: Helmut Coing and Walter Wilhelm (eds), *Wissenschaft und Kodifikationen des Privatrechts im 19. Jahrhundert*, vol. 4: *Eigentum und industrielle Entwicklung und Wettbewerbsrecht* (Frankfurt a. M.: Klostermann), pp. 206–35.

Polaschek, Martin F. (1992) *Die Rechtsentwicklung in der ersten Republik. Die Gesetzgebung im Verfassungs- und Strafrecht von 1918–1933* (Graz: Verlag für die TU Graz).

Pollock, Friedrich (1941) 'Is National Socialism a New Order?', *Studies in Philosophy and Social Science* 9, pp. 440–55.

——(1975a) 'Bemerkungen zur Wirtschaftskrise', in: *Stadien des Kapitalismus* ed. and introduced by Helmut Dubiel (Munich: Beck).

——(1975b) 'Die gegenwärtige Lage des Kapitalismus und die Aussichten einer planwirtschaftlichen Neuordnung', in: *Stadien des Kapitalismus* (see Pollock 1975a), pp. 20–39.

Portner Ernst (1973) *Die Verfassungspolitik der Liberalen 1919. Ein Beitrag zur Deutung der Weimarer Reichsverfassung* (Bonn: Ludwig Röhrscheid).

Postone, Moishe and Brick, Barbara (1993) 'Critical Theory and Political Economy', in: Seyla Benhabib et al. (eds), *On Max Horkheimer: New Perspectives* (Cambridge, Mass.: MIT Press), pp. 215–57.

Potthoff, Heinrich (1972) 'Das Weimarer Verfassungswerk und die deutsche Linke', *Archiv für Sozialgeschichte* 12, pp. 433–83.

——(1974a) 'Verfassungsväter ohne Verfassungsvolk? Zum Problem von Integration und Desintegration nach der Novemberrevolution', in: Gerhard A. Ritter (ed.), *Gesellschaft, Parlament und Regierung. Zur Geschichte des Parlamentarismus in Deutschland* (Düsseldorf: Droste), pp. 339–54.

——(1974b) *Kleine Geschichte der SPD*, vol. 1: *Die Sozialdemokratie von den Anfängen bis 1945* (Bonn/Bad Godesberg: Verlag Neue Gesellschaft).

Potthoff, Heinz (1925) *Die Einwirkung der Reichsverfassung auf das Arbeitsrecht* (Leipzig/Erlangen: A. Deichert'sche Verlagsbuchhandlung).

Prauss, Gerold (1983) *Kant über Freiheit und Autonomie* (Frankfurt a. M.: Klostermann).

Preller, Ludwig (1949) *Sozialpolitik in der Weimarer Republik* (Stuttgart: Franz Mittelbach).

Preuß, Hugo (1919) *Deutschlands Staatsumwälzung. Die verfassungsmäßigen Grundlagen der deutschen Republik* (Berlin: Central-Verlag).

——(1926) 'Die Bedeutung der demokratischen Republik für den sozialen Gedanken', in: *Staat, Recht und Freiheit: Aus 40 Jahren deutscher Politik und Geschichte* (Tübingen: J. C. B. Mohr), pp. 481–97.

Preuß, Ulrich K. (1973) *Legalität und Pluralismus: Beiträge zum Verfassungsrecht der Bundesrepublik Deutschland* (Frankfurt a. M.: Suhrkamp).

——(1984) 'Von den Grenzen des bürgerlichen Gehorsams: Ziviler Ungehorsam und Verfassung', in: *Politische Verantwortung und Bürgerloyalität: Von den Grenzen der Verfassung und des Gehorsams in der Demokratie* (Frankfurt a. M.: Fischer), pp. 26–144.

——(1993) 'Political Order and Democracy: Carl Schmitt and his Influence', in: Leszek Nowak and Marcia Paprzcki (eds), *Social System, Rationality and Revolution* (Amsterdam/Atlanta: Rodopi), pp. 15–40.

——(1994a) *Revolution, Fortschritt und Verfassung: Zu einem neuen Verfassungsverständnis* (Frankfurt a. M.: Fischer), pp. 80–99.

——(1994b) 'Zum Begriff der Verfassung', in: *Zum Begriff der Verfassung: Die Ordnung des Politischen* (Frankfurt a. M.: Fischer), pp. 7–33.

Pridham, Geoffrey (1977) *Christian Democracy in Western Germany: The CDU/ CSU in Government and Opposition, 1945–1976* (London: Croom Helm).

Puhle, Hans-Jürgen (1970) 'Parlament, Parteien und Interessenverbände 1890– 1914', in: Michael Stürmer (ed.), *Das kaiserliche Deutschland. Politik und Gesellschaft 1870–1918* (Düsseldorf: Droste), pp. 340–77.

——(1972) *Von der Agrarkrise zum Präfaschismus: Thesen zum Stellenwert der agrarischen Interessenverbände in der deutschen Politik am Ende des 19. Jahrhunderts* (Wiesbaden: Franz Steiner).

Rachfahl, Felix (1902) 'Der dualistische Ständestaat in Deutschland', *Jahrbuch für Gesetzgebung* 23, pp. 165–219.

Ramm, Thilo (1953) *Ferdinand Lassalle als Rechts- und Sozialphilosoph* (Vienna: Westkulturverlag Anton Hain).

——(1980) 'Die Arbeitsverfassung der Weimarer Republik', in: Franz Gamillscheg et al. (eds), *In Memoriam Sir Otto Kahn Freund* (Munich: Beck), pp. 225–46.

Rapport, Karsten (1992) *Im Dienst am Staat von Weimar: Das Zentrum als regierende Partei in der Weimarer Demokratie 1923–1930* (Düsseldorf: Droste).

Raschke, Joachim (1987) 'Zum Begriff der sozialen Bewegung', in: Roland Roth and Dieter Rucht (eds), *Neue soziale Bewegungen in der Bundesrepublik Deutschland* (Frankfurt a. M.: Campus), pp. 19–30.

Raschke, Peter (1978) *Vereine und Verbände. Zur Organisation von Interessen in der Bundesrepublik Deutschland* (Munich: Juventa).

Rasmussen, David M. (1996) 'How is Valid Law Possible? A Review of *Between Facts and Norms* by Jürgen Habermas', in: Mathieu Deflem (ed.), *Habermas, Modernity and Law* (London: Sage), pp. 21–44.

Rathenau, Walther (1918) *Die neue Wirtschaft* (Berlin: Fischer).

Raz, Joseph (1980) *The Concept of a Legal System: An Introduction to the Theory of Legal Systems* (Oxford: Clarendon Press).

Rehg, William (1994) *Insight and Solidarity: A Study in the Discourse Ethics of Jürgen Habermas* (Berkeley/Los Angeles/London: University of California Press).

Renner, Karl (1965) *Die Rechtsinstitute des Privatrechts und ihre soziale Funktion. Ein Beitrag zur Kritik des bürgerlichen Rechts* (Stuttgart: Gustav Fischer).

Repgen, Konrad (1976) 'Hitlers Machtergreifung und der deutsche Katholizismus', in: Dieter Albrecht (ed.), *Katholische Kirche im Dritten Reich: Eine Aufsatzsammlung zum Verhältnis von Pabsttum, Episkopat und deutschen Katholiken zum Nationalsozialismus, 1933–1945* (Mainz: Topos), pp. 1–34.

Revermann, Klaus (1959) *Die stufenweise Durchbrechung des Verfassungssystems der Weimarer Republik in den Jahren 1930 bis 1933: Eine staatsrechtliche und historisch-politische Analyse* (Münster: Aschendorffsche Verlagsbuchhandlung).

'Richtlinien der Deutschen Zentrumspartei vom 16. Januar 1922', in: Wilhelm Mommsen (ed.), (1960) *Deutsche Parteiprogramme: Deutsches Handbuch der Politik*, vol. I (Munich: Isar Verlag), p. 487.

Riedel, Manfred (1973) 'Die Aporie von Herrschaft und Vereinbarung in Kants Idee des Sozialvertrags', in: Gerold Prauss (ed.), *Kant. Zur Deutung seiner Theorie von Erkennen und Handeln* (Cologne: Kiepenheuer & Witsch), pp. 337–49.

——(1982) 'Hegels Kritik des Naturrechts', in: *Zwischen Tradition und Revolution. Studien zu Hegels Rechtsphilosophie* (Stuttgart: Klett-Cotta), pp. 84–115.

Riemer, Jeremiah M. (1982) 'Alterations in the Design of Model Germany: Critical Innovations in the Policy Machinery of Economic Steering', in: Andrei S. Markovits (ed.), *The Political Economy of West Germany. Modell Deutschland* (New York: Praeger), pp. 53–89.

Riley, Patrick (1982) *Will and Political Legitimacy: A Critical Exposition of Social Contract Theory in Hobbes, Locke, Rousseau, Kant and Hegel* (Cambridge, Mass.: Harvard UP).

Ritter, Gerhard A. (1976a) 'Politische Parteien in Deutschland vor 1918', in: Gerhart A. Ritter, *Arbeiterbewegung, Parteien und Parlamentarismus: Aufsätze zur deutschen Sozial- und Verfassungsgeschichte des 19. und 20. Jahrhunderts* (Göttingen: Vandenhoeck & Ruprecht), pp. 102–15.

——(1976b) 'Entwicklungsprobleme des deutschen Parlamentarismus', in: *Arbeiterbewegung, Parteien und Parlamentarismus* (see G. A. Ritter 1976a), pp. 158–89.

——(1978) 'Kontinuität und Umformung von Parteiensystem und Wahlergebnissen in Deutschland 1918 bis 1920', in: Otto Büsch et al. (eds), *Wählerbewegung in der deutschen Geschichte: Analysen und Berichte zu den Reichstagswahlen* (Berlin: Colloquium), pp. 362–90.

——(1985) *Die deutschen Parteien 1830–1914: Parteien und Gesellschaft im konstitutionellen Regierungssystem* (Göttingen: Vandenhoeck & Ruprecht).

——(1989) *Der Sozialstaat. Entstehung und Entwicklung im internationalen Vergleich* (Munich: R. Oldenbourg).

Ritter, Joachim (1969a) 'Moralität und Sittlichkeit. Zu Hegels Auseinandersetzung mit der Kantischen Ethik', in: *Metaphysik und Politik. Studien zu Aristoteles und Hegel* (Frankfurt a. M.: Suhrkamp), pp. 281–309.

——(1969b) 'Das bürgerliche Leben. Zur aristotelischen Theorie des Glücks', in: *Metaphysik und Politik* (see J. Ritter: 1969a), pp. 57–105.

——(1969c) 'Naturrecht bei Aristoteles. Zum Problem einer Erneuerung des Naturrechts', in: *Metaphysik und Politik* (see J. Ritter 1969a), pp. 133–79.

——(1970) 'Zum Primat des Rechts bei Kant und Hegel', in: Jürgen Blühdorn and Joachim Ritter (eds), *Recht und Ethik. Zum Problem ihrer Beziehung im 19. Jahrhundert* (Frankfurt a. M.: Klostermann), pp. 77–82.

Robert, Rüdiger (1976) *Konzentrationspolitik in der Bundesrepublik – Das Beispiel der Entstehung des Gesetzes gegen Wettbewerbsbeschränkungen* (Berlin: Duncker & Humblot), pp. 97–8.

Rockmore, Tom (1989) *Habermas on Historical Materialism* (Bloomington/Indianapolis: Indiana University Press).

Roehl, Christoph von (1988) *Große Depression und Stagflation. Eine kritische Analyse der deutschen Wirtschaftspolitik 1927/33 und 1970/86* (Göttingen: Vandenhoeck & Ruprecht).

Röhl, J. C. G. (1967) *Germany without Bismarck: The Crisis of Government in the Second Reich, 1890–1900* (London: Batsford).

Rommen, Heinrich (1935) *Der Staat in der katholischen Gedankenwelt* (Paderborn: Bonifacius Verlag).

Ronge, Volker (1975) 'Entpolitisierung der Forschungspolitik', *Leviathan* 3, pp. 307–37.

Rosenberg, Arthur (1928) *Die Entstehung der deutschen Republik 1871–1918* (Berlin: Rowohlt).

——(1955) *Entstehung und Geschichte der Weimarer Republik* (Frankfurt a. M.: Europäische Verlagsanstalt).

Rosenberg, Hans (1967) *Große Depression und Bismarckzeit. Wirtschaftsablauf, Gesellschaft und Politik in Mitteleuropa* (Berlin: de Gruyter).

Rossi, Pietro (1987) *Vom Historismus zur historischen Sozialwissenschaft: Heidelberger Max Weber-Vorlesungen* (Frankfurt a. M.: Suhrkamp).

Rossmann, Witich (1986) *Vergesellschaftung, Krise und gewerkschaftliche Gegenmacht. Studien zu Strukturveränderungen der 'industriellen Beziehungen' in der Bundesrepublik (1969 bis 1984)* (Marburg: Verlag Arbeiterbewegung und Gesellschaftswissenschaft).

Roth, Klaus (1994) 'Neue Entwicklungen der Kritischen Theorie', *Leviathan* 23, pp. 422–45.

Roth, Wolfgang (1979) 'Strukturräte als eine Fom der überbetrieblichen Mitbestimmung', *Zeitschrift für Parlamentsfragen* 10, pp. 544–8.

Rucht, Dieter (1994) *Modernisierung und neue soziale Bewegungen: Deutschland, Frankreich und USA im Vergleich* (Frankfurt a. M./New York: Campus).

Runge, Wolfgang (1965) *Politik und Beamtentum in Parteienstaat. Die Demokratisierung der politischen Beamten in Preußen zwischen 1918 und 1933* (Stuttgart: Klett).

Rupp, Erik (1976) *Technologietransfer als Instrument staatlicher Innovationsförderung* (Göttingen: Schwarz).

Rürup, Reinhard (1972) 'Entstehung und Grundlagen der Weimarer Verfassung', in: Eberhard Kolb (ed.), *Vom Kaiserreich zur Weimarer Republik* (Cologne: Kiepenheuer & Witsch), pp. 218–43.

Rüthers, Bernd (1990) *Carl Schmitt im Dritten Reich: Wissenschaft als Zeitgeist-Verstärkung?* (Munich: Beck).

——(1994) *Entartetes Recht: Rechtslehren und Kronjuristen im Dritten Reich* (Munich: DTV).

Saage, Richard (1982) ' "Gleichgewicht der Klassenkräfte" und Koalitionsfrage als Problem sozialdemokratischer Politik in Deutschland und Österreich zwischen den Weltkriegen', in: Horst Heimann and Thomas Meyer (eds), *Reformsozialismus und Sozialdemokratie. Zur Theoriediskussion des Demokratischen Sozialismus in der Weimarer Republik. Bericht zum wissenschaftlichen Kongreß der Friedrich-Ebert-Stiftung 'Beträge zur reformistischen Sozialismustheorie in der Weimarer Republik' vom 9. bis 12. Oktober 1980* (Berlin/Bonn: Dietz), pp. 145–66.

——(1983) 'Rückkehr zum starken Staat? Zur Renaissance des Freund–Feind-Denkens in der Bundesrepublik', in: *Rückkehr zum starken Staat* (Frankfurt a. M.: Suhrkamp), pp. 7–42.

——(1989) 'Besitzindividualistische Perspektiven der politischen Theorie Kants', in: *Vertragsdenken und Utopie. Studien zur politischen Theorie und zur Sozialphilosophie der frühen Neuzeit* (Frankfurt a. M.: Suhrkamp), pp. 192–234.

Saner, Hans (1967) *Kants Weg vom Krieg zum Frieden*, vol. 1: *Widerstreit und Einheit. Wege zu Kants politischem Denken* (Munich: Piper).

Sarcinelli, Ulrich (1979) *Das Staatsverständnis der SPD: Ein Beitrag zur Analyse des sozialdemokratischen Staatsverständnisses auf der Grundlage der SPD-Programm- und Grundsatzdiskussion in den Jahren 1969 bis 1975* (Meisenheim am Glan: Anton Hain).

Sassenbach, Ulrich (1992) *Der Begriff des Politischen bei Immanuel Kant* (Würzburg: Königshausen & Neumann).

Schaefer, Rainer (1990) *SPD in der Ära Brüning: Tolerierung oder Mobilisierung? Handlungsspielräume und Strategien sozialdemokratischer Politik 1930–1932* (Frankfurt a. M.: Campus).

Schäfer, Gert (1984) 'Ein Intellektueller an der Seite der Arbeiterbewegung. Über einige Motive im politischen Denken von Franz L. Neumann', in: Joachim Perels (ed.), *Aktualität und Probleme der Theorie Franz L. Neumanns* (Baden-Baden: Nomos), pp. 143–63.

Scharpf, Fritz W. (1973) 'Planung als politischer Prozeß', in: *Planung als politischer Prozeß. Aufsätze zur Theorie der planenden Demokratie* (Frankfurt a. M.: Suhrkamp), pp. 33–72.

——(1978) *Autonome Gewerkschaften und staatliche Wirtschaftspolitik: Probleme einer Verbändegesetzgebung* (Frankfurt a. M.: Europäische Verlagsanstalt).

——(1988) 'Verhandlungssysteme, Verteilungskonflikte und Pathologien der politischen Steuerung', in: Manfred G. Schmidt (ed.), *Staatstätigkeit. International und historisch vergleichende Analysen* (Opladen: Westdeutscher Verlag), pp. 61–87.

Schatz, Heribert (1974) *Politische Planung im Regierungssystem der Bundesrepublik Deutschland* (Göttingen: Otto Schwarz).

Schauff, Johannes (1928) *Die deutschen Katholiken und die Zentrumspartei. Ein politisch-statistische Untersuchung der Reichstagswahlen seit 1871* (Cologne: J. P. Bachem).

Scheler, Max (1921) *Vom Ewigen im Menschen*, vol. 1: *Religiöse Erneuerung* (Leipzig: Verlag der neue Geist).

Schelsky, Helmut (1965) 'Der Mensch in der wissenschaftlichen Zivilisation', in: *Auf der Suche nach der Wirklichkeit. Gesammelte Aufsätze* (Düsseldorf: Eugen Diederich), pp. 439–80.

——(1970) 'Zur soziologischen Theorie der Institutionen', in: Helmut Schelsky (ed.), *Zur Theorie der Institutionen* (Düsseldorf: Bertelsmann), pp. 9–26.

——(1973) 'Mehr Demokratie oder mehr Freiheit? Der Grundsatzkonflikt der "Polarisierung" in der Bundesrepublik Deutschland', in: *Systemüberwindung – Demokratisierung – Gewaltenteilung* (Munich: Beck), pp. 41–82.

——(1980a) 'Planung der Zukunft. Die rationale Utopie und die Ideologie der Rationalität' (1966), in: *Die Soziologen und das Recht. Abhandlungen und Vorträge zur Soziologie von Recht, Institution und Planung* (Opladen: Westdeutscher Verlag), pp. 288–307.

——(1980b) 'Die Soziologen und das Recht', in: *Die Soziologen und das Recht* (see Schelsky 1980a), pp. 77–94.

——(1980c) 'Die juridische Rationalität', in: *Die Soziologen und das Recht* (see Schelsky 1980a), pp. 34–76.

Scheuermann, William E. (1994) *Between the Norm and the Exception: The Frankfurt School and the Rule of Law* (Cambridge, Mass./London: MIT Press).

——(1996) 'Introduction', in: *The Rule of Law under Siege: Selected Essays of Franz L. Neumann and Otto Kirchheimer* (Berkeley/Los Angeles/London: University of California Press), pp. 1–25.

Scheuner, Ulrich (1967) 'Die Anwendung des Art. 48 der Weimarer Reichsverfassung unter den Präsidentschaften von Ebert und Hindenburg', in: Ferdinand A. Hermens and Theodor Schieder (eds), *Staat, Wirtschaft und Politik in der Weimarer Republik. Festschrift für Heinrich Brüning* (Berlin: Duncker & Humblot), pp. 249–86.

——(1977) 'Volkssouveränität und Theorie der parlamentarischen Vertretung. Zur Theorie der Volksvertretung in Deutschland 1815–1848', in: Karl Bosl (ed.), *Der moderne Parlamentarismus und seine Grundagen in der ständischen Repräsentation* (Berlin: Duncker & Humblot), pp. 297–340.

——(1978) 'Das Wesen des Staates und der Begriff des Politischen in der neueren Staatstheorie', in: *Staatstheorie und Staatsrecht. Gesammelte Schriften*, ed. Joseph Listl and Wolfgang Rüfner (Berlin: Duncker & Humblot), pp. 45–79.

Schieck, Hans (1972) 'Die Behandlung der Sozialisierungsfrage in den Monaten nach dem Staatsumsturz', in: Eberhard Kolb (ed.), *Vom Kaiserreich zur Weimarer Republik* (Cologne: Kiepenheuer & Witsch), pp. 138–64.

Schieder, Theodor (1980) 'Die Krise des bürgerlichen Liberalismus. Ein Beitrag zum Verhältnisse von politischer und gesellschaftlicher Verfassung', in: Lothar Gall (ed.), *Liberalismus* (Königstein: Athenäum), pp. 187–207.

Schiffers, Reinhard (1971) *Elemente direkter Demokratie im Weimarer Regierungssystem* (Düsseldorf: Droste).

Schiller, Karl (1973) 'Preisstabilität durch globale Steuerung der Marktwirtschaft', in: Frieder Naschold and Werner Väth (eds), *Politische Plannungssysteme* (Opladen: Westdeutscher Verlag), pp. 99–103.

Schilling, Otto (1933) *Christliche Sozial- und Rechtsphilosophie* (Munich: Max Hueber).

Schimkowsky, Reinhard (1974) 'Exkurs über Hilferding: Vom Generalkartell zur Konzeption des organisierten Kapitalismus', in: Rolf Ebbighausen (ed.), *Monopol und Staat. Zur Marx-Rezeption in der Theorie des staatsmonopolistischen Kapitalismus* (Frankfurt a. M.: Suhrkamp), pp. 279–92.

Schluchter, Wolfgang (1979) *Die Entwicklung des okzidentalen Rationalismus. Eine Analyse von Max Webers Gesellschaftsgeschichte* (Tübingen: J. C. B. Mohr).

——(1980) 'Bürokratie und Demokratie: Zum Verhältnis von politischer Effizienz und politischer Freiheit bei Max Weber', in: *Rationalismus der Weltbeherrschung: Studien zu Max Weber* (Frankfurt a. M.: Suhrkamp), pp. 75–133.

——(1991) *Religion und Lebensführung*, vol. 2: *Studien zu Max Webers Religions- und Herrschaftssoziologie* (Frankfurt a. M.: Suhrkamp).

Schmid, Günther (1970) 'Niklas Luhmanns funktional-strukturelle Systemtheorie: Eine wissenschaftliche Revolution?', *Politische Vierteljahresschrift* 11, pp. 186–218.

Schmidt, Axel (1981) *Militärdiktatur mit Massenbasis? Die Querfrontkonzeption der Reichswehrführung um General von Schleicher am Ende der Weimarer Republik* (Frankfurt a. M.: Campus).

Schmidt, Eberhard (1970) *Die verhinderte Neuordnung 1945–1952. Zur Auseinandersetzung um die Demokratisierung der Wirtschaft in den westlichen Besatzungszonen und in der Bundesrepublik Deutschland* (Frankfurt a. M.: Europäische Verlagsanstalt).

——(1971) *Ordnungsfaktor oder Gegenmacht. Die politische Rolle der Gewerkschaften* (Frankfurt a. M.: Suhrkamp).

Schmidt, Gustav (1964) *Deutscher Historismus und der Übergang zur parlamentarischen Demokratie: Untersuchungen zu den politischen Gedanken von Meinecke, Troeltsch, Max Weber* (Lübeck: Matthiesen).

——(1974) 'Parlamentarisierung oder "Präventive Konterrevolution"? Die deutsche Innenpolitik im Spannungsfeld konservativer Sammlungsbewegungen und latenter Reformbestrebungen 1907–1914', in: Gerhard A. Ritter (ed.), *Gesellschaft und Regierung. Zur Geschichte des Parlamentarismus in Deutschland* (Düsseldorf: Droste), pp. 249–78.

Schmidt, Manfred G. (1978) 'Die "Politik der Inneren Reformen" in der Bundesrepublik Deutschland 1969–1976', *Politische Vierteljahresschrift* 19, pp. 201–53.

——(1990) 'Staatsfinanzen', in: Klaus von Beyme and Manfred G. Schmidt (eds), *Politik in der Bundesrepublik* (Opladen: Westdeutscher Verlag), pp. 36–73.

Schmidt-Aßmann, Eberhard (1967) *Der Verfassungsbegriff in der deutschen Staats-lehre der Aufklärung und des Historismus: Untersuchungen zu den Vorstufen eines hermeneutischen Verfassungsdenkens* (Berlin: Duncker & Humblot).

Schmitt, Carl (1914) *Der Wert des Staates und die Bedeutung des Einzelnen* (Tübingen: J. C. B. Mohr).

——(1921) *Die Diktatur von den Anfängen des modernen Souveränitätasgedankens* (Munich/Leipzig: Duncker & Humblot).

——(1922) *Politische Theologie: Vier Kapitel zur Lehre von der Souveränität* (Munich/Leipzig: Duncker & Humblot).

——(1923) *Die geistesgeschichtliche Lage des heutigen Parlamentarismus* (Munich/ Leipzig: Duncker & Humblot).

——(1925a) *Römischer Katholizismus und politische Form* (Munich: Theatiner-Verlag).

——(1925b) *Politische Romantik* (Munich/Leipzig: Duncker & Humblot).

——(1927) *Volksentscheid und Volksbegehren: Ein Beitrag zur Auslegung der Wei-marer Verfassung und zur Lehre von der unmittelbaren Demokratie* (Berlin: de Gruyter).

——(1928) *Verfassungslehre* (Berlin: Duncker & Humblot).

——(1931a) *Der Hüter der Verfassung* (Berlin: Duncker & Humblot).

——(1931b) *Freiheitsrechte und institutionelle Garantien der Reichsverfassung* (Berlin: Reimar Hobbing).

——(1932a) *Der Begriff des Politischen* (Berlin: Duncker & Humblot).

——(1932b) 'Das Zeitalter der Neutralisierungen und Entpolitisierungen', in: *Der Begriff des Politischen* (see C. Schmitt 1932a), pp. 79–95.

——(1932c) *Legalität und Legitimität* (Berlin: Duncker & Humblot).

——(1935) *Staat, Bewegung, Volk, Die Dreigliederung der politischen Einheit* (Hamburg: Hanseatische Verlagsanstalt).

——(1940) 'Der Führer schützt das Recht', in: *Positionen und Begriffe im Kampf mit Weimar-Genf-Versailles 1923–1939* (Hamburg: Hanseatische Verlagsanstalt), pp. 199–203.

——(1958a) 'Weiterentwicklung des totalen Staates in Deutschland', in: *Verfas-sungsrechtliche Aufsätze aus den Jahren 1924–1954: Materialien zu einer Verfas-sungslehre* (Berlin: Duncker & Humblot), p. 359–66.

——(1958b) 'Machtpositionen des totalen Staates', in: *Verfassungsrechtliche Auf-sätze* (see C. Schmitt 1958a), pp. 367–71.

——(1958c) 'Grundrechte und Grundpflichten', in: *Verfassungsrechtliche Aufsätze* (see C. Schmitt 1958a), pp. 181–231.

——(1969) *Gesetz und Urteil: Eine Untersuchung zum Problem der Rechtspraxis* (Munich: Beck).

——(1982) *Der Leviathan in der Staatslehre des Thomas Hobbes* (Stuttgart: Klett-Cotta).

Schmitt, Hermann (1987) *Neue Politik in alten Parteien. Zum Verhältnis von Gesellschaft und Parteien in der Bundesrepublik* (Opladen: Westdeutscher Verlag).

Schmitz, Georg (ed.) (1981) *Die Vorentwürfe Hans Kelsens für die österreichische Bundesverfassung* (Vienna: Manz).

Schmitz, Karl, Richle, Rainer, Narr, Wolf-Dieter, Koch, Claus and Albrecht Ulbrich (1976) *Der Staat und die Steuerung der Wissenschaft: Analyse der Forschungs- und Technologiepolitik der Bundesregierung* (Göttingen: Otto Schwartz).

Schmitz, Matthias (1965) *Die Freund–Feind-Theorie Carl Schmitts* (Opladen: Westdeutscher Verlag).

Schönhoven, Klaus (1987) *Die deutschen Gewerkschaften* (Frankfurt a. M.: Suhrkamp).

Schorske, Carl F. (1965) *German Social Democracy 1905–1917: The Development of the Great Schism* (Berkeley/Los Angeles: University of California Press).

'Schreiben des Vorsitzenden der Zentrumspartei Dr. Ludwig Kaas an Reichskanzler v. Schleicher' (26.1.1933), in: Ernst Rudolf Huber (ed.) (1991) *Dokumente zur deutschen Verfassungsgeschichte*, vol. 4: *Deutsche Verfassungsdokumente 1919– 1933* (Stuttgart: W. Kohlhammer).

Schulz, Carola (1984) *Der gezähmte Konflikt. Zur Interessenverarbeitung durch Verbände und Parteien am Beispiel der Wirtschaftsentwicklung und Wirtschaftspolitik in der Bundesrepublik (1966 bis 1976)* (Opladen: Westdeutscher Verlag).

Schulz, Gerhard (1963) *Zwischen Demokratie und Diktatur: Verfassungspolitik und Reichsreform in der Weimarer Republik*, vol. 1: *Die Periode der Konsolidierung und der Revision des Bismarckschen Reichsaufbaus 1919–1930* (Berlin: de Gruyter).

——(1980) 'Einleitung', in: *Quellen zur Geschichte des Parlamentarismus und der politischen Parteien*, 3rd series, vol. 4/1: *Die Weimarer Republik: Politik und Wirtschaft in der Krise 1930–1932. Quellen zur Ära Brüning* (Düsseldorf: Droste), pp. ix–lxxxvii.

Schustereit, Hartmut (1975) *Linksliberalismus und Sozialdemokratie in der Weimarer Republik: Eine vergleichende Betrachtung der Politik von DDP und SPD 1919–1930* (Düsseldorf: Schwann).

Schwer, Wilhelm (1970) *Stand und Ständeordnung im Weltbild des Mittelalters. Die geistes- und gesellschaftsgeschichtlichen Grundlagen der berufsständischen Idee* (Paderborn: Ferdinand Schöningh).

Seibel, Wolfgang (1982) *'Regierbarkeits'-Krise und Verwaltungswissenschaft. Eine ideengeschichtliche Systematik der Stabilisierung krisengefährdeter sozialer Ordnungen und ihrer Berücksichtigung in den Wissenschaften vom programmierten Staatshandeln* (Marburg: dissertation).

Seifert, Jürgen (1967) 'Gegenmacht in der Verfassungsordnung', in: Peter von Oertzen (ed.), *Festschrift für Otto Brenner* (Frankfurt a. M.: Europäische Verlagsanstalt), pp. 75–93.

——(1977) *Grundgesetz und Restauration. Verfassungsrechtliche Analysen und dokumentarische Darstellung des Textes des Grundgesetzes mit sämtlichen Änderungen*, 3rd edn (Neuwied: Luchterhand).

Sened, Itai (1997) *The Political Institution of Private Property* (Cambridge: CUP).

Sheehan, James J. (1978) *German Liberalism in the Nineteenth Century* (Chicago/ London: University of Chicago Press).

Sieling-Wendeling, Ulrike (1976) 'Die Entwicklung des Eigentumsbegriffes vom Inkrafttreten des bürgerlichen Gesetzbuches bis zum Ende des Nationalsozialismus', in: Wolfgang Däubler, Ulrike Sieling-Wendeling and Horst Welkorborsky (eds), *Die Entwicklung des Eigentumsbegriffs im Kapitalismus* (Neuwied: Luchterhand).

Simmel, Georg (1989) *Philosophie des Geldes* (Frankfurt a. M.: Suhrkamp).

Sinzheimer, Hugo (1916) *Ein Arbeitstarifgesetz. Die Idee der sozialen Selbstbestimmung im Recht* (Munich/Leipzig: Duncker & Humblot).

——(1976a) 'Das Rätesystem', in: *Arbeitsrecht und Rechtssoziologie: Gesammelte Aufsätze und Reden*, 2 vols, ed. Otto Kahn-Freund and Thilo Ramm (Frankfurt a. M.: Europäische Verlagsanstalt) vol. 1, pp. 325–50.

——(1976b) 'Die Demokratisierung des Arbeitsverhältnisses', in: *Arbeitsrecht und Rechtssoziologie* (see Sinzheimer 1976a) vol. 1, pp. 115–34.

Smend, Rudolf (1955) 'Verfassung und Verfassungsrecht', in: *Staatsrechtliche Abhandlungen und andere Aufsätze* (Berlin: Duncker & Humblot), pp. 119–276.

Sohn-Rethel, Alfred (1973) 'Die soziale Rekonsolidierung des Kapitalismus', in: *Ökonomie und Klassenstruktur des deutschen Faschismus. Aufzeichnungen und Aufsätze*, ed. and introd. Johannes Agnoli, Bernhard Blanke and Niels Kadritzke (Frankfurt a. M.: Suhrkamp), pp. 165–72.

Söllner, Alfons (1979) *Geschichte und Herrschaft: Studien zur materialistischen Sozialwissenschaft 1929–1942* (Frankfurt a. M.: Suhrkamp).

——(1982a) 'Politische Dialektik der Aufklärung: Zum Spätwerk von Franz Neumann und Otto Kirchheimer (1950–1965)', in: Wolfgang Bonß and Axel Honneth (eds), *Sozialforschung als Kritik: Zum sozialwissenschaftlichen Potential der Kritischen Theorie* (Frankfurt a. M.: Suhrkamp), pp. 281–326.

——(1982b) 'Jürgen Habermas und die kritische Theorie des gegenwärtigen Rechtsstaates – Versuch einer wissenschaftsgeschichtlichen Einordnung', *Leviathan* 10, pp. 97–131.

——(1986) 'Jenseits von Carl Schmitt. Wissenschaftsgeschichtliche Richtigstellungen zur politischen Theorie im Umkreis der Frankfurter Schule', *Geschichte und Gesellschaft* 12, pp. 502–29.

Sombart, Werner (1925) *Die Ordnung des Wirtschaftslebens* (Berlin: Julius Springer).

——(1927) *Der moderne Kapitalismus. Historisch-systematische Darstellung des gesamteuropäischen Wirtschaftslebens von seinen Anfängen bis zur Gegenwart*, vol. 3: *Das Wirtschaftsleben im Zeitalter des Hochkapitalismus* (Munich/Leipzig: Duncker & Humblot, 1927).

——(1932) *Die Zukunft des Kapitalismus* (Berlin: Buchholz & Weißwange).

Song, Seog-Yun (1996) *Politische Parteien und Verbände in der Verfassungsrechtslehre der Weimarer Republik* (Berlin: Duncker & Humblot).

Sontheimer, Kurt (1962) *Antidemokratisches Denken in der Weimarer Republik. Die politischen Ideen des deutschen Nationalismus zwischen 1918 und 1933* (Munich: Nymphenburger Verlagshandlung).

Spael, Wilhelm (1985) *Friedrich Naumanns Verhältnis zu Max Weber* (Sankt Augustin: Liberal Verlag).

Spangenberg, Hans (1912) *Vom Lehnstaat zum Ständestaat. Ein Beitrag zur Entstehung der landständischen Verfassung* (Munich: R. Oldenbourg).

Spann, Othmar (1921) *Der wahre Staat* (Leipzig: Quelle & Meyer).

Sperber, Jonathan (1982) 'Roman Catholic Religious Identity in Rhineland-Westphalia, 1800–1870: Quantitative Examples and Some Political Implications', *Social History* 7, pp. 305–18.

Spieker, Manfred (1986) *Legitimitätsprobleme des Sozialstaats. Konkurrierende Sozialstaatskonzeptionen in der Bundesrepublik Deutschland* (Berne/Stuttgart: Paul Haupt).

Stammer, Otto (1957) 'Interessenverbände und Parteien', *Kölner Zeitschrift für Soziologie und Sozialpsychologie* 9, pp. 587–605.

Stegmann, Dirk (1970) *Die Erben Bismarcks: Parteien und Verbände in der Spätphase des Wilhelminischen Deutschlands. Sammlungspolitik 1897–1918* (Cologne: Kiepenheuer & Witsch).

Stein, Lorenz von (1959) *Geschichte der sozialen Bewegung in Frankreich von 1789 bis auf unsere Tage*, vol. 1 (Hildesheim: Georg Olms).

*Stenographische Berichte über die Verhandlungen des deutschen Reichstages* (1933) vol. 457.

Stolleis, Michael (1992) *Geschichte des öffentlichen Rechts in Deutschland*, vol. 2: *Staatsrechtslehre und Verwaltungswissenschaft 1800–1914* (Munich: Beck).

Stone, Lawrence (1972) *The Causes of the English Revolution 1529–1642* (London: ARK Paperbacks).

Stöss, Richard (1987) 'Parteien und soziale Bewegungen. Begriffliche Abgrenzung – Volksparteien – Neue soziale Bewegungen – DIE GRÜNEN', in: Roland Roth and Dieter Rucht (eds), *Neue soziale Bewegungen in der Bundesrepublik Deutschland* (Frankfurt a. M./New York: Campus), pp. 277–303.

Struve, Walter (1973) *Elites Against Democracy. Leadership Ideals in Bourgeois Political Thought in Germany, 1890–1933* (Princeton: Princeton UP).

Sturm, Roland (1993) *Staatsverschuldung. Ursachen, Wirkungen und Grenzen staatlicher Verschuldungspolitik* (Opladen: Leske & Budrich).

Stürmer, Michael (1974) *Regierung und Reichstag im Bismarckstaat 1871–1880. Cäsarismus oder Parlamentarismus* (Düsseldorf: Droste).

——(1980) 'Der unvollendete Parteienstaat – Zur Vorgeschichte des Präsidialregimes am Ende der Weimarer Republik', in: Stürmer (ed.), *Die Weimarer Republik. Belagerte Civitas* (Königstein: Athenäum), pp. 310–17.

Süß, Werner (1983) 'Wahl und Führungswechsel. Politik zwischen Legitimation und Elitenkonsens. Zum Bonner Machtwechsel 1982/83', in: Hans-Dieter Klingemann and Max Kaase (eds), *Wahlen und politischer Prozeß. Analysen aus Anlaß der Bundestagswahl 1983* (Opladen: Westdeutscher Verlag), pp. 39–83.

——(1991) 'Zukunft durch Modernisierungspolitik. Das Leithema der 80er Jahre', in: *Die Bundesrepublik in den achtziger Jahren. Innenpolitik, politische Kultur, Außenpolitik* (Opladen: Leske & Budrich), pp. 89–106.

Tanner, Klaus (1989) *Die fromme Verstaatlichung des Gewissens: Zur Auseinandersetzung um die Legitimität der Weimarer Reichsverfassung in Staatswissenschaft und Theologie der zwanziger Jahre* (Göttingen: Vandenhoeck & Ruprecht).

Taubes, Jacob (1995) *Die politische Theologie des Paulus* (Munich: Fink).

Teubner, Gunther (1979) 'Neo-korporatistische Strategien rechtlicher Organisationssteuerung: Staatliche Strukturvorgaben für die gesellschaftliche Verarbeitung politischer Konflikte', *Zeitschrift für Parlamentsfragen* 10, pp. 487–502.

Theiner, Peter (1983) *Sozialer Liberalismus und deutsche Weltpolitik: Friedrich Naumann im Wilhelminischen Deutschland (1860–1919)* (Baden-Baden: Nomos).

——(1986) 'Friedrich Naumann und der soziale Liberalismus im Kaiserreich', in: Karl Holl, Günter Trautmann and Hans Vorländer (eds), *Sozialer Liberalismus* (Göttingen: Vandenhoeck & Ruprecht), pp. 72–83.

Theunissen, Michael (1981) *Kritische Theorie der Gesellschaft: Zwei Studien* (Berlin: de Gruyter).

Thome, Helmut (1973) *Der Versuch die 'Welt' zu begreifen: Fragezeichen zur Systemtheorie von Niklas Luhmann* (Frankfurt a. M.: Athenäum).

Thompson, John B. (1981) *Critical Hermeneutics: A Study in the Thought of Paul Ricoeur and Jürgen Habermas* (Cambridge: CUP).

Thum, Horst (1991) *Wirtschaftsdemokratie und Mitbestimmung: Von den Anfängen 1916 bis zum Mitbestimmungsgesetz 1976* (Cologne: Bund-Verlag).

Timm, Helga (1952) *Die deutsche Sozialpolitik und der Bruch der großen Koalition im März 1930* (Düsseldorf: Droste).

Tischleder, Peter (1927) *Staatsgewalt und Katholisches Gewissen* (Frankfurt a. M.: Carolus Druckerei).

Tönnies, Ferdinand (1887) *Gemeinschaft und Gesellschaft. Abhandlung des Communismus und des Socialismus als empirischer Culturformen* (Leipzig: Fues's Verlag).

Tornow, Ingo (1979) 'Die deutschen Unternehmerverbände 1945–1950', in: Josef Becker, Theo Stammen and Peter Waldmann (eds), *Vorgeschichte der Bundesrepublik Deutschland. Zwischen Kapitulation und Grundgesetz* (Munich: Fink, 1979), pp. 235–60.

Tribe, Keith (1986) 'Franz Neumann in der Emigration: 1933–1942', in: Axel Honneth and Albrecht Wellmer (eds), *Die Frankfurter Schule und die Folgen: Referate eines Symposiums der Alexander von Humboldt Stiftung vom 10–15. Dezember 1984 in Ludwigsburg* (Berlin: de Gruyter), pp. 259–74.

Trippe, Christian F. (1995) *Konservative Verfassungspolitik 1918–1923: Die DNVP als Opposition in Reich und Ländern* (Düsseldorf: Droste).

Turner, Henry Ashby (1985) *German Big Business and the Rise of Hitler* (Oxford: OUP).

Ullmann, Hans-Peter (1976) *Der Bund der Industriellen. Organisation, Einfluß und Politik klein- und mittelbetrieblicher Industrieller im Deutschen Kaiserreich 1895–1914* (Göttingen: Vandenhoeck & Ruprecht).

——(1982) 'Deutsche Unternehmer und Bismarcks Sozialversicherungssystem', in: Wolfgang J. Mommsen (ed.), *Die Entstehung des Wohlfahrtsstaates in Großbritannien und Deutschland 1850–1950* (Stuttgart: Klett-Cotta), pp. 142–58.

——(1995) *Das deutsche Kaiserreich 1871–1918* (Frankfurt a. M.: Suhrkamp).

Ullrich, Norbert (1996) *Gesetzgebungsverfahren in der Bismarck-Zeit unter besonderer Berücksichtigung der Rolle der Fraktionen* (Berlin: Duncker & Humblot).

Ulmen, G. L. (1991) *Politischer Mehrwert: Eine Studie über Max Weber und Carl Schmitt* (Weinheim: VCH, Acta Humaniora).

Vaihinger, Hans (1911) *Die Philosophie des Als-Ob* (Berlin: Reuther & Reichard).

Varain, Heinz Josef (1956) *Freie Gewerkschaften, Sozialdemokratie und Staat. Die Politik der Generalkommission unter der Führung Carl Legens (1890–1920)* (Düsseldorf: Droste).

*Verhandlungen der verfassunggebenden Deutschen Nationalversammlung* (1920), vols 328 and 329 (Berlin: Druck und Verlag der Norddeutschen Buchdruckerei und Verlagsanstalt).

Vestring, Sigrid (1987) *Die Mehrheitssozialdemokratie und die Entstehung der Reichsverfassung von Weimar 1918/1919* (Münster: Lit Verlag).

Vierhaus, Rudolf (1983) 'Liberalismus, Beamtenstand und konstitutionelles System', in: Wolfgang Schieder (ed.), *Liberalismus in der Gesellschaft des deutschen Vormärz* (Göttingen: Vandenhoeck & Ruprecht), pp. 39–54.

Villa, Dana, R. (1996) *Arendt and Heidegger: The Fate of the Political* (Princeton: Princeton UP).

Voegelin, Erich (1927) 'Kelsen's Pure Theory of Law', *Political Science Quarterly* 42, pp. 268–76.

Vogel, Barbara (1983) *Allgemeine Gewerbefreiheit. Die Reformpolitik des preußischen Staatskanzlers Hardenberg (1810–1820)* (Göttingen: Vandenhoeck & Ruprecht).

Völtzer, Friedrich (1992) *Der Sozialstaatsgedanke in der Weimarer Reichsverfassung* (Frankfurt a. M.: Lang).

Wagner, Adolph (1911) 'Staat in nationalökonischer Hinsicht', in: *Handwörterbuch der Staatswissenschaften*, vol. 7 (Jena: G. Fischer), pp. 727–39.

Wallerstein, Immanuel (1980) *The Modern World-System* vol. 2: *Mercantilism and the Consolidation of the European World-Economy, 1600–1750* (New York: Academic Press).

Watkins, Frederick Mundell (1939) *The Failure of Constitutional Emergency Powers under the German Republic* (Cambridge, Mass.: Harvard UP).

Webber, Douglas (1987) 'Eine Wende in der deutschen Arbeitsmarktpolitik? Sozialliberale und christlich-liberale Antworten auf die Beschäftigungskrise', in: Heidrun Abromeit and Bernhard Blanke (eds), *Arbeitsmarkt, Arbeitsbeziehungen und Politik in den 80er Jahren, Leviathan*, spec. issue 8, pp. 74–85.

—— (1991) 'Das Reformpaket: Anspruch und Wirklichkeit der christlich-liberalen Wende', in: Werner Süß (ed.), *Die Bundesrepublik in den achtziger Jahren. Innenpolitik, politische Kultur, Außenpolitik* (Opladen: Leske & Budrich), pp. 153–70.

Weber, Max (1922) 'Der Sinn der "Wertfreiheit" der soziologischen und ökonomischen Wissenschaften', in: *Gesammelte Aufsätze zur Wissenschaftslehre* (Tübingen: J. C. B. Mohr), pp. 489–539.

—— (1972) *Wirtschaft und Gesellschaft: Grundriß der verstehenden Soziologie* ed. Johannes Winckelmann (Tübingen: J. C. B. Mohr).

—— (1986) 'Die protestantische Ethik und der Geist des Kapitalismus', in: *Gesammelte Aufsätze zur Religionssoziologie*, vol. 1 (Tübingen: J. C. B. Mohr), pp. 17–206.

—— (1988a) 'Der Nationalstaat und die Volkswirtschaftspolitik', in: *Gesammelte politische Schriften* (Tübingen: J. C. B. Mohr).

—— (1988b) 'Deutschlands äußere und Preußens innere Politik', in: *Gesammelte politische Schriften* (see M. Weber 1988a), pp. 178–91.

—— (1988c) 'Deutschland unter den europäischen Weltmächten', in: *Gesammelte politische Schriften* (see M. Weber 1988a), pp. 157–77.

—— (1988d) 'Parlament und Regierung im neugeordneten Deutschland', in: *Gesammelte politische Schriften* (see M. Weber 1988a), pp. 306–443.

—— (1988e) 'Deutschlands künftige Staatsform', in: *Gesammelte politische Schriften* (see M. Weber 1988a), pp. 448–83.

—— (1988f) 'Die Lehren der deutschen Kanzlerkrisis', in: *Gesammelte politische Schriften* (see M. Weber 1988a), pp. 216–21.

—— (1988g) 'Politik als Beruf', in: *Gesammelte politische Schriften* (see M. Weber 1988a), pp. 505–60.

—— (1988h) 'Deutschland unter den europäischen Weltmächten', in: *Gesammelte politische Schriften* (see M. Weber 1988a), pp. 157–77.

—— (1988i) 'Bismarcks Erbe in der Reichsverfassung', in: *Gesammelte politische Schriften* (see M. Weber 1988a), pp. 241–4.

—— (1988j) 'Wahlrecht und Demokratie in Deutschland', in: *Gesammelte politische Schriften* (see M. Weber 1988a), pp. 245–91.

—— (1988k) 'Innere Lage und Außenpolitik', in: *Gesammelte politische Schriften* (see M. Weber 1988a), pp. 292–305.

—— (1988l) 'Über das Verhältnis der Kartelle zum Staat', in: *Gesammelte Aufsätze zur Soziologie und Sozialpolitik* (Tübingen: J. C. B. Mohr), pp. 399–406.

Weber, Werner (1951) 'Der Einbruch politischer Stände in die Demokratie', in: *Spannungen und Kräfte im westdeutschen Verfassungssystem* (Stuttgart: Friedrich Vorwerk), pp. 39–64.

—— (1985) 'Der Staat und die Verbände', in: Rudolf Steinberg (ed.), *Staat und Verbände: Zur Theorie der Interessenverbände in der Industriegesellschaft* (Darmstadt: Wissenschaftliche Buchgesellschaft), pp. 64–76.

Wehler, Hans-Ulrich (1969) *Bismarck und der Imperialismus* (Cologne: Kiepenheuer & Witsch).

—— (1973) *Das deutsche Kaiserreich 1871–1918* (Göttingen: Vandenhoeck & Ruprecht).

—— (1995) *Deutsche Gesellschaftsgeshichte*, vol. 3: *Von der deutschen Doppelrevolution bis zum Beginn des Ersten Weltkrieges 1849–1914* (Munich: Beck).

Weisbrod, Bernd (1978) *Schwerindustrie in der Weimarer Republik. Interessenpolitik zwischen Stabilisierung und Krise* (Wuppertal: Peter Hammer).

Weisbrod, Bernd (1982) 'Die Krise der Arbeitslosenversicherung und der Bruch der Großen Koalition (1928–1930)', in: Wolfgang J. Mommsen (ed.), *Die Entstehung des Wohlfahrtsstaats in Großbritannien und Deutschland 1850–1950* (Stuttgart: Klett-Cotta), pp. 196–212.

Weiß, Johannes (1977) 'Legitimationsbegriff und Legitimationsleistung der Systemtheorie Niklas Luhmanns', *Politische Vierteljahresschrift* 18, pp. 74–85.

Weitzel, Otto (1967) *Die Entwicklung der Staatsausgaben in Deutschland. Eine Analyse der öffentlichen Aktivität in ihrer Abhängigkeit vom wirtschaftlichen Wachstum* (Erlangen/Nuremberg: dissertation).

Wenzel, Rolf (1979) 'Wirtschafts- und Sozialordnung', in: Josef Becker, Theo Stammen and Peter Waldmann (eds), *Vorgeschichte der Bundesepublik Deutschland. Zwischen Kapitulation und Grundgesetz* (Munich: Fink, 1979), pp. 293–339.

White, Dan S. (1976) *The Splintered Party: National Liberalism in Hessen and the Reich 1867–1918* (Cambridge, Mass.: Harvard UP).

White, Stephen K. (1988) *The Recent Work of Jürgen Habermas: Reason, Justice and Modernity* (Cambridge: CUP).

Wieacker, Franz (1967) *Privatrechtsgeschichte der Neuzeit unter besonderer Berücksichtigung der deutschen Entwicklung*, 2nd edn (Göttingen: Vandenhoeck & Ruprecht).

Wiesendahl, Elmar (1987) 'Neue soziale Bewegungen und moderne Demokratietheorie. Demokratische Elitenherrschaft in der Krise', in: Roland Roth and Dieter Rucht (eds), *Neue soziale Bewegungen in der Bundesrepublik Deutschland* (Frankfurt a. M./New York: Campus, 1987), pp. 364–84.

—— (1989) 'Etablierte Parteien im Abseits? Das Volksparteiensystem der Bundesrepublik vor den Herausforderungen der neuen sozialen Bewegungen', in: Ulrike C. Wasmuht (ed.), *Alternativen zur alten Politik? Neue soziale Bewegungen in der Diskussion* (Darmstadt: Wissenschaftliche Buchgesellschaft), pp. 82–108.

Wiggershaus, Rolf (1986) *Die Frankfurter Schule: Geschichte, Theoretische Entwicklung, Politische Bedeutung* (Munich/Vienna: Carl Hanser).

Wilhelm, Walter (1958) *Zur juristischen Methodenlehre im 19. Jahrhundert. Die Herkunft der Methode Paul Labands aus der Privatrechtswissenschaft* (Frankfurt a. M.: Klostermann).

Willke, Helmut (1996) 'Theoretische Verhüllungen der Politk – Der Beitrag der Systemtheorie', in: Klaus von Beyme and Claus Offe (eds), *Politische Theorien in der Ära der Transformation* (Opladen: Westdeutscher Verlag), pp. 131–47.

Willms, Bernard (1973) *Kritik und Politik. Jürgen Habermas oder das politische Defizit der kritischen Theorie* (Frankfurt a. M.: Suhrkamp).

Windell, George G. (1954) *The Catholics and German Unity 1866–1871* (Minneapolis: University of Minnesota Press).

Winkler, Heinrich August (1972) *Pluralismus oder Protektionismus? Verfassungspolitische Probleme des Verbandswesens im deutschen Kaiserreich* (Wiesbaden: Franz Steiner).

—— (1973) 'Unternehmerverbände zwischen Ständeideologie und Nationalsozialismus', in: Heinz Josef Varain (ed.), *Interessenverbände in Deutschland* (Cologne: Kiepenheuer & Witsch), pp. 228–58.

—— (1979a) 'Vom linken zum rechten Nationalismus: Der deutsche Liberalismus in der Krise von 1878/79', in: *Liberalismus und Antiliberalismus. Studien zur politischen Sozialgeschichte des 19. und 20. Jahrhunderts* (Göttingen: Vandenhoeck & Ruprecht), pp. 36–51.

—— (1979b) 'Bürgerliche Emanzipation und nationale Einigung: Zur Entstehung des Nationalliberalismus in Preußen', in: *Liberalismus und Antiliberalismus* (see Winkler 1979a), pp. 24–35.

Witt, Peter-Christian (1970) *Die Finanzpolitik des deutschen Reiches von 1903 bis 1913. Eine Studie zur Innenpolitik des Wilhelminischen Deutschland* (Lübeck: Matthiesen).

—— (1983a) 'Kontinuität und Diskontinuität im politischen System der Weimarer Republik. Das Verhältnis von Regierung, Bürokratie und Reichstag', in: Gerhard A. Ritter (ed.), *Regierung, Bürokratie und Parlament in Preußen und Deutschland von 1848 bis zur Gegenwart* (Düsseldorf: Droste), pp. 117–48.

—— (1983b) 'Bemerkungen zur Wirtschaftspolitik in der "Übergangswirtschaft" 1918/19. Zur Entwicklung von Konjunkturbeobachtung und Konjunktursteuerung in Deutschland', in: Dirk Stegmann et al. (eds), *Industrielle Gesellschaft und politisches System. Beiträge zur politischen Sozialgeschichte. Festschrift für Fritz Fischer zum siebzigsten Geburtstag* (Bonn: Verlag Neue Gesellschaft, 1978), pp. 79–96.

Wittmann, Walter (1982) 'Mechanismen wachsender Staatsaufgaben', in: Gottfried Bombach, Bernhard Gahlen and Alfred E. Ott (eds), *Möglichkeiten und Grenzen der Staatstätigkeit* (Tübingen: J. C. B. Mohr), pp. 294–316.

Wulf, Peter (1979) *Hugo Stinnes. Wirtschaft und Politik 1918–1924* (Stuttgart: Klett-Cotta).

Wyduckel, Dieter (1984) *Ius Publicum. Grundlagen und Entwicklung des öffentlichen Rechts und der deutschen Staatswissenschaft* (Berlin: Duncker & Humblot).

Zängle, Michael (1988) *Max Webers Staatstheorie im Kontext seines Werkes* (Berlin: Duncker & Humblot).

Zimmermann, Rolf (1984) 'Marx, Habermas und das Problem der gesellschaftlichen Emanzipation', *Praxis International* 4, pp. 395–411.

Zöller, Michael (1975) *Die Unfähigkeit zur Politik: Politikbegriff und Wissenschaftsverständnis von Humboldt bis Habermas* (Opladen: Westdeutscher Verlag).

Zunkel, Friedrich (1974) *Industrie und Staatssozialismus. Der Kampf um die Wirtschaftsordnung in Deutschland 1914–18* (Düsseldorf: Droste).

Zwehl, Konrad von (1983) 'Zum Verhältnis von Regierung und Reichstag im Kaiserreich (1871–1918)', in: Gerhard A. Ritter (ed.), *Regierung, Bürokratie und Parlament in Preußen und Deutschland von 1848 bis zur Gegenwart* (Düsseldorf: Droste), pp. 90–116.

# Index